Judy Meeken

PRAISE FOR

THE MORMON MURDERS—

the definitive account of the Salt Lake City car-bomb murders that rocked the foundations of the Mormon Church and unveiled one of the most bizarre cases of bribery, intrigue, forgery, and murder ever recorded.

"ENGROSSING . . . A BIG, ABSORBING TRUE-CRIME SAGA!"   *—Booklist*

"GRIPPING . . . A FIRST-CLASS PIECE OF REPORTING."   *—Greenwich Times*

"The authors' combination of law and journalism provides an excellent foundation for understanding this twisting and legally complex story."   *—Rocky Mountain News*

"FASCINATING, SENSATIONAL REVELATIONS . . . WELL-RESEARCHED."   *—Times Tribune*

"A MOST CONTROVERSIAL AND REWARDING ACCOUNT!"   *—San Francisco Record*

"INTRIGUING . . . FASCINATING READING . . . takes a huge cast of charac̶t̶e̶r̶s̶ ̶a̶n̶d̶ ̶g̶i̶v̶e̶s̶ life into them."   *—O̶g̶den Standard-Examiner*

① **Signet**   ⑩ **Onyx**

NAL BONUS BOOK
SHORE BETS
FREE BOOK

CHOOSE ONE:
INDIGO MOON by Patricia Rice
CHANDRA by Catherine Coulter
WORTH WINNING by Dan Lewandowski
FAMILY TRADE by James Carroll
ODESSA BEACH by Bob Leuci
MALLORY'S GAMBIT
by L. Christian Bailing
PREY
by C. Terry Cline, Jr.
BROTHERS AND SISTERS
by John Coyne
TWILIGHT CHILD by Warren Adler

FREE BOOK TITLE (Include $1 for handling)

_____

WIN $1,000 CASH!

Your coupon will automatically enter you in sweepstakes

Name_____

Address _____

City_____ State _____ Zip_____

Signature _____

The Mormon Murders

A TRUE STORY OF GREED, FORGERY, DECEIT, AND DEATH

STEVEN NAIFEH
AND
GREGORY WHITE SMITH

AN ONYX BOOK

NEW AMERICAN LIBRARY

A DIVISION OF PENGUIN BOOKS USA INC.

Photographs appear courtesy of the following:

Salt Lake City, LDS Visitors Center, Gary Sheets with portrait, Hofmann
with S. Flynn: MICHAEL O'BRIEN/© SUNDAY TIMES, LONDON; LDS Temple,
Ashworth, Throckmorton and W. Flynn: ANACLETO RAPPING/© 1987 LOS
ANGELES TIMES; Hofmann's car, Rust, Church officials at press confer-
ence: TOM SMART/DESERET NEWS; Farnsworth and Bell: © 1987 LONGIN
LONCZYNA, JR.; Salamander Letter, Oath of a Freeman, Mark and Dorie
Hofmann: JACK MONSON/DESERET NEWS; Tanners, Flynn: SALT LAKE TRI-
BUNE; Yengich with Rich, Cannon et al., Jacobs, Mark and William
Hofmann: RAVELL CALL/DESERET NEWS; D'Elia, Stott: DEREK SMITH; Yengich:
PAUL G. BARKER/DESERET NEWS; Hofmann at prison: PAUL FRAUGHTON/SALT
LAKE TRIBUNE; Kathy Sheets with family: GARY SHEETS; Steve and Terri
Christensen: TERRI LAUDER; Christensen children: ALAN MILLS/TERRI LAUDER.

IN MEMORY OF
STEVE CHRISTENSEN
AND
KATHY SHEETS

Acknowledgments

Before this book, our contacts with the Church of Jesus Christ of Latter-day Saints were limited but benign. One of us dated a woman who was a devout Mormon; the other was acquainted, through secular channels, with a senior member of the Church leadership, a man of considerable stature and integrity.

But books often take unexpected, even unwanted, turns.

In one of our last interviews, a respected Mormon historian asked us how the Church fared in our account. He obviously understood what we had come to understand—that there was much about the Mark Hofmann case the Church would prefer not to see in print.

We answered his question with another question: What is the Church? Is it the body of Mormon doctrine? If so, which doctrine—Mormon doctrine as currently held or Mormon doctrine as held at the time of the Prophet Joseph Smith? Or is it the current leadership of the Church, as most Church leaders maintain? Or is it the community of Mormons and the shared values that bind them together?

Each of these "churches" fares differently in our account.

This book is based largely on a series of interviews, most of which were conducted in Utah during nine months in 1987. Some were brief; some lasted days. No one was more generous with their time and recollections than Detectives Jim Bell and Ken Farnsworth of the Salt Lake City Police Department. We are also especially indebted to the members of the victims' families: Scott Christensen, Joan Gorton, Heidi Sheets Jones, Terri Christensen Lauder, Joseph Robertson, Katie Sheets Robertson, Gary Sheets, Gretchen Sheets, and Jimmy Sheets, all of whom went out of their way to make us feel comfortable in a situation that had to be as awkward for them as it was for us.

In addition, we would like to thank Julius Andersen, Richard Anderson, Carl Arrington, Leonard Arrington, Brent Ashworth, John Ashton, Ralph Bailey, James Barber, Brent Bateman, Lary Ann Bateman, Don Bell, Curt Bench, David Biggs, Davis Bitton, Jill Brady, Cherie Bridge, Mike Bridge, Wilford Cardon, Mike Carter, Betty Lynn Davis, Gerry D'Elia, Duffy Diamond, Sue Dunster, Fred Esplin, Mildred Evans, Ralph Feurer, Peggy Fletcher, William Flynn, Dick Forbes, Ernie Ford, Jack Ford, Jane Forsgren, John Foster, Mike George, Jennie Glover, Demoin Gold, Don Gottfredson, Paul Grant, Rick Grunder, Charles Hamilton, Mark Haroldsen, John Harrington, John Heinerman, Charles Honts, Bob Jack, Lyn Jacobs, Franklin Johnson, John Johnson, Chris Jones, Kyle Jones, Grant Kesler, Faye Kotter, Leslie Kress, Don LaFevre, Dean Larsen, Wade Lillywhite, Richard Lindsay, Leo Lindsey, Bruce Lubeck, Paul Markosian, Richard Marks, Michael Marquardt, Brent Metcalfe, Jill Metcalfe, Thomas Moore, Eric Nielsen, Jorgen Olsen, Mike Orchard, Lynn Packer, Bruce Passey, Hal Passey, Robert Pitts, Daniel Rector, Kirk Rector, Janet McDermott, Randall Rigby, Kenneth Rigtrup, Al Rust, Gaylen Rust, Jeff Salt, Darlene Sanchez, Donald Schmidt, Jeff Simmonds, Connie Smith, Jack Smith, Nick Smith, Diane St. Thomas, Gregory St. Thomas, Stephanie St. Thomas, Robert Stott, Don Tanner, Jerald Tanner, Sandra Tanner, Paul Toscano, George Throckmorton, Dawn Tracy, Bradley Volmar, Wesley Walters, Brent Ward, Brooke Wells, David West, Bud Willoughby, Kenneth Woolley, Ron Yengich, David Yocom, Michael Zinman, and Mark Zobrist, as well as a dozen other people who asked that their names be withheld.

While the conventions of storytelling require that books on criminal cases focus on the efforts of a few key investigators, such cases are almost always solved through the efforts of many. The Hofmann case is no exception. Among those whose contributions deserve recognition are C. Larson of the B.Y.U. Police Department; Steven Bauer, Clive Barnum, Jo Ann Becker, Elliott Byall, Richard Chase, John Dehaan, Allan Galyan, Michelle Guthrie, Larry Hall, Jordan Lowe, Jerry Miller, James Newberry, Carl Newton, Edward Peterson, Steve Pirotte, Mary Riker, Marvin Rennert, Joyce Seymour, Robert Swehla, Jerry Taylor, James Thompson, and Frank Wandell of the

Bureau of Alcohol, Tobacco and Firearms; Philip Dinan of the Denver City Police Department; Scott Bakken, David Barker, Ned Christensen, Steve Clark, Calvin Clegg, Russell Dalrymple, Robert Gallacher, Richard Graham, William Hanes, Al Jacobsen, Morris James, Melvon Jensen, Terry Knowles, Theresa Mack, Dennis Molder, Stephen Moore, Rhead Richards, Donald Roberts, Don Rogers, Jeffrey Sarnacki, William Walker, and Mark Wilson of the FBI; Paul Hardy, Rudy Reit, and Steve Sweeney of Utah's Office of the Medical Examiner; Craig Geslison of the Provo City Police Department; Steve Bartlett, Sam Dawson, Dick Forbes, Michael George, Jennie Glover, George Throckmorton, and Olin Yearby of the Salt Lake County Attorney's Office; Russ Adair, Chris A'Hearn, David Askerlund, David Aylor, Jim Bell, Jim Bryant, Don Cahoon, Joel Campbell, John Campbell, William Cawley, James Chandler, George Clegg, Billy Collier, Ray Dalling, Mike Davis, Steve Diamond, Ralph Evans, Ken Farnsworth, Jim Faraone, Mike Fierro, Mike Fithen, John Foster, Scott Foulger, Bob Gillies, Jim Grandpre, Bill Gray, Bo Grimes, Scott Hallock, Frank Hattonward, Sam Hemingway, Dave Hendrick, Mack Humphries, Jed Hurst, Jim Jensen, John Johnson, Kyle Jones, Kelly Kent, Joseph Kattenring, James Leary, John Longson, Edward Lyman, Doug Maack, Henry Mark, Scott Marks, Chris Martinez, Jerry Mendez, Louis Muniz, James Nelson, Nick Paloukos, Richard Parkin, Gordon Parks, Mark Peck, Oran Peck, William Peglau, Kim Plouzek, Morgan Sayes, Greg Smith, Doug Shupe, John Stoner, Veda Travis, Dan Varoz, Richard Walton, Scott Warensky, Dave Ward, Bud Willoughby, and Mark Zelig of the Salt Lake City Police Department; Glen Bailess, Fred Baird, Bart Bellon, Garth Beckstead, Vern Beesley, Dale Bullock, David Burdett, Dick Carlson, Dean Carr, Alex Churchich, Dennis Couch, Mike Crebbs, Barry Dalton, Ken Davis, Steve Debry, Gaylord Dent, Syd Elliott, Steve Fife, Dan Fletcher, Dennis Floto, Ben Forbes, Jim Glover, Jim Grant, Steve Grogan, Marv Hammer, Pete Hayward, Tube Horiuchi, Ron Huber, Robert Jack, Brian Jackson, Leigh Kilpack, Dennis Knudsen, Rex Nelson, Tim Nielson, Lloyd Prescott, George Sinclair, Dave Smith, John Terry, Jerry Thompson, Doug Townsend, and Larry Wadsworth of the Salt Lake County Sheriff's Office; Don

Bird of the University of Utah Police Department; and John Graber of the Utah Highway Patrol.

In fairness, we should acknowledge those major players whom we were not able to interview. Shannon Flynn and Tom Wilding both demanded payment for interviews, a precedent we could not afford to set. LDS Church officials in the Public Communications Department were helpful in answering routine questions, but currently active Church officials uniformly denied us substantive interviews. Finally, despite the repeated assurances of his attorney, we were not able to interview Mark Hofmann prior to his first parole hearing on January 29, 1988—too late for our purposes.

However, we were able to supplement our own interviews not only with the massive record from the preliminary hearing but also with transcripts of interviews conducted by police and prosecutors with all of the principals, including Hofmann and Church officials.

We owe a debt of gratitude to a number of books, including Leonard J. Arrington's *Brigham Young;* Fawn M. Brodie's *No Man knows My History: The Life of Joseph Smith;* Linda King Newell and Valeen Tippetts Avery's *Mormon Enigma: Emma Hale Smith;* and Robert Gottlieb and Peter Wiley's *America's Saints: The Rise of Mormon Power.* We benefited immeasurably from Jerald and Sandra Tanner's many publications, especially their principal work, *Mormonism: Shadow or Reality?* As a counterweight to the Tanners', we also used *The Story of the Latter-day Saints,* by James B. Allen and Glen M. Leonard, and *The Mormon Experience,* by Leonard J. Arrington and Davis Bitton.

In addition, we would like to thank the *Sunstone Review* for permission to reprint excerpts from its interview with Mark Hofmann.

For their herculean efforts in transcribing hundreds of hours of interviews, we thank all our typists, especially Mari Hoashi and Robert Kurilla. Our agent, Connie Clausen, read the book with her usual unerring eye, and our editors at Weidenfeld & Nicolson, John Herman and Dan Green, gave us that rarest of authors' rewards, genuine editorial support.

Wherever dialogue appears within quotation marks, it represents an exact transcription of a conversation as related by a participant. In a few instances involving Steve Christensen, the dialogue is based on the recollections of friends to whom Christensen related the conversation at the time.

Wherever dialogue exceeds a few lines, it is based on either a tape recording or a stenographic transcription. The sole exception is the conversation between Brent Metcalfe and representatives of LDS Church Security. There the dialogue is based on notes made by Metcalfe immediately following each session.

For obvious reasons, we have tried to make clear in the text those few instances where we have relied solely on the testimony of Mark Hofmann.

For a variety of reasons, we have felt it necessary to change the names of certain minor players in the Hofmann drama. Deborah Bowdoin, Brad Carter, Fred Harmon, Nancy Loden, Carl Lundquist, Eric Palmer, John Steiner, and Jill Stone are all fictitious names, as are Paradise Cove and Garden Park.

Contents

PART ONE

Blood Atonement

1 To her friends, she was the perfect Mormon. Generous, thoughtful, forgiving, community minded, she represented everything that was good and right about their unique religion. If only outsiders, who always seemed preoccupied with the Church's unusual doctrines, missionary zeal, and Victorian politics, could meet Kathy Sheets. Then they would understand the strength and appeal of the Mormon way of life.

She was certainly no ideologue. The *Book of Mormon* invariably put her to sleep. (Her children once gave her an audio cassette version to play in the car, but that proved dangerous as well as boring, so she gave it up.) When the "big questions" came up in conversation—Did a tribe of Israelites really cross the Atlantic and settle in America? Did Joseph Smith really discover gold plates on a hillside in upstate New York in 1823? Was he led there by an angel? Was the *Book of Mormon* really another gospel that belonged right beside the Old and New Testaments?—she let others fight over them. She preferred Agatha Christie's mysteries to Joseph Smith's, slept soundly even when she missed church, and, like the rest of the country, spent her Sunday evenings watching "Murder, She Wrote." Her only tie to the Mormon power structure was a passing friendship with Hugh Pinnock, an old college pal of Gary's, who had become a bigwig in the Church hierarchy. She considered him an insufferable, sanctimonious windbag. "He-you rhymes with P.U.," she would say.

Kathy's philosophy, if you could call it that, was summed up in the aphorisms she had carved on wooden plaques and nailed up around the kitchen and family room:

THE EARLY BIRD GETS ITS OWN BREAKFAST.

BE ALERT. THE WORLD NEEDS MORE LERTS.

FORGET THE DOG, BEWARE OF MEAN KIDS.

3

*   *   *

More than ideology, more than catechisms, the signs provided what she really needed in the morning: a good laugh.

She especially needed them this morning, the Tuesday after a long Columbus Day weekend in October 1985. Gary had run out the door at the ungodly hour of 6:50 to take Jimmy to volleyball practice. (Volleyball practice at seven in the morning!) Then Gretchen, her eighteen-year-old joy and heartache, had left separately in her own car. God only knew what crisis would befall her today. Kathy wondered how she had ever survived when there were *four* kids in the house.

WHEN YOU REACH THE END OF YOUR ROPE,

TIE A KNOT AND HANG ON.

She took advantage of the sudden quiet to sit at the kitchen counter, treat herself to a Hershey's Chocolate Kiss, and slowly recover her sense of humor. Then she called her sister, Joan Gorton. This was her other joy in the morning. "The Lovely Sisters" they called themselves—they had seen the name on an old print in a New England hotel. They traveled together every chance they got. Kathy would always ask, "Are we sorry we didn't bring the men?" and the answer was always, "Not on your life."

Without the men, they could play. "Now Joan," Kathy would say in an airport lounge, "you have to look at all the men who come through here and find one that you could have an affair with. It has to be someone our age. It can't be some young stud." That made it a frustrating exercise. "He might be pretty good," she would say when a prospect approached, "but no. Look at his dumb *shoes*." And then they would laugh for the millionth time.

This morning, Kathy was bursting to tell all about her recent trip to New York City with Gary. But somehow the conversation slipped into a subject she didn't want to talk about at all: their mother.

She was living—if you could call it that—in a nursing home and waiting at that very moment, they could feel it, for one of them to visit. "You just dumped me here," she would say. It wasn't that they didn't love her, it was just so hard to see her lying in the nursing home like a dead leaf clinging to the end of a branch, waiting to be blown away. They would have preferred to see her living on her own, but that was out of the question. After the last operation, she had left some grease on the stove and burned her house down.

The conversation brought the usual rush of guilt—about not seeing her more often, about expecting her to die anytime. After her visits to the home, Kathy always arranged to stop at her daughter Heidi's house to play with her grandchildren. That invariably got her thinking about life again, instead of death.

Joan had to run. Lloyd, her husband, was waiting to take her to the Department of Motor Vehicles. She had let her driver's license expire. Kathy thought that sounded like something *Gary* would do. They both leaped at the opportunity to laugh. WHEN GOD CREATED MAN, SHE WAS ONLY KIDDING. Joan said she would call back when she returned. "There's still lots I haven't asked you about your trip," she said, signing off.

A few blocks away, Faye Kotter waited. Kathy was late for their morning walk. That wasn't terribly unusual. More than once, Faye, an attractive, athletic-looking woman with cinnamon hair, had walked over to the Sheets house and rousted Kathy out of bed when she overslept or crept back into bed after the house emptied. Faye remembered another of Kathy's signs: THERE'S A CURE FOR A POOR MEMORY BUT I FORGET WHAT IT IS.

Maybe she was still mad about their argument the other day. Faye had come unglued when she heard that Kathy's daughter Gretchen was going to a school dance with a black classmate.

Kathy was shocked. "You mean to tell me that you, Faye. . . ."

"Listen," said Faye, suddenly on the defensive. "I have nothing against blacks. I don't have anything against any race. But I don't want my children dating them. I don't wish them ill, of course. I mean, I'm against *slavery*."

Foursquare against slavery, thought Kathy. How brave.

"I just don't know why she would want to do it," Faye said.

"Because he's a neat kid," Kathy ventured.

"I'm sure he's a neat kid."

The discussion had gotten pretty heated. But it wasn't like Kathy to hang on to something that way.

Maybe she was depressed again. The troubles at Gary's business, CFS—Coordinated Financial Services—had caught her off guard. One week she was jetting off in Gary's private plane and inviting friends to use the company condo in downtown Salt Lake City, the next week she was buying bread and cheese and "picnicking" in the park. In fact, she and Faye had planned to spend the Columbus Day weekend at a condo in California, but Kathy had to back out. "We don't have the money," she confessed. (Another company had picked up the tab for the New York trip.) It didn't help matters that finally, at fifty, her age was catching up with her: she was going through menopause.

Faye had been in the house yesterday when Gary called. All she heard Kathy say was, "When will it end?"

Whatever was holding Kathy up, Faye decided to take advantage of the delay to put in a load of wash. Just as she finished, about 8:25, Kathy appeared, hopping mad. "I am so *mad* at him," she sputtered, flinging her furry beret onto the sofa, exposing her short, salt-and-pepper hair. "He makes me so mad." Tuesday was garbage-pickup day, and Gary had absentmindedly put the garbage where the dogs could get at it. And they did. Kathy had spent the last fifteen minutes putting trash back in the cans. "If Gary had only put it out where he was supposed to," she fumed, "this wouldn't have happened."

In her anger, she had grabbed her gray winter parka, too heavy by half for an autumn day that was overcast and cold—you could see your breath—but not freezing by Utah standards. Faye had put on two sweat shirts.

Kathy had also brought her car, the one with the license plate URP GAG. She obviously didn't want to walk around Naniloa that day, she wanted to drive to some other neighborhood and explore. Faye wondered if it had anything to do with Gary's speech in church the previous Sunday. She wasn't there, but by now it was all over the community. As bishop of his ward (a kind of lay minister), Gary had told the congregation, "I am going through some really hard times, and I just don't know how things are going to look financially. I have a lot to struggle with, and I don't know what's going to happen."

That, of course, started Kathy Sheets's telephone ringing. "We feel so bad for you and Gary. Can we help? What can we do?" It was all meant well, but it made Kathy squirm. "I just don't want people to feel sorry for me," she had said during their walk yesterday. On their return, a friend from up the street had approached Kathy and said, "I just have to give you a hug." Faye and Kathy looked at each other with the same thought: she had heard Gary's speech. She knew all about the problems Gary was having with CFS. Kathy wanted more than anything to avoid a repeat of that scene.

So they drove to the Cottonwood area, a fashionable suburb nearby, parked the car, and started walking. Kathy didn't talk much—a sure sign of depression. Normally, they never ran out of things to gab about. As they passed some of the big houses with the huge yards, Kathy finally said, "I wonder what the people in these houses are doing?" Faye remembered a conversation they had had months before in the same area when Kathy was her more buoyant self, before Gary's problems had weighed her down. "Can't you just picture the ladies sitting around having a luncheon after coming off the tennis court, having their shrimp cocktails and chattering. . . ." She had done a whole routine.

But this gray morning she had a different take on the big houses with the huge yards. "You walk along here and you wonder what is going on in people's lives. I bet it's not really as rosy as it looks. People drive by *our* place, and they say, 'Gary and Kathy have really got it made. They have a neat house and wonderful kids.'" She paused a long time before adding, "If they only knew." Knowing that Faye and her husband had been through difficult times a few years back, Kathy turned to her. "Tell me. How bad can it get?"

Remembering how supportive Kathy had been, Faye offered, "It always seems worse than it really is. Anything you are imagining in your mind—even if you lose everything—imagining it is worse than actually losing it."

That seemed to help, Faye thought, so she continued. "It's not the end of the world. It really isn't. You live through it. We think we're so attached to everything, but life goes on. And people forget. You are worried about what people think. Who cares what people think? They think what they think anyway. It doesn't really matter."

Faye wanted to say more, wanted to say the perfect thing, but she couldn't think of it. "It's a matter of just being here, I guess," she told herself.

They returned to Naniloa Drive about 9:25. Faye had to get to school. At age forty, she had gone back to college at the University of Utah. Before getting out of the car, she reached over and took Kathy's arm. "Hey, you going to be okay today?"

"Yeah."

Faye jumped out of the car with a cheery "See you tomorrow, it'll get better," but couldn't help feeling guilty. *Kathy* never stinted on the time she gave friends in trouble.

Instead of going home, Kathy pulled back out onto Holladay Boulevard and drove to the bank. The long holiday weekend and the trip to New York had left her without cash. On the return trip, she stopped at the entrance to the cul-de-sac and took the paper from the mailbox. As she pulled her red Audi into the garage, she saw a package halfway onto the wooden catwalk that led to the main house. She had been in such a hurry on her way out, mad at Gary, she must have missed it. She parked the car and walked around to pick it up.

She had just enough time to tuck it under her arm before it exploded. A second later, shreds of her gray parka hung from the tree branches overhead.

It was the second bomb that morning. If Kathy Sheets had turned on the radio in her car, she would have heard the frantic news reports that were already throwing Salt Lake City into a panic.

2

"There's been an explosion at the Judge Building, and there's all kinds of people dead."

The police dispatcher sounded like her chair was on fire. She had to be new on the job, Jim Bell thought. Dispatchers were usually the coolest of the cool. They prided themselves on their deadpan delivery: "Riot in Temple Square, forty-seven dead, Tabernacle on fire, possible UFO, see the officer."

"All kinds of people dead?" Bell repeated to himself.

"There's at least one dead," she clarified, "but I think there's a bunch more." Bell guessed it was probably a boiler explosion, something like that.

"I don't need this today," he mumbled, tugging at his mustache, and then, to pacify the dispatcher, "Okay, okay, I'll go on over."

He really didn't need it. He and his partner, Ken Farnsworth, were just coming off two lousy weeks. A homicide detective's nightmare: decomposed body, no leads, probable transient. No one knew who killed him, and worse, no one cared. But they had solved it anyway. A bunch of the dead man's fellow transients had gotten drunk and shot him four times in the head. It was a damn good piece of police work and still no one cared. Papers didn't even mention it and TV. . . . The thought of Channel 5's Eyewitness News team doing a live report on the decomposed bum was enough to make even Jim Bell smile, even this morning.

On the way to the Judge Building, Bell remembered that the dispatcher wasn't a rookie. She was day shift. Not the kind to flinch at nothing. There might just be something to this explosion. When Farnsworth turned on the radio, it was already the number-one story in town. Then they turned left off Third South.

It was like driving off the edge of the world.

Every patrol car and fire engine from a fifty-mile radius had converged on the Judge Building. Policemen, firemen, emergency medics, and a roaming horde of news people. It was pandemonium, all right, but still not enough to agitate Jim Bell—until he saw the dog. It was sitting obediently in the back of a big airport truck that pulled up with all lights flashing and siren screaming. It was a bomb dog. *That* made Jim Bell's heart skip a beat. This wasn't any boiler explosion.

Inside the lobby, uniformed officer Jim Brand Preeney confirmed it. "It's a bombing, and it's definitely a homicide, and there's one guy dead upstairs," he told them. "You can't go upstairs because the bomb dogs and bomb techs are sweeping the whole building."

When the bomb crew gave the all clear, Bell and Farnsworth took the stairs to the sixth floor. (The elevator had been turned off. Someone said the bomber had been seen using it.) The hallway looked like a war zone. The walls were blown in, the ceiling blown down, and one door frame blown free of the wall. The door had blown off its hinges and dangled from the frame. The walls were pockmarked with shrapnel craters. Chunks of wallboard and ceiling tile were scattered everywhere. Bell whispered under his breath, "We're in deep shit."

The victim lay just inside the doorway, on his back, his hips rotated slightly to the right. He had a deep laceration in his chest area, and his face was covered with black soot and some blood. It would be hard to make a positive I.D. until the medical examiner cleaned him up. (Bell didn't want to rummage for a wallet for fear of disturbing the evidence.) The pants covering his right thigh had been ripped open by the explosion, and the leg underneath shone bright red in the harsh, artificial light. The tips of some of the fingers on his right hand had been blown off in the explosion. His right leg from the ankle down was badly mangled. The heel of his shoe, and of his foot, was missing.

Surrounding the body were two six-packs of crumpled Tab cans and the remains of a bag of doughnuts. The victim did not have good eating habits.

Bell and Farnsworth herded everyone else off the floor, strung yellow Do Not Cross tape, and commandeered an office at the opposite end of the hall as a control center. Within minutes, Bob Swehla, a thirteen-year man at the

Federal Bureau of Alcohol, Tobacco and Firearms, showed up. All bombings are federal cases, ATF cases, so Farnsworth was uncharacteristically deferential. "What do you want to do, Bob?"

Swehla, like most ATF men, was a professional. None of this interagency rivalry crap. He was used to cooperating with local law enforcement. It was a rare bombing that didn't bend some local noses. The Salt Lake police would retain custody of the evidence; ATF would provide its laboratory.

Farnsworth manned the control center while Bell and Swehla laid out the bomb scene. They ran fluorescent tape in a grid and made a chart so they could note with coordinates where each piece of evidence was found. They took Polaroids of the entire area, dozens of them. Bell drew a diagram of the floor plan. Each time he picked up a piece of evidence, it had to be labeled and a corresponding label placed on the map. He started with the big pieces: bomb parts, sack parts, cardboard box parts from the device, batteries, wires, chunks of plaster, bits of acoustic tile from the ceiling, shards of plastic from the overhead lights. Just the easy stuff took two and a half hours.

Meanwhile, they tried to identify the body. The office where the bomb went off had recently been rented by Rigby-Christensen, Inc., a small consulting company. Eyewitnesses placed Steve Christensen, one of the firm's principals, in the hall at the time of the explosion. But Bell needed a positive I.D. About ten, Shane Jones, a fellow officer and part-time male model who happened to know Christensen, provided it.

"Is it Christensen?" Bell asked.

Jones forced himself to look. "I can't tell for sure. It sure looks like him." Then his handsome face clouded over. "I'm sure that's Steve. His face is messed up, but that's his hair color; it's his size. I'm sure it's him."

Still, Bell didn't announce the victim's name officially until 1:30, when the body was finally moved and the wallet taken out of his pocket. Farnsworth followed the body to the medical examiner's office for the autopsy.

Now, with the body gone and the scene to himself, Bell could really get to work. With a magnifying glass in one hand and tweezers in the other, and a supply of plastic bags and vials, he got down on his knees and resumed the search.

For Jim Bell, this was almost heaven.

Heaven would have been standing knee-deep in a smelly bog somewhere along the shores of the Great Salt Lake at five on a frosty morning in November, waiting, 12-gauge shotgun in hand, often for hours at a stretch, for that rustle in the underbrush or that commotion in the sky, that moment when you raise your gun, aim, and bring down a big one. Duck, that is.

Jim Bell was a duck hunter.

The boys in the department got a lot of mileage out of that. "Hey, you know the only way to give Bell a hard-on?" they would joke. "Quack!"

During college at Weber State, Bell had gone duck hunting every day during the season, scheduling his classes so that he wouldn't miss a single frigid morning in the swamps of the Ogden Bird Refuge. When he married, his wife Patti found 250 ducks in his deep freezer, dressed and ready to cook.

But jokes or no jokes, everyone agreed that duck hunters made great cops. "When you do surveillance work, you want duck hunters because they're the only people who can sit still all day and not get bored," his fellow detectives would say. "They're used to it. They don't have any brain waves. They're perfectly content looking over the horizon for a speck in the sky." Bell himself admitted that duck hunting was for "slow people," people who could wait, people with patience and persistence, people who kept their own pace.

That was Jim Bell.

His parents had found that out early—to their dismay. Unlike most of the cops in his department who came from cop families, Bell was a crossover from the real world. His father was an executive with the Steelcase Corp., his brother also a prosperous businessman. Jim was supposed to follow in their footsteps, but he had his own ducks to hunt.

Being the only cop in the family didn't faze Jim. Nothing fazed Jim. It didn't even faze him when fellow detectives called him "Stretch"—an arch reference to his height, five feet, seven inches. As the shortest in his family, he was used to ribbing. He just kept at it, calmly ignoring the jokes, pursuing the cases—the more tedious, the more complicated, the more elusive, the better.

Like the murders of several young women in the Salt Lake area: they seemed unrelated at first, just random murders without rape. But the M.O. was precisely the same, and Bell was convinced a serial murderer was responsible. So he began his methodical pursuit, canvassing police departments across the country for similar crimes, similar M.O.s, anything that might tie in to his killer. He called agencies in Utah, Colorado, New Mexico, and Wyoming and brought officers from all the jurisdictions together for a meeting. Right away, two murders in Wyoming were solved. One of the cops had interviewed a man in a jail in Nephi, Utah, who confessed to killing two people in Wyoming.

That was the way Jim Bell liked to work: slowly, meticulously, patiently, tenaciously. He might have to spend all day wading through a swamp, but he had 250 ducks in the freezer to show for it.

So Bell moved slowly across the floor on his knees, picking up every fragment of evidence with tweezers and putting it in a plastic bag or a vial or a paper bag and carefully pinpointing its location on his map. In the end, there were 164 items on the floor plan: among them, pieces of wire, an Estes rocket igniter, and a mercury switch.

When that was done, he cut away pieces of the carpet and put them in plastic bags. Residue from the bomb powder was sealed in paint cans. Then he tore the hall apart looking for shrapnel. The bomb had been packed with two-and-a-half-inch carpentry nails—this bomber meant to kill—and the force of the explosion had driven them into walls, through the ceiling, and deep into the subflooring. Bell dug out as many as he could, using a huge pair of pliers on the stubborn ones, and left the rest. With a broom, he swept up small pieces of debris, and then used a vacuum cleaner to suck up anything he might have missed. Then he went back over the key areas with a magnifying glass for one last look.

Then, just to be sure, he arranged to have a search warrant issued for Christensen's office. They hauled away fourteen filing cabinets, a computer system, and fifty cardboard boxes full of materials. Eventually, he would have to wade through all that as well.

At 10:15 that night, after more than twelve hours, most of them spent on his knees, Jim Bell returned to his office to begin the paperwork.

3

For anyone else, the autopsy of Steve Christensen's body would have been a nightmare. In the time it usually took to complete the exam, Dr. Steve Sweeney, the state's chief medical examiner, hadn't even cleaned away the coagulated blood in order to see what he was doing. Pieces of evidence had to be pried out of the cavern where a chest should have been: lengths of wire, bomb parts, bits of a battery, and huge jagged shards of metal pipe. One piece proved particularly reluctant. It had entered through the chest and lodged under the armpit, where it bulged up beneath the skin, pressing the body out of shape. And there were nails everywhere. Some had gone in sideways, others straight, like arrows. One had entered through the left eye and lodged in the brain. That, at least, had killed him instantly.

Through it all, Ken Farnsworth's eyes never left the table.

For Farnsworth, gore was just a part of the game. His stomach for "goo spots" was legendary—not just dead bodies, not just decomposed dead bodies, but *goo spots*—bodies that have been left so long that they don't even look like bodies anymore, but more like puddles of slime. In the never-ending police search for litmus tests of machismo, tolerance for goo spots ranked high, and Ken Farnsworth held the departmental record.

Autopsies were his forte. One photograph that made the rounds showed the medical examiner cutting a body with one hand and holding his nose with the other while Ken leans over the rail, chin in hand, utterly fascinated, filling his nostrils with the experience. Someone had posted a cartoon on the wall showing two vultures sitting on the carcass of a dead hippo. "What could be better?" says one vulture to the other. "A hot day and a bloated body."

But the boys in the department had it all wrong. It wasn't the goo spots themselves that made Ken's day. It was the thrill they gave him—the sheer adrenaline rush he got from staring at something so horrible, so repulsive, so shocking.

It was the same rush he used to get as a patrolman. He loved the "controlled chaos" of patrol work, never knowing what was going to hit you next. He still told the story (a way of reliving the rush) about his brush with death—the ultimate adrenaline high. It was early morning, that last bleary-eyed hour before the end of an all-night shift. He had been on the force only eighteen months and was headed back to the station when he heard some shots just outside the Beehive Buck Club, a black hangout in downtown Salt Lake. He pulled around by the Greyhound bus terminal and waited for backup. At the end of an alley, he heard some arguing and saw two silhouettes dipping and dodging behind a pickup truck. He got out of his car, carrying a 12-gauge shotgun.

Then he did something only a rookie would do. He called out after them. They ducked out of sight, and he ran after them down the half-lit alley. When he got to the corner, he stepped out from behind a brick wall, completely exposing himself. Ten feet away, one of the men was standing there screaming at two others who were behind the pickup. He was holding a 410-bore shotgun, but it was pointing down.

It was a classic "shoot/don't shoot" situation. A split-second decision. If he shot, it would be to kill. That was the rule. Only cops on TV shoot to maim. The regulation was three shots: two in the chest, can't miss; then one in the head, no surprises. Farnsworth wanted to reverse the order, to shoot the guy in the face. No. A shotgun shoots high. Hit him in the throat. That can't fail. A shotgun blast from a 12-gauge, and he's history.

The gun was racked in, cocked, safety off, ready to blast off. If the guy moved that 410 even slightly, Farnsworth would blow his head off. No time for a warning. The 410 started to move up. Farnsworth's inner alarm said, "Shoot!"

But nothing happened. Something inside stopped his trigger finger at the last nanosecond.

The man droped his gun.

He had gotten the same rush when he worked undercover for seven months in Utah's first sting operation. That was one long adrenaline high, from the time he walked into a meeting with one of the nastiest drug dealers in the Southwest, fully wired, and the guy started to frisk him, to the time a crazy lady, strung out on cocaine, held him at knife point. It got so bad—or good—that he was actually sleeping with his hand on a gun on his nightstand. After that, homicide duty, with its goo spots, was a definite comedown.

He still got the old rush from shooting his gun. Although the product of a solid police family (three relatives on the force), Farnsworth didn't fire a shot until he was twenty-two. But once he started, he couldn't stop. He loved the noise, the jerk of the recoil, the little black hole in the target a split-second later. He fired off twenty thousand rounds a year to maintain his standing as one of the top 100 marksmen in the country. His wall full of trophies had earned him the nickname—everybody on the force had a nickname—"Trophy Boy."

He got the same rush from women. Not from women per se, but from *dating* them, dating new ones as often as possible, dating two or more at a time. He never seemed to run out of them. At six feet, three inches tall and 150 pounds, with a sharp wit, remarkable intelligence, and winning grin, Farnsworth was that rarest of commodities in marriage-mad Utah, an attractive bachelor over thirty. And he had every intention of staying that way. Friends attributed it to his two years in France when he was a younger man. Despite his own family's rather loose Mormon affiliation, he had gone on a mission to convert the French to Mormonism, and instead had been converted to everything French: French food, French wine, French women, even French philosophy. Somehow the Mormon ideal of wife, family, and hearth had never looked as good to him since he had seen Paris.

Besides, there was no rush in family life. "If they just gave me bed and food," Farnsworth would say of police work, "I'd work here for nothing."

He left the autopsy room at University Hospital about six that evening and headed back to the department carrying the blood-covered nails, wires, and clothing in paper bags. He arrived in time to catch some details of the other bombing that day, the one at the Sheets residence in Holladay. That one happened in the county, not the city, so it wasn't their problem, thank God. They had enough on their hands. He also saw his boss, Chief Bud Willoughby, on the evening news trying to calm a panic-stricken city that had already been dubbed "the Beirut of the West."

A huge man with big, clear eyes, startling energy, and rare patience, Willoughby had cop in every capillary of his bloodline: father, brothers, even his mother was a cop. That probably explained his gut approach to crime solving. He had no ideology, no fancy theories. His only rule was "Whatever it takes is what it takes." If his men needed more money, more manpower, even more time to do a job, he fought for it. He had even been known to consult hypnotists and psychics when all else failed.

If Willoughby had a flaw, it was overeagerness, especially when dealing with press and public. No one would forget his efforts to calm the city, especially its tiny black community, when two black joggers were killed. The murders are not racially motivated, he announced confidently. That turned out to be dead wrong. The murders had, in fact, been committed by an avowed white racist, Joseph Paul Franklin. Willoughby was forced to eat his words—in court no less—when the defense attorney called him to the stand.

Now he was at it again.

The bomb that killed Kathy Sheets was meant for her husband Gary, Willoughby explained. Both he and Steve Christensen were officers in an investment company, Co-ordinated Financial Services. Recently, CFS had lost a lot of money, and a lot of its investors were mad about it—mad enough to kill. Obviously, they had hired professionals, Mafia types, to do the job. The bombs were sophisticated devices, undoubtedly the work of paid assassins.

There was no crazed bomber on the loose randomly killing passersby, Willoughby concluded reassuringly. This was strictly business. To emphasize the point, Captain Bob Jack of the sheriff's office held up an inch-thick computer readout of three thousand CFS investors and said, "Here are the suspects in the case."

That sounded fine, but Farnsworth hoped this didn't turn out to be another of Willoughby's faux pas.

Farnsworth went home about 4:30 the next morning and grabbed an hour and a half of sleep. Jim Bell, who had come into the office around ten P.M., stayed the rest of the night, although at one point he lay down under the table and closed his eyes for a few minutes.

4 J. Gary Sheets, a gray-haired man with soft, friendly features and dark eyes, stood in the pandemonium of the Salt Lake County Sheriff's Office in Holladay and cried. "We think it was a professional hit man, Gary," a homicide detective tried to tell him. "A disgruntled investor in your company, probably." Kathy's killing had been a mistake: the bomb had been intended for him. Somebody wanted both him and Steve Christensen dead. Until a few months ago, when he left to form his own consulting firm, Christensen had been the president of Sheets's company, CFS.

A few minutes later, the detective overheard Sheets telling a friend, "I did it. My friend's dead and my wife's dead because of a situation I got them into."

Visitors came and went and he hugged each one and cried some more. Church leaders called and so did Senator Orrin Hatch—Sheets had worked on his last campaign. Hatch gave his condolences and said he had called the head of the FBI and told him to "Get those bastards." Sheets repeated the story to everyone who came in after that. He seemed untouched by the police warnings —"A professional hit isn't paid until the job's done." The killer would try again. But he welcomed the company of the bodyguard assigned by the sheriff's office, a policeman who had once moonlighted at CFS.

Strangely, Sheets wanted to know about the condition of the bodies: "Is it true that the blast took off the upper portion?" he asked Lieutenant Ben Forbes of the homicide division. "Is it true that it literally cut Steve's body in half?"

"I didn't see the body," said Forbes, "but that's what I understand."

"Is that about the same way Kathy was found?"

"I'm really not sure, Mr. Sheets, but I am sure that your wife didn't suffer at all."

Then suddenly Sheets's mind was in another place. He looked at the can of Cherry Coke in his hand. "This is going to be the biggest seller that Coca-Cola has," he said with genuine wonder. "This Cherry Coke is really going to sell. This is going to be the biggest seller ever."

Fifty years earlier, a towheaded little boy edged nearer a coffin, trying to get a look at the beautiful, serene young blond woman inside. He understood only vaguely why she was there and why she was so still. When Doc Gledhill slipped into the back of the crowded parlor to pay his respects, the little boy ran to him and hugged his leg. "Please bring back my mommy," he cried. "Please bring back my mommy!"

The boy was Gary Sheets. He was three years old.

There was no father for Gary to hug. Lloyd Sheets, a traveling salesman, had passed through Richfield, a small town in southern Utah, only long enough to fall in love with and marry a beautiful blond girl named Iris Peterson. He was the first man who had paid much attention to her. Despite her beauty, boys had avoided the local lame girl with the withered leg, a legacy of childhood polio. But Iris Peterson was an incurable optimist. Instead of dating, she learned to play the mandolin, the ukelele, and the banjo. And when Lloyd Sheets left her, soon after their son Gary was born in 1934, she set her sights on business college, polio or no.

She was on her way there when she contracted pneumonia and died.

Three months after taking in his orphaned grandson, George Peterson, a local businessman, died of a heart attack. That left Gary and his grandmother Eva.

It was Gary's first partnership. Before long, he was doing her taxes, managing her property, and running the businesses George had left her. Spurred on by his mother's Mormon faith, his father's salesman genes, his grandmother's relentless optimism—"You can do anything you want to do," she exhorted him—and the memory of the blond woman in the coffin, he started running and never stopped.

In college, he sold rattraps to farmers. Then he moved up to encyclopedias. His Sigma Chi fraternity brothers at the University of Utah used to joke there was nothing Gary Sheets couldn't sell. In the world's oldest profession, he was a natural. A salesman, not a hustler. Someone who says, "I really believe in this product," not "Here's an opportunity to con some people." Someone, in the words of an associate, who "cons *himself* first."

Then he tried selling real estate and fell on his face. The problem was that he couldn't work over the phone, in an office, across a desk. He was, at heart, a *direct* salesman. He had to be there, with the client, hands-on— hugging, grasping, touching, stroking. He had to put his arm around the customer, wrap him in that warmth, that optimism, that guileless sincerity. Let him do that, and there was nothing he couldn't sell. So he went back to encyclopedias, door to door, and the income poured in again, enough to buy a first house for his young bride, Kathy Webb, whom he had almost refused to marry because she wasn't blond.

Insurance was next, working for an old fraternity brother, Hugh Pinnock, who was smart enough to know a good thing when he saw it. But insurance was too easy for a natural like Gary Sheets. By the 1960s, the action was in securities so he went after a securities license. Pinnock, who had ambitions of his own, found the competition from his brightest young salesman too hot for comfort and told him that if he moonlighted in securities, Connecticut Mutual would have to let him go. But there was no stopping Gary Sheets. In 1966 he turned in his resignation and set up his own brokerage agency. For anyone else, it would have been an unnerving gamble, a leap into the unknown, but Gary didn't even blink. He knew it would work.

Within two years, he had sold so many securities to so many clients that he was ready to move into another new area: total financial planning. That's where the *really* big money is, Gary said. He wanted to be where the sales were hottest. After only three years with a big, Atlanta-based company, he was ready to strike out on his own again. With two friends, he formed his own financial services company: Coordinated Financial Services.

Nothing could stop him now. Not even timid partners. In 1975 he was ready to expand to meet the market demand, but his partners balked. They weren't naturals. They weren't blessed with Gary's boundless optimism. So one day, they locked themselves in an office and knelt down to pray. Then they began dividing the company. At the end of the day, they called in an attorney to add the boilerplate to the deal that God had made.

Gary Sheets and CFS were now on their own.

It was beautiful to watch. In ward houses and on college campuses throughout Utah, Nevada, Colorado, and Texas, there was Gary Sheets, in his blue suit, red tie, and white starched shirt "talking sense" about investments. Part teacher, part cheerleader, part seducer, he talked profits and portfolios the way Moses talked milk and honey. He would lead them out of the Wilderness of taxes, over the River of deductibility, and into the Promised Land of high returns. You could practically hear the audience gasp. They were mostly doctors, drummed up with an extensive advance promotional campaign, including good word of mouth on the Mormon grapevine.

Not everyone there was Mormon. Gary kept a copy of *The Best Doctors in the U.S.* on his desk, making extensive marginal notes beside the names of prominent individuals, knowing that for every one of the big fish he could attract, a school of M.D.s would follow. "Physicians are suckers for scams," said a CFS employee, using language Gary would never have used. "They've got a lot of money and very little time to manage it. So they get very excited, overly excited, by high rates of return."

They couldn't wait to give Gary their money.

These investment seminars, offered free throughout the Southwest, became the lifeblood of CFS. At the end of a lecture, Gary would hand out business cards to anyone who wanted the lecturer's expertise "on a more personal and permanent basis." Out of a typical audience of sixty or seventy, usually twelve or more would sign up.

Then those clients would bring in other clients. The money poured in like the Red Sea on the armies of Pharaoh.

Sheets hired a brigade of bright young men to help invest the money, syndicate deals, form partnerships, and manage properties: men like Steve Christensen, an eager, inexperienced twenty-eight-year-old who quickly became Gary's "boy wonder." More deals demanded more salesmen to bring in more money to fund more deals. It seemed that God truly was with him. Sheets turned the day-to-day management over to others so he could concentrate on sales and on reaching his new personal goal: $1 million in commissions—$10 million in sales. The new men, like Christensen, were all "high-quality people," as Gary liked to say, all active in the Mormon Church. By the early eighties, CFS had grown from two employees to 120, total syndications to almost 150, net worth to $6 million. The internal rate of return was running at a stratospheric 30 percent. To congratulate itself, the company bought the old Auerbach's Department Store building downtown and converted it, sparing no expense, into a gleaming new "headquarters" where the men were always handsome, the secretaries always "immaculately decked out," the plants always green, the restrooms always clean, and the receptionists always answered the phone cheerfully.

Even the building, where salesmen (they were called consultants) brought admiring clients, was a sharp investment. According to John Naisbitt's megaseller, *Megatrends*, Salt Lake City was one of the country's "top ten growth areas." Among the others who thought so was Adnan Khashoggi, the Saudi billionaire. His Triad America Company had just bought a huge chunk of downtown with plans for an immense new multi-use development. With new corporate offices for American Express, Sperry-Rand, and Western Airlines just opening up, downtown Salt Lake City was taking off the way Denver had ten years before. It was heady company for Gary Sheets's CFS, but anything seemed possible.

By 1983 Gary was earning $600,000 a year in commissions. It wasn't yet his goal of $1 million, but it was enough to build a beautiful rambling house by a fast-running creek in the toniest section of the tony suburb of Holladay. It was enough to buy fistfuls of season tickets to Utah Jazz basketball games, and to buy himself a seat on the board of the Utah Symphony—no one seemed to care that he didn't know anything about music. It was enough to give tens of thousands away to charities of every stripe, including $10,000 to the Osmond Foundation, set up by the singing Osmond family to benefit children's hospitals (a gift for which they made him chairman of the foundation). It was enough to merit glowing profiles in Church-owned publications like the *Deseret News* and evenings with Orrin Hatch, one of the many Republican politicians whose campaigns he supported generously.

But the choicest recognition came from even higher up. In April 1983, the same year he made $600,000, Gary Sheets was "called" by God to serve as a bishop in the Mormon Church. And there were whispers that one day, if his star continued to rise (and his fortune continued to accumulate), Gary Sheets might become a General Authority.

5   In 1837, a newspaper editor in Kirtland, Ohio, criticized Joseph Smith and the local Mormon community for "hav[ing] too much worldly wisdom connected with their religion—too great a desire for the perishable riches of the world—holding out the idea that the kingdom of Christ is to be composed of 'real estate, herds, flocks, silver, gold,' etc., as well as of human things."

On a cool Southern California night almost 150 years later, prosperous Mormons from all over the Los Angeles area filled a meeting hall in Pasadena. They had come from as far away as La Jolla to hear G. Homer Durham, a member of the First Quorum of the Seventy, address his fellow saints. Only the Council of the Twelve, known as the Apostles, and the three members of the First Presidency, including the Prophet, were more exalted. Together, these eighty-five men who governed the Mormon Church were known as the General Authorities.

When Durham spoke, he spoke with true authority, authority rooted in both this world and the next. His opposition to liberal politics, to the ERA, and to Democrats in general was well known and widely admired among the faithful. Many thought: If only the men in Sacramento or Washington had such vision.

The subject of the sermon tonight was money. Not the evils of money, but the joys. The sixty-nine-year-old Durham praised local Church members both for their devotion to God and for their balance sheets. He congratulated them not just because of their good works, which were considerable, but also because they belonged to one of the most affluent stakes in Mormondom. That, said Durham, was a direct reflection of God's favor, a sign that the Church of Jesus Christ of Latter-day Saints was, in fact, the *true* Church of Christ on earth.

At each accolade, the crowd squirmed deeper and deeper into the comfortable seats. Elder Durham had apparently failed to see, scattered among the $400 suits and designer dresses, a considerable number of darker faces wearing clothes from Sears and K mart, most of them recent immigrants from Mexico and other Central American countries. After the speech, the word was discreetly passed to Temple Square in Salt Lake City: please don't send us G. Homer Durham again.

Durham wasn't *wrong*, he was just too blatant. Everyone knew that the Church equated bank accounts and blessings; that, as one Church official put it, "The accumulation of wealth" was "a sacred obligation." Why else would God call only successful businessmen to positions of authority? Why else would Church publications so relentlessly profile Mormon success stories like George Romney, J. Willard Marriott, and the Osmonds? Why else would the Church be so ironfisted about tithing, the rule that every good Mormon give 10 percent of his income to the Church?

Everyone knew where these vast sums of tithing money went. Not to orphanages or old-age homes or hospitals. Not to young missionaries in the field—they were generally expected to pay their own expenses. Not to welfare or disaster relief. In times of crisis, Mormons were expected to look to one another for help, not to the Church's tithing chest.

Everyone knew that Church money went into the

Church's business, which was *business:* television stations, newspapers, banks, farms, ranches, real estate, and a stock portfolio to match that of the government of Saudi Arabia. The Church was, in fact, a giant conglomerate, freed by its religious, "nonprofit" status from both reporting requirements and taxes.

God had indeed been generous with his favor—from $15 billion to $50 billion generous, depending on who did the estimating. Whatever it was, it was a truly inspirational figure. More than a few of the Brethren agreed with Durham that "if [the Church] is rich, it must be true," and must eventually triumph over other churches. Fifty billion compounded at 9.2 percent, tax free. In a few hundred years, the Mormon Church wouldn't need to convert the world, it would *own* the world.

With the Lord on his board, there was nothing Gary Sheets couldn't do. What worked for real estate, the bulk of CFS's investments, would undoubtedly work for other investments as well. Besides, good real estate deals were getting harder to find. Investors were eager to branch out into new areas. If CFS didn't oblige them, some other outfit would. The magic word became "diversify." Soon Gary Sheets, encyclopedia salesman, was doing deals in alternative fuels, gold mines, airplanes, horse-breeding farms in Kentucky, and express lube shops in Las Vegas.

Instead of hiring people with expertise, Gary sent his able young men in their starched white shirts and Temple garments out on week-long "get-acquainted" trips. When they returned, they became in-company experts, each with his own pet project. Somebody thought solar energy looked promising, so CFS bought $700,000 worth of solar panels. The plan was to rent them out to heavy users of electricity, meter their usage, and charge only 70 percent of what the big utilities charged. It sounded fail-safe. Rich James, CFS's president, had seen a high-tech waterslide, or "hydrotube," at a mall in Portland, Oregon, and thought it was "neat." So CFS syndicated a $750,000 investment in a similar slide for a mall in Denver. They bought airplanes—a Citation and a Lear—for a million and a half. Nobody knew anything about planes, but a good Mormon pilot, Brent Bateman, told them they could make a killing by leasing the planes to companies like Purolator and stars like Robert Redford. Their eyes twinkled.

One of CFS's salesmen put the company in touch with John Steiner, the son of the salesman's bishop and a missionary companion. Steiner had a Thoroughbred breeding farm in Kentucky that he was syndicating. Investors could buy a piece of a stud, and each time it bred—about forty times a year on average—they would get a piece of the fee, plus a tax break (if they borrowed) and depreciation. A CFS entourage went to Kentucky to see for themselves—and, as long as they were there, take in the Kentucky Derby.

They liked what they saw. Steiner was just the kind of guy CFS admired: so young, so good looking (in the white-bread, Midwestern insurance man way that so many Mormons are), so all-American, so *Mormon*. His operation was first class: fancy hotel, fine restaurant, a huge house with a swimming pool and a beautiful wife. And the guy was only thirty-three. CFS officers bought into the deal and came away thinking: Yet another gilt-edged investment found through the Mormon network. It had to be divine intervention.

Eric Palmer, a former mortician or shoe salesman, depending on whom you spoke to, introduced Gary and CFS to the wonders of ethanol, a gasoline substitute distilled from grain. The numbers were staggering. Because the government offered an 11 percent alternative-energy tax credit on top of the usual 10 percent investment tax credit, an investor could put $10,000 into an ethanol plant, borrow $90,000, and get $21,000 in tax credits *the first year*. So you could actually *make* money by investing. Then every year after that, you took out $10,000 in profits and saved $10,000 in taxes. This was truly a deal made in heaven.

Just to be sure, CFS sent a private investigator down to Portales, New Mexico, where Palmer already had one plant in operation. But when the investigator returned with grave doubts about Palmer's reliability, CFS officers were too busy fighting one another over who would get what cut of the action to notice. (Gary grabbed much of it for himself.) Besides, Kirk Rector, who put the deal together, was a smart, hard-working, young Mormon— the son of a General Authority, no less. Within a few months, CFS had plans for five ethanol plants in the works.

Meanwhile, the company continued to acquire commercial property despite a softening market. The men responsible for bringing properties into the company continued to pitch them—they made their commissions whether or not a property subsequently made money—and Gary continued to buy, sometimes over the objections of his own acquisitions board. After all, he had the magic touch.

But even if there were a few doubting Thomases, Gary Sheets was hardly the only officer who felt that CFS couldn't fail.

At a meeting to discuss the acquisition of a property called Paradise Cove, John Conrad, a young Mormon salesman who had only recently joined the company, looked at the projections and scratched his head. "What's wrong with me?" Conrad wondered. "This property is a *dog*. Why do I look at these numbers and see absolutely no purpose for anyone to buy it? What have I missed?"

The numbers showed a $52,000 investment that after five years, even if one accepted the projections—a true act of faith—would repay only $54,000 in a cash sale. "Why was this property purchased?" Conrad asked at the next meeting. "I am apparently missing something. Can somebody explain it to me? Why would I want to buy this thing? Two thousand over $50,000 over five years?—according to *your* figures. No cash flow in the interim. A little tax savings, but no profitability."

"We *stole* this property," said the man from the real estate committee. "We bought it cheap."

"Then I assume you're planning to sell it cheap," said Conrad, "because these numbers don't show the windfall return we should expect if we're buying it cheap. What am I missing?"

Just then, Steve Christensen walked in.

Someone said, "Steve, you were down there, explain it. Tell us about Paradise Cove."

"We *stole* it," said Christensen.

"Can you elaborate?" asked Conrad, still calm. "Where is that reflected in the numbers?"

Just then Tom Heal walked in. Christensen turned to Heal. "Tom. Tell us about Paradise Cove."

"We *stole* it," said Heal.

Perhaps they believed, Conrad thought, that if they said it often enough, that would make it true.

When an early real estate project went into bankruptcy, it wasn't a mistake, it was merely a "setback." To prove it, CFS resyndicated the property, Garden Park, signing on new investors to bail out the old ones. When profits started slipping, the company merely increased its share in partnership investments, from 2 percent to 3 percent.

When salesmen like Conrad started asking too many questions, Gary decided that the solution was to give them less information. What they really needed was more positive thinking. More *faith.* "If you give them facts," a company attorney warned him, "all they'll do is ask questions. They're not smart enough to understand the deal anyway. You put the deal together, and just don't tell them any more than you have to. Just go in and sell them the deal. Then you go run it and make it a success."

At a meeting to sell the Garden Park resyndication scheme to the salesmen, Conrad raised his hand again: "Gary, give us some facts. Give us some numbers. I haven't heard anything said that would convince me that this is a good investment. And please don't give me a sales job. No more hype."

Gary stood up, pointed his finger at Conrad, and said, "John. I *have* to do a sales job on you, because you're so damned *stupid* you can't recognize the best investment your clients will ever put their money into."

End of discussion. How do you challenge someone who has been called by God? "We were dealing with prominent members of the Church," says Conrad, a devout Mormon. "I admit that I put some faith in that. I felt that these guys were trying to do what was right. I knew I wasn't associated with a bunch of crooks."

6   The good Mormons of Kirtland, Ohio, undoubtedly told themselves the same thing when Joseph Smith, Prophet and founder of the Church, opened a bank.

Smith knew a good thing when he saw it, and in 1836, the best thing by far was land speculation. With the westward drive, land values were shooting up at such a frenzied rate that fortunes could be made virtually overnight. By the mid-thirties Smith had already spent every dollar he had buying up land around the Mormon community in Kirtland, hoping that a railroad would run a line somewhere across his property and make him a rich man. When he ran out of his own money, he started looking for other people's money to use. The best way to attract money, of course, was to open a bank, and in 1836, coincidentally, the Lord commanded him to do just that.

There was just one problem: you had to *have* money to open a bank. Never a stickler for details, Smith went out and borrowed the money to open the Kirtland Safety Society Bank and have plates made up for printing the currency the bank would issue. To assure depositors that their money would be secure, he filled several strong boxes with sand, lead, old iron, and stones, then covered them with a single layer of bright fifty-cent silver coins. Prospective customers were brought into the vault and shown the heaping chests of silver. "The effect of those boxes was like magic," claimed one witness. "They created general confidence in the solidity of the bank, and that beautiful paper money went like hot cakes. For about a month it was the best money in the country."

Smith wasn't fazed a bit when the state legislature refused to grant his bank a charter. With only a few additions to the printing plates (why waste the money to have new ones made up?), the Kirtland Safety Society

Bank became the Kirtland Safety Society Anti-Banking CO. As far as Smith was concerned, a company, unlike a bank, didn't need a charter.

The faithful, of course, didn't care what it was called. It was enough for them that the bank was run by Joseph Smith. What safer place could they put their money than in the hands of the Prophet? Lest they miss the message, Smith wrote an article for the Mormon newspaper inviting his flock to "take stock in our safety society. . . . We would remind them also of the sayings of the prophet Isaiah, . . . which are as follows: 'Surely the isles shall wait for me, and the ships of Tarshish first, and to bring thy sons from afar, their silver and their gold (not their bank notes) with them, unto the name of the Lord thy God, . . .'" Smith added the parenthetical to the biblical text as a discreet reminder that his bank wanted deposits in hard coin, not in notes drawn on other banks.

After only a few months of operation, the Anti-Banking Co. collapsed. The single layer of silver coins didn't last long once the notes started coming in. Meanwhile, the Ohio state legislature, unamused by Smith's semantic games, charged him with operating an unchartered bank and fined him $1,000. To collect, however, they had to get in line with the other investors who were suing Smith (thirteen suits were filed against him between June 1837 and April 1839). On the night of January 12, 1838, Smith, like many other speculators, declared bankruptcy with his feet, fleeing Kirtland with his followers under cover of darkness. In his imaginative account of the event, Smith later claimed he left Kirtland "to escape mob violence, which was about to burst upon us under the color of legal process to cover the hellish designs of our enemies."

To prevent his creditors from hounding him to his new home in Nauvoo, Illinois, Smith declared legal bankruptcy, but not before transferring many of his assets to his wives, children, friends, and associates—some 105 people in all. (In 1844, the year of Smith's death, these transfers were declared fraudulent and illegal.)

"If Joseph Smith were alive today," says a prominent Mormon businessman, "he wouldn't start a religion, he would be a leverage buyout king on Wall Street."

* * *

A hundred and fifty years later, the U.S. Attorney's Office declared Salt Lake City "the fraud capital of the nation." Between 1980 and 1983, the Utah U.S. attorney estimated that about ten thousand investors lost approximately $200 million in fraudulent deals. Many of them involved or implicated Church figures, even General Authorities. Scam artists had a name for it: "the Mormon marketing strategy." Any scheme, they discovered, no matter how outrageous or flimsy, would fly if it could be tied to the Church—What safer place to put one's money than in the hands of the Prophet? Investing money in a scheme that had the blessing of a General Authority was as good as handing it to the Lord.

So eager were many Mormon faithful to accumulate wealth (and blessings), and so trusting of Church leaders, that they would buy the Brooklyn Bridge—twice. Or better yet, "gold certificates" worth, according to the nice young Mormon man who sold them, a hundred or even a thousand times the up-front investment. When he was finally caught, the nice young man had unloaded $612 *billion* worth of bogus certificates—an amount equal to half the national debt. "What you have out here," says a local newspaper reporter, "is a bunch of people who are basically educated from birth to unquestioningly believe what they're told, and they do, right up through adulthood. The conditions for fraud are perfect." In 1981 alone, Utah was third in the nation for business-loan defaults and suffered eleven major business frauds. SEC officials labeled Salt Lake City "the sewer of the securities industry."

The Church finally had to take note of the stink when in the early 1980s, a member of the Church's elite found himself embroiled in a multimillion-dollar mortgage fraud. Believing that Elder Paul Dunn, a member of the First Quorum of the Seventy, had blessed the deal, hundreds of trusting Mormons had mortgaged their houses and given the proceeds to a Mormon entrepreneur named Grant Affleck who promised to invest their money, make their mortgage payments, and give them a substantial profit to boot. In his sales pitch, Affleck showed pictures of himself, Dunn, and some of the Osmonds cutting a ribbon at the opening of one of his housing developments.

Like most Ponzi schemes, Affleck's scam went smoothly as long as new money poured in, but as soon as the flow of gullible investors stopped, the whole pyramid collapsed, leaving many without their money and some without their homes.

Fortunately for the Church, Dunn had pulled out of the company before the roof caved in, but the "Grant Affleck Affair," as it became known, was enough of an embarrassment that the Church felt compelled to make a rare public statement: "Beware of smooth talk," said the editorial in the *Church News,* a weekly supplement to the *Deseret News,* "claims of endorsements or participation by Church leaders are often false. . . . Some Church members think normal business formalities should be suspended when they are dealing with 'brothers and sisters.' This can lead to fraud." The author of those cautionary words was Gary Sheets's old frat brother, Hugh Pinnock.

7

But Gary Sheets was no Grant Affleck.

Even as the price of oil plummeted, the inflation rate fell, and real estate values began to tumble, Gary kept the faith. In a depressed market, the CFS building, once the company's pride, became a costly white elephant. Properties in Houston followed the whole oil-based Houston economy down the proverbial tubes. Everybody was hurting, but aggressive firms like CFS with high debt-to-equity ratios found themselves particularly far out on the limb when they finally heard the sawing. The project that Gary had approved over the objection of his acquisitions board went bankrupt, as did the resyndication of the Garden Park project and many others. The $700,000 worth of solar panels sat in the basement of the CFS building gathering dust. Not a single one was ever rented.

At first, everyone tried to blame the catastrophe on the economy, OPEC, or poor management. Rich James, the comptroller turned president, had been too mired in detail; he failed to delegate; the various parts of the company were too compartmentalized. In December 1984, Sheets dumped James (who was smart enough to transfer his assets to other members of his family) and handed the reins to his fair-haired boy, Steve Christensen.

But things only got worse.

Christensen discovered that large sums of money had been "borrowed" from solvent partnerships to prop up losing ventures. The officers responsible argued that these were merely loans—"plugs" was the word they used—from one company to another. Arm's length transactions. All very proper and above board. So what if none of them was ever paid back? That didn't make them illegal—just bad business decisions.

Not everyone took such a benign view. John Conrad was stunned when he heard about it. "It was like some-one telling me that my mother, a sweet old farm lady in West Mountain, Utah, was a prostitute." Gary, too, was shocked by the extent of the "plugging," although when a $300,000 plug turned up and he loudly demanded to know who was responsible for it, his name was on the check. "I sign some things I haven't seen," he explained limply.

Meanwhile, the ethanol plants, the golden investments over which corporate officers had fought, followed the fortunes of the oil market. Profit projections that looked great when oil was $40 a barrel looked dismal when it fell to $15. The company made a recision offer and prayed that no one would grab it. Meanwhile, the plants them-selves continued to consume vast quantities of increas-ingly hard-to-come-by cash. When a team of accountants flew to Portales, New Mexico, to find out what was going wrong, Eric Palmer ran them off.

The airplanes, another glamour investment, turned out to cost far more and be worth far less than everyone had expected—everyone, that is, except Brent Bateman, the good Mormon pilot who had brought the deal to CFS in the first place. What Bateman had failed to reveal was that the Learjet they had purchased for $800,000 had sold previously for only $650,000. In his enthusiasm for the deal, he had also overlooked the need for a mainte-nance reserve, an oversight that meant the plane began to lose money almost from the moment CFS bought it. When Nick Smith, the man in charge of the deal for CFS, found out about Bateman's "mistake," he couldn't believe it. "Brent was such a good Mormon, a religious person. Such a personable, likable fellow. I just didn't expect bad things to happen."

In Lexington, Kentucky, John Steiner, the good-looking young Mormon horse breeder and son of a bishop, stood up and gave a speech at a banquet following the Kentucky Derby. The next morning, he packed all the valuables he could into his Cadillac and drove off. More than $1 million in investor money disappeared with him, including about $200,000 that belonged to the CFS officers he had wined and dined. In his enthusiasm, Steiner had sold the same package to several different investors.

But nothing could shake Gary Sheets's confidence.

At every new piece of bad news, he would give another pep talk. "All we need to do is sell more product," he would say. "If the money keeps flowing in, then we can solve these problems." No one could tell him that investors weren't about to put more money into a failing company.

When told about a pathetic $5,000 debt that had to be paid with scarce cash to avoid a lawsuit, Gary offered, "Why don't I just show him my financial statement? That ought to satisfy him. Because I'll personally guarantee it."

"You can't personally guarantee anything," his attorney, Paul Toscano, told him. "Your financial statement is terrible."

"But I have assets worth millions of dollars," Gary complained.

"Sure, but you can't just show him the asset side. You've got to show him the liability side as well."

Sheets stared at Toscano for a long time. It hadn't occurred to him, the consummate salesman, that you had to show both sides of any statement.

At another meeting, Gary suggested that he could personally borrow enough money to keep the company afloat. He looked shocked and hurt when someone explained that he couldn't borrow any money personally with a personal financial statement in the red.

"It was like Hitler's bunker," Toscano recalls. "Here was Gary talking about moving the Ninth Panzer Division in—and there was none."

But Gary dismissed such talk. No matter what happened, no matter how bleak things looked, he still had faith that somehow CFS would be saved.

Steve Christensen tried to make him see the light—or the darkness. He formed a secret committee to draw up a plan for saving the company, or at least its most viable assets, by selling them off to a new independent entity—an entity independent of Gary Sheets and his "pathological optimism." Christensen called it the "White Knight" plan. On August 1, 1985, he presented it to Gary.

Sheets was shocked at first, then angry. More defeatism, he thought.

"The only way to make this work is to be more optimistic," he insisted. "There's got to be a better alternative. I'm gonna come up with it. I can save this. I made this company happen and I'm gonna make it happen again." Then he ordered Christensen to: "go back and come up with a plan that's based on a more optimistic view of the company."

Gary just didn't get it. Optimism was no longer enough. Christensen retreated to his computer and gave it one last try, but the numbers were inescapable. He went back to Gary and said it again, "It's all over."

"Steve, can't you tell people we're gonna pull through?" Gary asked.

"But we can't pull through," said Christensen.

"Can't you just tell them we might have a chance?"

"But we don't have a chance."

"The only way to solve the problems is to get people to believe we can do it, that there's a fighting chance."

"But there isn't a fighting chance."

"If you're that negative," said Gary angrily, "if there's absolutely no chance at all, why stay around?"

"Either you accept what needs to be done, or I'm going out the door," said Christensen.

"So go out the door."

Gary Sheets would do it himself. He would take the reins again and turn the company around—a comeback to end all comebacks. He had brought CFS this far. Like H. Ross Perot and Lee Iacocca (whose autobiography he was reading at the time), he would turn defeat into victory and lead his company to even greater triumphs.

His strategy? *Sell!* "We've got to go out and continue to sell product," he told his salesmen, "and by doing that we'll be able to make money and solve the problems of the past."

Gary Sheets couldn't go under. God wouldn't let him. "I don't know how it *can't* work," said one of CFS's attorneys. "We have a stake president and a couple of bishops in this thing. I don't see how the Lord would ever let this thing sink."

Once in control again, Sheets finally realized just how dire the situation was. He tried to implement Christensen's plan to sell off the viable parts of CFS and repay at least some investors but it was too little too late. A letter went out to investors advising them of the company's dire situation. Salesmen glumly began giving their clients the devastating news. "There have been fabulous losses," the Salt Lake *Tribune* reported. "One man lost $500,000 in one of the partnerships in one hit. . . . There were marked mass losses and unhappy people."

One of those unhappy people, police suspected, had hired a killer.

The bombings put an end to any last-ditch efforts to save CFS. Potential buyers for the viable pieces disappeared overnight. Bankruptcy became inevitable. Not long afterward, Gary Sheets was asked to resign as a bishop in the Mormon Church.

8

On the day after the bombings, Brad Carter, a twenty-four-year-old florist, picked up a shipment of tulips from Holland at the Salt Lake airport and then drove downtown. He parked his truck in the usual spot, in front of the McCune Mansion on Main Street, just north of Temple Square, and walked down the hill to the Crossroads Mall, where he had lunch with a friend. A little after two, he left the mall and headed back up the hill to his truck, passing on the way newspaper machines displaying the latest headline in the story that had all of Salt Lake jumpy: 2 KILLED IN S.L.-AREA BOMBINGS: POLICE SUSPECT "HIRED ASSASSIN." It was about 2:45.

Halfway up the hill, in front of the Deseret Gymnasium, he remembered what was wrong with this parking spot. It was lovely coming down, but murder going up. At the top of the hill, he had to stop to catch his breath. He saw a postman, a meter maid, a few others on the street—and, in the vicinity of the gymnasium, a white male, average height, a little stocky.

He saw the man go to his car, a sleek blue sports car, open the door and lean inside, keeping one foot outside on the pavement. His arms and shoulders were moving. It looked as if he was shifting something off the driver's seat. At that point, Carter looked away—he had been hit twice by cars when he wasn't paying attention, and besides, he had just broken up with his girlfriend. He had a lot on his mind.

He had time to cross the street before he heard the explosion. It sounded like a car backfiring and a gunshot combined—double that sound. He spun around and saw only smoke and debris where the blue car had been, and a man lying in the street. Some pieces were still airborne.

Carter hightailed it down the road to the scene of the wreckage. "It looked like somebody was in sad shape," he later told the police, "and that's all I cared about." The man was lying flat on his back, legs bent and spread apart. He had a gaping hole in his knee, one of his fingers had been blown off, exposing the bone. There was a gash in his head that bled badly, and some kind of wound in his chest. He was covered with powder burns. It wasn't clear if he was alive or dead.

Carter wanted to leave him where he was until the ambulance came, but the flames in the car were spreading, and the heat was already overwhelming. With the help of two passersby, he dragged the man across the street and onto the grass in front of the gym. He took one last look at the car before flames engulfed it. He could see the bottom half of a box, a cardboard box, on the floor of the passenger's side. The top had been blown off. There were also some papers crumpled up, and a pile of papers in the back behind the seat. Flames quickly consumed them.

Carter heard faint sounds of breathing coming from the man. People came running out from the Deseret Gym with towels and he applied them to the wounds, which had begun to bleed what seemed like gallons. When he tore the man's clothes off to get at them, he saw he was wearing his Temple garments, the holy underwear that all good Mormons wear every day, everywhere, under their street clothes. So he took out the vial of consecrated oil that he always carried with him and anointed the man with it, saying, "I command you to live until the proper medical help gets here."

9   Ken Farnsworth, who had spent the morning at Kathy Sheets's autopsy, was on his way back to the department when he heard the news over the car radio. There had been a third bombing at 200 North Main Street.

Farnsworth recognized the victim's name: Mark Hofmann.

The investigation was only a day old, but Hofmann's name had already come up as a business associate of Steve Christensen's. In his entire life, Christensen had only done two things that might make someone want to kill him, his friends said. One was taking the helm of Gary Sheets's sinking company. The other was buying the Salamander Letter, a letter written by an early Church leader that undermined some of the major tenets of the Mormon faith. Although Christensen eventually donated the letter to the Church, it received national publicity, embarrassed the Church deeply, and upset many faithful Mormons. Upset them enough, perhaps, to want revenge.

And the man who sold Christensen the letter was Mark Hofmann, a respected dealer in rare books and documents, especially ones relating to Mormon history.

Police had dismissed the letter as a motive in the Christensen killing because it had nothing to do with Gary or Kathy Sheets. But the bombing of Hofmann changed everything. Now it looked like they were facing not some disgruntled investor, but some disgruntled believer.

When Jim Bell heard that the victim of the third bombing was alive, he jumped in his car and headed straight to Latter-day Saints Hospital. Bombings were rare. Survivors of bombings were even rarer. He didn't know how badly Hofmann had been hurt but hoped he could hang on long enough to answer a few questions.

He arrived at LDS Hospital about 3:40 and tracked down a friend of his wife's who worked in the emergency room. "Where's Hofmann?" he demanded, skipping the pleasantries. She led him to a huge room filled with doctors and nurses and one uniformed officer, all in masks and gowns. On the left wall, a battery of X-ray viewers was covered with films. Bell assumed they were Hofmann's. He noticed one in particular: a knee with a round piece of metal imbedded in it, probably the end cap from a pipe bomb.

Through a large window on the other side of the room, he could see Hofmann (it had to be him) lying on a gurney surrounded by doctors and nurses. He asked a nearby nurse, "What kind of condition is he in? Is he in a position for me to talk to him?"

She asked one of the doctors, who said, "It's fine with me." Did he need a gown and mask? She said it wasn't necessary. Then she led him into the X-ray room, where he spoke to Hofmann directly.

"I'm a detective with the police department," he began softly. "Do you feel like talking to me?"

"Sure," said Hofmann, surprisingly lucid. Two nurses were dressing a head wound and some IV lines ran into his arm. The technicians were setting up for the next round of X rays.

"Do you feel okay?"

"I guess so."

"Can you understand me?"

"Yes."

"Can you hear me?" Hofmann seemed to be having a hard time hearing him.

"I'm having some problem in one ear. You'll have to speak louder."

"Do you own a—is your car blue in color?"

"Yes."

"Where were you going when your car exploded?"

"I was going to sell some documents to an attorney here in town. The documents I intended to sell were in my car when it exploded."

"Can you go over your movements from the time you got out of bed today?"

"I got up at 7 A.M., left home, and drove to a Dee's Restaurant at about 60th South and Highland Drive. I got there about eight. I had eggs and hash browns and a glass of orange juice for breakfast."

Bell was dumbfounded by how clearheaded Hofmann seemed. He had had witnesses down at the Hall of Justice who were more befuddled than this man lying here badly wounded in the emergency room. "What did you do after you left the restaurant?"

"I just drove around for a while."

"Where were you driving around?"

"Around."

Maybe not so clearheaded. "Where's around? You know, east, west side of town or what?"

"I don't know. Just around." Bell was a good enough cop to know that Hofmann wasn't just befuddled, he was being evasive. He was coherent enough to remember what he had for breakfast, but not where he had been all morning.

But why would a *victim* be evasive?

"You must remember some of the places you went," Bell pressed.

"Well, I was up in Emigration Canyon."

"What were you doing up in Emigration Canyon?"

"Just driving around."

"Just driving around?"

"Thinking."

"What were you thinking about?"

"Just things."

At that point, Bell had to leave the room for a few minutes while the technicians took another set of X rays.

When they were through, he came back and started again. "Do you feel okay? Do you want to begin again?"

Hofmann said, "Yes, I'll talk to you."

"Okay. Let's talk about what happened when you got to your car?"

"I went to the car, opened the door, and something fell off the seat onto the floorboard. It was a package and I reached for it and it blew up."

"Give me a description of the package."

"Well, it was just a package, I can't remember anything special about it."

Bell decided to try again with Emigration Canyon. "What were you doing up in Emigration Canyon?"

"Just driving around."

"You said you were driving around thinking. What were you thinking about?"

"Things."

This was getting nowhere, and Bell couldn't understand why. Of course, he'd never dealt with a *living* bombing victim before. Maybe it was the effect of a concussion or some sort of limited amnesia. There had to be an explanation.

When they wheeled Hofmann into another room for a CT scan, Bell sat outside thinking about what he had said—or hadn't said. A doctor detailed Hofmann's injuries for him. Pointing to the X ray with the end cap, he explained that the knee had been severely damaged, that it had been pinned back together and large clips attached to the outside to hold the leg in place. More surgery would be required, but Hofmann was out of danger.

Jim Bryant, the uniformed officer in the surgical gown, filled Bell in on what had happened before he arrived. Bryant had been the first person other than medical personnel to join Hofmann in the trauma room. He had told the same story about opening the door and a package falling out.

But there was something else.

Hofmann had told Bryant about a brown pickup truck that had been following him earlier that day. He described it in detail: a full-size, tan pickup truck with some damage on the right front bumper. The driver was a white man, about thirty-five or forty years old, and he was wearing a white shirt. The license plate number was TW something, something, with two 3s in it.

"I pulled over at about 200 South West Temple," Hofmann said. "The truck stopped in the traffic lane and waited for me to pull away again. I didn't think the truck had followed me to the area of the Deseret Gym, and I didn't see the truck when I left my car there."

Finally, he asked Bryant for a favor. He wanted the policeman to rely a message to some friends.

"What's the message?" asked Bryant.

"Tell them to get out of town."

10 When television and radio stations began interrupting their programming to flash the astounding news that there had been a third bombing and Mark Hofmann was the victim, Salt Lake City's small community of Mormon dissidents flew into a panic. Like the police, they immediately saw the terrifying logic of it: the Salamander Letter had touched off a spark in some crazed Mormon fanatic, and he had declared open season on the Church's enemies.

That night, Jerald Tanner, one of the most prominent dissidents, was startled from a restless sleep by the faint sound of a car outside his house. Wide awake, he looked at the clock. It wasn't even four yet. Beyond the windows of his small Victorian house on West Temple Street, Salt Lake City was black and quiet—except for the unmistakable sound of footsteps approaching his front door.

He had lived in fear of this moment ever since settling for good in Salt Lake City in 1960, ever since he and his wife, Sandra, began their crusade of information against the Mormon Church, publishing a newsletter and scores of books and pamphlets. They had attacked the Church's policy of denying blacks the priesthood. They had brought many of the Church's historical skeletons out of the closet, like Joseph Smith's 1831 revelation instructing Mormons to marry American Indians (a "dark, and loathsome, and filthy people") because intermarriage would make them "fair and delightsome." They had exposed the Masonic roots of the secret Temple-endowment Ceremony. At one point, one of the Twelve Apostles, the Church's ruling body, had given them an ominous order: "I'm warning you—don't start anything against this Church."

But nothing happened. And after a few years of sleepless nights, the fear went away.

The bombings had brought it all back.

Like everybody else, the Tanners had dismissed the first two bombs as CFS related—just some irate, unbalanced investor. Then came the third bomb, the one in Mark Hofmann's car. It's finally begun, they thought. The Day of Retribution. A Mormon crackpot had finally reached the end of his fuse. The Lord had sent an avenging angel to smite the critics of the Church.

Others wondered if the Church itself was behind the bombings. It was hard, almost impossible, to believe that the Church, given its obsession with public relations, would stoop to murder. But at a time like this, no scenario, no matter how outrageous, seemed truly impossible. After all, the Church Security force was a notorious hotbed of Mormon fanaticism, just the kind of crazies to rid the Church of its enemies—with or without authorization. By now dark rumors were already circulating through the underground that a Church Security truck had been seen tailing Mark Hofmann the day before *his* bomb went off.

The Tanners' phone hadn't stopped ringing since. People from all over the country: "Are you all right?" "Have you got police protection?" "Is everything okay?" "Do you have a gun?" CBS News wanted to interview them. A friend of George Bush's with CIA connections called to offer "special security" if police protection proved inadequate.

Their employees, the ones who ran the presses and collating machines in the basement, spent the following days in a state of sheer terror. The husband of one wouldn't let her come to work unless he came with her and sat beside her all day. Another checked her car from top to bottom before starting it—and even then, closed her eyes when she turned the key.

Many of their friends in the small but vocal Mormon dissident community had already left town. All feared for their lives, feared that they would be the next to hear footsteps in the night, that theirs would be the next name on the avenging angel's list.

Trembling, Tanner woke his wife.

Sandra Tanner was a fifth-generation Mormon, a direct descendant of Brigham Young, founder of Salt Lake City and builder of the Tabernacle, a larger-than-life figure that all Mormon children are taught to revere. As a young girl raised in a cloistered Mormon community in

Los Angeles, she had never doubted her religion. In fact, she grew up thinking that it made her superior. "I knew *my* church history," she recalls. "The other kids, the Catholics especially, were dupes who were being spoon-fed altered history, but *I* was in the true Church. *I* had the inside scoop. *Our* leaders had nothing to hide."

And so she continued to believe until one day, over-come with curiosity, she began to ask questions. That led inevitably to trouble. In class after class, teachers scolded her for "confusing" the other students. Finally, after much soul searching, she left the Church, married Jerald Tanner, and enlisted in his mission to "give people knowl-edge so they can find the way."

How odd, she thought as she saw the fear on her husband's face, that the great-great-granddaughter of Brig-ham Young should be fearing for her life at the hands of his most zealous followers.

The noise was on the porch now. Someone leaving something at the door? Devout Christians, the Tanners thanked God that their children were not in the house that night. With his wife trailing him, Jerald padded down the stairs, his tall, gangly body stumbling in the darkness—without his contacts he could barely see his way to the door. Sandra would have to be his eyes.

In the midst of his terror, he wanted to catch the murderer in the act, actually laying the package at his doorstep.

It was Joseph Smith himself who put the death sentence on the Tanners' heads.

Sometime in 1839, while conversing with Saint Peter—he held frequent dialogues with biblical figures—Smith hap-pened to mention the problems he was having with dissi-dent members of the Church. According to Smith's own telling, Saint Peter said, in effect, "You should have *seen* the problem we had with Judas Iscariot." When Smith asked Peter how he handled his problem, Peter replied that he had personally "hung Judas for betraying Christ." That was enough for Joseph Smith. From that day for-ward, the punishment for dissent in his Church would be death.

Smith's successor as Prophet, Brigham Young, a bril-liant leader but a huge bully of a man, spelled out the new theory in a series of bloodcurdling sermons. "There are sins that men commit for which they cannot receive forgiveness in this world, or in that which is to come, and if they had their eyes open to see their true condition, they would be perfectly willing to have their blood spilt upon the ground."

When a few brave souls suggested that such a doctrine was perhaps too harsh, Young replied,"I know, when you hear my brethren telling about cutting people off from the earth, that you consider it a strong doctrine, but it is to save them, not to destroy them." (Young, of course, had other reasons for imposing such a hard rule. He was determined not to lose converts at a time when settlers were badly needed to populate Salt Lake City.)

What exactly were the sins that required "cutting off from the earth"? In addition to dissent, they were murder, adultery, theft, taking the Lord's name in vain, miscegenation, breaking covenants, leaving the Church, lying, counterfeiting, and condemning Joseph Smith, his Church, or any of its leaders. Any one of these, according to the doctrine of Blood Atonement, required that a man be killed in order to be saved.

And not just killed. His blood had to be *spilled:* specifically, "his throat cut from ear to ear, his tongue torn out by its roots, his breast cut open and his heart and vitals torn from his body and given to the birds of the air and the beasts of the field and his body cut asunder in the midst and all his bowels gush out." (In practice, slitting a throat usually proved sufficient.)

For those who didn't catch on, Young and his followers provided many instructive demonstrations.

Only days after announcing his intention to leave Springville, Utah, for California in 1857, William Parrish was "interviewed" by three Mormon officials who found his beliefs "unsatisfactory." Soon afterward, he and his son were shot and their bodies loaded into a wagon. When the corpses finally turned up, Mr. Parrish had been stabbed forty-eight times, and his throat cut "from ear to ear." No one missed the point. Mrs. Parrish later recounted, "There had been public preaching at Springville, to the effect that no apostates would be allowed to leave; if they did, hogholes would be stopped up with them. . . . My husband was no believer in the doctrine of killing to 'save,' as taught by the teachers."

Failing to believe in Blood Atonement was one of the sins that demanded Blood Atonement.

William Parrish wasn't alone. During the early years of Salt Lake City, when new construction was everywhere, builders were constantly digging up skeletons, not in coffins, not in cemeteries, but just a few feet deep in what had been open fields. Local sheriffs looked the other way, but the U.S. marshal at the time, Sam Gilson, was convinced that "the leaders of the Church were the guilty party." He decided to prove it by bringing one case to trial, the murder of a man named Yates, in 1871. Yates had committed the sin of selling ammunition to government soldiers who had been sent by President Ulysses S. Grant to enforce the laws against polygamy and foil Brigham Young's plans to create a "spiritual and temporal Kingdom" of his own and secede from the United States. To Young, those troops were "the enemy" and so was anyone who supported them. Consequently, according to a contemporary account, Yates's "brains were knocked out with an ax."

A man named William Hickman, who did the actual "saving," confessed that he did so on orders from the Mormon leaders, and the U.S. district attorney had the temerity to indict not only the mayor of Salt Lake and several others, but the Prophet himself, Brigham Young. Before they could arrest him, however, Young, who had already been arrested and released on charges of "lewd and lascivious cohabitation" with sixteen of his wives, fled to the Mormon stronghold of St. George, Utah.

Meanwhile, in Salt Lake City, his followers did their best to persuade the authorities to drop the charges. The appeal was simple and direct. Heavily armed men visited all the local Gentiles (non-Mormons) who had supported the federal authorities "in opposing the Mormon system" and told them that if Young was arrested, they would all be killed.

Persuaded, the Gentiles ran to the U.S. attorney, R. N. Baskin, and implored him to drop the charges against Young. Baskin, a man not without a sense of humor, told their spokesman, "You would make a splendid angel, and as I do not intend to grant the request, you had better prepare to go to Abraham's bosom." (Young, the so-called Lion of the Lord, was eventually arrested for murder. But before his case was brought to trial—Baskin was certain the government would have won in court—he was released on a technicality.)

As the Tanners knew all too well, the bloodthirsty, vengeful spirit of Brigham Young was still alive in the vast outback of rural Utah. There were still polygamists out there, thirty thousand of them by some estimates. Although most were peaceful, decent people, a small core of fanatics believed that the current Prophet of the Church, Spencer W. Kimball, was an agent of the Devil because he had succumbed to the federal government on the issue of polygamy. On more than one occasion, they had threatened to blow him up.

By comparison, Blood Atonement was downright mainstream. In fact, it was still a part of the Temple Ceremony, the secret religious service established by Joseph Smith. Just as in Smith's day, modern worshipers ritually agreed during the ceremony to "suffer" their lives "to be taken," if they revealed its secrets. The P.R.-minded men On Temple Square didn't like to talk about it, and many of the insurance salesmen and housewives who went through the motions didn't know what they meant. But a few did. And in a state filled with guns and religious fanatics, it only took one.

11

One like Ervil LeBaron.

At age twenty-eight, LeBaron, a Mormon polygamist, founded the Church of the First Born of the Fullness of Times. Claiming divine inspiration, he waged a campaign of death, terror, and Blood Atonement unmatched since the days of Brigham Young. It began with the murder of his brother, Joel, in 1972. Six years later, God ordered LeBaron to have one of his wives, Vonda White, "Blood Atone" an apostate named Dean Grover Vest. God spoke to LeBaron, as he did to

Joseph Smith, very specifically. Tell White to "fix Vest a hot meal," God said, and then, "while he is at the table enjoying the dinner," get behind him and "shoot him in the back of the head until he is dead."

When another of LeBaron's followers, Lloyd Sullivan, began having problems with his wife Bonnie, God interceded again. He told LeBaron to tell Sullivan: take Bonnie to the "Deep South and deep-six her there." In another revelation, God ordered the death Of LeBaron's own daughter, Rebecca. The Lord's exact words: Send her a "one-way ticket."

As many as twenty-nine people may have been "Blood Atoned" under LeBaron's ministry of terror.

More recently, in 1984, two polygamous brothers, Ron and Dan Lafferty, had become infuriated at their sister-in-law, Brenda, for refusing to encourage their brother, Allen, to take on additional wives. To remove the obstruction and advance the cause of polygamy, they broke into Allen's home and killed both Brenda and her fifteen-month-old daughter, slashing their throats from ear to ear.

When Ron Lafferty was arrested, the police found a written revelation in the pocket of his shirt:

Thus sayeth the Lord unto my servants the prophets. It is my will and commandment that ye remove the following individuals in order that my work might go forward, for they have truly become obstacles in my path and I will not allow my work to be stopped. First thy brother's wife Brenda and her baby, then Chloe Low and then Richard Stowe. And it is my will that they be removed in rapid succession that an example be made of them in order that others might see the fate of those who fight against the true saints of God. . . .

Not all the fanatics were as crazy as the LeBarons and Laffertys, but, unfortunately, not all the fanatics were safely out in the countryside. Some were right downtown, working in the Church Office Building.

They may have looked like drab office workers, in their white shirts, old suits, too-wide ties, and too-tight belts, but underneath they were the Lord's foot soldiers— some would have said God's gumshoes. Some were, in fact, former FBI agents and proud of it. They were led by J. Martell Bird, a former Fed who, upon retiring from the bureau offered to run the Church's security operation. Bird had been one of J. Edgar Hoover's right-hand men back in the good old days, before the bureau was high-teched and yuppified. It was said, with some awe (and often by Bird himself), that he was one of only seven men in the FBI that Hoover actually trusted—if he trusted anyone. He had been on the surveillance team that bugged Martin Luther King's hotel room and listened in on the moans of white call girls. He had also bugged communist college kids, those peaceniks and fairies who opposed the war in Vietnam. "Bad people have to be watched," Bird was fond of saying.

Bird had been appointed to his position as head of Church Security by Ezra Taft Benson, a man who made even J. Edgar look conciliatory, a man who considered Eisenhower "a socialist," the civil rights movement "a communist conspiracy," and the John Birch Society just a bunch of patriots. With Benson's backing, Bird had helped turn a tiny security operation that used to spend most of its time tracking down kids who stole from the candy machines into a mini-FBI, and the Church offices, especially the offices of the First Presidency, into a veritable fortress. When the Prophet was being moved from his official residence in the Hotel Utah to a new apartment, windows were replaced with bulletproof glass and walls fitted with sheets of steel—enough to stop a bomb.

"When you are at war," Apostle Boyd K. Packer said publicly, "and we are, security is crucial."

When a fire alarm went off on the fifth floor of the Administration Building, one man from Church Security came running out of his office yelling, "We're under attack! We're under attack!" In public, the Prophet was surrounded by more security men than the President of the United States. Offices were constantly being swept for electronic bugs. There were always rumors of phones being tapped and even of listening devices being placed in rooms of the Temple to overhear the plotting of radical fundamentalists.

More ominous were the Church's increasing efforts—like those of the Nixon White House—to "keep track of" its critics. A secret "Intelligence Division" was created within the security office for just that purpose and staffed with the purest of the pure, the same kind of nonsmoking, nondrinking, hypercommitted Mormon shock troops that Howard Hughes had surrounded himself with in his last paroxysms of paranoia.

Only this time, they were working for God.

On November 6, 1975, afraid that his phone was being bugged, Jerald Tanner had picked up the receiver to call an ex-Mormon who knew something about bugging. Between the second and third rings, he heard a woman's voice saying softly, "They're trying to call out."

A few months later, the Tanners received a letter from a young man in California named Stan Fields, inquiring about their activities. For the next four years, Fields corresponded and visited often. He was a bright, scrubbed young man, a former missionary who claimed to be a refugee fleeing from the Church.

He was, it turned out, a mole spying for the Church. His name was Steve Mayfield, not Stan Fields, and he had worked for both the Church and the FBI. On July 16, 1980, Tanner confronted him in the Church Office Building. He denied spying for the Church but confessed that some of the material he had gotten from the Tanners might have "floated upstairs."

Some time later, the Tanners also discovered that the FBI had opened a file on them as potential "threats to the national security." All it would have taken was a phone call from Martell Bird to one of his buddies still at the bureau, or, better yet, from a Church leader to a powerful Mormon politico in Washington—"God has asked me to ask you. . . ."

To sic the FBI on the Tanners was one thing; to blow them up was something else. But there were so many unanswered questions. Why did Church Security men materialize at the scene of the Hofmann bombing almost instantly? What about the report by the state legislator that Church Security had kept Hofmann under surveillance? That didn't make them bombers, but it didn't make them look good either. Did they see it happening and not try to stop it? At least one federal investigator from the Bureau of Alcohol, Tobacco and Firearms thought it looked more than just suspicious. He almost ignited a fistfight in the police department when he declared the murders were the work of the "Mormon Mafia"—a group of "hit men" from Church Security sent by their leaders to "off the enemy." Shades of Brigham Young. More level heads saw the possibility of a rogue operation: something unauthorized, something to protect the "plausible deniability" of higher-ups.

The night of October 16, the night of the third bombing, Jerald Tanner laid his trembling hand on the doorknob while Sandra peered out the window.

It was a man in a black uniform—a limousine driver. He was there to pick them up for their appearance on CBS's "The Morning Show." Apparently, someone had forgotten to tell the limousine company that the appearance was canceled.

Which again raised the question of why the appearance —to be taped at the Church-owned CBS affiliate, KSL-TV—had been canceled in the first place.

12 When Jim Bell heard that Hofmann's scans would take at least another hour or two, he stationed a uniform at the door and drove down to the bomb site on North Main to join his partner. The whole way, he kept replaying the bizarre conversation with Hofmann. Despite being surrounded by nurses and doctors and IVs and X rays, he just didn't look or sound like a victim.

In fact, although Jim Bell didn't know it yet, Mark Hofmann was already the number-one suspect.

Two witnesses at the Judge Building the previous day, Bruce Passey and his father, Hal, had ridden up in the elevator that morning with a man carrying a package addressed to Steve Christensen. They told the police, and the press, that the man was wearing "a Kelly green, letter-type jacket with brown leather sleeves, blue jeans, and tennis shoes."

Early the next morning, Ed Ashment, a Mormon historian, called Dawn Tracy of the Salt Lake *Tribune*. "Dawn, it says on the news accounts that a man was seen carrying a package in the Judge Building with a green letter jacket on. Mark Hofmann has a green letter jacket. Mark Hofmann would fit that description."

The suggestion seemed "totally off the wall" to Tracy. Not *Hofmann*. But she told her fellow reporter at the *Tribune*, Mike Carter, about it anyway. "That's Mark's trademark. The green letter jacket."

Carter, a thirty-year-old reporter in wire-rim glasses who covered the courthouse beat for the *Tribune*, relayed the news to Detective Don Bell—no relation to Jim Bell—later that morning. Bell took it nonchalantly. Like the rest of the Salt Lake City police, he was still working on the assumption that the bombings were CFS-related, not documents-related. But four hours later, when the third bomb went off, Bell collared Carter. "It's Mark Hofmann. We may need you to swear as a witness on a search warrant."

Carter said he couldn't do that, ethically. "I can't burn my sources."

Not long afterward, Carter appeared at the bombing scene and told Ken Farnsworth, "I hear Hofmann wears a green letter jacket just like the one in the description."

And he matched the composite.

The same two witnesses, Passey Senior and Junior, had taken their turns with Detective John Johnson, who doubled as the department's sketch artist. Johnson wasn't a likely man for the job, with his massive barrel chest, overbuilt arms, drill-sergeant posture, and steel-blue eyes. But with practice, he had grown extremely adept with the little kit of plastic overlays of mouth, eyes, hair, nose, chin that allowed even deep-chested military types to play artist.

Bruce Passey gave a general description first. "The man was about thirty to thirty-five, white, with a medium build, about 175 pounds, brown hair cut pretty short, and I think he had a thin mustache." Using the overlays, Johnson constructed the face feature by feature, then showed it to Passey's father, Hal. "It's a real good likeness," he said, "except he didn't have the mustache." So the mustache remained a question mark.

And except for the mustache, the police thought, the composite matched Hofmann to a tee.

* * *

Back at the bombing scene, all activity came to a temporary standstill.

Jerry Taylor had arrived from San Francisco.

What Joe Namath was to football, what Bobby Orr was to hockey, what Joe DiMaggio was to baseball, what Stallone was to *Rocky*, Jerry Taylor was all these and more to the Salt Lake City cops. Even a young bull like Ken Farnsworth had to pay his respect. This was a cop's cop. He didn't look like much—early forties, dark curly hair with a few touches of gray, thin, a bit of a paunch, glasses—not the kind of guy to stop traffic or bring a bar to its feet when he walked in. But appearances could be deceiving.

Jerry Taylor was the two things every cop wants to be: *professional*— totally, uncompromisingly, shit-kicking professional; and *tough*—really tough, not TV tough, a harddrinking, tough-talking, fast-moving, no-bullshit kind of a guy with a chain tattooed on his wrist. He was also the best at what he did, the very best, and he wasn't shy about telling you so. No false modesty about Jerry Taylor. Expertise was expertise and he wasn't the top ATF man in the Western United States for no reason. *No one* knew bombs like Jerry Taylor knew bombs. Cops in fifty states knew that, and they respected it.

They especially respected the way he spoke his mind, never pulled punches, never minced words, never hedged. That was the luxury of working with bombs. Bombs weren't subtle, they weren't gray, they weren't ambiguous, and neither was Jerry Taylor. He would look you straight in the eye and give you a straight answer, no matter who you were, no matter what your rank. If you tried to argue, he would shoot back, "What are you, some kind of shithead? Don't you understand what I'm telling you?"

When he fingered a criminal, he stayed fingered. When he said a guy was guilty, he stayed guilty. And when he came around to the courtroom to back it up, looked the jury in the eye, and said, "That man did it," they *always* believed him because he was Jerry Taylor and he goddam knew his business.

Without wasting any time, he and Bob Swehla, the local ATF man, examined the bomb site and checked the car, which was still smoldering. The braking mechanism had been damaged in the fire, and the car had rolled down the hill a few feet since the explosion. Taylor knew precisely where it had been at the time of the explosion from a small impact rut in the asphalt. From the lines of the pellet shots and fragmentation of the bomb, he pinpointed the direction of the explosion. All that in the first minute.

Then he divided the scene into sections with chalk marks on the pavement. They would map the scene and tag the evidence just as Jim Bell had done in the hallway of the Judge Building. ATF men fanned out over the scene tagging and packing items for the lab. Taylor, and Taylor alone, decided which pieces were of potential evidentiary importance. When the immediate vicinity was scoured clean, he sent men throughout the surrounding area, as far as the rooftops of nearby buildings, looking for more. Later, he had the storm drains checked in case the water that had been used to put out the fire had carried any important evidence into the gutter.

It was a joy to watch.

Taylor was still there when Jim Bell arrived from the hospital.

"Look," said Bell, grabbing Taylor away from the others. "I talked to Hofmann," he began. "He said he came back to his car and found a package on the driver's seat. When he opened the door, the package fell on the floor and he reached to catch it. That's when it blew up."

Taylor rubbed his chin and looked long and hard at the burned-out car. Then he turned to Bell. "The designer of these three bombs is different from any other in the United States," he said, seeming to ignore what Bell had told him. "This last bomb wasn't exactly the same size. And the Christensen bomb was the only one with nails. But other than that, all three bombs were the same. All three bombs had the same kinds of pipes, the same kinds of powder, the same kinds of mercury switches, the same kinds of battery packs, the same kinds of igniters, the same kinds of wiring systems, the same kinds of packages. Put all that together, and you have a unique bomb design, even though the elements aren't that unique. It would be an exercise in futility for a defense attorney to try to distinguish them.

"Now tell me again where Hofmann said the bomb was when he got in the car?" Taylor had that hard-eyed look.

"He said it dropped on the floor and went off when he got in the car."

Taylor drew in his breath and smiled. "Then you've got your bomber."

Bell was dumbstruck. "What do you mean?"

Taylor took him to the car and explained. It was clear, he said, that at the time of the explosion the bomb had been at the right edge of the seat, tilted against the console that separated the left seat from the right. "Hofmann is lying when he says it fell on the floor when he got in the car. He was kneeling on the seat fiddling around with the bomb when it went off. The guy just made a mistake. He dropped the bomb, and he knew it. He had a few milliseconds, but just long enough for his brain to say, 'Here it goes.' "

"You mean it was the biggest Oops! ever heard," said Bell. "The biggest Oh, shit! ever recorded?"

"That's about it."

Taylor showed him the indentation near the right side of the seat, which showed where the bomb was at the time of the explosion. It was a tight, cramped little car, with a console between the two seats and a tiny ledge behind them. "The bomb went off there," he said. "Do you see this depression, going this way here and down? That means the bomb was right up on the seat—not *on* the seat exactly, but right at the edge of the seat, resting against the console. If the bomb was really on the floor when it went off, it would have blown straight down, and there wouldn't be any impression here."

The door had to be ajar, Taylor added, otherwise Hofmann would have been hoisted straight through the roof by the force of the blast. He had looked at countless homicide victims who had been in car explosions with the doors closed. They had shot through the roof but were usually caught halfway, at the waist.

In a flight of virtuosity, Taylor reconstructed for Bell the last few minutes before the explosion. "Hofmann comes back to the car. The bomb is probably in the back. He kneels down on the seat, twists to the back to get the bomb. It's moving forward, then he bobbles it, drops it by mistake, and . . . boom."

Taylor went on to play with a variety of scenarios,

from the crazy—that Hofmann brought the bomb fully armed, propped between his leg and the console—to the more likely, that he armed it on the spot. "He rests it on the ledge behind the seat. Then he goes away and comes back, and needs to arm the device. So he has a simple protective mechanism—a couple of wires sticking out of the box, and all he has to do is twist them together. So he arms the device while it's resting on the ledge, then he brings it forward and drops it."

There it was, the Taylor conclusion: absolute, no hedging, no ifs, no maybes. Hofmann did it.

13

After that, everything the police turned up only confirmed what Jerry Taylor already knew.

Christine Hayes, an attractive woman in her twenties, was on metermaid duty in the area at the time of the explosion. She saw a man near the McCune Mansion carrying a briefcase. In her rear-view mirror, she watched him head west down the street and walk around behind the blue sports car (which she had noticed because it was such "a cool car"). He bent over the car as if unlocking the door. A moment later she heard the explosion, so close she could feel the heat. When she looked back, the man was lying beside the car. So she turned around, drove back to the scene, and called for help on her radio.

Hayes was absolutely certain no one was standing outside the car at the time of the explosion. So Hofmann was lying when he said the bomb went off just after he opened the door. He had to have been sitting *inside* the car.

There was one problem: Hayes remembered the man as being blond and six feet tall. Hofmann was short and brunette.

Richard Evans had been staring at the little blue sports car from his apartment window just before the explosion.

He confirmed it: there was no one standing outside the car in the moments before the explosion. No more than two seconds elapsed between the time he turned away from the window and the explosion. He turned back and there was a man lying in the street.

A postman and a friend had been walking along the sidewalk no more than twenty feet from the car when it blew. They agreed: no one was standing outside the car at the time. Ditto Maureen Clark, who was standing across the street. Ditto two women in a car on Main Street. Ditto Keith Sorensen, a truck driver who was turning onto West Temple, half a block away, when he heard and felt the explosion: no one outside the car.

Lori Loftin had been looking directly at the car and saw Hofmann *inside* at the time of the explosion. He was kneeling down on the driver's seat reaching for something, Loftin remembered. He had taken something from behind the front seat, turned slightly, and then boom, he was thrown from the car.

That was *exactly* the way Jerry Taylor had said it happened.

Later, when the warrant to search the trunk of the car arrived, they found an elbow of pipe, like the pipe used to make the Sheets and Christensen bombs; a black Magic Marker, like the one used to address the bomb packages; and two rubber surgical gloves, like anyone would use to avoid leaving fingerprints. They also found an old, dark, crinkled piece of paper (no one recognized it as papyrus) along with armfuls of other papers, all of them soaking wet from the drenching of the fire hoses. Hofmann clearly dealt in paper of some kind.

By seven that night, they had a warrant to search Hofmann's house, and Bell and Farnsworth joined the huge team that headed out to Holladay. With the warrant in hand, they were inside the house five minutes after arriving. Lucille Hofmann, Mark's mother, had already given them the key.

With men from the police department, sheriff's office, and county attorney's office, it looked like a marauding horde going through the little three-bedroom bungalow on Marie Avenue, but Bell had planned the operation with his usual care. Each officer was assigned a separate room and, when he was done, reported to one of the search officers. Bell assigned one officer to act as evidence custodian and collect the evidence, another to take photographs. Bell made it clear he did not want any foul-ups that would give some cowboy defense attorney a chance to exclude the evidence they found.

He knew it was a no-win situation. If they closed down the house and went through it piece by piece, it would take a week and the family would howl to the press, "The cops have taken over our house." If they took everything back to the police department and went through it there, a clever defense attorney could say the search was too broad, they took too much, so all the evidence was seized unlawfully.

The only thing to do was stick to the warrant, which listed bombs or materials that could be used in making bombs and the letter jacket. Nothing else. That meant no fishing. No papers, no records, no letters. They searched Hofmann's office in the basement and found hundreds of strange documents, but left them where they lay.

What they seized was an empty tape recorder (the parts could have been used to construct a bomb), some gun parts, and, most bizarre, an Uzi machine-gun manual. (What was a documents dealer doing with a machine-gun manual?) They also dismantled the security system. (Some of the parts could have been used to make a bomb.)

About fifteen minutes into the search, they opened the closet near the stairs. Sergeant Glen Bayless called out to the other officers, most of whom were in the basement, "You should come upstairs. We just opened a closet and there might be some items of interest to you in here." There, in the very back corner of the closet, on the floor, turned inside out, was a green letter jacket.

That afternoon, Chief Willoughby had held another press conference, to reassure the public again that no mad bomber was loose in Zion. "I think it's important that we not unnecessarily alarm our citizens. I think we have things well in hand." The chief said that the main focus of the investigation had indeed shifted away from CFS and toward the Salamander Letter, adding that the case was becoming so complex, it was "like something out of 'Miami Vice.'" He added, evasively, that it would be "99 percent accurate" to say that "the person making the bombs" was "under surveillance." When a reporter asked, "Isn't it Mark Hofmann?" he coyly refused to answer.

Late that evening, Willoughby and ATF Agent Jerry Miller were speaking to the press again. And this time they were willing to name names. "We've found enough evidence that Jerry Miller is going to the U.S. Attorney's Office to file charges," Willoughby announced. "Jerry feels in his gut that we have more than enough to charge Mr. Hofmann. We're not saying the investigation is concluded." But, he added, with at least as much confidence as the night before, "We know who the players are and other charges will be filed—other than Mr. Hofmann."

But weren't the first two bombs supposed to be the work of a professional hit man? Weren't those bombs, like today's bomb, too sophisticated for a presumed amateur like Mark Hofmann?

"It's a proven fact that it was sophisticated," Willoughby quipped. "So much so that he blew himself up."

Ken Farnsworth left Hofmann's house about three that morning, when the search was finally called off. On his way home, he phoned the LDS Hospital and found out that Hofmann had just come out of surgery. He and Joe Everett, another cop, decided to swing by and get a fuller reading on his condition. Jerry Taylor had said he wanted a detailed description of Hofmann's injuries so he could plot precisely the position of his body at the time of the blast. The longer they waited to get it, Taylor said, the more time the evidence would have to heal.

If Jerry Taylor wanted it, Ken Farnsworth wanted to get it for him, even at three in the morning.

They arrived at a good time. The attending nurse, Deborah Bowdoin, had held off redressing Hofmann's wounds following surgery in order to let him sleep. He was lying in the brand-new special procedures room—a large space with two surgical lights above and outlets for oxygen, nitrous oxide, and air in case the room had to be used for surgery. It was big enough to hold three or four beds but right now held only one. Hofmann had a "C" collar around his neck and a fixator device on his knee, which was propped on pillows and still bleeding. There was a light dressing on his right upper arm with blood seeping through, and the fingers of his right hand, visible despite the splint, were bright red at the tips. He was attached to a blood pressure/heart rate monitor, a respiration monitor, and an intravenous-pump monitor.

Farnsworth took shorthand mental notes: "Right leg blown to shit, right hand blown to shit." He had a laceration across his forehead, which he must have banged on something very hard. He had a piece of shrapnel still stuck behind his shoulder blade, according to Bowdoin, and couldn't rotate his arm.

"He could have died," said Bowdoin, sympathetically. "But at this point, it's clear he won't."

In the last two days, Farnsworth had sat through both the Christensen and Sheets autopsies, separated by only an hour and half of sleep. He wasn't feeling sympathetic. As far as he was concerned, this man had just killed two people and obviously intended to kill a third when he blew himself to hell instead.

"He got what he deserved," muttered Joe Everett with a black laugh.

Farnsworth remembered Gary Gilmore, another Utah killer, who tried to commit suicide just before he was supposed to face the firing squad. Doctors had worked frantically to bring him back just so the authorities could get on with the execution. Farnsworth knew this was another capital case, probably another death penalty case, and here they were working a miracle of modern medicine for a guy they would end up executing. It was just weird.

He looked at Bowdoin, an emergency-room nurse as hard as any cop. "You patch him up," he said in a voice laced with sarcasm, "and we'll stand him up and execute him."

PART TWO

Too Good to Be True

14 Eighteen-year-old Mark Hofmann sat in the planetarium-like "Creation Room" of the Mormon Temple in Salt Lake City, surrounded by murals of swirling clouds in pinks and grays, dressed in the full splendor of his Temple clothing: white shirt, white pants, white belt, white tie, white moccasins. He had already been washed and anointed and was now ready for the Temple-endowment Ceremony, the super-secret ritual that faithful Mormons perform at least twice a year beneath the Buck Rogers spires of their Temples, beyond the prying eyes of a skeptical world.

If any of the worshipers objected to the aesthetics or to the sexism (men were anointed "to become hereafter kings and priests unto the Most High God," women "to become queens and priestesses to your husbands"), none dared speak out. This wasn't just ceremony, it was rehearsal. Rehearsal for entrance into the Celestial Kingdom. And when that day came, nobody wanted to fluff his lines.

It began with prologue, a retelling of Creation—although not a version most Christians would recognize. Joseph Smith believed there were many gods, generations of gods; that the God of this world was once a man, just as all good Mormons will one day be gods in their own worlds. Smith also believed that the God of this world, the Bible's God, was really three gods: Elohim, Jehovah, and Michael. This was partly the result of Smith's idiosyncratic reading of the Hebrew phrase *Elohim Jehovah*—"Lord God"—to mean two Gods, Elohim *and* Jehovah, Lord and God. Michael's origins were less clear.

All of these gods were, of course, married, many times over, although there was a principal God/wife, or "Eternal Mother." She wasn't mentioned in the Bible because God was afraid humans would take Her name in vain.

So, in the version of Genesis that Mark Hofmann saw,

as acted out in the Temple Ceremony, God, or Elohim, didn't actually *do* the creating, he ordered it done.

Jehovah, Michael. See yonder is matter unorganized. Go ye down and organize it into a world like unto the other worlds that we have heretofore organized. (If there were other gods, there had to be other worlds.)

When the drama was over, Mark and the other worshipers gave the secret salute—right arm "to the square" (forearm at shoulder level, parallel to the ground)—and Elohim reminded them of their mission: "You do sacrifice all that you have, including your own lives, if necessary, for the building up of the Kingdom of God on the earth."

Now it was time for the real ceremony to begin: the first of the secret tokens and signs.

They are most sacred and are guarded by solemn covenants and obligations of secrecy to the effect that under no condition, even at the peril of your life, will you ever divulge them. . . .

A Temple worker demonstrated the First Token of the Aaronic Priesthood by clasping the hand of another worker, placing the joint of his thumb over the first knuckle of the hand. By any other name, it was a secret handshake.

Then came the sign of the First Token. The worker demonstrated by bringing his right arm to the square, palm to the front, fingers closed, and thumb extended.

Finally came the "execution of the penalty" for revealing the First Token or the Sign of the First Token. The worker placed his thumb under his left ear, palm down, and drew his thumb quickly across his throat, from ear to ear.

There was no mistaking *that* gesture.

I, Mark, do covenant and promise that I will never reveal the First Token of the Aaronic Priesthood, together with its accompanying name, sign and penalty, rather than do so I would suffer my life to be taken.

Then came another morality play, acted out by Temple workers, this one a curious parable in which Lucifer tries to bribe a preacher to sway Adam to his cause. Lest the audience titter, the worker playing Peter instructed them to "avoid all lightmindedness, loud laughter, evil speaking of the Lord's anointed, the taking of the name of God in vain and every other unholy and impure practice."

Once again, Mark and the others gave the secret salute—right arm to the square.

Then there was a Second Token of the Aaronic Priesthood, another secret handshake, another sign of the token, another penalty sign, and another oath.

Next came the part of the ceremony devoted to the higher Melchizedek Priesthood with its special garments (white robe; white, turban-like cap with a bow over the right ear; apron; and white moccasins) and more complicated signs and tokens like the Sign of the Nail (cupping the left hand and bringing it forward to form a square while placing the right thumb over the left hip); the Patriarchal Grip, or the *Sure* Sign of the Nail (interlocking little fingers); and the sign of the Second Token (raising both hands and then lowering them while repeating the incantation "Pay lay ale" three times).

Eventually, Mark was brought before the Veil of the Temple, a gauzy curtain embroidered with symbols and pierced by three holes. The symbols corresponded to the symbols on the Temple garments: the square, symbolic of the covenants he entered into in the Temple; the compass, a reminder that "all truth is circumscribed into one great whole and that desires, appetites, and passions are to be kept within the bounds the Lord has established; the navel mark, placed on the right side of the garment, over the navel, symbolic of the "constant need for nourishment to body and spirit"; and the knee mark, placed over the kneecap and indicating that "every knee shall bow and every tongue confess that Jesus is the Christ."

The holes in the veil were for the final test. Through one, a worshiper gave the secret tokens to Temple workers on the other side. Through another, the workers asked questions, and through the third, the worshiper gave the secret passwords. If all the responses were correct, there would be three taps on the magic mallet, like knocks on a door, and the person would be led around the veil—into the Celestial Kingdom.

When it was Mark's turn, he gave the five points of fellowship: inside of right foot by the side of right foot, knee to knee, breast to breast, hand to back, and mouth to ear.

He said the magic incantation: "Health in the navel, marrow in the bones, strength in the loins and in the sinews, power in the priesthood be upon me and upon my posterity through all generations of time and throughout all eternity."

He gave the secret password: "The Son."

And the Lord said, "That is correct."

Three taps with the mallet.

"What is wanted?" asked the Lord.

"Adam, having conversed with the Lord through the veil, desires now to enter His presence," intoned a Temple worker.

"Let him enter," said the Lord.

And Mark was brought into the Celestial Room, a Victorian hotel lobby filled with heavily padded chairs, for a few moments of introspection.

15 By all accounts, Mark William Hofmann was the ideal Mormon child. A little reticent socially, perhaps, and a little awkward physically, but studious, hardworking, and, above all, exceedingly deferential to his elders.

His was certainly the ideal Mormon family. His devout Mormon father, Bill, a salesman for Pitney-Bowes, had married his equally devout Mormon mother, Lucille, a seventh-generation Mormon housewife, and raised an obedient—if small—Mormon family of two girls and one boy in the ideal Mormon community of Millcreek, a prosperous suburb of Salt Lake City.

Like many Mormon men, William Hofmann ran his life with a combination of naiveté and rigidity—the former at work, the latter at home. Whether cheerleading in high school or peddling the latest get-rich scheme, salesmanship was in his blood. No promise was too extravagant, no sell too hard, no shot too long for Bill Hofmann.

At home, however, there were no deals. Most Mormons believe that they will be rewarded in the next life with worlds of their own, but in the little house on Marie Avenue, Bill Hofmann had decided to get a head start on the afterlife. Within its walls, he was already God. "Everything was black and white with Bill," according to a friend. "He couldn't deal with gray." Especially where religion was involved. When Mark, at thirteen, came home with questions about Darwin's theory of evolution and how it didn't square with Mormon doctrine, Bill Hofmann refused to hear about it.

"Your faith's not strong enough," he insisted. "If you have a testimony, your religion doesn't *need* proof." When Mark pressed, his father flew into a rage. No one remembers seeing him hit his children exactly, but he had a reputation for a low flashpoint, a tendency to become "a little unhinged" in arguments, especially over religion. "If it wasn't what he wanted to hear, then it just wasn't true," recalls one family friend. "And everybody else around him had to feel that way too or else they were *bad*—not just wrong, but evil."

Like many Mormon women, Lucille Hofmann obeyed her husband, loved her children, and clung to her religion, rising every morning at five to read the Bible and pray. A slight, red-haired woman with big, intelligent eyes, she accepted the wifely role prescribed by Mormon doctrine, leading tours in Temple Square and serving as Relief Society president for her stake, the Mormon equivalent of a diocese. Everyone knew that Lu was smarter, better read, and more thoughtful than her husband, but that, unfortunately, didn't count. In a Mormon household, it was the husband who held the priesthood. Other wives finessed the doctrine by playing Donna Reed, all wifely deference on the outside, while ruling with a mailed fist on the inside. But Lu Hofmann was too pious for pretenses.

Their second child, Mark, was born on Pearl Harbor Day, December 7, 1954, and grew up, like most Mormon children, in a house filled with dutiful family outings, frequent prayer sessions—led by Bill Hofmann—and endless Church activities. At Sunday school, he sang the usual songs—"I hope they call me on a mission"—with the other children at the ward house (the local church) and joined the usual Explorer Boy Scout troop. Although an avid reader, he languished safely in the middle of the class, or a little below the middle. His weak chin, mincing walk, high-pitched voice, and glasses would have marked him as a nerd if his grades hadn't been so low—Cs and even Ds. Except that somehow everyone, from his friends at school to his family at home, *believed* his grades were very good.

He wasn't a bad athlete: "untalented but determined," according to one of his few friends. In the end, though, he didn't have much choice but to be a loner. Even his own cousin shunned him in the halls. In high school, he chose a loner's sport, track, and lifted weights.

To others, it looked like a bland but happy and typical Mormon adolescence—typical hobbies for a boy growing up in Utah: hunting (rabbits), camping, waterskiing, coin collecting. Typical summer jobs: roofing houses, bagging groceries (he was promoted to head of the vegetable department). Even his troublemaking was typical: a run-in with a teacher who caught him with his head down during class, a speeding ticket, flashing fake SOS signals to a park ranger on a camping trip to East Canyon Reservoir, harassing cats and dogs with buckshot, shooting off illegal firecrackers.

And some overeager experimenting with his chemistry set. Once, when he was fourteen, he poured some wood alcohol into a heated beaker, covered it, and waited too long. The explosion sounded like a hard-hit baseball shattering a plate-glass window, somewhere between a pop and a ping and the end of the world. Mark tried to take cover but a jagged hunk of glass caught him under the chin, simultaneously tearing a gash in the skin and filling it with scalding wood alcohol. The miscalculation had left a thick, ugly yellow scar on his neck.

But even by Bill Hofmann's standards, a young boy was allowed to be rambunctious every once in a while. Nothing strange in that. At the appropriate time, he would settle down and act responsibly.

When he graduated from high school in 1973, Mark planned to go to college and study to be a doctor. "I want to save lives," he told a friend.

16

Mark Hofmann did have one secret. A secret so deep and filled with shame that he never told a soul about it.

The trouble began in 1836 when an attractive servant girl named Fannie Alger walked into Joseph Smith's life. Smith, who had moved his new religion from Palmyra, New York, to Kirtland, Ohio, instantly took a shine to the attractive young Fannie, as he had previously to a number of the female members of his flock. There was just one problem: Smith's wife Emma. Not long afterward, Joseph had a revelation from God:

> Verily, thus saith the Lord . . . if any man espouse a virgin, and desire to espouse another, and the first give her consent, and if he espouse the second, and they are virgins, and have vowed to no other man, then is he justified; he cannot commit adultery for they are given unto him. . . .

In other words, Joseph Smith could marry Fannie Alger *in addition to* Emma. For good measure, the Lord added a postscript addressed to Emma. "And let my handmaid, Emma Smith," He said, "receive all those that have been given unto my servant Joseph." Fearing the worst, Joseph sent his brother, Hyrum, to deliver the revelation to the hot-tempered Emma. "I believe I can convince her of its truth," Hyrum said to Joseph before setting out, "and you will hereafter have peace."

Joseph knew better. "You do not know Emma as well as I do," he said to Hyrum.

Joseph was right. When Hyrum read the revelation, the only "piece" Emma Smith wanted was out of Jo-

rum a tongue lashing and when
the written revelation, promptly
ce. When asked why he would let
elation from God, Smith replied he
at any time if necessary." Eventually
En___ ___, and Joseph went on to marry not only
Fannie ___ at least forty-seven other women (hundreds mo___ ___re "sealed" to him in eternity).

By 1844, the year Joseph Smith was martyred by an angry mob in Carthage, Illinois, polygamy, or "plural marriage" as the Mormons preferred to call it, had become the best-known and certainly most titillating feature of Mormonism. Salt Lake City, where the faithful settled in 1847 under the leadership of Smith's successor, Brigham Young, became the Plato's Retreat of the Wild West. Farmers threw lavish parties at which their wives could inspect the newest nubile prospects and help choose, in a kind of sorority rush, their husband's next bride.

Not surprisingly, the demand for brides soon outstripped the supply of new converts from Europe and the East. The problem was compounded, apparently, by libidinous missionaries who were "skimming off" the inventory. "The brother missionaries have been in the habit of picking out the prettiest women for themselves before they get here, and bringing only the ugly ones for us," complained Heber C. Kimball, an early Church official. Speaking for all the men of Salt Lake City, Kimball ordered the missionaries: "Hereafter you have to bring them all here before taking any of them, and let us all have a fair shake."

Mormon male leaders proved endlessly inventive in justifying their "peculiar institution." They argued that Jesus himself was a polygamist (they could name only Elizabeth, Mary Magdalene, and Martha as wives, but insisted there was "a host of others"). Even *God* was polygamous. "We have now clearly shown," declared Orson Pratt, an early Church leader, "that God the Father had a plurality of wives . . . by whom He begat our spirits as well as the spirit of Jesus His first born. . . ." In support of his claim, Pratt offered a simple mathematical calculation: " [I]t would have required over one hundred thousand million of years for the same mother to have given birth to this vast family." So, of course, God simply *had* to have not one wife, but hundreds.

Some even tried to portray polygamy as a moral boon, attacking the one-wife system as a "source of prostitution and whoredom." Polygamy, they argued, was a bulwark against promiscuity. Polygamy reduced the temptations that beset married men, eliminated the need for mistresses and adultery, *and*—and this was the best part—it kept men strong and virile. "I have noticed that a man who has but one wife, and is inclined to that doctrine, soon begins to wither and dry up," Kimball told the *Deseret News,* "while a man who goes into plurality looks fresh, young, and sprightly."

The sprightly men of Salt Lake City bought every word, but to Victorian America it all added up to one thing, legalized prostitution.

For a while, Mormon leaders thumbed their noses at the Gentiles in Washington and their laws against polygamy. "I live above the law," declared Brigham Young, who had accumulated twenty-seven wives, "and so do this people." Polygamy was divinely ordained, he insisted, and "no power on earth can suppress it, unless you crush and destroy the entire people. . . . A man that enters this Church ought to be able to die for its principles if necessary." "Polygamy was revealed by God," the Church announced in the *Deseret News* in 1865. "To ask them to give up such an item of Belief, is to ask them to relinquish the whole, to acknowledge their priesthood a lie, their ordinances a deception, and all that they have toiled for, lived for, bled for, or hoped for, a miserable failure and a waste of life." Just to make sure there was no doubt about where He stood, the Lord spoke to Wilford Woodruff, fourth president of the Church, at least twice to reiterate that plural marriage was nonnegotiable.

But all that changed in 1887, when the federal government seized all Mormon property, including Temple Square. To the hardworking, materialistic Mormons, dying for principles was one thing, but surrendering their property was something else. Eventually, the Lord came around to the government's view. He appeared to Woodruff and "showed me by vision and revelation exactly what would happen if we did not stop this practice," said Woodruff. In 1890 the Church issued a manifesto banning plural marriages.

But nothing really changed. The manifesto was just a ruse for Washington's sake, a public relations ploy, a sop to Congress on the eve of Utah's application for statehood. In fact, the Mormons had no intention of giving up their wives. Church leaders continued to perform polygamous marriages even as they condemned the practice in public. Joseph F. Smith, the sixth president of the Church, had eleven children by five wives and performed plural marriages on ships in international waters long after the practice was supposedly banned by God.

To ensure that witnesses could not inform on those who performed these illegal marriages, the vows were often read from behind a curtain. Polygamy became the Church's little secret, something to be hidden from the outside world, from the federal marshals who came snooping around, and from the congressional committees investigating Utah's statehood.

In defense of the deception, Church leaders claimed they were "lying for the Lord."

In the end, however, not even Congress was fooled. Its report concluded: "The leaders of this church, the first presidency and the twelve apostles, connive at the practice of taking plural wives, and have done so ever since the manifesto was issued which purported to put an end to the practice."

Gradually, as the Church was transformed from a radical sect into an ultraconservative social institution, the crackdown on polygamy grew teeth. By 1904, a man could be excommunicated for taking a second wife. References to polygamy were expunged from official Church histories, students at Church-sponsored schools like Brigham Young University who had the effrontery to mention it in their papers had the references crossed out with the remark, "Too controversial." Professors were forbidden to write or speak of it.

Meanwhile, the human cost was devastating. Years of hypocrisy and deception threw generations of Mormon husbands and wives into legal limbo. Children suddenly found themselves illegitimate. To avoid federal agents, they took on false names, wore disguises, and developed an elaborate early-warning system. Children had to be brought into the conspiracy at an early age. According to one account, "Not talking to strangers, being part of a warning system, and being taught outright falsification were all elements in their training during those years." Like their leaders, they learned to lie for the Lord.

Far worse than the hiding, however, was the sense of spiritual abandonment as the Church reversed its position. Now their souls were in jeopardy. They felt betrayed by their leaders. For many families, polygamy became a secret shame.

One of those families was Lucille Hofmann's.

Her parents had been married from behind a curtain. From the time she was old enough to talk, they had told her repeatedly, Don't talk to strangers, don't say anything, and if anyone asks you if your father has two wives, deny it. At all costs, she was to guard the family's dark secret.

Mark Hofmann may have respected his father, according to family friends, but he adored his mother. Her shame was his shame. Anything that hurt her, hurt him. That's why, when she finally confessed the family secret that had tormented her for so long, he was furious at the Church. "Institutionalized deceit," he called it. He ran to the Church genealogical libraries, determined to find out who, in fact, had married his mother's parents. He made a list of all the Church officials who had the authority to perform marriages at the time. Then he began eliminating names: one was on a mission, one was at a conference, another was on a trip. Finally he eliminated every name but one: Joseph W. Summerhays, a prominent businessman and Church leader. The hypocrisy of it all outraged him.

He confronted his father.

"You just need more faith," Bill Hofmann told him. It takes faith to follow the Church's teachings.

Which teachings, Mark demanded, the old ones or the new ones?

"Whatever the current Church believes."

Subject closed.

But like many Mormon boys with doubts, Mark was already caught up in the intriguing, Masonic-like initiation rites of the Mormon priesthood, the secret passwords, the secret handshakes, the special garments. On December 2, 1973, in a Temple Ceremony, he was received into the Melchizedek Priesthood. In his blessing, Patriarch Frank Carl Berg (a building contractor who worked out of his home on Preston Street), informed

Mark that he was "descended from worthy ancient patri-
archs that lived upon the earth anciently, even from
Abraham, Isaac, and Jacob." Specifically, Mark's ances-
tor was Ephraim, "a worthy son of Joseph." "Ephraim
was given an important blessing," intoned Elder Berg,
"in which he was told that through him and his posterity
the righteous would receive their knowledge of truth.

"You will rejoice in the special work you will be called
to do. A burning will come into your soul and you will
know that you are about your Heavenly Father's business. . . . Yes, you are truly a worthy son that has been
given a special assignment to fill in this mortal world. . . ."

The next step was a "mission."

Almost every good Mormon male is "called" by God
to perform missionary duty in another state or another
country. (God rarely calls young Mormon women.) God's
summons is very specific. He not only tells you to go, He
tells you where to go.

In 1974, God told Mark Hofmann to go to southwest
England.

He made a good missionary, though not a great one.
In a report listing the number of hours each missionary
spent on the road proselytizing, he ranked forty-ninth out
of 208. It wasn't easy work, especially for a diffident
loner. Like a pack of young lions tracking a herd, the
young missionaries preyed on the old, the sick, and the
lame. The Church's research had shown that the most
likely converts were blue-collar, lower-class workers unhappy with their low station in life, and those whose
"ramparts were broken." "Your rampart is your circle of
friends and your sense of a coherent life," explains a
former missionary. "When people move, change jobs,
get divorced—their ramparts are broken, and that's when
they're most susceptible to conversion. Those were the
people they told us to go after."

Hofmann spent the next two years making banal entries in his journal, engaging in occasional "Bible bashes"
—heated debates with missionaries from other sects,
especially the Jehovah's Witnesses—and studying Mormon doctrine. His fellow missionaries considered him
quiet, intelligent, and bland—typically Mormon.

And he returned from his mission in 1976 with typical

doubts. "I guess the Mormon Church only wins by default," he told a fellow missionary. "I just can't find any other Church that is true, that I can feel is true. At least the Mormon Church is better than any other."

For many young Mormons, the mission is an eye opener. After eighteen years in the Mormon stronghold of Utah, they discover that not only is there a world outside of Mormonism—a world that drinks and smokes and swears and fornicates and stays up late—but that that world is, at best, skeptical of, at worst, hostile toward Mormonism. Many never recover from the shock. A high school friend of Hofmann's, Jeff Salt (who had gone no farther than Florida), was one of many missionaries who in the process of trying to convert the benighted, almost joined their ranks.

When Hofmann entered Utah State in 1976, he chose to room with Jeff Salt. There were endless late-night, soul-searching discussions of religion that first semester. Hofmann admitted that he had first doubted when he picked up a book on Darwin at age thirteen and realized that Darwin's survival-of-the-fittest theory directly contradicted Joseph Smith's eternal progression from the Pre-Existence to the Celestial Kingdom.

Once again, Mark tried to bring his doubts home, to family dinners, to Bill Hofmann.

What about these discrepancies? Mark would demand.

"Nit-picking," Bill Hofmann would say.

Mark would run to his room to get a book or an article to bolster his point.

But Bill Hofmann never looked at them. "He was intimidated by ideas," according to a family friend, "by thoughts, intellectualism. Everything was from the heart, not the head."

"Concentrate on the value of the Church as a whole," he would tell his son, according to the same family friend.

But the books. . . .

"Put your faith in the living Church."

But the history. . . .

"Don't get hung up on history. Look at it as it is now, and as it affects your life now."

But the Prophet said. . . .

"Don't be so concerned about what some Prophet said or didn't say."

But it keeps changing. . . .

"What you need is more faith."

Subject closed.

Infuriated, Mark went back to school and wrote out his beliefs in a page-long letter. He was an atheist. He didn't trust the Church or its leaders. Why did they hide things from its members? Like the truth about polygamy. It was dishonest. He planned to send the statement to his mother. She was a victim herself. Surely she would understand.

Bill Hofmann must have tried to tell himself that this was all normal; that Mark was just finding himself. It was typical for missionaries to return with doubts. Mark was just going through a trial. His faith was strong, and it would triumph in the end.

When Lu Hofmann read the letter, if she read it, she put it away and never said a word to her husband. As for any doubts about the Church she may have shared with her son, they would undoubtedly be resolved in time.

Right now, what Mark needed, they agreed, was a good wife.

17

One Sunday that first year at Utah State, Bill and Lu Hofmann drove up from Salt Lake City to Logan, about eighty miles, to visit their son. Like most of their visits, it was unannounced. If Mark knew in advance they were coming, he might make some special arrangements, so it was better if they just surprised him. Mark understood the real purpose of the no-warning policy. On their last visit, he hadn't had time to take down his Farrah Fawcett-Majors poster. Lucille Hofmann took one look and it was down. She didn't have to say a word. It was replaced by a poster she gave him with a Mormon devotional message.

This Sunday, the Hofmanns made another, similar discovery.

"Mark's not here," Jeff Salt told them.
"Where is he?" In church perhaps?
"Sunday afternoons, he's at Jill's," said Salt.

For a twenty-one-year-old boy who had never dated, never even kissed a girl before, Jill Stone was quite a catch. Friends called it "beginner's luck." How could Mark Hofmann, a detached, often arrogant, somewhat wimpy science major, attract this tall, tanned, dark-haired girl with a shapely body and pretty face? He was usually quiet, she was extremely verbal; he was sarcastic (if seldom funny), she was always serious; he wore T-shirts and jeans, she wore anything tight and black; he was aloof toward girls, she was flirtatious toward boys; he was a cultural cipher, she played the piano, and well. On the surface, about the only things they seemed to have in common were blue eyes and a taste for off-beat people.

Mark didn't just woo her, he laid siege to her. For whatever reason, he wanted to have a wife—and Mark Hofmann had a way of getting what he wanted. He wrote her cute little notes telling her how much he loved her, bought her flowers—"Not just the red-roses-once-a-year routine," she says—and thoughtful presents like a copy of the *Book of Mormon* bound in white leather and a gold teddy bear on a chain. He told her how much he liked her long dark hair, the way she did her makeup, the way she dressed. She was such a *lady*. At that, Jill surrendered without a fight.

She was the oldest of three daughters raised by an Idaho rancher. Inevitably, that meant being raised like an eldest son, so Jill found being treated like a lady a new and exhilarating experience. "Oh, Markie," she gushed. She told him how selfless and noble he was for giving up a lucrative future in medicine in favor of a life of helping people through medical research. To friends she bragged about her gallant young beau from an excellent Mormon family.

Maybe they didn't share the same intellectual interests, but at least he could talk—so many boys couldn't—and talk very intelligently, at that. Maybe he was a little on the nerdy side, but then, with her interest in classical music and her serious outlook on life, she was hardly the frivolous, fun-loving, sorority type herself.

When Jill threw out his dirty jeans and unkempt T-shirts

and bought him the kind of preppy clothes that befitted a boyfriend of hers, Mark didn't complain. His mother had always bought his clothes anyway.

In April, only four months after they started dating, Mark popped the question, and Jill said yes. Yes, *but:* she wanted a long engagement "so we can get to know each other better." Mark reluctantly agreed to wait one year. To mark his claim, however, he bought her a huge one-carat diamond ring. Jill was touched by the gift but troubled by the message that accompanied it. "You're too flirtatious," he told her. "This ring will let everybody know you're already taken."

That was Jill's first hint that Mark was "dealing from two decks."

What, for example, did he think about the Church?

On the one hand, he railed against it. "It's all a joke," he would say. "The *Book of Mormon* is a fairy tale." And then—as if it came to him as an afterthought—"God is dead." He always wanted to argue with her about it. He showed her books and articles and research papers. He took her to visit well-known anti-Mormon activists. "Don't you see how strongly I feel?" he protested. "It's important to me to find things out about the history of the Church so I can prove it's not true." He seemed to think these were explosive ideas and waited for Jill to counter-attack.

Jill wondered what all the fuss was about. Although she considered herself a good Mormon, she didn't really *believe* that Joseph Smith had found gold plates on a hillside in New York State. She wondered if *anybody* did, except maybe a few old relics at Church headquarters. The real strength of the Mormon Church wasn't the doctrine, anyway; it was the people, the family and community values. "I am a Christian first; that's my real priority," she told him. "All I really care about is living a good life, having a nice family, and being, you know, a useful member of society."

Why did Mark take every little thing so personally? "Why are you getting so fanatical?" she would ask. "It's just history."

What she truly didn't understand was why he still considered himself a Mormon. Why did he still go with her to church every Sunday? Why did he still pay his tithe?

Why did he still present himself to the outside world as a good and faithful Mormon if he had such strong antagonisms? Why was he so obsessed with appearances? Surely it wasn't for her sake. She had been raised in a split family: Protestant father, Mormon mother, and they had gotten along just fine. As long as he let her raise their children as Christians, they could live together happily, Mormon or not.

"If you're really not into the Mormon faith," she told him impatiently, "don't devote your life to tearing it down. Walk away from it."

But for some reason Mark couldn't do that. He couldn't let go.

Once they were engaged, she couldn't do anything right. "Tone down the way you dress," he commanded. "Don't be so visible." One day she came home and found him in her apartment uninvited. When she went to her closet, she noticed some things were missing: a halter top, a sheer blouse—just the kind of flashy clothes Mark always complained about. When she accused him of taking them, he didn't even bother to deny it.

She was too independent. "Let's go get our blood tests," she suggested one day.

"We can put it off," he said.

Procrastinating as usual, she thought. "Let's just go do it and get it over with," she insisted.

She just plain *thought* too much. When he mentioned that he was considering dropping out of school, she had the gall to have her own opinion on the subject. "I think it's a lousy idea," she said.

She was bossy and overbearing. "Grate the cheese," she told him one night when they were fixing pizza at his apartment.

"Why are you always telling me what to do?" he exploded, his face turning bright red. Suddenly Mark was frothing at the mouth, gesticulating wildly. "I'm sick of you trying to control my life," he screamed. "Sick, sick, sick, SICK!" While Jeff Salt stood and watched, his jaw dangling in disbelief, Mark grabbed Jill's arms and threw her against the wall.

Not about to be manhandled by this crazed choirboy, she grabbed the nearest thing in reach, a dishwasher-safe plate, and batted him over the head, hoping maybe a good lump would bring him to his senses.

But two weeks later he did it again.

She was "too social." She had too many friends. When an old boyfriend came to visit her, Mark and Jeff Salt hid in the bushes and kept an all-night vigil with a pair of binoculars. Mark took down the boyfriend's license plate number and somehow traced it through the Department of Motor Vehicles. The next day, with the boyfriend's name in hand, he accused Jill of sleeping with him. She tried to slough it off—"You're ridiculous," she told him—but Mark was sure he was right. Not long afterward, he walked into the room when she was on the telephone with the same old boyfriend.

"Who was that?" he demanded.

"I don't have to tell you," she said and hung up.

"Then I'll find out for myself." He grabbed the phone and dialed the operator. "My twelve-year-old daughter just made a call that I shouldn't be paying for. If you could give me the number, I can charge her for it. She needs to learn to be responsible for her own expenses." The operator gave him the number.

Jill was furious. Mark was even more furious.

But he never stopped planning the wedding.

He chose the place—the Temple in Salt Lake, where his parents had been married (even though Jill's parents would have to wait outside during the ceremony, since her father wasn't a member of the Church). *He* chose the time—September 1977, instead of the original date the following June. *He* even chose the wedding dress—a Victorian extravaganza with a high neck, ruffles at the top and bottom, long lace sleeves, faux pearls, a huge train, and a profusion of slips forming a glorious full poof. It was a sixteen-year-old girl's fantasy—and just like the dress his mother had worn. There would be two wedding receptions, one in Idaho, the other in Salt Lake. More than five hundred people were invited.

But Lucille Hofmann was having second thoughts. Finding a wife for Mark was one of her highest priorities, but it had to be the *right* wife.

All along, Lu Hofmann had been concerned that Mark's relationship with Jill was too "liberated," that Jill was too "negative," too "willful," not *Mormon* enough. Once she even took matters into her own hands, telling Jill, "You'll have to be more respectful if you want to make a marriage work." But that wasn't enough. As the wedding date approached, Mark pointedly reported to Jill the negative feedback he was getting from home: "They think you aren't religious enough, or traditional enough, or subservient enough to make a good wife for me."

Or socially prominent enough. Bill and Lu Hofmann thought their brilliant, young pre-med son deserved nothing less than the daughter of a leader of the community— preferably the daughter of a General Authority.

Eight days before the big day, Mark called Jill and canceled the wedding. No explanations, no apologies, no wedding.

Three days later, he called back. "Jill, you question me too much. You question what I do. You disagree with what I feel religiously. And you're way too *visible*. You have a huge circle of friends. You're way too extroverted. You could never be what I have to have in a wife. You could never be more compliant, more . . . more. . . ."

"More like Lucille Hofmann," she completed the sentence under her breath. It was almost as if he had some plans for the future, she thought, plans that required a wife who wouldn't ask questions, who wouldn't have friends traipsing through the house, who would rely on him utterly, who could be trusted to keep some secret. And he was right: that wasn't her.

Two years later, Mark married Doralee Olds, a freshman at Utah State whom he had met the previous fall in the laundry room of his apartment complex. She couldn't have been more different from Jill: small and skinny with mouse-brown hair and a wardrobe filled with worn jeans and old T-shirts. When asked about her good points, friends would say, "She's a very simple girl" or "She's good at planning things." "Dorie's not an aggressive sort of person," says one friend. "She just wanted to get married and stay home and have kids and make cookies and not have to worry about taking care of herself in the big, bad world."

In July 1980, Mark and Dorie moved to Sandy, a suburb south of Salt Lake City.

Like the typical young Mormon wife, Dorie bore three

babies in quick succession: Michael, Karen, Lisa. Like the typical young Mormon husband, Mark ignored her, put on weight, and played with the babies. (Feeding, diapering, and bathing them he left entirely to her.) Like the typical young Mormon couple, they went to church and to Sunday school every Sunday and were reasonably active in the ward. Dorie became a counselor in the Relief Society Presidency, teaching homemaking skills— cooking, quilting and sewing, home decorating, budgeting, and health. Mark served in the Elders Quorum Presidency.

Neighbors didn't see much of them, but what they saw they liked. Dorie was "sweet and wholesome" they thought, "a typical girl next door." Mark "kept to himself" but "loved his kids." They remembered the time, in 1981, when he came to the aid of a lady down the street whose house needed new shingles but who couldn't afford a roofer. Mark organized a work crew at the ward house. "Don't you worry about a thing," he told her. "You just let me take care of it." The day they planned to do the work, a storm blew up and it poured rain, but Mark just kept working through the lightning and thunder. He was afraid if they didn't finish, the roof would leak.

"Mark, get down from there and go home!" the woman called to him as he worked in the rain, soaking wet.

"No, no. There's only a little bit more to do."

"Let me pay you," she insisted when he was finished.

"Oh, no," Mark said pleasantly. "Helping your neighbor is what Mormonism is all about."

18 Mark Hofmann's obsession with the past began simply enough, with coin collecting —the perfect activity for a nonathletic, socially inept, and overly controlled twelve-year-old boy. Except Mark didn't do it for the same reason other boys played football or dated girls. He didn't even do it for the same reason other boys collected stamps or baseball cards. Mark did it for one reason and one reason only: money. He would buy rolls of pennies and sit quietly for hours, days, in his room, going through tens of thousands of pennies looking for the defect, the mint mark, or the date that might make a penny worth a nickel or a dollar, or maybe even a hundred dollars.

One day, Mark took a friend, Ralph Feurer, down to his basement workshop.

"This is my electroplate set," he said proudly, pointing to a stainless-steel tank, a rectifier, some wires, and several bottles of solutions.

"What's it do?" asked Feurer, an affable, athletic boy who was always bemused by Mark's mysterious projects.

"You put these clips on and you can build up metal."

"That's great, but what do you use it for?"

Mark, who had been waiting for that question, held up a dime. "You see this mint mark," he explained, pointing at the tiny letter on the head side of the coin. "If that says one thing, this dime's worth about two dollars. But if it has a different mint mark, it would be a much, much rarer coin and would be worth hundreds and hundreds of dollars. With this electroplate set I can change the mint mark. I can take an old one off and build a new one up."

Not long afterward, Mark sent a rare dime to the American Numismatic Association in Colorado Springs for authentication. They sent back a letter stating the coin's value and instructing him, "Please send us 3 percent of the value of the coin." Mark sent them the money, and they returned the coin, along with a certificate verifying its authenticity.

When Feurer heard the story, he asked Mark if the coin was genuine. "Of course it's genuine," Mark said with a smile. He had an unpleasant way of smiling without showing his teeth. The corners of his mouth would tighten, as if on a drawstring, and his lips would thin to a line that looked more like an incision than a smile. "If the American Numismatic Association says it's genuine, why then it's genuine."

It wasn't long before Mark's remarkable success in coin collecting merged with the other great preoccupation of his life. In 1967, at the age of thirteen, he began collecting

Mormon memorabilia. His very first purchase was a $5 note from Joseph Smith's short-lived bank, the Kirtland Safety Society. It was signed by Smith himself. Mark paid what was, for a thirteen-year-old, the huge sum of $250.

And that was just the beginning. Before long, he was selling and trading little "odds and ends" of Mormonabilia and studying the collection of early Church materials at the Wilford C. Wood Museum in Bountiful. By the time he graduated from high school, Mormon history was no longer just a hobby, it was an obsession.

19

And what a history it was.

Beginning with the story of Israelites sailing to America in 600 B.C. on a boat designed by God, as related in the *Book of Mormon*, it was a curious history indeed.

There were those hundreds of revelations from God to Joseph Smith, many of them amounting to little more than "Stop bothering Joseph Smith" or "Give Joseph Smith your money" or "Let Joseph Smith marry your daughter." Never in the history of religion had a supreme being found it necessary to talk at such length and with such specificity to one of his servants.

There was that awkward passage in the Book of Abraham, "translated" by Joseph Smith, that cast blacks into eternal disfavor for sinning in the Pre-Existence. The Church's policy of excluding blacks from the priesthood had stood against all attempts at reform during the civil rights movement. But then, in the 1970s, a Stanford University official declared that if the B.Y.U. basketball team ever wanted to play Stanford again, the Mormon Church would have to "reinterpret God's word and establish doctrines compatible with Stanford's policies." After a decent interval, the Prophet *did* have a new revelation reversing the Church's position on blacks.

It was only the most recent embarrassment in a history

already marred by murder, forgery, fraud, boundless lust, betrayal, and power politics—to say nothing of polygamy. With a history like that, it wasn't surprising that the Church in which Mark Hofmann grew up, was, to put it mildly, *ambivalent* about its past. Rather than study history, early Mormon historians preferred to rewrite it—or just forget it.

The process of revision began soon after the Church began. Joseph Smith himself recounted at least three different versions of the all-important First Vision, his initial encounter with God at age fourteen. In one version, for example, God appeared to him with Jesus and some angels, in another version the angels stayed home.

When Smith died, the Church immediately set to work revising *his* story—more than doubling the length of his *History of the Church,* for example, putting the additions into the first person and claiming that they were Smith's own. The Church also deleted some material. In his version, Smith had written that he drank a "glass of beer at Moesser's." The line was dropped in later editions. When a memoir by Lucy Mack Smith, the Prophet's mother, was published in 1853, word went out from the First Presidency that all copies of the book should be "gathered up and destroyed, so that no copies should be left." Brigham Young later appointed a "committee of "committee of revision" to "correct" the book. The commission added 436 words, changed 220, and deleted altogether another 1,379.

Over the years, other revisions were made in Smith's biography: the fact that he declared Missouri, *not* Utah, to be Zion, the land promised by God to His people; the fact that he urged moderation, not abstinence, in drinking; and especially the fact that he broke his own rules to confer priesthoods on Elijah Abel, a black man, and, according to some accounts, Emma, his wife.

Brigham Young, too, left a trail of embarrassing historical facts that had to be excised from the record, among them the cover-up of the Mountain Meadows massacre, an Indian raid planned and supervised by Young's men in which 150 men, women, and children were killed; various murders; counterfeiting charges; bizarre plans to create a wilderness kingdom and crown himself king; and dipping his rather large hand into the

Church's tithing till. (While sponsoring communitarian values for the faithful, Young himself amassed a vast personal fortune.)

Around the turn of the century, even the revisions had to be revised. In the drive for statehood, Church leaders had decided that the time had come to enter the mainstream, to become respectable, and thus began a period known as the Great Accommodation. That meant no discussion of polygamy or Blood Atonement or communitarianism or anything else that sounded even vaguely cultish. Great chunks of Mormonism's lusty and colorful but decidedly fringe history disappeared overnight.

The Church was forced to deny its common roots with the secret society of Masons, a fraternal organization with elaborate ceremonies and arcane symbology. Smith had "restored" an ancient Christian ceremony that the Masons had bungled. When it was pointed out that Joseph Smith had joined the Masons just two months before devising the Temple Ceremony, the Church claimed it was just coincidence. And the dozens of exact parallels in the two ceremonies (including many word-for-word borrowings)? Just coincidence.

Why did the Mormons flee from Missouri in 1839? The official Church response was that persecution by local non-Mormons forced them out. Which was the truth, but not the whole truth: the fact that Joseph Smith formed a small band of storm troopers called the Danites, who robbed and burned the property of local non-Mormons, was simply dropped from the histories. As were Smith's orders to "murder and plunder the enemies of the Saints." Officially, the Church denied that the Danites existed at all. When confronted with documents proving their existence, the Church argued that Joseph Smith knew nothing about their activities. When confronted with evidence that he did, the Church argued that their activities were justified.

What couldn't be denied or justified was simply not talked about, like the Mountain Meadows massacre. The official Church policy was, according to one historian, to "shrink from it, to discredit any who try to inquire into it, to refuse to discuss it," and to refuse "to accept all the evidence. . . ."

The early Church, like many utopian sects of the nineteenth century, had practiced blatant communism: not just good community values, not just helping people in need, but red-blooded *communism:* "From each according to his abilities, to each according to his needs." The idea came to Joseph Smith himself in a revelation from God (later called the Law of Consecration and Stewardship): Church members were to hand their property over to the Church (i.e., to Joseph Smith), who would then give them back what they needed, making them "stewards," while keeping the rest in the hands of the Church (i.e., his hands) for the benefit of the poor.

Communalism was taken up more eagerly still by Brigham Young as a solution to taming the hard frontier of 1860s Utah. Even as he himself became a highly successful frontier capitalist, Young created a series of experimental frontier cooperative communities, including, notably, Brigham City, in which, according to one historian, "the entire economic life of this community of 400 families was owned and directed by the cooperative association."

Needless to say, especially during the McCarthy era, a mainstream institution couldn't be seen as embracing communism. So yet another important aspect of the early Church conveniently disappeared from the record.

Where it could, the Church simply rewrote the history books. In 1965, for example, Parley P. Pratt's 1855 *Key to the Science of Theology* was rewritten to remove the lengthy discussion of polygamy. Missionaries fanned out to libraries across the country offering to exchange old publications for "more up-to-date material." To most librarians, the deal offered by the young missionaries was too good to pass up. The missionaries would hand them the new books, then suggest helpfully, "Now that you have these books which tell the truth about our religion, undoubtedly you would like to discard other books in the library which tell lies about the Mormon Church. Other libraries have been glad to have this pointed out to them."

When a Mormon historian, Fawn Brodie, dared to write a neutral—and widely acclaimed—biography of Joseph Smith, *No Man knows My History,* the Church promptly excommunicated her and published a shrill pamphlet in response called *No, Ma'am, That's Not History,* written by the Church's most beloved historian, Hugh Nibley. The pamphlet made up in sarcasm what it lacked in historical argument or analysis, referring variously to the author, a respected professor at UCLA, as "Mrs. Brodie," "Mrs. B.," and "the lady."

But what about those things the Church couldn't deny, delete, or discredit? What about the documentary record that proved all the embarrassing truths? The Church had a place for those too.

The Vault. It sounded like the title of a Kafka novel. The Vault was the final resting place of all the uncomfortable truths. Its contents, according to legend, would shake the foundations of the Church of Jesus Christ of Latter-day Saints. Any document, letter, record, or journal that was too "hot," that might cast doubt on the Prophet or on Church doctrine, was locked up forever in The Vault. No one knew exactly where it was—except that it was somewhere in the First Presidency building, a great stone, banklike structure near Temple Square, the sanctum sanctorum of Church business. The Vault's walls were said to be sixteen feet thick. It was filled with gold. It was as big as an underground garage. Only the Prophet himself knew the combination.

No one knew exactly what was in it, either, and in the absence of information, speculation ran wild. According to one account, it contained the Urim and Thummim, the seer stones that Joseph Smith had used to "translate" the *Book of Mormon*. Others thought it must contain the missing 116 pages of the *Book of Mormon*. Some even suggested that the golden plates themselves had disappeared into The Vault. But why would the Church want to hide such things? What could be so damaging that it had to be kept secret from the faithful?

Church spokesmen, of course, denied everything. At first, they even denied there was such a vault. Then they denied that it contained anything. Then that it contained anything sensitive. Then that they ever bothered to go inside. When asked why no one, not even their own historians, was allowed to review the materials, they argued that the contents were personal, mostly private journals of early Church leaders that contained embarrassing "intimate revelations." They cited in particular, the diary of George Q. Cannon, a former high official of the Church. The diary contained repeated references to members of the Church who had confessed to some sin or other, and it was felt that those confessions deserved something like priest-penitent confidentiality.

True or not, few believed it. Some tested the explanation and requested to see the journals of their own ancestors. Hugh Nibley asked to see a relative's diary that he himself had given to the Church only a few years before. His request was denied. A descendant of Frederick G. Williams, an early first counselor to the First Presidency of the Church, asked to see Williams's journal. The Church denied having it. It later turned up in the custody of Joseph Fielding Smith, the Church historian for forty-nine years before becoming president in 1970. Dozens of similar requests were turned away with polite circumlocutions or, if one pressed, outright lies. "If you had the discourtesy to ask them a direct question," according to one critic, "they had a right to tell you what they needed to tell you in order to make you go away."

That approach worked fine—as long as nobody dug up any new skeletons.

20

The policy of "lie and deny" kept the lid on Mormon history, but it was a public relations disaster. Anti-Mormon groups had a field day, accusing the Church of stonewalling its own members. What thinking person could believe a church that was afraid of its own past? From the other side, polygamists accused the Church of denying its true heritage at their expense. To the world, the LDS Church was looking more and more like an institution with something to hide.

Finally, the Church caved in. Nothing that might come out could possibly do more harm than all the bad P.R. and speculation about the Church's secrets. In 1972, the Council of the Twelve appointed a new head of the Church Historical Department: Leonard J. Arrington.

The son of an Idaho farmer, Arrington was hardly a radical, but he was unlike anything the Historical Department had ever seen. For years, it had been staffed exclusively by "a bunch of shirttail relatives of the General Authorities and people who had drifted there because they couldn't drift anywhere else," according to one insider. "Basically, they were people who had the combinations to the locks."

In marked contrast, Arrington was a genuine historian—there had never been one in the Historical Department—and a good one. Although a devout Mormon, he had criticized the Church for not being more open about its past, and especially about the contents of The Vault. "It is unfortunate for the cause of Mormon history," he had written, "that the Church Historian's Library, which is in possession of virtually all of the diaries of leading Mormons, has not seen fit to publish these diaries or to permit qualified historians to use them without restriction." He also refused to heap the ritual scorn on Brodie's biography of Joseph Smith, calling it more credible than the official biographies, which he described as "undeviating pictures of sweetness and light."

He even had the gumption to make some demands. His publications would not pass through the process known euphemistically as "Church correlation." They would not be censored by a panel of Church functionaries. "I won't have the publications submitted to people who will take out facts that are facts," he declared. "*I* will be the correlation committee. I will attest to the factual accuracy of the books." Although he would allow an "advisory member," chosen by the General Authorities, to read his books before publication, the advisor would not be allowed to edit them—something that General Authorities had always done as a matter of divine right.

To everyone's astonishment, especially Arrington's, the Church agreed to his demands, although they did appoint Apostle Boyd Packer, sometimes known as "Darth Packer" for his imperial views on Church authority and dogma, to act as advisor to the department. When asked how he would deal with the special sensitivities of Church leaders like Packer, Arrington—equal parts optimist and diplomat—would say: "There are ways to say things that are more discreet than others, and we will try to be discreet about what we do. But we won't compromise our integrity."

Fired by the conviction that "you could turn over any rock in Mormonism and you could easily find something that would support the traditional story," Arrington laid out an ambitious slate of new projects: a one-volume history of the Church for a mainstream Mormon audience (told in "a way to educate Latter-day Saints while still leaving them feeling good"); another one-volume history for a non-Mormon audience to be written by Arrington himself; and, finally, the *pièce de résistance*, a massive, definitive, sixteen-volume scholarly history of the Church to be written by various scholars.

It was a thrilling idea—actually throwing the spotlight of history on all aspects of the Mormon experience, and it sent chills of anticipation down the spines of all but the most conservative Mormon scholars. Even before the major projects got under way, magazines like *Sunstone* appeared to test the new *glasnost*—journals of Mormon "thought" outside of direct Church control. They featured articles on the Church's early communitarian efforts, the role of women in the history of the Church, discrepancies between the various accounts of the First Vision, and other formerly forbidden topics.

Almost overnight, Mormon history became the rage. Even the most obscure episodes, like Joseph Smith's money-digging activities, became the subjects of research and writing. Every scrap of paper, every historical document, every word ever penned by Church leaders became the subject of intense scrutiny for historical clues—not just by scholars, but by a legion of history-obsessed para-scholars, devout Mormons who followed every new discovery in the magazines. In a feeding frenzy, they devoured every fragment of the past that could be scared up from family chests and attic shoe boxes.

But through it all, The Vault stayed closed. Arrington was allowed access to *some* Church documents ("Before, you practically had to have a blood relationship to Joseph Smith to see even casual documents," says one insider), but the legendary treasure trove of early history remained inaccessible—which only added to the fury of the search.

Documents had become the magic link to the past, the long-denied, long-hidden past. Dormant for so long, suddenly the market for Mormonabilia came alive. And Mark Hofmann was right in the middle of it.

21

In 1978, a young man walked into the bookstore run by Jerald and Sandra Tanner, the leading Mormon apostates and publishers of anti-Mormon literature, out of the parlor of their house. There was nothing distinctive about him; he seemed to be a typical young Mormon male, probably back from his mission, suddenly asking himself questions and hoping maybe the Tanners would have some answers. With the explosion of interest in Mormon history, they were seeing more and more of them lately.

They all looked lost and uneasy, but this one seemed unusually nervous. His glance bounced from the pale green walls to the stained ceiling, to the drab bookshelves where the Tanners stacked their homemade books.

"I have a document," he finally said to Sandra Tanner. He had the high, nasal voice of a boy half his age. "It's from my grandpa's collection." He held out a piece of paper.

It was a photocopy of a handwritten "second anointing," a ceremony performed in the early years of the Church only for V.I.P.s. Unlike the first anointing, the ceremony performed by all good Mormons in which they prepare for the Celestial Kingdom, the second anointing virtually *guaranteed* a position of prominence in the hereafter. It was the religious equivalent of an American Express Platinum Card. To maintain strict secrecy, the words of the second anointing ceremony were always memorized. Although a crib sheet still existed, it was never supposed to leave the Temple. At one time, a

Church member caught copying or revealing those words could have been put to death.

"My family wouldn't be comfortable with me being here," the young man explained, his eyes darting around the room again. "My grandpa has died, and my family has been sorting through all these papers and they came across this and I realized its significance and I don't want to see it buried and locked away so that no one would ever see it again. I thought someone should be aware of it."

"Why did you come to us?" Sandra asked.

"I know who you are," he said, gaining confidence. "I know about your work. I don't necessarily agree with what you're doing except that you are preserving history and making it available for all scholars."

So this nice Mormon boy was willing to risk his family's wrath, as well as his place in the Celestial Kingdom, by revealing this document to known apostates. And for what? For history? Sandra Tanner was skeptical.

"What's your name?" she asked.

"I can't tell you who I am," the boy said quickly. "I am from a prominent Mormon family, and you'd recognize the name of my grandfather."

"Can you tell me the family name?" After several generations of polygamous marriages and huge families, giving your last name in Salt Lake City was like giving the name of your community—a general identification at best.

But the boy balked again. "My family would be embarrassed that I am associated in any way with the Tanners," he said. "So why don't you just take it?" He seemed anxious to have it over with.

Sandra looked at the paper again. It had "Salt Lake Temple" written across the top. It was probably genuine, she thought, but how could she ever prove it? If she didn't know the name of the family, there was no way to verify that it really was what this man claimed it was, no way to trace it back to the family. Without a provenance, it was useless.

"Thank you," she said, taking the piece of paper with the certainty that she would never use it. "It's very interesting."

The young man smiled a weird smile and walked out.

*　　*　　*

A year later, Mark Hofmann appeared in the office of Jeff Simmonds, the curator of special collections and archives at Utah State, with a document he wanted to sell. It was a second anointing.

Simmonds knew Hofmann about as well as anybody at Utah State. The two had spent hours together talking about Mormon history, especially the early period from 1839 to 1844, when Joseph Smith moved the Church to Nauvoo, Illinois. Although a sixth-generation Mormon by birth, and closely related to Smith, Simmonds was no Mormon—not even close. He not only liked to drink, he liked to talk about drinking ("I just drank lunch"), he cussed now and then, and he downed blasphemous amounts of coffee.

But he was fascinated with Mormon history. Over the years, he had built what he called, tongue-in-cheek, "the third best collection of Mormon materials on earth." the only problem was nobody wanted to use it. "I'm less likely to get a student researching Brigham Young," he used to say, "than one studying the otters in southern Utah."

Then along came Mark Hofmann. Hofmann not only knew loads about the most esoteric aspects of early history, almost as much as Simmonds himself, he wasn't a stuffed shirt about it. He didn't object when Simmonds referred to the Church Office Building as the "Power Tower," or E. T. Benson, future Prophet of the Church, as "Extra-Terrestrial Benson" for his serene dissociation from the real world. Simmonds realized early that Hofmann wasn't one of those upright, uptight Mormon *Bundesjungen*, whose eyes flared with disdain every time someone ordered a Coke. In fact, in one of their few conversations about doctrine, Hofmann had made it clear that he "didn't buy" the Book of Abraham, a portion of the *Pearl of Great Price*, which, along with the *Book of Mormon* and *Doctrine and Covenants* constituted the three gospels, or "triple combo," of the Mormon faith. "Joseph Smith just made a mistake with that one," Hofmann said fliply.

At times, Hofmann was *so* cool that Simmonds had to look and make sure he still had that "little smile"—the telltale semicircular impression of the low-cut Temple garments under his shirt. Mormons and non-Mormons alike keep a sharp eye out for the little smile that sets the Saints apart. Hofmann always had one.

After a while, teacher and student became like two jocks in a bar, swapping baseball stories about the spread of polygamy, obscure court records, and Kirtland bank notes. Every so often, especially when the conversation turned to Mormon money, even Simmonds's eyes glazed over and he was reminded of a sign in an Idaho Falls antique shop: BROWSING, FREE. $25 AN HOUR IF I HAVE TO LISTEN TO ALL THE THINGS YOUR GRANDMOTHER HAD. But most days it was "Hello, how's the weather, and let's get down to Nauvoo in 1840."

But Nauvoo wasn't the only thing they had in common. There was *The Word*.

Both Simmonds and Hofmann had devoured Irving Wallace's 1972 thriller about ancient manuscripts, forgeries, and murder. In the fall of 1979, they discussed the CBS mini-series, based on the book and broadcast the previous year, and relived together all the excitement of Wallace's potboiler. How the impoverished Frenchman, Robert Lebrun, was betrayed by the evil priest, Père Paquin. How he plotted his revenge by planting a brilliant forgery that would rock the foundations of Christendom. For two men whose lives were wrapped up in documents, it was a delicious treat to read of Lebrun's meticulous forgeries; of the authentic papyrus leaves that he stole from museums; of the careful planning that went into the text of the forged document, the "lost" Book of James; and of his recipes for making and aging ink.

Especially fascinating was the way Lebrun planted the forgery so that a professor of archaeology would "accidentally" discover it. Hofmann was particularly impressed with how brilliantly he planned every detail. Not even the greatest experts in the world could detect the forgery. They all pronounced it genuine. "Their egos would not let them do otherwise," Lebrun declares just before he is killed.

"When I get ready to retire," Simmonds joked, "I'm going to forge the ultimate Nauvoo diary and sell it to B.Y.U." He and Hofmann had a good laugh over that.

It didn't bother Simmonds that his wife, Jeannie, a shrewd judge of people, took an "instant dislike" to the bookish, bespectacled new student, or that his usually blasé staff "couldn't stand the guy." To Simmonds, Mark was always a model of thoughtfulness, deference, and scholarly dedication. So when he brought in a second anointing "from a relative's attic" in excellent condition, Simmonds snapped it up for what he considered an excellent price: $60.

Hofmann made him promise not to tell anyone where he got it.

22 On April 17, 1980, less than a year later and two weeks before the medical school entrance examinations, Hofmann again came running into Simmonds's office in the library at Utah State. He seemed agitated and out of breath. Simmonds knew immediately something was up. It was so strange to see any kind of emotion on Mark's placid face.

Carefully, portentously, Hofmann laid an old Bible and a folded piece of paper on Simmonds's desk and then began to tell his breathless but remarkably lucid tale.

A month before, he had bought this 1668 Cambridge edition of the King James Bible from a Salt Lake City man. The man had occasionally sold him Mormon odds and ends in the past, but Hofmann was particularly struck by this Bible when he saw some handwriting inside and a signature in the name of Samuel Smith—the name of Joseph Smith's grandfather. Not wanting to seem too nosy, he had inquired casually, "Where did you get this Bible?"

"In Carthage, Illinois," the man replied, naming the town in which Joseph Smith had died at the hands of an angry mob.

Simmonds's heart was already fluttering. But the best was yet to come.

"I was in my apartment yesterday, about 4:30," Hofmann continued, "when I saw that two of the pages in the Bible were stuck together with this funny black glue."

Simmonds wondered for a split-second why someone as sophisticated as Hofmann hadn't examined the book more carefully when he bought it.

"I don't know why I never saw it when I flipped through the Bible before," Hofmann went on without pausing. "I was trying to separate the pages as carefully as I could when I saw this piece of paper, stuck between the pages because of the glue."

Simmonds was on the edge of his chair. Maybe the folded sheet had been bound in by accident. The old book looked like it had been rebound at some point in its three-hundred-year history.

Hofmann continued: "I managed to pry off the top page and there, on the paper, was the name 'Joseph Smith Jr.' "

Simmonds had already seen the signature on the folded piece of paper in front of him. It set his pulse pounding. He had seen Smith's signature on a host of documents, but this was different, this was a *discovery*.

Hofmann told how he had carefully separated the document from the Bible with a razor blade but dared not go any further. The piece of paper had been folded in fourths and sealed with glue and he was terrified of damaging it. So he had brought it to his friend and mentor for help.

There, clearly written on the outside was an inscription: "These caractors were dilligently coppied by my own hand. . . ." It was signed "Joseph Smith Jr." Just by coincidence, a copy of Robert N. Hullinger's *Mormon Answer to Skepticism* was lying nearby on his desk, and Simmonds turned to the inscription by Joseph Smith: the word *character* was spelled without the *h* and with an *o* instead of an *e*.

After ten seconds of silence in which Simmonds's mind raced in a thousand directions at once, Hofmann leaned over the desk and asked in a solemn sotto voce, "Do you think the signature is authentic?"

Simmonds ran to his vault to fetch the only authentic signature by the Prophet that he had in his collection, one on a Kirtland bank note. The moment he laid the note next to the brown piece of folded paper, his heart nearly stopped. It *was* authentic.

The two men stood looking at the two signatures for a

long time before Hofmann finally asked, "How can we get this thing apart?"

The problem was the adhesive. Simmonds had never seen anything like it, except maybe the tar that his father had used to seal the horse troughs on his family's farm.

The closer he looked, the less it looked like an accident. Maybe the person who had rebound the Bible had glued the paper into the book for safekeeping, and then, over the years, the glue had oozed through, bonding the bottom of the document to the top, sealing it shut for what, a hundred years? a hundred and fifty?

This wasn't a dream, he thought. This wasn't a novel. This was real, and it was happening to him.

"How do you think you could remove the glue?" Hofmann asked, surprisingly calm and directed in the middle of such momentous events.

Simmonds tried dissolving the glue with toluene, a mild solvent. Nothing. He took an X-Acto knife and tried scraping the glue. Nothing. Here I am, confronted with the archival find of the century, he thought, and *I can't get it open!*

Finally, in exasperation, he turned to Hofmann. "What would you say if I just *cut* the damn thing?" It was like Simmonds to be so aggressively un-Mormon at a moment like this.

Hofmann looked at him gravely, then nodded an okay.

Simmonds was a little surprised and a little sorry he agreed. Now *he* would have to cut it. He brushed the wisps of hair from his forehead, swallowed hard and picked up the knife. Fighting to control his trembling hands, he slit the document open along the side where the tarlike glue had sealed it shut. He felt like a surgeon. The old, yellow paper yielded with frightening ease. "If this document is what I think it is," he kept repeating to himself, "this is like wiping up a coffee stain with the Declaration of Independence."

Then he leaned down and peered into the slit.

It *was* what he thought it was.

Joseph Smith's problems did not end the moment the Angel Moroni directed him to the place on Hill Cumorah where the golden plates were buried. Even after he translated the tablets and began to spread the word of his new religion, converts did not exactly flock to his door. The solution, he decided, was better publicity. He just needed to get the *Book of Mormon* into more hands. But to do that, he needed money.

That was where Martin Harris fit in. A well-to-do and somewhat gullible farmer who was constantly chasing after new religions, Harris was prepared to sell his farm, worth $10,000, and give the money to Smith to finance the publication of the *Book of Mormon*. Harris would have done so if it weren't for his wife, who was outraged at the notion. To placate her and to satisfy his own nagging doubts, Harris demanded to see the gold plates. Smith refused to allow that, but he did offer to show Harris a transcript of a small part of the *Book of Mormon* that Smith claimed to have hand-copied from the gold plates.

Harris may not have been too bright, but he was industrious. He took Smith's transcript east to show it to some experts, one of whom was Professor Charles Anthon at Columbia University. Anthon was not impressed by what he saw. He told Harris that the strange conglomeration of symbols given him by Smith belonged to no known language, and he suspected that the whole story of the gold plates was either a hoax or a fraud. Harris brought that bleak assessment back to Smith, but the Prophet had an answer for everything. The process of engraving the golden plates was so long and tedious, he explained, that the Nephite prophet Mormon (the ancient author of the *Book of Mormon*) had turned to a "shorthand" Egyptian obviously unknown to Anthon. Smith called it "Reformed Egyptian."

That sounded good to Martin Harris. So good, in fact, that he began saying that Professor Anthon had, indirectly, *confirmed* that the characters were genuine. When Anthon later learned that Harris was misrepresenting his opinion, he was furious. "The whole story about my having pronounced the Mormonite inscription to be 'reformed Egyptian hieroglyphics' is perfectly false," he wrote. In his opinion, the story of the gold plates was either "a hoax upon the learned" or "a scheme to cheat the farmer of his money." Hoax or not, the transcript did succeed in parting the farmer from his money. Harris put up $5,000 for three thousand copies of the *Book of Mormon*. Soon thereafter, the so-called Anthon Transcript disappeared.

* * *

Now, 150 years later, it was on Jeff Simmonds's desk.

Simmonds rushed to his bookshelf, found his copy of Fawn Brodie's *No Man knows My History,* and turned to page 51. He knew just where to find Professor Anthon's description of the transcript that Harris had showed him. Simmonds's eyes jumped electrically from the book to the paper. Every detail matched up perfectly:

> all kinds of crooked characters disposed in columns. . . . Greek and Hebrew letters, crosses and flourishes, Roman letters inverted or placed sideways, were arranged in perpendicular columns, and the whole ended in a rude delineation of a circle divided into various compartments, decked with various strange marks. . . .

This *was* it. This was *it*—the high point of his career as an archivist.

Simmonds handed the book to Hofmann, who took it as if it was some new and strange object and then read the passage with intense, childlike attention. When he looked up, his eyes were wide with excitement. "Do you think it could be?"

Two days later, Hofmann arrived at the Church Office Building in Salt Lake City wearing the white shirt and tie he would always wear in dealings with Church officials. He walked into a hero's welcome. Dean Jessee, the Church's expert on Joseph Smith's handwriting, had seen the transcript the day before and pronounced the inscription authentic (pending more careful examination). Leonard Arrington, a man of considerable understatement, now took one look at the document and said, "Well, well. This looks very important. We ought to go tell Elder Durham." He and Hofmann paraded to G. Homer Durham's office on the second floor of the east wing of the Church Office Building, where they explained the significance of the discovery in terms that grew more glowing at each telling. Hofmann, of course, remained quiet and deferential throughout, smiling awkwardly, as though the publicity made him uneasy, as if he longed for the fuss to be over.

Durham nodded wisely and said in his sententious voice, "Well, well, we ought to have a meeting of the First Presidency and let them know about this. This is very important."

In fact, few could remember any document quite so important. The meeting was set for 1:30 *that* afternoon. For an institution that usually moved at a glacial pace, that had only recognized the equality of blacks *two* years before, this was the equivalent of exultation.

Hofmann's discovery could not have come at a better time.

Ever since the previous December, when Sonia Johnson was excommunicated for espousing the Equal Rights Amendment, the Church had been under media siege. Johnson appeared on the "Donahue" show, and every day, national papers carried more damaging revelations about the Church's bitter campaign against the ERA. Mormon women had been bused into neighboring states to lobby legislatures where the amendment was under consideration. Substantial Church funds had not only been spent but had been secretly transferred from California to Florida to help defeat the amendment in that state. Journalists uncovered "irregularities" in the Church's lobbying practices, especially in Virginia, where Johnson lived. And when the Church sent one of its own, Apostle Gordon B. Hinckley, out to calm the Gentile press, he wasn't treated with anything like the deference that was due a man appointed by God. On the "Today" show, Tom Brokaw had the temerity to ask him if the Church wasn't largely responsible for the ERA's defeat. Hinckley, of course, denied it.

After six months of this relentless bashing, the LDS Church desperately needed some good press.

Mark Hofmann provided it.

At 1:30 in the afternoon, April 18, the governing board of the Church of Jesus Christ of Latter-day Saints met in extraordinary session with Mark W. Hofmann. Two days before, he was an obscure student at Utah State. Now he was sitting with the representatives of God on earth in the boardroom of the First Presidency.

Spencer W. Kimball, the twelfth Prophet, Seer, and Revelator of the Church, stood unsteadily over the document, looking at it through a magnifying glass. Although widely admired and surprisingly progressive, the eighty-five-year-old Kimball was known for wafting in and out of coherence.

Gathered around Kimball at one end of the big corporate-style table were the "younger" men who really ran the Church. Men like N. Eldon Tanner, a former Canadian who, in his better days, had overseen the vast expansion of the Church's corporate empire but now, as Hofmann later told a friend, looked "kind of comatose." The octogenarian Marion G. Romney, first cousin to George Romney, former Michigan governor and presidential candidate, sat in the corner humming to himself during most of the meeting. Apostle Boyd K. Packer, one of the most conservative of all the Church's leaders, was there, as was Gordon B. Hinckley, the former railroad CEO and media savant, still in favor despite the embarrassments of the Sonia Johnson–ERA debacle.

The meeting lasted forty-five minutes. The elderly men asked questions and milled around one another to get just one more look at the little piece of yellow paper laid out on the enormous table. Someone commented, "Isn't it marvelous that this important document should have been brought to light during our sesquicentennial year?" A Church photographer took pictures. Hofmann hovered over the document to the side, never straying far from it, answering questions with a combination of shyness and formality that delighted the Brethren. Nothing would have been more inappropriate in such august company than an open display of emotion. Hofmann was suitably humble. They were suitably pleased.

Leonard Arrington explained that Hofmann's find was not only the earliest known example of the Prophet's handwriting, it was nothing less than the document from which Smith *personally* transcribed the characters from the gold plates. "In 1828," Arrington said, "this very piece of paper had lain on a table top alongside the sacred tablets." The leaders liked the sound of that. That pleased them *very* much. It was an inspiring image, a wonderful thought, especially in the way it made the gold plates so real. It would be repeated often, by Church officials and by Mark Hofmann.

The Church, of course, couldn't wait to add this treasure to its collection. They would have preferred it if Hofmann

had donated the document, but they soon discovered that
Hofmann wasn't nearly so self-effacing at the bargaining
table as he was at the photo opportunity. He wanted
$20,000. With rich businessmen, the Brethren could be
powerfully persuasive. After all, they had a direct line to
God—one bad word from them and the "reserved" sign
could be taken off a man's place in the Celestial Kingdom. That tended to discourage the faithful from hard
bargaining with the Church despite its vast wealth. But
Hofmann could be excused. He was a young man with a
family, just heading out into the world. Besides, $20,000
was a steal.

Still, an exchange of money would not look suitably
reverent, so they agreed instead on a trade. Hofmann
would give them the transcript and they would give him
materials from their archives worth about $20,000—a
first-edition *Book of Mormon,* a $5 gold piece, and some
Kirtland Safety Society bank notes. That way Church
publications could honestly report that the Church had
not *paid* for the document.

Somewhere in all the excitement, someone suggested
that perhaps they ought to authenticate the document
before buying it. But that idea got nowhere. They wanted
that document, and they wanted it *now*.

On April 22, only two business days after Hofmann
first brought it to them, Church officials signed the agreement. The next day, G. Homer Durham wrote to thank
Hofmann for his "gift":

> I am happy to write confirming the execution of the
> acquisition sheet and instrument of gift which was
> executed April 22, 1980 by yourself and Leonard J.
> Arrington.

Once the document was safely in their hands, Church
leaders rushed to make it public. The formal announce-
ment came at the Mormon History Association meeting,
which was being held that sesquicentennial year, suitably
enough, in Palmyra, New York—the very place where,
exactly 150 years before, Joseph Smith had penned the
Anthon Transcript. It was a public relations coup, or-
chestrated brilliantly by the Church's public relations spe-
cialist, Gordon B. Hinckley.

On May 3, 1980, the Salt Lake papers ran articles on

the discovery, along with the picture taken in the boardroom showing Hofmann leaning protectively over the transcript while Kimball examines it with his magnifying glass. UTAHAN FINDS 1828 WRITING BY PROPHET, trumpeted the *Deseret News*.

Suddenly Hofmann's face was everywhere: in Church publications, in newspapers, even on the television—in particular, the Church-owned CBS affiliate KSL. "It appears to be the earliest Mormon document," he explained one night on the news, looking uncharacteristically rakish in a sporty print shirt. "Also I think it's exciting to think apparently this piece of paper was copied by Joseph Smith's own hand—the characters were. Just *right* from the golden plates that were *right* there."

Jeff Simmonds watched the outpouring of attention and stewed. The next time he saw Hofmann, he joked, with just a touch of bitterness, "I should have murdered you and added the manuscript to the special collections."

Eventually, Don Schmidt, the Church archivist, took the new acquisition to B.Y.U. and had the photo studio run it through the standard ultraviolet and infrared examinations—ultraviolet to check for alterations or additions, infrared to see if the ink was appropriate to the time period. It passed. Dean Jessee, the Church's handwriting expert, examined it again and gave it a definitive thumbs-up. The inscription was indeed written by Joseph Smith, he announced, and the paper was consistent with the 1828 date.

When Hofmann heard the results of the test, he seemed pleased but not entirely convinced. He suggested that maybe they ought to test the tarlike glue as well. He thought NASA's Jet Propulsion Laboratory in Pasadena, California, could probably do the job. Church officials admired his conscientiousness. "Isn't that just like Mark," one of them said. "Never satisfied."

23 Nine months later, on February 12, 1981, Hofmann called Michael Marquardt, postal employee, documents investigator, and arguably the most important terminus in the Mormon underground, the network of liberal Mormons and former Mormons who trade gossip about Church politics and photocopies of damaging Church documents. The two men hadn't spoken since their first meeting, one week after the sale of the Anthon Transcript.

After six months of silence, Hofmann wanted to talk about "the succession problem"—the question of whether Joseph Smith, Jr., the Church's founder and Prophet, should have been succeeded by his son, Joseph Smith III, or Brigham Young. He also wondered if Marquardt, a "walking encyclopedia" on Mormon trivia, happened to know what Joseph Smith was doing on January 17, 1844. The conversation seemed strangely "out of the blue" to Marquardt, but he checked on the information and two days later, when Hofmann called again, told him that Smith was at home that day.

The next time Hofmann visited Church leaders, the occasion wasn't nearly so joyous.

A year had passed since the discovery of the Anthon Transcript. Mark had forsaken his plans for medical school, dropped out of college, and set up shop as a full-time documents dealer. He had moved with Dorie, now pregnant, to Sandy, a small suburb south of Salt Lake City. Riding on the celebrity of the transcript, he had quickly established himself in the small community of collectors, doing a brisk business mostly in books and Mormon money. He had even done a few deals with the Church—although nothing like the Anthon. That had been a "once-in-a-lifetime find," he told friends. Now he was in the documents business for the long haul.

Then lightning struck again.

On February 16, he drove to the Church Office Building and walked directly into Don Schmidt's office. He didn't have to make an appointment. No one stopped him; his face was well known by secretaries and guards. He handed Schmidt the photocopy of a document, and Schmidt read it without expression.

"Have you showed this to anybody else?" he asked when he was finished.

"You're the first person."

"How much do you want for it?"

Hofmann suggested somewhere in the neighborhood of $5,000—and he would take it, as before, in trade. But he also had something else to offer, something more than just the document, something equally valuable. "I promise I won't breathe a word of its existence to anyone," he told Schmidt.

To Hofmann's surprise, Schmidt hesitated.

Trying hard not to sound threatening, Hofmann added, "You know there are people who would be willing to pay me a lot more for this document."

When Joseph Smith died in 1844, a dispute erupted over who should succeed him. On one side was Brigham Young, Smith's chief lieutenant and a powerful, charismatic leader. On the other side was Smith's eldest son, Joseph Smith III, an eleven-year-old boy overly attached to his domineering mother and chief sponsor, Emma Smith. While avowing allegiance to the young Smith, Young wasn't about to serve as regent to a callow pre-teen. Seizing the initiative, he had himself declared Prophet and led most of his people on the arduous trail to Salt Lake City, where he founded an empire. Joseph III, Emma, and a small group of supporters stayed behind in Independence, Missouri, and fared considerably less well.

Young's church became the huge, wealthy LDS Church with more than five million members worldwide and, by some reports, ten thousand times that many dollars in the bank. Smith's church, the Reorganized, or RLDS, Church, remained an obscure sect, with less radical ideas (no polygamy), fewer members (about 200,000), and not enough money to build a proper Temple. But they continued to claim, much to the chagrin of the General Authorities in Salt Lake City, that *they* were the true Church, that Brigham Young was a false prophet, that Joseph Smith III and his descendants were the true heirs to Joseph Smith's church.

And now Mark Hofmann had found a document that proved they were right.

To Hofmann's surprise, Schmidt said he wasn't interested. The document wasn't important enough, and the price was too high.

But Hofmann was persistent. He came back twice more, the second time on February 23. This time, he said that if Schmidt wasn't interested in the document, he knew someone who would be very interested. "I think the RLDS Church might possibly trade a *Book of Commandments* for it." This was a rare, early version of Joseph Smith's revelations from God, which was later enlarged and "corrected" by the First Presidency to become the *Doctrine and Covenants*. It was worth at least $30,000.

"If you think you can get a *Book of Commandments* for it," Schmidt chuckled, "then you ought to try."

As Hofmann expected, the RLDS Church wanted the blessing and wanted it badly. Madelon Brunson, Schmidt's counterpart at the RLDS Church, was a bit taken aback when Hofmann said he wanted a *Book of Commandments* though. "Oh, my, that is quite a price," she said over the phone when he called the next day. But within twenty-four hours, Richard Howard, the historian of the RLDS Church, was on the line, agreeing to meet with Hofmann on March 2 at the Church Office Building in Salt Lake City to arrange the deal.

In the meantime, Hofmann decided to give the LDS Church one last try.

This time, he took the letter to Dean Jessee, ostensibly to ask his opinion of the handwriting. But Jessee couldn't help reading the startling contents:

A blessing, given to Joseph Smith, 3rd, by his father, Joseph Smith. . . .

Blessed of the Lord is my son Joseph, who is called the third,—for the Lord knows the integrity of his heart, and loves him, because of his faith, and righteous desires. And, for this cause, has the Lord raised him up; . . . For he shall be my successor to the Presidency of the High Priesthood: a Seer, and a Revelator, and a Prophet, unto the Church; which appointment belongeth to him by blessing, and also by right.

The handwriting was neat and precise, nothing like Smith's hasty script. Jessee agreed with Hofmann that it must have been dictated by Smith to his secretary, Thomas Bullock. As if to remove any doubts, Smith had obligingly signed his name on the back and written the date: January 17, 1844.

Unlike Schmidt, Jessee knew a bombshell when he saw it. He immediately called Earl Olsen, Schmidt's superior, and asked if he knew Schmidt had turned it down. Could Schmidt have bungled such a momentous decision on his own?

Olsen knew nothing about it, but he wasn't going to make the same mistake himself. He took the matter to G. Homer Durham, who saw the letter's "importance" right away and called the Church's man for sensitive matters, Gordon B. Hinckley.

Hinckley was no theologian, but he knew a public relations debacle when he saw it. The Reorganized Church in Missouri could blow this up into a national media circus. SALT LAKE CHURCH BASED ON BOGUS CLAIM. OLD FEUDS REKINDLED BY NEW DISCOVERY. The Mormon bashers back East would have a field day. It would be Sonia Johnson all over again.

The word came down from above: of course the Church was interested in this document, very interested. On February 28, duly chastised, Don Schmidt called just about every dealer and collector of Mormon documents he knew and put out the message: "Mark Hofmann was here and offered us something and wanted us to buy it. We're interested. If he comes to you, grab it." Then he called Hofmann: the Church had changed its mind, he said. It wanted the blessing after all. Was it still available?

Hofmann mentioned his pending negotiations with the RLDS Church. He had written Howard giving him a deadline of March 8 and didn't feel that he could withdraw his offer before that time. Schmidt could only agree that, under the circumstances, it would be unethical for the LDS Church to interfere with Hofmann's negotiations with the RLDS Church. But that same night, Schmidt called back, more anxious than ever: Could Hofmann possibly meet with G. Homer Durham on March 2, *before* he met with Howard?

On the morning of March 2, Durham made the Church's position very clear: "The Brethren very much want to acquire the document. Could you possibly free yourself from your negotiations with the RLDS Church?"

Hofmann was the very model of deference. "Well, I see one possible way out of my agreement with them," he ventured. "In my last conversation with Howard, he indicated that it would require perhaps several weeks before the blessing document could be authenticated." If the authentication couldn't be completed by the March 8 deadline, the LDS Church could have it. Based on their experience with the Anthon Transcript, of course, they wouldn't need to bother with authentication.

Hofmann repeated how uncomfortable he felt being sandwiched between the two Churches, but Durham waved his concerns aside. All that mattered was that Hofmann free himself from his agreement with the RLDS Church. Durham and his bosses wanted that document.

Hofmann went directly from his meeting with Durham to see Richard Howard, who had just received the letter with the March 8 deadline. "It will be impossible for the RLDS Church to authenticate the blessing document before that date," Howard said. Hofmann didn't say anything. If Howard took his silence to mean that the deadline wasn't binding, Hofmann later explained, that was *his* problem.

Four days later, on March 6, Howard got a call from Lorie Winder of *Sunstone*, asking for any possible statement he might be willing to make on the Joseph Smith III blessing. "I have learned that the LDS Church acquired it from Mr. Hofmann this morning," she said.

Howard was dumbstruck. Then furious. As far as he was concerned, the document had been sold out from under him. On March 3, he had told Hofmann that the tests couldn't begin until March 17, and Hofmann had agreed to bring the document to Missouri at that time.

Howard called Hofmann, who confirmed what Winder had told him. Then he called Don Schmidt and asked him for a certified photocopy of the blessing along with permission to publish it. Schmidt balked. "I'll forward your request to my superiors," he said, referring to Olsen and Durham. "But you'll have to put the request in writing first."

Howard not only fired off a letter to Schmidt requesting the photocopy, and letting him know what he thought of this kind of ecclesiastical cooperation, he also publicly accused Hofmann of "duplicitous negotiating" and threatened to bring legal action against him for breach of contract. For a few anxious days, the incident threatened to explode into full-fledged sectarian warfare—just the kind of publicity that Hinckley dreaded most. The last thing the Church needed was a bitter custody battle fought in open court.

But the cat was already out of the bag. Within days of the "secret" March 6 signing, calls started coming in from *Time,* the *New York Times,* the *Los Angeles Times,* and other magazines and newspapers across the country. Clearly it was too late for a cover-up. A lengthy court battle might keep the document out of the hands of the RLDS Church, but nothing would keep it out of the papers.

Under the circumstances, Hinckley must have decided it was better to release the document to the press immediately rather than be killed slowly by leaks and innuendo. Of course, Church officials strived mightily to put the document "in context," as they liked to say. Jerry Cahill, the Church spokesman, described it to the press as merely "an interesting historical footnote." Gordon B. Hinckley himself, waxing sentimental, called it "a father's blessing given upon the head of a son he loved" —the equivalent of a Hallmark greeting card: sweet and touching, but hardly historic.

Less than two weeks after acquiring it, Hinckley decided to turn the document over to the RLDS Church in exchange for the *Book of Commandments* Hofmann had demanded. Richard Howard was summoned again from Independence, and the two Churches held a joint press conference to announce the exchange. It was yet another public relations coup by the Church's P.R. genius. What better way to play down the document's importance and put an end to media coverage than to give it up?

And the Church made almost $10,000 in the bargain.

And most important, Hinckley had learned an important lesson. In the future, he would deal with Mark Hofmann personally.

During the negotiations between the two Churches, Richard Howard asked Don Schmidt to provide a provenance for the document. Schmidt called Hofmann and asked, "Could you provide an affidavit from the person who sold it to you? Would that be possible?"

"No problem," said Hofmann.

Sometime later, he produced a notarized statement from Allen Bullock of Coalville, Utah, the descendant of Thomas Bullock from whom he had bought the document. *But,* he told Schmidt, you must never, under any circumstances, make this affidavit public. You can only inform the RLDS Church that it exists. Later, when Schmidt telephoned to get some additional information on Allen Bullock, Hofmann supplied him with a middle name, Lee, and a year of birth, 1918. But, he cautioned again, the name must never be made public. "Allen Bullock also has some important papers concerning Brigham Young's finances that would be very embarrassing to the Church," he warned. Better not to stir those dirty waters.

24

Mark Hofmann had the golden touch. If it had anything to do with Mormon history, Hofmann was the man to see. If you were a dealer or a collector and you wanted a particular kind of document, Hofmann was the man to see. If you had a lead on a rare document and you wanted someone to track it down, Hofmann was the man to see. Of course, it wasn't *all* luck, he would say. He was, after all, "the only person on earth who is actively, and on a full-time basis, pursuing Mormon documents." Other collectors had jobs or businesses to tend to, but Hofmann was out there, twenty-four hours a day, sifting through public records, flying around the country, even canvassing Utah towns door to door, beating the bushes of history.

And what about his close ties to the Church? No one could remember Hofmann actually bragging—that wasn't his style—but somehow everyone knew how tight he was with Church officials, especially Hinckley. They knew about their regular phone calls and meetings. Everyone knew that since the Anthon Transcript deal he had virtually unlimited access to the First Presidency archives. (According to one source, Hofmann had actually seen the fabled seer stones. "They're like brown chocolate eggs with white stripes," he reported.) What better source for leads on missing artifacts than the one who had access to the confidential journals and other secrets of The Vault?

Even with all that, though, Hofmann's knack for finding just the *right* document for the *right* collector was truly beyond belief.

Since his arrival in Utah in 1953 with all his earthly possessions stuffed in the back of his car, Al Rust had parlayed a love of coins into a $6 million-a-year business with two stores—one for each of his sons. A sweet-tempered, affable man with a face as elastic and disarming as the Cowardly Lion's, Rust had only three passions in life: the LDS Church, his family, and Mormon money.

Like many collectors, Rust looked forward to Mark Hofmann's unannounced visits. Not just because Hofmann was a good source, although he was; and not just because Hofmann promised to cut him in on some fabulously profitable deals, although he did. (Rust, in fact, had loaned him $10,000 to buy the Joseph Smith III blessing.) Rust saw Hofmann as a kindred spirit, someone who could, like Rust, spend hours talking about obscure issues of Mormon currency—a service that Rust found especially helpful at a time when he was trying to put the finishing touches on his five-year magnum opus, *Mormon and Utah Coin and Currency*.

Among the few items missing from Rust's book were "valley notes," the earliest printed money used in Utah. Also known as white notes, these two-inch by four-inch handwritten bills had circulated only briefly for a few years starting in 1849, when the dies used to strike gold coins broke. Although descriptions existed in various journals, no examples had ever been found.

In March 1981, Mark Hofmann walked into Rust's Coin Shop in Salt Lake City with eight of them.

Rust thought he had died and gone to heaven. What the Holy Grail was to the Crusaders, what the Ark of the Covenant was to archaeologists, these eight little slips of paper were to a Mormon-currency collector. At the mere sight of them, Rust went breathless. When he regained his composure, he handed them back to Hofmann. "Don't tell me what you want for them," he said. "They're too valuable." A devout Latter-day Saint, he insisted, "They should go to the Church."

Later the same day, Hofmann appeared in Don Schmidt's office and told him he had found *four* valley notes. Schmidt bought all four for $20,000. It was a steep price, but they were, Hofmann didn't fail to point out, the only four in existence. He then returned to Rust and sold the remaining four for an additional $12,000. Rust considered it a bargain price—after all, there were only eight in existence.

Until several months later, that is, when Hofmann returned to Rust's shop and said he had discovered nine *more* valley notes. This time, Rust received the news with considerably less enthusiasm. When there were only eight in existence, half of which were locked away in the Church archives, $3,000 apiece was a steal. Now with *seventeen* in existence . . . But if he didn't buy them, Hofmann would sell them to someone else for less and the price of his notes would go down. The only way to protect the price was to take them off the market. That cost him an additional $27,000. But he was grateful that Hofmann had brought them to him in the first place.

In late 1982, Hofmann showed up with another find of a lifetime: Spanish Fork Cooperative notes.

Brigham Young had established scores of small utopian communities, or cooperatives, all over Utah, some of which issued their own primitive currency. Yet no examples had ever been found. "Wouldn't it be great," Rust had fantasized to Hofmann one day, "if some of those notes actually showed up."

Not long afterward, as if by a miracle, Hofmann returned with copies of notes issued by the cooperative at Spanish Fork, Utah.

Rust could hardly believe it. How exciting it was to be in on the discovery from the very beginning. What an exciting life Mark Hofmann led. What a reasonable price $2,500 was for such rare items.

It didn't seem to diminish the thrill too much that Hofmann returned in early 1983 with yet another set of notes that he was sure Rust would want to include in his book—it was, after all, the only other set in existence; and the price was only $1,500 this time. Later, Hofmann sold still another set of the notes to a collector in Arizona, and still another set to the Church.

Brent Ashworth also had a wish list—although looking around the Philippine mahogany walls of his study, one wouldn't have thought so. Behind the floral-patterned, L-shaped sofa were rows of framed documents: a bill from Paul Revere; letters from Thomas Jefferson, Benjamin Franklin, and George Washington; an original copy of the Thirteenth Amendment to the Constitution, including all the original signatures. The bookcase on one wall was stocked with dozens of first editions, including a 1611 first edition of the King James Bible. It was just the blue-chip collection one would expect from a well-heeled lawyer who, at age thirty-one, had already landed a job he would probably have the rest of his life: vice-president and legal counsel for Nature's Sunshine Products, a company owned by his cousin.

What could a young dealer in Mormon documents like Mark Hofmann possibly have that would interest a man who already had it all?

Salvation.

For Ashworth, Hofmann wasn't just selling documents, he was selling status within the Church—status in this world that could eventually be cashed in for status in the next. An astonishingly honest man, Ashworth would come close to admitting as much in conversation: Mormon documents were his entrée to the Celestial Kingdom. He had almost missed the boat once, at age nineteen, when he skipped the two-year mission expected of all able Mormon males.

Hofmann's documents gave him a second chance. That's why he wasn't interested in anything that wasn't what the Church called "faith promoting." Hofmann could bring him Joseph Smith's teen diary, but if it didn't hew to the Church line, if it didn't support the Church's version of its own history and doctrines, Ashworth wasn't interested. If he wanted history, he could buy another Washington or Lincoln. When it came to his religion, there had to be, in his phrase, a "religious-spiritual payoff."

On March 6, 1982, Hofmann drove to Ashworth's home in Provo, an hour south of Salt Lake City and home to B.Y.U. The house was an odd one for Utah: more solid than most, all cut stone and mahogany boards, but idiosyncratically arranged. Like the Temple and the Tabernacle in Salt Lake City, it was a building designed by a man who believed good materials and hard work were incapable of producing bad results. A mural with a Mormon theme over the staircase announced the family's devoutness, and the long row of photographs in the living room, of Ashworth's beautiful dark-haired wife and six handsome children, proved his adherence to the Mormon ideals of family and fruitfulness.

Hofmann settled on the edge of the L-shaped sofa in front of the Revere and the Washington and very carefully pulled a sheet of paper from his portfolio. Ashworth took it and peered at it closely through his huge, horn-rimmed glasses. As he read, his fleshy cheeks and chin began to tremble. He was always a little nervous, on edge about doing the right thing, but this wasn't nerves. It was sheer elation.

Suddenly, he leaped from his chair and reached for the nearest frame, the letter from Abraham Lincoln making Sherman a general. Would Hofmann take that in exchange? He ran to the three-page letter by George Washington, written a week before Washington's death. What if he threw that in as well? It was the latest Washington letter known to be in private hands. *And*—he ran across to another wall—the letter from Robert E. Lee to Jefferson Davis saying the Confederate cause was lost. "I *have* to have this," Ashworth pleaded, hugging the document Hofmann had shown him.

When Joseph Smith began telling people that an angel had led him to the golden plates from which he translated the *Book of Mormon,* not everyone believed him. It didn't help that when they asked to see these golden plates, Smith explained that he had given the plates back to the angel.

To buttress his claim, he had two groups of men attest to the fact that they "beheld and saw the plates, and the engravings thereon." The first three—Martin Harris, David Whitmer, and Oliver Cowdery—were reportedly shown the plates by an angel. A second group of eight men—all but one relatives of either Whitmer or Smith himself— were reported only to have seen the plates. But there was very little direct evidence of these events. There was no direct evidence from Harris, for example, that he had done anything more than hold a box that Smith told him contained the plates, not that he had actually seen them, certainly not that he had seen an angel.

It didn't help much that two of the three key eyewitnesses, Martin Harris and Oliver Cowdery, were later excommunicated from the Mormon Church and that the third, David Whitmer, left of his own accord. Harris, in particular, was no Rock of Gibraltar. When he became a Mormon, he had already tried out four or five other religions. Even the conservative Mormon historian Richard Anderson later admitted that Harris was disposed to a certain amount of "religious instability." Joseph Smith put it more bluntly, calling Harris "too mean to mention" and telling people that God Himself had called Harris "a wicked man."

The document Brent Ashworth "had to have" was a one-page letter from Martin Harris, written in 1873, forty-six years after the momentous events in Palmyra, New York.

I now solemnly state that as I was praying unto the Lord that I might behold the ancient record, lo there appeared to view a holy Angel, and before him a table, and upon the table the holy spectacles or Urim and Thummim, and other ancient relics of the Nephites, and lo, the Angel did take up the plates and turn them over so as we could plainly see the engravings thereon, and lo there came a voice from heaven saying 'I am the Lord,' and that the plates were translated by God and not by men, and also that we should bear record of it to all the world, and thus the vision was taken from us.

If Mary had recorded her version of the Annunciation, if the Apostles had penned letters home about the Last Supper, if the soldier guarding Christ's tomb had written a memoir, that's how important Harris's letter was. Here for the first time was written, firsthand confirmation by Martin Harris of Joseph Smith's First Vision, the golden plates, and, most important, the divine origin of the *Book of Mormon*—all from a man who was known to be resentful of his treatment at the hands of Smith and his followers, a man who had every reason to cast doubt on the Mormon religion.

The letter even quoted God.

If anything would ever elevate Ashworth in the Church's grace, if anything would ever make up for the undone mission, this was it. That's why he had to have it.

When Mark Hofmann finally left that night, he had $27,500 worth of Ashworth's documents under his arm.

In July, Hofmann was back with another astonishing discovery: a letter from Joseph Smith's mother, Lucy, to her brother, Solomon Mack, dated January 23, 1829, which described some of the material in the lost 116 pages of the *Book of Mormon*. (When Martin Harris returned from showing the transcript to Professor Anthon, he served as Joseph Smith's scribe while Smith "translated" the first 116 pages of the *Book of Mormon*, dictating to Harris from behind a screen. To appease his skeptical wife, Harris implored Smith to let him take the pages home to show her and, when he did, promptly lost them. Some suspected the shrewish Mrs. Harris of destroying them. In any case, they hadn't been seen since. If they ever did turn up, this letter from Smith's mother could be used to validate them.)

It was also the earliest known letter by the Prophet's mother, anticipating by some two years an 1831 letter, also to her brother, containing some surprisingly similar passages, but no mention of the contents of the 116 pages. In fact, it was the first-known document from *anyone* to *anyone* relating to the history of the Church.

To those who knew anything about Mormon history, it was a truly historic find. For years skeptics had been saying that Smith waited a suspiciously long time before recording his First Vision. If he really had a vision from the Lord in 1820, why wasn't it described in writing until 1838? Here was a description written as early as 1829 that conformed exactly with the version that the Church had selected—among the several Smith left behind—as the *genuine* version.

Ashworth later recalled that he "fell out of his chair" when he saw how important the letter was. Once again, he had to have it.

But Hofmann hesitated. "Don't you think maybe the Church ought to have it?" he suggested.

"Oh, no, Mark. This is one I really have to have." At that moment, he didn't seem to care about the Church, the cost, or the Celestial Kingdom. He wanted that letter.

And he went to the wall to get it.

He pulled down his pride and joy, the framed original copy of the Thirteenth Amendment to the Constitution. "Would you take this?" he asked breathlessly. Before Hofmann could answer, he pulled two letters off the wall, the Benjamin Franklin and an Andrew Jackson. Then he went to the bookshelf. How about the *Solomon Maximarius*, the book Joseph Smith's grandfather wrote in 1811? It was the only copy in private hands.

All the time Ashworth was running around the room, Hofmann was totting up values in his head. He wanted $30,000 for it, and Ashworth was short. No problem, said Ashworth. Hofmann added some items to the list. By the time he was done, the total had climbed to well over $30,000 by Ashworth's estimate, but he didn't care. The letter was priceless.

But Ashworth did have one request. He insisted that Hofmann's role be kept strictly confidential; that Hofmann let him take credit for the discovery.

To his delight and surprise, Hofmann agreed without an argument.

When Ashworth's discovery of the Lucy Mack Smith letter was announced at a press conference in August, the Church was so pleased that the First Presidency invited Ashworth and his wife to a meeting afterward. It was the Mormon equivalent of an audience with the Pope. For a devout Mormon, there was nothing more thrilling this side of death.

The Church leaders muttered their congratulations. "Nice job." "It's very exciting." "We like what you're doing." Gordon Hinckley, since elevated to the First Presidency, shook Ashworth's hand and looked deep into his eyes. "Keep up the good work," he said. "What you're doing is a positive thing for the Church." Ashworth smiled his nervous smile and unstuck his tongue long enough to say, "The real joy to me is getting something that the Church that I believe in can use."

The Prophet, Spencer W. Kimball, now eighty-seven and feeble, entered the room slowly, looked at the Lucy Mack Smith letter—he was, in fact, related to her—and posed for a picture with Ashworth and his wife. (The picture was later sent to all the stakes in the Church to show that President Kimball was still, in Ashworth's word, "viable.") Not that he was all that "viable." Mostly, he wandered around the room, ignoring the letter. At one point, he turned to Ashworth and mumbled, "I love you, I love you."

Later, Ashworth would tell friends that there, in the presence of the Prophet, he had had a "spiritual experience."

Shrewdly, Ashworth held off announcing the Martin Harris letter until October, at the General Conference, a twice-yearly convocation of Mormons from around the world. It was also the conference at which the Church planned to announce, with great fanfare, the new subtitle of the *Book of Mormon: Another Testament of Jesus Christ.* (There had been an Old Testament, then a New Testament; now there would be Another Testament.) What could be more appropriate for such an occasion than the discovery of Martin Harris's written testimony that the gold plates did, in fact, exist? It was so fortuitous that some devout Mormons attributed it to divine intervention.

With the round of interviews and the spotlight of national media coverage on him, Ashworth felt like a "personal crusader for the Church." At the press conference, he played his part well, telling reporters, "I feel like the letter supported that new title, that this is also a testament of Christ. I felt like the Church would use the letter in the way the writer intended." Letters poured in from Church members all over the United States and around the world, congratulating him on his find. The document was featured in Church publications and both local papers, as well as on local television stations. In the *Deseret News*, it merited a full-page write-up, accompanied by heartwarming words from G. Homer Durham: "Because it is a signed statement, it represents one of the most significant documents regarding [the] coming forth of the *Book of Mormon, Another Testament of Jesus Christ.*" Another commentator called it a veritable "festival" of faith promotion.

After the hubbub died down, Hofmann tried to persuade Ashworth to donate both the Harris letter and the Lucy Mack Smith letter to the Church—or at least *sell* them to the Church. "You know, you ought to try to do that before G. Homer Durham dies," he prompted. "I think you could get a complete set of Mormon gold for them." But Ashworth wouldn't hear of it. He loved too much the limelight they brought. Instead, he had thousands of copies printed up—on yellow paper, to make them look old—and gave hundreds of talks to Church groups about how these documents had reaffirmed his faith.

It wasn't any wonder that collectors like Ashworth and Rust put up with unreturned phone calls; erratic, unannounced visits; occasional bounced checks; bizarre behavior; and especially Hofmann's stubborn refusal to reveal his sources. That was, they told themselves, part of the business. And besides, the profits—however you calculated them—were too good to question.

25

Every Wednesday morning, Ashworth would come to Hofmann's house and sit in the cramped living room while Mark reclined in one La-Z-Boy and Dorie in another. They talked mostly about things "in the woodwork"—collector talk. Then they would meet again every Wednesday afternoon at the Crossroads Mall in downtown Salt Lake City. It was such a routine that Mark's three kids had come to think of Ashworth as a kind of uncle.

Only this Wednesday, Mark wasn't home.

Ashworth was willing to wait, but he had to rearrange his schedule. He asked Dorie if he could use the phone.

"The one up here doesn't work," she told him. "You'll have to use the one in the basement."

The phone hung on the wall in the hall next to the door to Mark's workroom. The door was open. Ashworth looked inside and saw a clutter of papers, including a stack of old cover letters lying on the floor. It would be so easy, he thought, just to walk in and see what Mark had in the pipeline. Knowing Mark, there were probably some valuable things lying around. It was tempting. Extremely tempting.

No, he decided. That's Mark's business. He shouldn't butt in.

Mark came home while he was still on the phone. When he saw Ashworth, he became suddenly agitated—more agitated than Ashworth had ever seen him. As soon as he was off the phone, Mark nervously hustled him up the stairs. I guess that area's off-limits, Ashworth thought.

26 Hofmann was on a roll. Profits from the big deals with the Church, Rust, Ashworth, and others, plus dozens of little deals began to add up. He was doing more and more business out of town as well—jetting off to New York on a moment's notice. In March 1983, he bought his father's old house in Millcreek, the house in which he had grown up, and moved his family back to Salt Lake City. Within a year or so, he bought himself a racy blue Toyota MR2 and installed a cellular phone—a necessity for fast-breaking deals, he told Dorie. Some friends wondered why Hofmann, the ultimate low-profile pragmatist, would buy such a snappy, impractical car. Wouldn't he want something less cramped for his long document-hunting expeditions into rural Utah? And how would it fit his family, now grown to five? But as long as he was successful, nobody fretted too much over such questions.

Nor did they complain that he wasn't seen around the ward house very much. The rumor had spread quickly through the Mormon grapevine that Mark Hofmann was on a first-name basis with several General Authorities and that he was doing the entire Church an invaluable service in hunting down documents. So if he kept to himself, missed church now and then, rarely entertained, and spent inordinate amounts of time in his basement study, nobody was going to make a fuss. Hofmann, the neighbors agreed, had his own way of working. Strange, perhaps, but undeniably successful.

In September 1982, Peggy Fletcher, editor of *Sunstone* magazine, managed to catch the high-flying documents dealer for an interview, subtitled "How to avoid medical school but still make the bucks."

* * *

How do you go about finding documents? Do you have specific items in mind which you actively pursue or do you simply cover whole geographical areas where there might be documents?

When I first got started there were very few sources for the material I was interested in. Then I started getting more aggressive. I have gone door to door in places like Cedar City looking for things rumored to be there. I didn't know any other way of finding them.

Mostly what I do nowadays, though, is just track down leads. In fact, I now have someone working for me strictly to pursue leads. And I could probably afford to hire even a few more people.

Hofmann met Lyn Jacobs at Deseret Book, a watering hole for dealers, collectors, students and various other eccentrics who shared an obsession with Mormon history. The son of a Church-employed electrical engineer, Jacobs worked in the Church's genealogical library to help pay his way through the University of Utah and support his passion for collecting foreign-language books on Mormonism—a *Book of Mormon* in Hindi or a *Doctrine and Covenants* in Czech—an esoteric specialty even by Mark Hofmann's standards.

Jacobs was what people in Salt Lake City called flamboyant. He had been on a mission to Quebec, had visited Los Angeles often, and knew big-city life. With his stylish, skintight European clothing, tight, dark ringlets of hair, calibrated walk, and roller-coaster patter, he seemed to be on a personal mission to bring the flamboyant life-style of the Sodoms and Gomorrahs of the coasts to Brigham Young's backward kingdom. Jacobs wasn't the kind to hide his lights. If nothing else, even his detractors admitted, he was a welcome relief from the great, grinning goodness of Mormon culture, a crystal of salt on a vast landscape of mashed potatoes.

It was really this distinctiveness, more than the usual mutual obsession with Mormonabilia, that drew Hofmann to Jacobs. Hofmann, too, seemed to Jacobs somehow outside the mainstream. Unlike Jacobs, he could "pass" —he looked so unassuming, almost dopey, Jacobs thought. He would walk in with that black-hole look on his face and say in the most unassuming voice, "Oh, dear, I found something today . . ." then drop a bombshell on you. Jacobs wasn't nearly so adroit with people—but he was smart. Hofmann used him mostly to handle the minor documents. "He was too busy to take care of every one of his dippy little things," says Jacobs. "He had so much going on every day he would shove something off on me."

And it was okay with Jacobs that Hofmann didn't want his name involved in the deal. That just made Jacobs look better. He took his cut—usually in the form of some little pamphlet he wanted for his collection—and signed the check, if there was one, over to Hofmann.

Once you have found an item, how do you determine if it's authentic?

Actually, to authenticate a Mormon item—at least so far—has been easier than the same process for, say, Lincoln or Washington letters. There have been all kinds of Lincoln forgeries around and even though I'm in the business, I wouldn't buy a Lincoln letter without getting one of the few persons I respect as experts to authenticate it. To date that hasn't been a real problem with Mormon documents. Now, however, with the publicity that's been given the tremendous amount of money to be realized . . . there may be some temptation to forge.

More than a year after discovering the Anthon Transcript, Hofmann drove back to the site of that first triumph, the special-collections archive at Utah State University, to see Jeff Simmonds. He had yet another startling find to show his old mentor. It was a letter from Joseph Smith himself, addressed to Maria and Sarah Lawrence, two of his plural wives, ages nineteen and seventeen.

Dear Maria & Sarah:—I take opportunity this morning to communicate to you two some of the peepings of my heart; for you know my thoughts for you & for the City & people that I love. God bless & protect you all! Amen. I dare not linger in Nauvoo Our enimies shall not cease their infernal howling until they have drunk my lifes blood. . . . I want for you to tarry in Cincinnati untill you hear from me. Keep all things treasured up in your breasts. burn this letter as you read it. I close in hast. Do no dispare. Pray for me as I bleed my heart for you.

*   *   *

The letter not only added weight to the argument, which made the Church very uncomfortable, that Joseph Smith was an ardent polygamist, it also shed some new light on one of the more colorful incidents in his exceedingly colorful life. After being appointed legal guardian to Maria and Sarah Lawrence upon the death of their father, Smith was discovered *in flagrante delicto* with the elder daughter, Maria. One of the other guardians, William Law, filed charges against Smith, and an indictment was issued accusing him of "adultery and fornication."

Simmonds examined the document and looked at Hofmann. "I think it's a fake."

Hofmann looked surprised, but not upset. "Do you really think so?"

Not long afterward at a restaurant in Boston, where they were attending a book fair, Hofmann gave Lyn Jacobs and a group of friends a basic lesson on the ins and outs of forgeries—to help in detecting them, he said. On the paper tablecloth, he drew them a George Washington, an Abraham Lincoln, a Walt Whitman, and a Joseph Smith. "He talked about lifts and pressure points and a whole host of things," Jacobs recalls. "He really knew his stuff."

Do you keep any of the documents you find for your own collection?

My basic technique is to turn over material as fast as I can. If you buy things at a good price, there's a tremendous amount of money to be made. I try to sink as much of it as I can back into the search. My strategy isn't necessarily to get top dollar for every item but just to sell it so I have more money to keep looking. The real reward in the whole business is being able to see things that no one else knows about. It gives me a kick to know that this is original stuff, that no one else on earth has pieced this together or knows what this says. So there's the pleasure. It's like being a detective.

Sounds like a fascinating life.

Although I do have fun, it's really not as romantic as it sounds. It seems like you always have people who hate you or are mad at you.

*   *   *

One day, Hofmann handed Lyn Jacobs a small piece of paper with the words *Maid of Iowa* printed on it. Jacobs recognized it instantly.

It was a ticket from a Mississippi steamboat, the *Maid of Iowa*, of which Joseph Smith was half owner. Smith gave out tickets like favors: if he liked you, you got a ticket with your name written on it and signed by him. If he didn't like you, you had to figure out a different way to get across the river. Jacobs did some quick estimating in his head. The Joseph Smith signature: $1,000. Nauvoo imprint (rare): another $1,000. The ticket had Brigham Young's name on it (rarer still): another $500. It had been co-signed by Emma Smith (extremely rare): a couple of thousand at least.

Then there was the uniqueness factor: no *Maid of Iowa* ticket had ever been found.

Not long afterward, Don Schmidt bought it for the Church for $2,500. "Only one?" Schmidt asked abruptly.

"Just the one," Hofmann assured him.

A few days later, when Jacobs congratulated him on the sale, Hofmann gave him a wink. "Guess what? There's another one."

The second one went to Brent Ashworth.

At their next meeting, Hofmann told Jacobs about the sale to Ashworth. "Too bad there aren't more," Jacobs lamented.

"Guess what?" Hofmann said with another wink. "There's a third."

Hofmann took the third one back to Schmidt. "Guess what? I found another ticket," he said in his dippiest, most disarming voice. When Schmidt started to boil, Hofmann explained, "This one doesn't have Emma's signature on it—it's slightly different."

Schmidt wanted that one too.

If a document is of significance to the Church, do you give them the first chance to purchase it?

If I think the Church should have it, I do. My experience is, however, that the Church usually doesn't pay as much as a private collector would for an item. There are exceptions. I know of the collecting interests of the Church historians, things which they are pursuing or are interested in. Those things they will pay top dollar for. But there have been a lot of things which I think are historically significant which I haven't even given the Church a crack at. A lot of historians, I'm sure, aren't happy with me for this, but I'm in this for the money.

Are there any documents other than court records from Joseph's early money-digging days?

There is other material that I know about, but I don't want to say anything about what it is because I am actively seeking it.

27 Of all the many rumors about Joseph Smith, none was more damning than the one about money digging. Not that money digging was rare in the early 1800s. It was, in fact, all the rage. As one Mormon historian put it, "While the Founding Fathers were busy putting the finishing touches on the nation, the rest of the country was busy poking around in their backyards for Captain Kidd's buried treasure."

If Smith had merely gone out in his yard and dug a few holes, he would have been guilty of nothing more than gullibility. But the rumors were far worse than that. The rumors were that Smith, like his father, hired himself out to superstitious farmers and offered to search their fields with a divining rod or a looking glass or a seer stone, feeling for the vibrations of precious metals. That wasn't just unethical—even by the standards of the time—it was illegal. There was even a rumor that Smith was brought to trial for money digging and *confessed*.

This was serious stuff. If Smith did, in fact, engage in money digging as an ongoing enterprise, running around the farms of Palmyra with a seer stone looking for buried gold, it didn't speak well for his story of *finding* gold plates buried in the land around Palmyra and "translating" them with the help of a seer stone. It all began to sound less like a divine revelation and more like a publicity stunt. And what did it make of the "testimony" of the other witnesses to the gold plates, many of them members of Smith's family?

Mormon scholars shuddered at the thought. They agreed that if anyone could ever substantiate any of those dreadful rumors that Smith had actually confessed to money digging in a court of law, it would be catastrophic for the faithful. Said one Mormon scholar: "If any evidence had been in existence that Joseph Smith had used a seer stone for fraud and deception, and especially had he made this confession in a court of law as early as 1826, or four years before the *Book of Mormon* was printed, and this confession was in a court record, it would have been impossible for him to have organized the restored Church."

In fact, such a trial record had existed for some time, had even been reprinted in several nineteenth-century journals. But the Church claimed it was an early forgery, that no such trial had ever taken place. Then, on July 28, 1971, Wesley P. Walters, a Methodist minister from Marissa, Illinois, while rummaging around the records in the basement of the county jail in Norwich, New York, found two boxes of county bills from the early 1800s. There, in a bundle of bills from 1826, were the records of the court trial of "Joseph Smith, The Glass Looker" on March 20, 1826.

That left one Mormon scholar arguing desperately that the Joseph Smith in the 1826 trial record couldn't be *the* Joseph Smith, and praying that no new evidence turned up to prove him wrong.

Sometime between January 11 and January 14, 1983, Hofmann brought another document to Temple Square. This time, instead of stopping at Schmidt's office in the Historical Department, he went straight to Elder Durham's door. Durham took one look at the letter and marched Hofmann directly over to Gordon Hinckley's office in the First Presidency building and placed the letter on Hinckley's bare desk. It was addressed to Josiah Stowell and signed "Joseph Smith, Jr." The date: June 18, 1825. If nothing else, it was the earliest known writing of the Prophet.

As described by one associate, Hinckley was "no Mahatma Gandhi. No waves of spirituality emanated from his person. No one came away from meeting him claiming their faith had been renewed." He was, first, last, and always, a bureaucrat—cool, precise, difficult when necessary; diplomatic, even charming, when appropriate; extremely effective at cutting through red tape and getting the job done. He was also notoriously shrewd about people.

Hofmann had every reason to expect that Hinckley, who had written a short history of the Church earlier in his career, would recognize the name Josiah Stowell. A wealthy farmer in Bainbridge, New York, Stowell was the customer whose dealings with "Joseph Smith, The Glass Looker" resulted in the complaints documented in the court records from 1826. Now Hofmann had found a letter, *in the Prophet's own hand,* proving that "Joseph Smith, The Glass Looker" and Joseph Smith, Prophet of God, were the same man.

Hinckley took up the letter, sat back in his ample chair, and read.

Dear Sir.

My Father has shown me your letter informing him and me of your Success in locating the mine as you Suppose but we are of the oppinion that since you cannot ascertain any particulars you Should not dig more until you first discover if any valluables remain you know the treasure must be guarded by some clever spirit and if such is discovered so also is the treasure so do this take a hasel stick one yard long being new Cut and cleave it Just in the middle and lay it asunder on the mine so that both inner parts of the stick may look one right against the other one inch distant and if there is treasure after a while you shall see them draw and Join together again of themselves let me know how it is Since you were here I have almost decided to accept your offer. . . .

"We would be interested in making a purchase," Hinckley said when he finished. He told Hofmann to return the following Monday. At the second meeting, no one else was present. Just Hinckley and Hofmann. Hinckley pulled out a checkbook and wrote a check for $15,000 from a Church account. He handed the check to Hofmann and took the letter. "The Council of Twelve, and the First

Presidency, and Elder Durham, and my secretary, Francis Gibbons, will be the only ones to know about this document," he said, according to Hofmann's account. "Have you mentioned it to anyone?"

"No," Hofmann assured him.

"Not even to your wife?"

"No."

"Does anyone else know about it?"

"No one else within the Church." Hinckley knew, and he knew, and the original owner knew. That was it.

"Where did you get it?"

"From an Eastern source." Hofmann assured him that it had been authenticated by an autograph expert in New York.

"Can you get me a copy of the authentication?"

"I can."

And the deal was done.

No press conference, no picture with the Prophet, no headlines, no articles, no interviews this time. For the 1829 letter by Joseph Smith's *mother,* there had been official proclamations—"The earliest known dated document"—and solemn, long-winded testimonials—"The vindication of Joseph Smith's work." But for this much earlier statement from the Prophet himself, nothing.

When Hofmann came out of the First Presidency building and rendezvoused with Lyn Jacobs across the street in the Crossroads Mall, he was smiling. He told Jacobs that Hinckley's parting words were: "This is one document that will never see the light of day."

Hofmann's *Sunstone* interview concluded with several questions about his testimony.

Do you consider yourself an active Latter-day Saint?

Yes. I'm an eighth-generation Mormon, and my mother is a stake Relief Society president right now.

Has your profession affected your beliefs at all?

I guess I am a lot more calloused than I was. But generally I just don't worry about some things. I don't have to figure everything out, have an explanation for everything. I can just say, "Well, that's the way it is."

* * *

Do you look for specific documents to substantiate Mormon historical claims?

You can't really do that; you have to take what you can find. I don't think documents really change anyone's mind anyway. For example, the Anthon Transcript. The anti-Mormons used it for their purposes and the Mormons used it for theirs. The same with the Lucy letter. I think most people are a little like me. You have your beliefs and you don't really let things change them too much.

If you found a document that was potentially embarrassing to the Church, would you consider hiding or destroying it?

Oh, no. That gets into a matter of ethics. It's not my role to burn a document just because I don't like what it says—not to mention that it's not a very profitable thing to do in the business world. The closest I've come was the Joseph Smith III blessing which shook up a few people in the Church. It surprised me a bit that the Church didn't buy it up quick and stash it away somewhere, but I guess the Historical Department is trying to be more objective and get away from that sort of thing.

28

Dawn Tracy believed that too—until Thursday, May 19, 1983.

That was the day Tracy, then a reporter for the Provo *Daily Herald,* heard a rumor from a B.Y.U. professor that liberal Mormon writers and intellectuals were being called in by their bishops. Like most newspaper writers in Utah, Tracy, a Mormon herself—but one who had questions about the way her Church was being run—had always had to contend with its vast power. Not that the Church owned the *Daily Herald.* It didn't need to. The paper served a readership in Utah County, the county with the highest percentage of active Mormons in the state. The mayor of Salt Lake City once called it the most conservative county in the most conservative state in the nation. If anything, the readership was more conservative and more devoutly Mormon than the readership of the Church-owned *Deseret News* up in Salt Lake. So the *Daily Herald* tended to steer clear of the Church. Sure, there were occasional little articles about a new bishop or a Church-related barbecue, but where was the real news, Tracy wondered.

This was one rumor she wasn't going to let get away. She grabbed her copies of *Sunstone* and *Dialogue*, the two liberal reviews, made a list of the authors, and started dialing. "Hi, I'm Dawn Tracy from the *Daily Herald*. Have you been quizzed by your bishop on your testimony?" she asked, using the Mormon shorthand. Every good Mormon is supposed to have a testimony, a heartfelt belief that the *Book of Mormon* is "true," that Joseph did translate it from golden plates, and that the LDS Church is the only true Church. If your faith wanes, you lose your testimony. From an early age, children are warned that "losing your testimony" is a fate worse than death. Twice a year, bishops call in ward members to review, along with the record of their tithing, the status of their testimonies. Without a testimony, you can't get a Temple recommend, and without a Temple recommend, you can't get into the Celestial Kingdom.

Tracy called twenty-five or thirty writers, from California to Virginia, and all of their stories sounded strikingly similar. Clearly the local officials were acting on orders from higher up. Tracy stayed at her word processor until past midnight making more calls and writing the story for the next day's edition, but no amount of arguing could convince her editors to run with it. Then, an hour before the Sunday edition went to press, they decided that the story was too big to sit on and gave her the go-ahead.

> Latter-day Saint stake presidents and bishops are warning Mormon writers who publish intellectual material to write faith-promoting stories or their church membership will be in jeopardy.
> The writers say the stake presidents and bishops are acting under orders from high-

ranking general authorities, a charge LDS officials neither confirm nor deny.

That was only the beginning of the story. Before long, it was on the UPI wire and a reporter from the *New York Times* was burning up the phone line to Provo. Pieces began to fall into place as the first article scared up more stories from a stunned community. Tracy was no longer dealing with a few isolated incidents. This was much bigger than that. The first word that came to mind was "crackdown."

It had begun in February when university officials banned the liberal newspaper *Seventh East Press* for "offend[ing] our sponsor, which is the LDS Church." After the newspaper folded, many of its writers were called in for "personal interviews" by their bishops and told they were "on the road to apostasy." One was forced to resign from a job with the Church. The editor of another paper, *BYU Today*, was dismissed. Then came the warnings to writers and historians off-campus who had written for liberal magazines and newspapers. Along the way, at least three professors at B.Y.U. were swept into the net, called in by Church officials and questioned on their writings.

Devout Mormons didn't know whom to be angrier at: the writers and professors for complaining, or Dawn Tracy for reporting their complaints. Richard Cracroft, dean of the College of Humanities at B.Y.U., lectured the malcontents: "If this is what the Brethren [the Prophet and his Apostles] want, then good Latter-day Saints must say it is appropriate. This may be difficult for scholars, but obedience is an important concept of the Mormon Church." Dr. Keith Perkins, chairman of the Church History and Doctrine Department, couldn't understand why all scholars didn't share his view: "I want to write what the Lord wants written. I don't want to offend the Lord."

But in Provo and Salt Lake City and Logan, all along the Wasatch Range, a second word was being whispered more and more frequently as the chilling details piled up. Tracy heard it for the first time over the phone from J. D. Williams, a highly respected Mormon professor at the University of Utah: "It's an inquisition."

* * *

Dawn Tracy didn't know it at the time, but the inquisition had begun long before.

Almost from the day in 1972 when Leonard Arrington took over as Church Historian and ushered in the so-called Camelot of Mormon history, the Brethren didn't like it.

Ezra Taft Benson, the former Secretary of Agriculture in the Eisenhower Administration and the Prophet-in-waiting, railed against "humanistic philosophy" and "contextual history." Ever since seeing the phrase "communal living" used to describe early Mormons, he had suspected the Historical Department was a hotbed of communists anyway. (Benson had once proclaimed, much to the embarrassment of his colleagues, that a good Mormon, "if he is to follow the Gospel, cannot also be a liberal Democrat." His son, Reed, had once served as public relations director for the John Birch Society.)

The fact that Benson would soon replace the ailing Spencer Kimball as Prophet did not augur well for the historians.

Elder Boyd Packer was every bit as distrustful as Benson, but less discriminating. He didn't like intellectuals of any stripe. In fact, he didn't even like *ideas* if they weren't his own. "Are you here to lobby or to listen?" he would demand of people who dared disagree with him. "Because if you're here to lobby, you can leave. If you're here to listen, you may have an audience."

There were some among the Church leadership who didn't care that much about the religious implications of the historical digging. To them the mission of the Church was to lay down a moral regimen for people, lead the political effort against pornography and other social ills (the ERA, for example), and promote a comfortable group identity that could be glamorized on the pages of the *Reader's Digest* and in television ads. They were businessmen at heart. Any talk of religion—from the historians or the anti-historians—made them uncomfortable, and they wished that people wouldn't bother themselves with such questions.

But there was one thing that *everybody* cared about: the bottom line. More than politics or theology, it was the bottom line that finally turned pragmatists like Hinckley, who had been reading almost everything that came out of the Historical Department, against Arrington's Camelot.

The Mormon Church runs the most active and successful missionary program of any denomination in the world. In 1981, a Church press release boasted, "In an era of increasing disinterest [sic] in organized religion, someone joins the Church of Jesus Christ of Latter-day Saints every two minutes and thirty seconds." One insider calls the missionary effort "the driving force of the contemporary Church."

And it didn't take a genius to know that what the historians were uncovering about money digging and polygamy didn't exactly lend itself to the all-important missionary effort. In fact, the reports were coming back from the field. These newspaper articles about Mormonism's colorful, cultish past were killing them in Polynesia.

In 1976 Hinckley appointed his old missionary buddy, G. Homer Durham, to rein in Arrington and his band of historians. Hinckley was smart enough P.R.-wise to know that mass executions in the Historical Department would only bring down the wrath of the national media. He had a better plan.

Durham was just the man for the job. When he wasn't in the field congratulating wealthy stakes for being wealthy and therefore blessed, he was in the First Presidency building, clawing his way up through the dense, sanctimonious jungle of the Church hierarchy. By general agreement, there had not been a more ambitious, more arrogant, more disagreeable, or more conniving General Authority since the wild days of Parley P. Pratt, an early Apostle who decided to take on a "plural" wife who was already married, adding bigamy to polygamy, and so enraging his new bride's first husband that he hunted Pratt down and sent him prematurely to the Celestial Kingdom.

Although considered flexible and kindly during his terms as Commissioner of Education in Arizona and president of Arizona State University, Durham had been transformed by the fierce competitiveness of the Church's inner circle into a Mormon Machiavelli. The closest he ever ventured to humility was a "holy gaze" with which he liked to receive visitors, especially groups of schoolchildren. When asked to give a brief speech at a devotional, he would invariably spend thirty minutes talking about himself and his accomplishments. Staff members down to secretaries and mail clerks, considered him "slimy," "mean," and "sneaky." Even the benign Arrington referred to him as "Pharaoh."

Durham wasted none of his charm on the Historical Department. He demoted Arrington from Church Historian to head of the Church's Historical Department. He cut the department's budget and staff. New publishing projects were held up indefinitely waiting for approval "from higher up" that never came. Writers were summarily cut off from Church-controlled historical records. A spy on the librarian's staff underlined "controversial passages" and sent copies to the General Authorities.

Slowly, out of the public eye, Camelot was dismantled. Durham ordered that all publications be submitted to the Church Correlation Committee. Deseret Book (whose president, Lowell Durham, was G. Homer's nephew) withdrew the contract to publish the sixteen-volume history of the Church. Arrington's book for non-Mormons was allowed to proceed (it was under contract to a non-Mormon New York publisher). But the corresponding history for Mormons was subjected to heavy editorial pressure and then, despite its surprising commercial success, eased out of print.

On July 2, 1980, the Salt Lake *Tribune* announced the coup de grace: "The history research division of the Mormon church's historical department will move to Brigham Young University. . . ." To demonstrate its commitment to history, the Church had decided to create a new Joseph Fielding Smith Institute for Church History based, appropriately enough, at the Church university. And who more appropriate to head this new institute than Dr. Leonard J. Arrington, distinguished church historian— now lower case. The crucial news was buried further down in the press release: "The department's library and archives and arts and sites division will remain at the church's Salt Lake City headquarters, said church President Spencer W. Kimball. . . ." In other words, if you can't take the documents away from the historians, take the historians away from the documents. At B.Y.U., they would still be within the fold—Church employees— but out of harm's way.

It was a brilliant stroke, another public relations coup: a knockout punch delivered in a good-news press release. And the author, of course, was Gordon Hinckley.

For those historians who might have missed the subtle message of Hinckley's maneuver, Elder Boyd Packer spelled out the Church's new attitude in a speech on August 22, 1981.

> I have come to believe that it is the tendency for many members of the Church who spend a great deal of time in academic research to begin to judge the Church, its doctrine, organization, and leadership, present and past, by the principles of their own profession. . . . In my mind it ought to be the other way around. . . .
>
> There is a temptation for the writer or the teacher of Church history to want to tell everything, whether it is worthy or faith promoting or no.
>
> Some things that are true are not very useful. . . . Be careful that you build faith rather than destroy it. . . .

For the truly thickskulled who *still* didn't get the message, Packer brandished the big gun.

> A destroyer of faith—particularly one within the Church, and more particularly one who is employed specifically to build faith—places himself in great spiritual jeopardy. He is serving the wrong master and unless he repents, he will not be among the faithful in the eternities. . . . In the Church we are not neutral. We are one-sided. There is a war going on, and we are engaged in it. . . . [T]here is a limit to the patience of the Lord with respect to those who are under convenant to bless and protect His Church and kingdom upon the earth but do not do it.

In 1982, Arrington was dismissed from his position in the Church Historical Department. His replacement: G. Homer Durham.

With their own house in order, the General Authorities set out to bring the rest of the flock to heel.

29 Brent Metcalfe couldn't imagine what the meeting was for. Sure, once or twice, he had slipped off to the men's room without permission. But did they have to make a federal case out of it? How typical of the FBI types in Church Security. A simple reprimand wasn't enough. They had to call a meeting in the personnel rep's office.

But the meeting wasn't about trips to the men's room. As soon as Metcalfe sat down, his boss, Ron Francis, began reading from a piece of paper: You are *ordered* not to associate any further with groups that exhibit "anti-Church attitudes." Something like that.

When Francis was done, Metcalfe asked to see the paper.

"You can't," said Francis.

Metcalfe, a soft-spoken, dark-haired, eager-looking young man, wasn't sure he understood what was happening. He had written some articles six months before for the *Seventh East Press* and had recently been asked to contribute to *Sunstone*. But not even Francis could consider either one of those publications subversive—could he?

Francis continued: "You are to sever yourself from involvement with people, groups, or publications that teach doctrines, privately or publicly, which are contrary to those of the Prophet." Even at fifty, Francis was six feet of military clichés and proud of it. He always said, in a way that was simultaneously menacing and incoherent, there was *nothing* he wouldn't do for his job. "Furthermore, you are not to write, publish, speak publicly, debate, etc. on controversial Church-related topics, and you are prohibited from serving on boards, committees, staffs, etc. of any controversial organizations."

Metcalfe was tempted to invoke the name of his father,

who was, after all, the managing director of the Temple Department, the man who supervised Temples all around the world. But it was clear these men already knew who his father was—and didn't care. Which meant that this meeting had been authorized very, very high up.

"Your employment will be subject to termination if you don't cease these activities immediately."

"My employment means a great deal to me," Metcalfe said, thinking immediately of his wife, Jill, and their two-year-old daughter, Michala. "I am willing to do what you want." He agreed to the terms that were set and was placed on thirty days' probation.

The next day, he told his editors at *Sunstone* that he would no longer be available as a writer. Two days later, he resigned from the *Seventh East Press* and asked the editor to remove his name from the masthead. Then he went to the personnel rep's office to report what he had done.

Metcalfe heard nothing more until March 10, the last day of his probation. On that day, he was summoned to a meeting with Francis and the head of Church Security, Martell Bird. The presence of the martinet Bird omened ill. The two men had butted heads a year before when Bird instructed Metcalfe to cease writing rebuttals to anti-Mormon groups in New Zealand, Metcalfe's native country and the site of his mission. Apparently, higher-ups thought his "defenses" of the Church were doing more damage than the critics' attacks. "You are not to give firesides or speak publicly responding to anti-Mormons," Bird had commanded. At the time, Metcalfe had insisted that he was just a seeker after truth whose only wish was to "pursue historical research with a great deal of honesty and to let history lead me rather than me to lead history." Well, Martell Bird wasn't buying any of *that* doubletalk.

Ron Francis acted as spokesman for the group: "Brother Bird and I are all very pleased with your total compliance with the rules and guidelines given to you. And with the openness and honesty expressed during our previous meeting on February 11. With the completion of this probation, all is forgotten. This probationary period will in no way stay in your record or affect your pay increases or job promotions."

That night, for the first time in a month, Metcalfe slept soundly.

But three weeks later, he was summoned to the office of Russ Homer, the managing director of Personnel.

"The Brethren have told us to call you in," Homer began. "They have reason to believe that you have violated your probation. They feel an inquisition is necessary."

Metcalfe went a little breathless at the sound of the word. He considered himself a historian. How could they use that word so lightly? Did Homer realize what he was saying?

In fact, Homer was oblivious to anything other than the task at hand. "They've asked us to determine," he continued, "if your historical research and scriptural studies are such as to warrant your termination."

Inquisition *was* the right word.

Once the questioning began, it was fast and furious. "What do you research?" "How?" "Why?" "Have people assisted you?" "Who?"

There were questions about his friends and associates. "Who are they?" "What are their names?"

The questions were not based on any concrete information, but instead fired randomly in the hopes of finding something, anything, to show that he had violated his probation.

"How often do you go to the Historical Department?"

"My visits to the Historical Library are sporadic."

"How much time do you spend there?"

"Sometimes I will spend as much as four to five hours a week studying there."

"Have you had any further involvement with *Sunstone?*"

"No. But I did drop by to see if their new magazine had been published."

"You shouldn't even be *reading* these magazines. You want to avoid the very appearance of evil."

Metcalfe began to wonder what country he was in, let alone what Church he belonged to. His back stiffened. "If you're telling me what I can and cannot read," he said, "then something is very wrong, and you'll have my resignation tomorrow."

Utter silence. He realized he had expected them to say, "Oh, no, no, that's not what we're telling you." They didn't.

Homer, apparently frustrated by the fruitlessness of

the enterprise, began reading from a list of prepared questions.

"Do you have a Temple recommend?"

"Yes."

Metcalfe could see immediately where this was headed. In order to have a Temple recommend, you must pledge that you have "sustained the General Authorities"—meaning that you haven't questioned the Church leaders in any troublesome way. If they couldn't get him for something substantive, they would get him for perjury.

"Now, what books have you been reading in the Historical Department during the last week?"

Metcalfe listed each book he had read.

"Were any *old* books used in your studies?"

This was the crux. In Homer's calculus, old books apparently meant unedited books, "uncorrelated" books, dangerous books. When somebody used old books they were rummaging too far back into the true history of the Church. Terror of the past was palpable in Homer's voice.

"Your research is what is known as 'delving into the mysteries,' " Homer said.

"I didn't realize that researching Church history was considered that way."

"It is. The Brethren feel it is harmful to the Church."

With that, the inquisition came to an abrupt end.

Until April 8, when Metcalfe was again summoned to the Personnel office.

"You are being terminated from Church employment," Ron Francis informed him.

It wasn't really a surprise. A shock, but not a surprise.

"What are the grounds for the termination?" Metcalfe asked, struggling to remain composed.

There was no answer.

"What are the grounds for the termination?"

Again, no answer.

He asked one last time. "What are the grounds for the termination?"

Finally someone spoke up. "You are being terminated because you didn't conform to the spirit of the things discussed in our previous meetings."

That was a lie, Metcalfe was certain, and he was suddenly indignant. "I fulfilled every requirement you asked of me."

"You conformed to the *letter* of the things that were previously discussed, but not the spirit."

"Give me specific examples of my neglect in conforming to the spirit."

Long pause. Much discomfort and many sidelong looks. Finally, weakly: "Your support for the General Authorities is questionable."

On May 16, 1983, Brent wrote President Gordon Hinckley a seven-page letter, describing his ordeal in detail and asking for his help. It concluded:

> I cannot emphasize too emphatically that in all the detailed researching and studying that I have done, nothing can approach the detrimental effect on the spiritual well being of my family and I resulting from the events described herein. . . . As of this date, May 16, 1983, I remain unemployed.

May 16 was his birthday.

Hinckley never responded. But within a month, Metcalfe was offered a job by Steve Christensen at CFS. Hinckley, it was said, didn't like loose ends.

30 To Lyn Jacobs, who had moved to Cambridge, Massachusetts, in the fall of 1984 to begin a divinity degree at Harvard, Mark Hofmann's soprano on the other end of the line sounded like a voice from another world. It reminded him again how far the Harvard Divinity School was from the LDS Church, how far Harvard Square was from Temple Square. One thing was the same, though. His first-semester study of early

Christian history had reconfirmed for him that much of what Christians now believe, like much of what Mormons now believe, was imposed on their religion long after its founder died.

The voice sounded excited—very unusual for the cool, unflappable Hofmann. Something was up.

When Jacobs left that fall, Hofmann asked him to be on the lookout for stampless covers—letters that were mailed prior to 1850, before postage stamps were introduced, and therefore bore only the imprint of the post office where they were mailed, the date, and the cost of mailing, which varied depending on the number of pages and how far the letter was going. Hofmann was particularly interested in any stampless covers coming out of Palmyra, New York. "You know, not everybody back East knows who Joseph Smith is," he said with his usual edge of sarcasm. "Something important might have gone unnoticed."

In his first hectic months of school, Jacobs wasn't able to do any looking, but he did give Hofmann a few names of dealers who might help him find something.

That was the last Jacobs had heard from him until this day. Just by the sound of his voice, it was clear that he had contacted those dealers and had found something—something big.

Hofmann described an "incredible" find, a letter dated 1830, written by Martin Harris, the same farmer and Smith intimate who had taken the Anthon Transcript to New York for verification. Hofmann didn't have to go any further. Harris's name was enough to make it a spectacular discovery even if it was only a laundry list. But this was much more than that. This was nothing less than *Harris's version of the finding of the gold plates*.

"Get a load of this," Hofmann clucked as he began to read:

> . . . Joseph often sees Spirits here with great kettles of coin money it was Spirits who brought up rock because Joseph made no attempt on their money I latter dream I converse with spirits which let me count their money when I awake I have in my hand a dollar coin which I take for a sign. . . .

*   *   *

Jacobs's first thought, as he listened to the long document, was, "I can't believe it, Mark's done it again." His second thought was, "I'll never see a dime." He should have asked for some kind of agreement when he provided Hofmann with the names of those dealers, he thought. Now it was too late.

He tuned out on the rest of the letter.

Michael Marquardt, however, was all ears when Hofmann called him in late November. He scribbled notes frantically as Hofmann read tantalizing excerpts:

To W. W. Phelps, postmarked Palmyra, October 23rd, 1830. . . . . . in the fall of the year 1827 I hear Joseph found a gold bible I take Joseph aside & he says it is true I found it 4 years ago with my stone but only just got it because of the enchantment the old spirit come to me 3 times in the same dream & says dig up the gold but when I take it up the next morning the spirit transfigured himself from a white salamander in the bottom of the hole & struck me 3 times. . . . Joseph found some giant silver specticles with the plates he puts them in a old hat & in the darkness reads the words & in this way it is all translated & written down. . . .

Something had to be wrong, Marquardt thought. This couldn't be the story of *the* golden plates. This story didn't sound Mormon at all. It didn't even sound *Christian*. There was no vision of God, no mention of Christ. Where was the kindly Angel Moroni who, as all Mormon children learn, showed Joseph where to dig? This story sounded more like a Grimms' fairy tale than a Sunday-school lesson: kettles of money guarded by spirits, seer stones, enchanted spells, magic "specticles," ghostly visitations. And instead of a benevolent angel, a cantankerous and tricky "old spirit" who transforms himself into a *white salamander!*

This was just the link that was needed to connect Joseph Smith's early involvement in money digging and folk magic, proved by the Glass Looker trial records, with the folk magic at the core of the *Book of Mormon*. No longer able to deny Smith's connection to money digging and magic, the Church had tried to palm it off as "youthful indiscretion," unrelated to his later religious activities. This new letter showing that Smith had never abandoned his interest in the occult blew a gaping hole in that explanation.

Marquardt couldn't dial the Tanners' number fast enough.

"You won't believe this one," he exulted in his bizarre, singsong voice. "A letter has been found, a letter from Martin Harris, and it says the money-digging thing and it refers to this old spirit."

"Doesn't it mention an angel?" Jerald Tanner asked, remembering Fawn Brodie's theory that Joseph Smith's "angel story" evolved from his illegal money-digging activities.

"Not a word," reported Marquardt.

"When was it dated?"

"Eighteen-thirty."

"Boy, that's kind of late," said Tanner. Although fascinated by Smith's early involvement with folk magic (he had written a book on the subject), Tanner was by nature a suspicious man, whether he liked what he heard or not. "It seems like the story would have evolved more by then. Are you sure it doesn't mention an angel at all?"

"No. Nothing about an angel. Just this old spirit who transforms himself into a white salamander."

There was a pause on the other end as Jerald assessed the startling news. "That's *amazing*," he finally said—a rave from the undemonstrative Jerald Tanner. "Quite a sensational find."

At ten in the morning, December 11, Marquardt arrived at Hofmann's house, questions swarming in his mind. Was the letter in Harris's handwriting? Were there examples against which to compare it? What did the rest of the letter say? Where did Mark get it? From the Phelps family? Where was it postmarked? Did it have the correct postage?

The meeting lasted for five hours. Hofmann didn't have the document itself, only a typescript and a photocopy. The original was still in the seller's hands. The price was $18,000. With a check already made out, Hofmann was ready to jump on the next plane to Boston. But before he did, he wanted Marquardt's advice on "getting the letter out," i.e., making it public.

"Who should I leak it to?" Hofmann wondered aloud.

"The *New York Times? L.A. Times? Newsweek? Time?*"
The list of names sent him into a reverie.

"It's up to you," said Marquardt, his mind on whether
the typescript was accurate.

"You know the Church isn't going to like this,"
Hofmann said at one point. "How do you think we could
soften the blow?" It was an awkward question for
Marquardt. He was used to bird-dogging the Church and
rushing into print whatever he could get his hands on.
Why was Hofmann talking to *him,* one of the Church's
archenemies, about "softening the blow"?

Marquardt suggested accentuating the positive. "Say
something about the fact that Harris was a witness to the
Book of Mormon," he suggested lamely. "Emphasize the
faith-promoting aspects of it."

"What faith-promoting aspects?" Hofmann looked
surprised.

"It confirms the Anthon Transcript."

Hofmann smiled his strange smile.

When Marquardt asked where he had found the document, Hofmann talked elusively about "a dealer back
East." Surely Marquardt understood, he couldn't reveal
the name. But at one point in the conversation, something very curious happened. After flourishing the envelope that the copy had supposedly come in, he turned it
face down on his desk within easy reach of Marquardt
and abruptly left the room. Marquardt looked at it for a
long time, turning it over in his mind, then decided he
"couldn't afford to be caught looking at it."

If he had looked at it, he would have seen Lyn Jacobs's
address.

Despite all his protests, Marquardt realized, Hofmann
hoped that he would see the letter in tomorrow's *New
York Times.* He hadn't been giving Hofmann advice on
how he should leak it, Hofmann had been giving him tips
on how *he* should leak it. After all, hadn't Marquardt
leaked the inscription on the Joseph Smith III blessing,
the letter from Joseph Smith making his son heir to the
Church? Soon after Hofmann showed it to him, it appeared in a pamphlet published by the Tanners. "Boy,
the Church was sure upset that that got out," Hofmann
said to him afterward, with everything but a wink and a
nod.

What Marquardt didn't realize was that Hofmann wanted

to make sure that when the letter did leak, the name attached to it was Lyn Jacobs, not Mark Hofmann.

That night Hofmann called Jacobs in Cambridge. "I just wanted to reassure you," he said. "You had a part in finding the letter, you should have a share in the profits." Jacobs was surprised and thrilled.

Two days later, Hofmann called Marquardt in a tiff. "*Someone* has leaked," he said in the voice of a playground bully. Even worse, the leak had gotten back to the seller and, for a while, it looked like the deal was off. But, fortunately, Hofmann had calmed him down and saved the sale.

When Lyn Jacobs arrived home for Christmas vacation on December 16, he saw for the first time the document that, according to Hofmann, he, Jacobs, had discovered. To appreciative eyes, it was an exquisitely fragile fragment of history: a single folded sheet of foolscap, worn and creased and penned in faded brown ink. Hinckley's going to want this, Jacobs thought, the adding machine starting up again. If there was ever a document that the Church would want off the streets and safely locked away in The Vault, this was it. Jacobs felt a twinge of sadness. It really was too bad: holographic documents weren't his passion, but he had to admit, it was a beautiful piece of work. Hofmann, too, seemed proud of it in a strange way—which was one reason his request came as such a surprise.

"I want you to do the selling."

Jacobs was shocked. He wanted to know why.

"I don't want the publicity," Hofmann said. "There have been some threats on my family."

Together they decided what to ask for it. Jacobs took the high road, Mark the low. They never came any closer than "anywhere between $25,000 and $60,000." Jacobs thought Mark was surprisingly casual about price—the only thing he seemed to care about was that his name be kept out of the sale.

In early January, Jacobs took the letter into Donald Schmidt in the Church archives. When Schmidt heard the asking price, he said exactly what Jacobs knew he would: "You know I'm not able to make decisions in that price range."

Jacobs liked this act. With this bombshell under his

arm, people paid attention to him. They treated him differently. He wasn't just a local eccentric whom people tolerated. He got respect. "That's okay," he told Schmidt with a toss of his shiny ringlets. He would take it up with Hinckley.

It was a memorable encounter. The hushed, paneled rooms of the First Presidency had not often, if ever, been a backdrop for such high-camp theater. From the moment Jacobs bounced into Hinckley's softly lighted, minimally decorated office in baggy Italian pants and purple-and-black shirt—he liked to wear dark colors with his dark hair—Hinckley moved about like a man caught in a freezer.

There were a few words of introduction and then an awkward pause. "Are you a member of the Church?" Hinckley asked, trying, apparently, to establish Jacobs's pliancy. "I understand that you were a missionary in the Canadian mission."

Hinckley had obviously done his homework. But it wouldn't work: the first few times Jacobs had sold items to the Church archives, Schmidt had tried to make him feel that, as a member of the Church, he should simply "give the stuff up." It hadn't worked then, and it wouldn't work now.

"Do you know Mark Hofmann?" Hinckley asked.

"Yes, I do."

Another awkward pause, then Hinckley, his hands clasped in front of him, knuckles white, said quietly, "The letter, the letter." But when Jacobs finally handed it to him, he read it without the slightest sign of emotion. He could have been reading an insurance policy.

When he finished, he slid the letter onto his slick, empty desktop and clasped his hands together.

"Well, what should we do about it?" he finally asked, without a trace of emotion in his voice. Another day, another problem. Running a church was much like running a railroad.

If that was supposed to be a philosophical question, Jacobs wasn't going to pay any attention to it. He had only one thing on his mind, and he answered the question he wanted to hear.

"What I'd like is one of the coins that Brigham Young minted." Without Hofmann there to control him, Jacobs's greed was getting the better of him. Those coins—$40 and $20 Mormon gold pieces—were worth somewhere between $25,000 and $100,000. The warm-up with Schmidt had made him feel invincible.

For the first time, Hinckley showed an emotion: a shadow of disgust passed over his benign, bureaucratic face. He didn't look astonished at the high price, just perturbed that anyone would demand it. Obviously, he, too, knew how much those gold pieces were worth. "That's a little high," he said very slowly, very much in control.

Jacobs burst into justifications. "Look, if I sell the coin, I'll have to pay almost 50 percent, you know, capital-gains tax. So you have to understand that the real profit on this is only half." Hinckley didn't look as if he appreciated the lesson in tax accounting. "Besides," added Jacobs, "you've got two sets."

"No way," Hinckley said firmly. "We have that as an investment."

"Okay," Jacobs relented, too quickly. "Good-bye to that one. Okay, I want a *Book of Commandments*."

Hinckley looked at Jacobs suspiciously. There was only one question on Hinckley's mind, it seemed, and it had little to do with price: Could *this* man be trusted to keep quiet about the contents of the document and about the Church's involvement?

At the first opportunity, Hinckley broke in. Jacobs read the look on his face as "I don't want this document unless you make it a donation." The meeting was not going well. "Well," Hinckley began portentously. "I don't really think we can do any business here. I'm not sure the Church would be interested in acquiring the letter at this time."

Trying to stay in control of the negotiations, while pumping new life into them, Jacobs said, "The other person we might offer the letter to is Brent Ashworth, since he's bought so many documents before." Jacobs didn't really believe that. He knew that Ashworth collected *faith-promoting* documents. This wasn't even close.

"Well, that might be a good idea," Hinckley said, to Jacobs's surprise. "Brent might not be averse to donating it to us." That wasn't any more likely than Ashworth's buying it in the first place.

Then Hinckley stood up: "This meeting is over."

Jacobs was stunned. Didn't Hinckley realize how explosive this letter was? Could he be so dense? Was he willing to dismiss the only chance the Church would have to bury this bombshell?

In fact, Hinckley wasn't dense, nor was he dismissing anything, especially not this bombshell.

31

Lyn Jacobs didn't know what had gone wrong.

"Well, Mark, I mean, you know, what can I say? No gold coin, no *Book of Commandments*. What are we going to do now?"

Hofmann sat on the other side of the booth, paying more attention to his hamburger than to Jacobs's excuses. "You asked for too much," he said absently, thinking that Jacobs had been the wrong man for the job all along. "It'll be a neat experiment," he had told himself at the time. The idea of putting Jacobs together with Hinckley had appealed to his sense of humor. Now he realized it was a mistake. How could Hinckley trust someone like Jacobs to keep the deal a secret? He was hardly the picture of a faithful, do-as-you're-told Mormon.

But Hofmann had other problems. He was still brooding over his meeting with Brent Ashworth earlier that day.

"It's selling for $50,000," he had told Ashworth. "The Church wants to buy it."

Ashworth read the long typescript of the letter from Martin Harris. In all the years the two men had been dealing, Hofmann had always shown him originals.

"Lyn has the original," Hofmann anticipated. "But we want to offer it to you first."

Ashworth shook his head. "Well, that's great, because I don't want it. It's obviously a non-faith-promoting document, and I am buying faith-promoting documents."

Hofmann tried a different tack. "It's a very major

document," he said, leading to Ashworth's taste for publicity. "*Time* magazine says they may be interested in doing a story on it."

"Well, I hope not," Ashworth said, laughing. "I mean the Church doesn't need that kind of publicity.

"Besides," he added. "I think it's a fake."

Hofmann looked intrigued. "You think so?"

Ashworth had recently reread *Mormonism Unvailed,* a famous early attack on the Church, and there were just too many similarities between the "old toad jumping out of the box" in E. D. Howe's 1834 account and this silly white salamander. "It's probably a very early forgery," Ashworth said, "but I think it's a forgery."

Hofmann jumped in. "Dean Jessee's seen this already. Lyn's shown it to Dean, and Dean has authenticated it. He spent a lot of time on it. There may be some similarities, but this has been authenticated. It's gonna be in *Time.*"

"Personally, I think it's a fake," Ashworth repeated, more softly this time. "But you know, I could be wrong."

"The Church wants to buy it," Hofmann pressed.

"Well, they really ought to have it. Because they ought to be the ones to own that letter. That's something that no collector should be stuck with having to explain or mess with."

Not a very encouraging response.

The next morning, Hofmann decided to try again. If the real problem was Jacobs's sales pitch, then maybe the Church would buy it from him. He called Don Schmidt and told him he could obtain complete control over the document and then he, Hofmann, would sell it to the Church. They could trust him, as they had in the past.

Schmidt wanted to know the price for this service.

"I think I can get it for ten or fifteen," Mark said.

Schmidt had to check with his superiors.

In the meantime, Hofmann tried to develop another buyer, maybe get an auction going. He remembered that Brent Metcalfe, whom he had gotten to know better since he left Church Security, was doing historical research for a rich businessman who was eager to buy Mormon documents—especially controversial documents. So eager, in fact, that he had supplied Metcalfe, and Metcalfe had supplied Hofmann, with a list of the topics he was interested in.

It was quite a shopping list: the coming forth of the *Book of Mormon,* Joseph Smith's involvement with money digging, the early practice of polygamy, the Adam-God theory, and the priesthood in the Temple. In short, *every* area of special Church sensitivity.

At the time, it seemed a little strange that an established Mormon businessman (a bishop in the Church, according to Metcalfe) would want to collect such *verboten* materials, especially at a time when the Church was cracking down. But now Hofmann was too desperate to afford the luxury of a lot of questions. He called Metcalfe.

"You're not going to believe this document Lyn and I found. It's made to order, so to speak," Hofmann told him. "It has to do with early Mormonism."

"Does it have to do with the origins of Mormonism?" Metcalfe asked.

"Yes."

"Does it have to do with the coming forth of the *Book of Mormon?*"

"Yes."

"Does it have to do with the money digging?" Metcalfe was getting more excited with each question.

"I'll just bring it down and show it to you."

Hofmann drove over to Metcalfe's office in the CFS building and showed him the document.

Metcalfe sat and read it. All he could say was, "Oh, my gosh." And when he was done, "I can't believe this."

Metcalfe ran down the hall and returned in a few minutes with a handsome, stout, surprisingly young man.

"Mark Hofmann," he said, barely able to contain his excitement, "this is Steve Christensen."

32

Gordon Hinckley had to consider Steve Christensen just about as perfect as a Mormon could get—in this world, at least. Handsome, in a kind of overstuffed way that bespoke a manly appetite and an absence of vanity, well dressed, well groomed, well spoken, and, best of all, impeccably deferential to his elders. Thanks to his meteoric rise at CFS, he could now safely be considered "successful" despite being only thirty. He had a wife, Terri, who wasn't just stunningly beautiful, but smart and sensible too, and three handsome young sons, Joshua, Justin, and Jared.

Among the elders of the Church like Hinckley, Christensen was already something of a legend. A former Boy Scout and president of his senior class, Steve had left a conspicuous trail of good works and warm feelings in his rapid rise up the Church ladder. There was the time on his mission to Australia when the local teenage kids were vandalizing the ward house. Young Christensen solved the problem not by going to the local police, but by organizing Church-sponsored soccer matches—with punch and cookies after the game. There was the time in Centerville, the suburb where he lived, when a fire consumed a nursery and Christensen mobilized the community to help rebuild. There was the time of the great flood, when he led the sandbagging effort, saving dozens of homes and businesses.

The legend was helped enormously, of course, by the fact that Steve's father was "Mr. Mac," the owner of a chain of clothing stores in the Salt Lake City area and a fixture on television advertisements in which he hawked his wares with the fervor of a TV evangelist. Men like Hinckley had grown up with Mr. Mac. They had bought their suits from him—when he would let them pay. Their pictures hung on the walls of his stores like pictures of sports stars in a bar or of movie stars at Sardi's.

As soon as Steve learned to drive, his father had sent him out with truckloads of suits to the homes of important General Authorities. They could shop at home, pick the ones they liked. When the bill came, it was always dramatically reduced—if it came at all. What was good for the Church was good for business, Mac Christensen believed. In fact, in his mind, the two were practically indistinguishable. It was said of him, admiringly, "Going to work and going to church are pretty much the same thing for Mac."

It was on those home-shopping visits that Church leaders first met Steve Christensen. He was the serious, diffident young man driving the Mr. Mac truck, his tie pulled up tight around his neck, his hair recently cut (every two weeks) and neatly combed, speaking in hushed tones, shaking their hands solidly. He impressed them even then.

Steve Christensen had a knack for doing that—impressing older men. In Australia, his mission president was so taken by his knowledge of Church history and doctrine that he took the young man under his wing and appointed him district leader. In college, Steve made a deep impression on a history professor when he went out and bought a multivolume history of the Popes instead of merely "taking a look at it," as the professor had suggested. At CFS, he won his way into Gary Sheets's heart with a slick, bound report listing the "ways he could make Sheets's life easier." (The list included chauffeur service for Sheets's peewee baseball team.) Sheets rewarded him by making him president of the company at age thirty-one.

Christensen worked the same magic with the father figures on Temple Square. While still in his early twenties, he was appointed to the General Church-Writing Committee and, at twenty-four, chosen to head the highly important Church Doctrinal-Resource Committee, a group of much older academics and theologians who prepared doctrinal briefing papers for the General Authorities. Three years later, even God responded to Christensen's charms, "calling" him to serve as the bishop of his ward in Centerville. At twenty-seven, he was the youngest bishop in the Church outside of college wards.

With Hinckley's backing, Christensen was sure to reach regional representative within a few years, and the Quorum of the Seventy soon after that. Gary Sheets had said it: "Steve Christensen was *born* to be a General Authority." But everyone knew that was only the beginning. Once in the Seventy, advancement would be largely a matter of seniority, and it wasn't stretching a point to guess that with his head start, Christensen might someday be a likely candidate for the First Presidency, or, dare anyone speculate, the *capo di tutti capi,* Prophet, Seer, and Revelator.

Gordon Hinckley knew that if anyone could succeed at a delicate task involving sensitive documents, it was Steve Christensen.

But there were, in fact, two Steve Christensens, and men like Gordon Hinckley saw only one of them. As the oldest of eight children of a tyrannical, ungiving father, Christensen had learned everything there was to know about deference and accommodation, about the appearance of obedience and the reality of resistance. Underneath the Boy Scout uniform, there was, by Mormon standards at least, a closet rebel.

Gordon Hinckley would have been astonished at the way Bishop Christensen, Apostle-in-training, ran his ward. The Church maintained that ward jobs were assigned by God. Not Steve Christensen. "Look," he told a Sunday-school class soon after being called, "you might as well know, speaking at least about myself and about 90 percent of the bishops, we're *not* inspired when we call you to a Church job. So if you covet another job, don't covet it, just come ask for it." The Church maintained that people with serious psychological problems should seek counsel from their bishop. Apostle Bruce R. McConckie had gone so far as to describe psychiatry as "the Church of the Devil." But when members of Christensen's ward came to him with serious problems, he ignored McConckie's warnings and sent them to a psychiatrist. He even offered to help pay the bills.

The Church ordered that young people who engaged in premarital sex should be denied their Temple recommends. Christensen told members to "just keep quiet about it." When one young man came to him just before heading out on a mission and said he was planning to make a confession to the stake president, Christensen advised against it. "If you confess to him, he'll make you stay behind for six months. Only God can really forgive you, so work it out with Him."

The Church exalted businessmen. Christensen excoriated them. "Why should a businessman who bilks people out of their money but who is righteous in his own mind go to the Temple instead of someone who is conscientious enough to be aware of his own sins?" he asked once. "The honest one is going to come in and confess all of his sins. He's the one who really ought to be able to go to the Temple. *He's* the one who's truly worthy."

Christensen knew he was straying from the path. "It's only a matter of time," he told close friends, "before they fire me as bishop." But so far his luck had held. His superiors were so taken with his charms and with his bottom line (tithing went up substantially after he became bishop), that every time he offered to quit, they pleaded with him to stay. "If you ever want to release me from my job as bishop," he told his stake president, "I'm ready and willing to be released any day. Just say the word." But the answer was always, "Oh, no, no, no. You're doing great." It was another of the many tactics he had learned in Mac Christensen's shadow.

And that wasn't the worst of it. If Hinckley would have found Steve's anti-authoritarian methods disappointing, he would have found his ideas appalling. Christensen's vast readings in Mormon history had convinced him that the golden plates were not ancient, if in fact they existed at all, and that the *Book of Mormon,* while it may have been divinely inspired, certainly wasn't what Joseph Smith claimed it was. He also knew that the modern Mormon Church bore only the most superficial resemblance to the Church that Smith founded. With social Mormons and friends among the anti-Mormon underground, he shared these heretical views. But to the men in power, to Gordon Hinckley and the other father figures in his life, he never breathed a word of doubt or dissent.

In his rare, immodest moments, Christensen considered himself representative of modern, thinking Mormons. He believed in the culture, if not in the doctrine—at least as the current leaders of the Church conceived it. But he didn't know if he could separate the two, and was afraid to try. "I won't do anything that might get me excommunicated," he told a friend. "I would rather lie publicly and recant my personal beliefs than allow myself to be excommunicated and hurt my family."

Christensen took the document Hofmann handed him to his office and read it quietly. Like Hinckley, he said nothing. He just looked up, his face a blank, and asked, "How much do you want for it?"

"Twenty thousand." Hofmann realized immediately that he had answered too quickly. "That's what *Lyn* wants for it," he corrected himself.

"How about $25,000?" Steve said. "That way Lyn can get $20,000 and you can get $5,000 for your efforts."

"I'll have to check with Lyn."

Later the same day, Hofmann met with Don Schmidt in the Church Office Building.

Schmidt had good news. He had spoken with Durham and Hinckley. They had agreed to buy the letter for $15,000 *if* Hofmann could guarantee confidentiality. Had he shown the letter to anyone? No, said Hofmann. Can Jacobs be trusted? On the phone that morning, Hofmann had reassured Schmidt that Jacobs could be "sworn to secrecy." The fact that he was asking again only verified what Hofmann had suspected all along: Hinckley didn't trust the flamboyant Harvard student even as far as tomorrow. This time, with Christensen's offer on the table, Hofmann hesitated.

There is another way, he said.

"If the Church would prefer," he began in a speculative tone, as if the idea were just coming to him, "we could see that it was sold to a faithful member of the Church. If Hinckley doesn't want . . ."—better not to be too specific. "If the Church is afraid of the publicity. . . ." He knew that Hinckley would never trust Jacobs to keep quiet, no matter how many oaths he swore. "We could arrange to have it sold to a faithful member who would . . ." Would what? Keep quiet? He thought it best to take a tactful approach, " . . . who would handle it the way the Church thought appropriate." Schmidt was arguably naive but certainly not stupid. He understood. "That way Church officials wouldn't be officially making decisions."

Once again, Hofmann was offering them what they most wanted: plausible deniability.

Schmidt said he would check with his superiors.

* * *

The next day, he called with the news Hofmann was expecting. "My superiors think it would be more appropriate to have that happen to it—so far as a faithful member making the purchase."

Now the only question was, How badly did Christensen want it?

Hofmann returned to the CFS building the next day with some startling news. "I was wrong," he told Christensen. "Lyn wants $100,000."

Steve Christensen had walked out of negotiations over less. But he wanted this document.

"You know the Church is interested in buying this," Hofmann said ominously. He had done his homework. Someone had told him, probably Metcalfe, that Christensen sided with the new historians who wanted to investigate the Church's past, even the dark corners of Joseph Smith's money digging. If the Church bought the letter, Hofmann intimated, no one would ever see it again.

Christensen knew better. He had been on the phone already with Spencer Kimball's secretary, Arthur Haycock, and G. Homer Durham. Durham had warned him that this was a "sensitive document" and had to be treated accordingly. Christensen had reassured him that his intentions were entirely "faithful," that he had no intention of embarrassing the Church. His mission was to get that letter and keep it out of "enemy hands."

Christensen shared none of this with Metcalfe or Hofmann.

After a day or two of negotiations, Hofmann informed Metcalfe that Jacobs would take $40,000. Christensen agreed to pay that amount—almost precisely the value of the *Book of Commandments* Jacobs had originally asked for from Hinckley. The night before the contract was to be signed, Hofmann called Jacobs and broke the news. "I've made all the arrangements," he said. This was the first Jacobs had heard of it. "A contract is drawn up, and Christensen will be paying $40,000, with $10,000 payments every six months." Jacobs was startled but pleased. His share, $5,000, would pay for his first-term tuition at Harvard Divinity School.

On January 6, 1984, Metcalfe met Hofmann and Jacobs in the reception area of the CFS building and escorted them to Christensen's office to sign the contract.

Hofmann hung back and let Jacobs take center stage. It was, after all, Jacobs's discovery.

On January 9, Christensen wrote G. Homer Durham to inform him that the document was safely in his hands and to reassure him that if and when the document was made public, it would only be after a thorough analysis by " faithful historians" and accompanied by a "careful commentary." In the long run, he added, "it is my intention and desire to donate the document to the Church of Jesus Christ of Latter-day Saints."

When Peggy Fletcher, the editor of *Sunstone* magazine, heard that a letter linking Joseph Smith to money digging and folk magic was being suppressed by the Church, she went straight to the top.

"President Hinckley, I really, really think this letter should be released to the public. You could call a press conference and say, 'We have this letter, we don't know what the implications of it are. It's just of interest, and we're not ashamed of it.' It's so much better if we do that as a Church. A lot of people are talking about this. I have been called by people from all over, including *Time* magazine, who are going to do a story on it. Why don't we just do it ourselves? That way we won't look like we're hiding it or are ashamed of it."

Hinckley paused for a moment. "We don't own the document," he finally said. "And so we can't call a press conference. Christensen has it."

"I know that," Fletcher pressed. "But you know Steve, and I know Steve. If you called him and said, 'Let's have a press conference, a joint press conference,' you *know* he would do it."

Hinckley took another long pause, the very model of patience. "It's out of my hands," he said. "It's not my problem."

33 Now that they had the document, the two Steve Christensens couldn't agree on what to do with it.

One hired a team of researchers to study the "historical context" of the letter with the objective of writing "the ultimate book on early Mormonism, especially on the magic connection." The panel reflected all of Christensen's guarded hopes for more openness in Mormon scholarship. The group included, on the one hand, Dean Jessee, the Church's favorite handwriting expert, and on the other, Ron Walker, a senior research historian at the Joseph Fielding Smith Institute, who was reported to be deeply troubled by the Church's hostility toward independent scholarship. After much pleading, Christensen even included Brent Metcalfe, whose borderline apostasy was well known—especially to the Church.

On January 24, Christensen charged his team of truth seekers: "I believe that the work that you Brethren do will be of significance to Mormon scholarship in the years to come, that this can and will become a standard cited reference, and that the Church will be blessed as a result of the honest, accurate historical foundation which the three of you men will provide to the study of early Mormon origins."

Meanwhile, the other Christensen was busy ensuring that the document stayed out of the public eye for as long as possible. Only days after the purchase in January, he sent it East for an extensive (and extended) examination by Kenneth Rendell, of Newton, Massachusetts, one of the world's foremost document dealers. Rendell rarely agreed to authenticate a document he wasn't selling, but he made an exception out of deference to his respected colleague, Mark Hofmann.

Where one Christensen had quickly invited Walker

and Jessee to join the research team, the other delayed formalizing the offer until May, almost five months later, offering each man $6,000 and 25 percent of the profits from the sale of the book that would come out of their efforts. That gave them a stake in not leaking anything to the press in advance of publication.

If there was a weak link in the chain of silence, Christensen knew, it was Mark Hofmann.

As if sensing his client's doubts, soon after the deal was signed, Hofmann came by with another offer. He had a document that he thought Christensen would be interested in. It was a typescript of a legal agreement between a group of men, including Joseph Smith and Josiah Stowell, dated November 1, 1825, on how to divide the profits—"Suppossd to be a valueble mine of either Gold or Silver & also to cont[ain] Coind money & bars or ingot of Gold or Silver"—that resulted from Smith's money-digging efforts "at a certain Place in Pennsylvania."

It was enough to give doctrinaire Mormons heart failure. This was the agreement for the business deal that went sour and ended up in a New York courtroom in 1826. *This* was the much-dreaded confession. At best, this document proved yet again, and beyond a doubt, what the anti-Mormons had been saying all along, that Joseph Smith was, for a period at least, a money digger and penny-ante con man. At worst, it was evidence of imagination and ambition running out of control, suggesting all too vividly a young Joseph Smith, failing to dig up any real "Gold or Silver," simply digging some gold plates out of the same rich soil of his imagination.

Hofmann was prepared not only to give Christensen all "legal rights of ownership" in the transcript, but also to offer him a right of first refusal on the actual document at a fixed price of $15,000 *if* Hofmann was able to pry it away from its current owners, "a couple of elderly sisters." And all Hofmann wanted in return was the next $10,000 installment of the Salamander money, which, under the terms of the contract, wasn't due until July 20. It was a gracious, generous act, Christensen thought, one that clearly showed Hofmann's good intentions.

Just to be sure, however, Christensen checked with his lawyer, Alan Smith, at the Salt Lake City office of the prestigious New York firm LeBoeuf, Lamb, Leiby &

MacRae. Just what were Hofmann's—and now Christensen's—legal rights of ownership in the documents? Could he sue Hofmann for revealing the contents of either document? Three weeks later, Smith wrote to say that the legal questions involved were "difficult" but that he was still working on them "methodically, albeit gradually." All Smith had to do was check with Jerald and Sandra Tanner. For obvious reasons, they had researched the question thoroughly and discovered that there was no legal way to control the contents of the documents or their reproduction. At least one other person knew about the results of the Tanners' research: Mark Hofmann.

Christensen was fighting a losing battle.

In early February, before she asked Gordon Hinckley about the Salamander Letter, Peggy Fletcher called Christensen. "Steve, I'm trying to reach Mark Hofmann," she said. "I heard from someone that there's this letter and that Mark Hofmann has sold it to someone."

"Yeah, me," Christensen confessed.

"Why don't you tell me about it? We want to do a story on it."

"I can't release anything about it now, but I'll give you first rights to the story. Maybe we can do the research and do a session at the symposium in August." (In April and August each year *Sunstone* sponsored a conference in which Mormon and non-Mormon scholars of Mormon history and doctrine would give lectures on recent research.)

Fletcher knew better than to press. She had worked with Christensen during his stint on the Doctrinal-Resource Committee and knew his philosophy on sensitive documents well. "This is how I'm handling it," he would say whenever something controversial came up. "It's okay to keep ideas quiet in the short run, with the intention of revealing them at a time, and in a way that is most palatable to believers."

Christensen had hoped at least to get through the summer before word leaked out. Here it was only weeks after the deal, and he was already making excuses. The Church had been right: this was a hot potato. He knew the research wouldn't be done by August, but he would cross that bridge when he came to it. This would at least keep things quiet until then.

Within days, Richard Ostling, the religion editor at *Time* magazine, called to say he had heard rumors of a sensitive letter and he planned to do an article on it. The so-called rumors were stunningly specific. He knew the letter in question was dated October 23, 1830, was written by Martin Harris to W. W. Phelps, and dealt with the revelation of the golden plates. Ostling had also heard about the Church's curious policy of buying controversial documents and squirreling them away. (Unknown to Christensen, Ostling's anonymous tipster had also helpfully directed him to Lyn Jacobs, who, when Ostling interviewed him the following week, claimed that his decision to withdraw from negotiations with the Church was based entirely on the failure to agree on an acceptable price.)

Christensen tried to contain the damage. "I don't want to publish the letter until I can also publish some explanations."

That might work with Peggy Fletcher, but Ostling wasn't buying it, so Christensen tried another tack. "Besides, I promised Peggy Fletcher that I would give it to her first, either for use in the *Sunstone Review,* or, preferably at the next conference." Trying to buy time, Christensen lied, " . . . which isn't until early April." The next conference was in April, but he hadn't promised anything to Fletcher until August—at the earliest. A little white lie for the Lord.

He closed with a plea: "Can't you sit the story out for a while?"

Ostling called Peggy Fletcher. He didn't want to scoop her but he couldn't sit on the story forever. Theirs was a competitive business. When was the earliest she could publish the letter? The March issue of the *Review,* which went to press on March 9. Fine. Ostling agreed to hold off on his account until March 12.

Ostling wrote Christensen back and explained the deal: "This will serve *Sunstone's* interests, give me a journalistic reward for sitting on an important story for a month, and give you time to complete a thorough historical article to accompany release of the text."

A month! Gordon Hinckley's Steve Christensen couldn't believe what he was hearing. Here he was conducting a full-scale rethinking of the founding years and early doctrine of the Mormon religion, and *Time* magazine expects it to be done in a month! That may be a long time by the yellow journalism standards of Time Inc., he thought, but it was a split second in the eyes of the Church that would ultimately judge the work.

Ostling was unmoved. "I think it would be unrealistic," he added ominously, "to suppose this will keep until the next *Sunstone* deadline, in early April. . . . I might be forced to go ahead with a story any time this appears in another publication before your official release date. I can tell you from much experience as a journalist that we would be very lucky if it remains bottled up that long."

They weren't lucky. In early March, Jerald and Sandra Tanner blew the story open in their monthly newsletter, the Salt Lake City *Messenger*. They called the Harris letter, of which they had seen excerpts, "one of the greatest evidences against the divine origin of the *Book of Mormon*, if authentic."

Christensen was furious. He couldn't believe that the *text* of the document had already leaked—to the Tanners, no less. Clearly, he had fumbled the ball for the Church. On May 7, feeling cornered, he issued a terse public statement.

> It is true that I am the owner of a letter written by Martin Harris to William W. Phelps, dated October 23, 1830. While it is hoped that the letter is authentic, professional tests have not yet been performed on the document. Before I will release transcripts or photographs of the document to the public, I wish to first determine the document's historicity as much as possible. I have therefore sought the help and advice of competent historians to assist me in determining the reliability of the contents of the letter.
>
> Until the above-referenced research and tests have further progressed, I do not feel at liberty to share the full contents of the letter. It is unfortunate that publicity of the document has preceded its historical authentication. This has lead [sic] to some cases of misstatement as well as numerous phrases being taken out of context.

To demonstrate to Church leaders just how angry he *really* was, Christensen also threatened legal action against the Tanners for violating his copyright to the Harris letter, and offered to testify in the lawsuit of another

TOO GOOD TO BE TRUE • 165

researcher who was suing the Tanners for publishing without permission sensitive material the researcher had obtained from the Church. Perhaps in courtroom questioning, he could find out who had leaked the excerpts from the letter.

In the end, neither Christensen nor the Tanners ever testified on the matter. If they had, Christensen would have been shocked to discover that the Tanners' source was none other than Mark Hofmann. The March article had been based on the notes Michael Marquardt had made at his five-hour meeting with Hofmann the previous December, before Christensen bought the letter.

Christensen didn't have any better luck tracing the source of the leak to Ostling at *Time*—one of the publications that Hofmann had mentioned to Marquardt in December. At one point, Lyn Jacobs helpfully suggested that perhaps Leonard Arrington, whose son and daughter-in-law both worked for Time Inc., was the source, but Christensen could never establish the link.

With the cat now well out of the bag, Peggy Fletcher approached Christensen again.

"I was the first journalist to hear about this," she said. "You asked me not to print anything about it, and I didn't. How about letting me print a story about the letter, then say you are doing all this research."

"I can't," he said. "I'm under a lot of pressure."

"From whom?" Fletcher had heard the rumors that the Church was pressuring Steve to keep the whole thing quiet, and that now, with the Tanners' revelation, the heat was on.

He wouldn't say.

She tried again. "Why not at least get the basic information out to the audience?"

He was adamant. Too much was out already. The debacle with the Tanners was exactly what he knew would happen if the text preceded the explanation. As one Church leader had put it, "Meat before milk always produces indigestion." "No," he said. "I want to do it my way. When we release the information, I want to release it in a context that people can understand."

Meanwhile, Jerald Tanner had decided that it was a moot point. The Salamander Letter, he said, was probably a fake.

There were just too many parallels between Harris's account and E. D. Howe's *Mormonism Unvailed,* which was published four years later. He also thought it strange that Harris, a religious man, didn't mention God or angels or devils *even once.* "This just isn't the Martin Harris I know," said Jerald. Sandra disagreed, and in the June issue of the *Messenger,* they wrote a divided editorial, Jerald calling it a fake, Sandra calling it genuine.

Now it was Hofmann's turn to be furious.

He approached Sandra Tanner, who had been passing out copies of Jerald's list of parallels between the Harris letter and the Howe book, at the *Sunstone* symposium in August.

"I just don't *understand* how there can be any question about this," he complained, his high voice uncharacteristically filled with emotion. "It's so *obvious* that it's all been verified and proved. Christensen did all these tests and has all this confirmation."

"Well, we need some specifics on this, Mark," said Sandra, her schoolteacher manner seeming even more solid and businesslike next to Hofmann's schoolboy petulance. "Who did you get it from?"

"It would be so easy to find out," he insisted. "There are only three dealers in New York that I could have gotten this kind of thing from. It's easy to verify all this stuff."

He is a *beautiful* salesman, Sandra thought. He seemed so convinced. "Christensen has had this thing all tested," he repeated.

Sandra went back to what was for her the key: "But who did you get it from?"

Hofmann straightened up, as though regrouping. "I can't divulge where I got it," he said, suddenly very straight, very professional, very officious. "Steve Christensen has the letter, he bought it, and I don't have a right to tell. When I sell a document to anybody, I always give them the right to control what they want to do with the document and what they want to divulge. I turn over to them a statement saying just where I got it and the background of the document and everything. It's their document and their background, and it's up to them to do what they want with it. Christensen has all that information, and you'll have to get it from Christensen. That's just the way I do business."

He paused and looked at her. His lower lip crept forward. "I can't understand why you, of all people, would be the ones to question me," he said slowly. He looked, Sandra remembers, "crushed and practically in tears."

Around the same time, a number of Mormon scholars, some of them connected to the underground, received in the mail typed copies of Joseph Smith's 1825 letter to Josiah Stowell, the letter that Hofmann had sold directly to Gordon Hinckley in January 1983, the letter that would "never see the light of day." The letters were not signed and bore only a New York City postmark. With its references to money digging, clever spirits, and detailed instructions on how to use a hazel stick to locate buried treasure, the Stowell letter seemed to confirm all the wild rumors about the Salamander Letter. Surely this would satisfy the skeptics.

But it didn't. On August 22, 1984, the Tanners published *The Money-Digging Letters,* in which they once again questioned the authenticity of the Salamander Letter.

To Christensen's great relief, Richard Ostling's article never did appear in *Time.* His editors twice pulled the story due to "lack of documentation." But it was only a temporary victory.

On the heels of the Tanners' publication, the full story hit in the August 25 issue of the *Los Angeles Times*—another of the papers Hofmann had mentioned to Marquardt:

> A letter purportedly written in 1830 by Mormonism's first convert is now threatening to alter the idealized portrait of church founder Joseph Smith. . . .
>
> The First Presidency's Gordon Hinckley said the Church of Jesus Christ of Latter-day Saints had earlier indicated that no comment would be made until the letter's analysis was completed.
>
> But insiders here say there are indications that the letter may be valid.
>
> Even if it is not, a respected non-Mormon authority on Mormon origins said the white

salamander letter is consistent with other evidence that Joseph Smith had his occult side.

The article in the September 22 *Arizona Republic* (a paper with a large, affluent Mormon readership) was even worse:

> White salamanders, ancient spirits, peep stones and divining rods are the stuff of magic and 19th-century American frontier folklore.
> According to two recently discovered letters dating from the beginnings of the Church of Jesus Christ of Latter-day Saints, they were also the stuff of prophet Joseph Smith's early life and the origins of Mormonism. . . .

Christensen tried to respond to the deluge of speculation. "What happened was not that unnatural or uncommon given what was going on in Joseph Smith's day," the release concluded. "To anyone who has studied the Joseph Smith period there are not a lot of surprises in the letter." Official Church spokesmen toed the same line, trying, as they had with the Joseph Smith III blessing, to pass off the document as an historical curiosity. "It certainly sounds consistent with the times," said spokesman Jerry Cahill, "and possibly is an interesting sidelight to what is known."

When asked if Church leaders were upset by the most recent round of bad press for Smith and his Church, Christensen said, "I frankly don't think the Brethren have had the time or the interest to even worry much about the letter."

In fact, they could think about little else.

Hinckley had to be furious. The drubbing in the press had continued right through September and up to the time of the General Conference in October, a time when thousands of well-groomed Mormons from all over the world make the pilgrimage to the vast, egg-shaped Tabernacle, famous for its organ and choir; a time when the General Authorities make one of their rare public appearances, like the Politburo at Lenin's Tomb; a time to reassure the flock that all is well with the true Church.

But all wasn't well. And in between the usual benign,

noncontroversial testimonials and rededications to the good life, Hinckley issued a stern warning concerning the dangers inherent in too much digging into the past. On Sunday morning, October 7, Hinckley noted in his conference speech that "for more than a century and a half, enemies, critics, and some would-be scholars have worn out their lives trying to disprove the validity of [Joseph Smith's] vision. Of course they cannot understand it. The things of God are understood by the spirit of God."

Hinckley's generalities were fleshed out by Elder Bruce R. McConkie, a senior Apostle, in his conference speech later that afternoon:

> On every issue it behooves us to determine what the Lord would have us do and what counsel he has given through the appointed officers of his kingdom on earth.
>
> No true Latter-day Saint will ever take a stand that is in opposition to what the Lord has revealed to those who direct the affairs of his earthly kingdom.
>
> No Latter-day Saint who is true and faithful in all things will ever pursue a course, or espouse a cause, or publish an article or book that weakens or destroys the faith.

At least one person in the audience took McConkie's words to heart: Christensen's boss, Gary Sheets. Always generous with his money, Sheets had been bankrolling the research project on the Salamander Letter, not so much out of historical curiosity as out of fondness for Steve. But when he began to hear the water-cooler gossip about Brent Metcalfe "losing his testimony" as a result of his work on the project, he decided it was time to act. Souls were at stake. As a bishop, he had no choice but to fire Metcalfe and terminate the project. And it had to be done quickly, before still others were "deprived of their testimonies." He told Christensen about McConkie's talk and, according to Christensen's later account, hinted about other, more direct pressures from elsewhere in the Church hierarchy. The project had to be shut down, and that included the book that Christensen planned. "It just isn't politically wise," Sheets stressed.

Christensen capitulated. Two days later, he terminated the project and called Metcalfe into his office. He blamed the debacle entirely on Sheets and offered generous severance terms of full pay for three months and $1,000 a month for six months after that. Christensen wanted no disgruntled leakers or, as Hinckley might have said, no loose ends.

Soon afterward, Peggy Fletcher asked Christensen why he had fired Metcalfe.

"The materials are too sensitive," he said. "Gary was being leaned on as a bishop—he was told to back off, since the subject matter is so controversial."

When the dust cleared, Christensen sat down to write a damage report. On October 16, he hand-delivered it to Hinckley's office. Starred and underlined at the top of the three-page letter were the words **Personal & Confidential**.

First, he reassured Hinckley, the Church's P.R. genius, of his discretion: "During this whole period I have been extremely unfriendly to the media." Then he reported the cataclysmic events of the previous week. "Last Thursday I had the unpleasant experience of terminating the working relationship with Brent Metcalfe. The main reason is that Gary Sheets and myself became uncomfortable with many of Brent's personal opinions relating to Church History and Doctrine. More important, we did not want to financially underwrite a book relating to the early origins of the Church and the coming forth of the *Book of Mormon* if the work had the potential of doing more harm than good. . . ."

Christensen gave Hinckley credit for bringing him to his senses. "I was extremely impressed with your Conference talk," he wrote. "I believe that the Church has more pressing work to accomplish than to be consumed by questions and contradictions from the past. While it is better that we lead forth in historical inquiry rather than leaving the task to our enemies, those so engaged must have sufficient faith that the day will come when all is revealed and then the pieces will all fit together."

Finally, Christensen asked Hinckley what he should do with the Salamander Letter.

"I am still not eager to thrust the document in the hands of the media. Personally, I would like to stay as low profile as is possible. . . . If the Church would like it, it is yours for the asking—just tell me when."

The next day, October 17, at a United Way luncheon, Christensen was surprised to find himself seated next to Hinckley. Through most of the meal they apparently talked little. Then suddenly, with hardly a word of introduction, Hinckley turned to him and said in a low voice, "We would like to see the letter come to the Church."

34 The market for Mormon documents was getting too hot. In 1984, with all the controversy surrounding the Salamander Letter, Hofmann decided it was time to step out and let things cool down for a while. Of course, he left open the possibility that something truly spectacular might lure him back.

In the meantime, he turned his skills and uncanny good fortune to the larger and even more lucrative Gentile documents market. He began trading the autographs of well-known historical and literary figures. He had particular success in uncovering obscure but valuable signatures like that of Button Gwinnett, a man who signed the Declaration of Independence but very little else, making his signature an expensive must for collectors assembling a complete set of signers. He discovered previously unknown, inscribed first editions of books like Jack London's *Call of the Wild* and Mark Twain's *Tom Sawyer*.

In was a fabulously rich market, with thousands of collectors, including such "deep pockets" as the Library of Congress and Malcolm Forbes. Now, instead of digging through attic trunks in Coalville, Utah, Hofmann jetted off to manuscript auctions at Sotheby's in New York. He bought tens of thousands of dollars' worth of rare books from prestigious dealers like Schiller-Wapner Galleries in New York and Mark Hime in Los Angeles.

He met the leading lights in the documents business, men like Charles Hamilton, the country's foremost handwriting expert and the author of *Great Forgers and Fa-*

mous Fakes, a book for which Hofmann expressed keen admiration. Hamilton was the man who had finally unmasked the famous Hitler diaries after experts all over the world declared them genuine. A venerable septuagenarian with a full head of white hair and a persona of Dickensian complexity who had filched his first autograph from a trash can at age nine, Hamilton looked forward to Hofmann's unannounced visits. The two would sit and talk for hours about history, literature, science, or music. Hofmann showed particular interest in Hamilton's recent book on Shakespeare's handwriting. (To Hamilton's surprise, Hofmann already knew there were only six known signatures of the Bard's.)

How encouraging, Hamilton thought, to find such an "unassuming, modest scholar, eager to add to the store of knowledge that the heritage of our country requires for its sustenance." In a business filled with hype and borderline claims, it was so refreshing to find someone who took a soft, low-key, and impeccably honest approach to his documents. When Hofmann brought something in, he always seemed uncertain about its value. "What do you think?" he would ask, or "Could it be genuine?"

One day, Hofmann handed him a letter signed "Joseph Smith."

Hamilton took one look and handed it back. "It is the wrong man," he said in his theatrical Irish tenor. "There were enough Joseph Smiths in upstate New York to create a regiment out of them. The name doesn't mean a damn thing. You've got the wrong man."

Later, Hofmann asked him to take another look.

Out of affection, Hamilton obliged. But his answer was the same. "Mark, this just isn't Joseph Smith's handwriting," he concluded. "It's too upright. The letters are too clear. It's not smudged enough. It does not have that precipitous movement toward the margin that Smith's handwriting had." Then Hamilton looked at the date. "Are you aware that Smith was nineteen at the time that this document was written?"

"Yes," said Hofmann tentatively, as if he expected more.

When Hamilton began to read the document—something he didn't always find necessary—he noticed the double consonants characteristic of Joseph Smith and a reference to a 'spirit.' "

"Jesus Christ, Mark, this *could* be a very early Smith and a different handwriting. The handwriting looks labored, as though the writer had taken hours and hours to write. Which would make sense, for someone who hadn't done much writing."

"Do you really think it could be?"

Hamilton eventually authenticated the letter.

Hofmann was always asking questions—"picking my brains," Hamilton called it. What should he be on the lookout for? "Mr. Hamilton, sir, you know I have such good luck at finding things," he would say. Hamilton told him one time, "I never knew a guy who had such good luck as you have, except one—a guy named Carl Williams, and Williams was, unbeknownst to me, stealing from the Philadelphia city hall."

Hofmann laughed hysterically at that.

With new contacts, new leads, new deals, new clients, Hofmann needed a new number two—someone to take the place of Jacobs, who was both too busy with his school and too wrapped up in his Mormon pamphlets to be of more than occasional use. The botched deal with Hinckley had clearly shown the limits of his usefulness.

Hofmann found his man in Shannon Flynn, a fat, friendly, seemingly harmless young man who laughed easily—too easily some thought. The two first met in 1982 when Lyn Jacobs introduced them. Jacobs had introduced Flynn to the joys of collecting Mormonabilia, and Flynn had asked for an audience with the "King of Mormon memorabilia," Mark Hofmann.

To Hofmann, Flynn was the perfect lieutenant: not too smart, not too curious, but very eager. To Flynn, Hofmann was a savior. He had been working as a salesman at a photography studio owned by relatives for longer than he cared to calculate. He would have followed anyone, anywhere, to get away from the calm and the boredom and the predictability of it all. Because underneath the considerable girth and the amiable grin lurked a different person altogether.

Flynn's apartment was filled with stacks of *Soldier of Fortune*, piles of camouflage clothing, an arsenal of guns and pistols, and enough smokeless powder to blow up a small town. Even walking around the pacific streets of Salt Lake City, Flynn carried his favorite weapon: a Philippine butterfly knife, a mean, double-bladed switchblade that posed more danger to the untrained owner than to an armed assailant. But Flynn had mastered the deadly flick of the wrist that turned him into a lethal fighting machine. He may have looked like the Pillsbury Doughboy, but underneath, Shannon Flynn was Rambo.

Like any good soldier of fortune, Flynn had to prove his loyalty.

In late September 1984, he called Wilford Cardon, a man of considerable wealth—oil, construction, convenience stores, etc.—and impeccable Mormon credentials. Cardon had been Flynn's mission president in Brazil in 1978, and the two had taken to each other like father and son.

In his eagerness, Flynn spilled the whole deal over the phone: his friend Mark Hofmann had found an extremely rare and valuable letter signed by Betsy Ross. According to Hofmann, he could sell it for at least twice the purchase price. All he needed was an investor. Cardon was noncommittal but pleased to hear from Flynn. He invited him and his new friend to come to Mesa, Arizona, and pitch the deal in person.

Flynn and Hofmann made plane reservations, and on October 6, left for Arizona. Flynn was off and running. This was just the life he had been dreaming of. Big deals, quick trips, jetting off on a moment's notice to exotic destinations to sign big-money, flick-of-the-pen deals with movers and shakers. He told friends he felt like James Bond.

At the meeting with Cardon, Hofmann descibed the 1807 letter signed by Betsy Ross.

"What makes this letter so valuable?" asked Cardon, who knew, he admitted, a lot about investments but nothing about documents.

"It's the only signed letter that's ever been found," said Hofmann.

"Where did you get it?"

Hofmann refused to give the source.

Flynn quickly piped up, "That's common in the documents business. A dealer never reveals his sources."

As an astute businessman, Cardon could understand that.

This was the deal: Hofmann could buy the letter for $18,000. Each of them—Hofmann, Flynn, and Cardon—would put up a third of the money. Each would receive a third of the profits from the sale.

"What about finding a buyer?" Cardon wanted to know.

"No problem," said Hofmann.

There was one more thing. Flynn wanted to ask a favor of his old mission president. Since he didn't *have* $6,000, and couldn't put his hands on it anytime soon, could Cardon loan him the money?

What's $12,000 between a father and a son? thought Cardon. He'd lost that much, and more, on any number of investments. If he could help Shannon get into a lucrative and fulfilling business, it was well worth the risk. If he made money from the investment, so much the better. On October 30, he sent Hofmann a check for $12,000.

On his next visit to New York, Hofmann dropped in on Charles Hamilton.

"What should I be looking for?" he asked, as he always did.

This time, Hamilton had a specific suggestion. "A signature of a mountain man who led the Mormons to Salt Lake City, Jim Bridger, is so damn rare that I never saw one in my life," he said. "However, Bridger was illiterate, so you're looking for an X mark."

"I'm going to really make an attempt," Hofmann said in his most determined, Andy Hardy voice.

Several months went by before Cardon heard anything more about his investment. He never did see the Betsy Ross letter, although Flynn sent him a photograph of it in December. Around the same time, Hofmann finally called, his voice quivering with excitement.

"Someone has offered to buy the Betsy Ross letter in exchange for sixteen promissory notes to a company called Livingston & Kincaid Co."

"Is that good news?" Cardon wondered.

Hofmann, apparently, thought it was great news. These weren't just any notes. "They're signed by Jim Bridger," he announced, then felt obliged to explain, "Of course, they're signed with an X, Bridger being illiterate. But that X is so rare that they're worth much more than the Betsy Ross letter."

On his next trip to New York, Hofmann returned to Charles Hamilton's gallery on 57th Street.

"Mr. Hamilton, I have located a very large collection of receipts, and all of it's worthless—except for three Jim Bridgers in it."

Hamilton's ears pricked up.

"I have to buy the whole collection to get them," Hofmann continued. "But I don't want them to know why I'm buying this collection of receipts. What do you think I could get for them?"

"Five thousand each," Hamilton answered without hesitation. Then he looked at his newest and brightest student: "For that information, I trust you're going to offer one of them to me."

"Of course," Hofmann offered cheerily.

Not long afterward, Hofmann sold one of the notes to Brent Ashworth for $5,000. "How many are there?" Ashworth asked.

"This is the only one," Hofmann·said.

A week later, he arrived at their regular Wednesday meeting at the Crossroads Mall with some bad news: there were, in fact, four Bridger notes. Ashworth bit his tongue and agreed to pay a second $5,000 for a second note. Not long afterward, he bumped into Hofmann coming out of Cosmic Aeroplane, a bookstore in Salt Lake that occasionally dealt in rare books and documents. Then Ashworth went inside.

"What was Mark doing here?" he asked the proprietor, Steve Barnett.

"What's Mark always doing?" said Barnett, a pleasant if mousy man, well suited to his business. "Selling something."

Ashworth was almost afraid to ask. "What was it this time?"

"Jim Bridger notes."

Ashworth looked at the two notes Barnett had bought. They weren't like the ones he had bought, but they weren't like the ones he *hadn't* bought either. That meant there were *six*. At least. Infuriated, Ashworth stopped payment on a check for the last $1,250 installment for the notes.

When Hamilton heard about the sale to Ashworth, he called Hofmann. "Look, why don't you let me sell one of those notes? Why don't you let me sell one at auction? I could get $7,500 for it."

35 Mark Hofmann was the talk of the town. Rumors ricocheted around the market about the dizzying profits to be made in document deals—Hofmann's deals. Collectors scrambled over one another to get a piece of the action. So what if he was a little evasive about his sources, hard to get ahold of when he owed you money, a nut about secrecy? What were a few personal idiosyncrasies when you were looking at double your money in six months, or four months, or less.

Hofmann brought Al Rust the Salamander contract signed by Steve Christensen. It called for four $10,000 payments. "But, hey," Hofmann said, "I need $5,000 right now. I'll give you this contract, which is for $10,000, and you'll be paid within ninety days, $10,000 for $5,000."

Rust was understandably suspicious. "Why would you want to do that, Mark?" he asked. "You can go to a bank and borrow $5,000. In ninety days you're gonna have to pay back maybe $600 interest at the most."

"I need the money right now," Hofmann insisted.

Rust wasn't going to put up a fight. Something about gift horses. "Fine, give me the contract."

The deal was done, and ninety days later Hofmann came up with the money: 100 percent return in three months. But Hofmann had a better idea. "How about turning around and putting the profit back in?" he suggested. With returns like that, who could refuse? The deals were just too good to be true.

*   *   *

Deals like the one Hofmann offered his old Utah State schoolmate, Thomas Wilding.

Since working his way through college selling insurance, Wilding had developed a successful financial advisory service. As Hofmann's insurance agent, he saw just how lucrative the documents business was—Hofmann had increased his coverage to a quarter of a million. He saw the glowing newspaper accounts. He heard the dizzying rumors. It was high time, he decided, for his clients to get a piece of the action.

The deal involved eighteen rare books that were coming into the U.S. from Germany through Schiller-Wapner in New York, one of the country's most prestigious galleries dealing in rare books and documents. Hofmann said he could purchase them for only $22,500 and sell them immediately for at least $40,000. "I already have buyers for some of the books," he assured Wilding, mentioning Yale University, "but I need some funding in order to obtain the collection." The bottom line was terrific—as good as Wilding had heard: 50 percent to 100 percent return over a few months. In addition, there was Hofmann's unbeatable track record. Wilding had known him for years, knew his wife, knew his parents, even knew his wife's parents. And if that wasn't enough, there was the additional security of Hofmann's "reputation with the LDS Church." If ever there was a sure thing. . . .

Of course, Wilding still wanted 200 percent collateral.

On March 15, Hofmann gave him the collateral, in books, and he gave Hofmann checks totaling $22,500.

Only a month later, Hofmann called with good news: he had sold the books already and Wilding's group would get the full 100 percent return that Hofmann had predicted. Almost a *hundred percent in one month!* Hofmann said he could take his profit or, if he preferred, reinvest it, or a part of it, in another, equally lucrative deal. Wilding decided to play it safe and let Hofmann have only half the profits, $8,750, to play with. The rest, $31,250, he wanted in cash.

The same month, Hofmann offered another can't-miss deal to Ralph Bailey, a Salt Lake City orthodontist.

"I need $40,000," he said one day showing up unexpectedly in Bailey's office. "I have a hot deal in New

York and need to get some money in a hurry. If you loan me the forty, in six months I'll pay you back fifty."

But that wasn't all.

Again Hofmann was willing to offer double collateral —$80,000 worth for a $40,000 loan. All in rare books.

"I want to see your bills of sale and invoices," Bailey insisted.

"No problem," chimed Hofmann.

The next day, he brought in the books. Bailey checked them off against the list: a *Peter Rabbit*, a first edition of *Tom Sawyer* inscribed by Twain to his close friend, Joe Twitchell, and, the star of the lot, a *Call of the Wild* by Jack London containing what book dealers called a "dream inscription": from the author to one of his closest friends in words that cut to the core of the author's vision, "To Buck and his human friend Austin Lewis, who often said his dog is the best friend he knows of. In appreciation, Jack London." Bailey cared more about the invoice than the inscription. When the inventory was finished, he wrote out a promissory note and carried the books to his vault. He couldn't wait to see what Hofmann would do with his $40,000.

The deals just kept getting bigger and better.

In May, Hofmann went back to Wilford Cardon in Arizona with the biggest and best deal yet. He had been offered a rare Charles Dickens manuscript, the original holograph of one of five Christmas stories written by Dickens and called "The Haunted Man." Surely Cardon had heard of Scrooge and the Ghost of Christmas Past and Tiny Tim. Well, this wasn't quite that famous, but it was the last such manuscript in private hands and, as such, quite a treasure—a $300,000 treasure to be precise. Its credentials couldn't have been better: formerly owned by the Carl H. Pforzheimer Foundation in New York and offered for sale by Justin Schiller of the Schiller-Wapner Galleries (for a 10 percent commission).

The deal was just like the one before: Cardon would put up one-third of the purchase price and reap one-third of the rewards. The only difference was, this time his share wasn't $6,000; it was $110,000. But the rewards would be commensurately spectacular, Hofmann assured him. There were already several collectors and institutions begging for a chance to bid on it.

After Hofmann's success with the Betsy Ross letter and the Jim Bridger notes, Cardon decided this, too, must be a winner. Mark had certainly proved he could pick them. It was reassuring to know that his former missionary, Shannon Flynn, had tied his star to someone as astute and ambitious as Mark Hofmann. On June 5, Cardon wired $110,000 to Schiller-Wapner in New York.

On May 9, 1985, Hofmann approached Thomas Wilding with the same deal. Same pitch: "Christmas Carol," Scrooge, Tiny Tim, last manuscript in private hands, eager collectors, Pforzheimer Foundation, Schiller-Wapner, $300,000 (plus $30,000 commission).

Like Cardon, Wilding wasn't a man to argue with success. But this was a lot of money, and he had some questions. He asked Hofmann if he could call the gallery in New York to verify some of the information.

"No problem."

With Mark listening in, Wilding called Schiller. He may not have been a documents dealer but he was a sharp businessman, and he knew what questions to ask. Why does the Pforzheimer Foundation want to sell it? Is the manuscript genuine? Is it in your possession? Is it really worth $300,000? What's its history? (Later, Wilding called around and asked about Schiller-Wapner. They checked out too.)

This was the deal: Wilding would put up $160,000. Mark would put up the remaining $170,000. They would share the profits proportionately.

"Are there any other investors involved?" Wilding asked at one point.

"None," Hofmann avowed.

Wilding insisted on collateral, of course, so Hofmann added to the store of books from the previous deal, providing the necessary invoices (most of them from Schiller-Wapner). In addition, Wilding insisted on a personal guarantee from Hofmann to cover the $160,000. The money came from several investors and was either wired directly into Hofmann's account or came in the form of cashier's checks.

Hofmann did caution Wilding that a big-ticket item like this wouldn't sell overnight. "This will take some time," he said. "It's a major manuscript, and it has to be marketed properly." For Wilding, memories of 100 percent return in one month would make the waiting a lot easier.

In New York, Schiller and Wapner waited for the money as long as they could. Cardon had wired $110,000. But all they had received from Hofmann was a check for $20,000. The money from Wilding must not have come through, they figured. In order not to lose the deal, they put up the remaining $170,000 themselves and purchased "The Haunted Man." Hofmann had promised to reimburse them.

36

"I need $50,000, right away." Hofmann seemed unusually anxious, Ralph Bailey thought, almost out of breath.

When he saw him come into his office that day in May 1985, Bailey was sure it meant good news, which to Bailey was a check. Great news was cash. It had been only a month since the $40,000 loan, but Bailey couldn't help thinking, maybe it hadn't taken as long as Mark thought for the deal to go through. At the mere prospect of 50 percent interest in *one month*, his heart leaped in anticipation. Now, Hofmann was before him again, begging for fifty thousand more.

"I need it right away," he said, "because there are these ten Joseph Smith letters I want to buy that are being sold by a family back in New York. If I am there on time, I can buy them, and I can at least double my money."

He was offering the same irresistible terms as before: 50 percent interest and double collateral. There were only two differences: this time it was Lyn Jacobs's book collection that went into the vault, and Bailey insisted on having a lawyer draw up the agreement.

When Jacobs came by not long afterward to retrieve

one of the books, a first-edition Descartes, so he could sell it, Bailey demanded $10,000 to make up the difference. Hofmann gave him a check.

It bounced.

Ralph Bailey was not a man to play games with, especially when money was involved. He called Hofmann's bank, Rocky Mountain State, and was told the account contained sufficient funds to cover the check. Determined to get his money immediately, Bailey jumped in his car and drove directly to the bank on 33rd South. When he got there, however, the bank officer refused to make the check good. The funds, apparently, had been withdrawn in the interim. Fuming, Bailey tried both of Hofmann's numbers but got only an answering machine. For lack of a live target, he tore into the machine: "Mark, you either get this check good in the next little while or I am going to turn it over to. the police."

Within five minutes, Hofmann was on the line. "I have made arrangements. They will take care of the check. Just take it back out there. I apologize." It was typical Mark, Bailey thought. Completely cool. Never angry. Always submissive and always apologetic.

And, most important, the check was good. The deal was back on track. He couldn't wait to see what Hofmann would do with his $90,000.

Was Mark Hofmann losing his touch?

By the spring of 1985, people were beginning to wonder openly. Always hard to reach, Hofmann was now virtually incommunicado. Despite having phones in both his car and his van, his numbers were perpetually out-of-service or disconnected. He seemed to change numbers as often as other businessmen changed shirts. His personal checks were considered worthless, and the fabled payoffs were taking longer and longer.

For some strange reason, he wasn't finding Gentile documents as profitable as Mormon documents. Perhaps the margins were slimmer. Or the competition rougher. Or astounding discoveries harder to come by. Old friends and customers in Utah began to wonder if maybe his overhead had gotten out of control—all those trips to New York, all those books at premium prices from Manhattan dealers. Wade Lillywhite of Deseret Book had seen Hofmann at the April book fair in New York, looking "on top of the world," buying books and documents as if he were Malcolm Forbes.

In the early days, he was strictly a K mart man. In New York, he would stay at the Empire Hotel on Broadway (sharing a room whenever possible). Now he was laying down $15,000 cash for *Motor Trend's* "sports car of the year" and sending Shannon Flynn, at $1,000 dollars a day, to New York just to pick up some legal papers that could have been Federal Expressed.

It was a sad but familiar story: good Mormon boy hits the bright lights, big city and can't handle it.

Some even began to suspect that all the glamour and high life might have shaken Mark's testimony. They had heard about his breaking the "word of wisdom" and experimenting with alcohol, starting with martinis—shaken, not stirred, because that's how James Bond liked them. They had seen him ordering drinks in restaurants on trips to New York and loading up on mini-bottles during the flight home. The Lillywhites had come late to one of Mark's hot-tub parties—a game of Mormon trivia followed by a jump in the tub—and saw empty wine bottles in the trash can!

At the 1985 New Year's Eve party given at the ward house, friends were surprised to see the reclusive Mark Hofmann sitting in a chair with five party horns in his mouth, bouncing up and down and blowing in time to the music.

The good Mormons who knew Mark shook their heads. They recognized the pattern: as the testimony goes, so goes the bottom line.

The only thing that would save him, both financially and spiritually, everyone agreed, was another big score, another brilliant bolt of Mormon luck. But what were the chances of that?

37 On March 15, 1985, Hofmann called Justin Schiller in New York City. But you just left here, said Schiller, the highstrung owner of the Schiller-Wapner Galleries. Yes, said Hofmann, but in the interim something possibly very important has happened. Schiller, a shrewd, experienced dealer, had learned a certain respect for the disingenuous choirboy from Utah, and he listened with interest to Hofmann's strange tale.

The day before he left, on March 13, he had been browsing in the second-floor broadside, or print, department of the Argosy Book Store on East 59th Street. As was his custom, he selected a few trifles from the chaos of old maps and etchings ripped out of old books: two old illustrations at $5 apiece, portrait etchings of George and Martha Washington ($12.50), and a broadside headed simply "Oath of a Freeman" ($25).

Fortunately, when he took them to the cash register, he thought to ask for an itemized receipt. Total, with tax: $51.42.

Later, on the plane back to Salt Lake City, he was flipping through the catalog for an upcoming auction of "Printed and Manuscript Americana" at Sotheby's and happened to notice, under the caption for Lot 32 (a copy of John Child's *New England, Jonas Cast Up in London*, dated 1647, estimated price $1,500 to $2,000), a small footnote:

> The book also provides the earliest reprint of "The Freeman's Oath," the first issue of Stephen Daye's Cambridge Press, of which no copy of the original survives.

Hey, I've got something similar to that, Hofmann thought. Could it be?

By now Schiller was so giddy he could hardly keep the receiver pressed to his ear. "God, Mark," he yelped, "if you've got something like this, send it to me!"

To Schiller's astonishment, Hofmann was nonchalant. "Well, when I get around to it."

If what he was hearing was true, Schiller had every reason to be giddy. The "Freeman's Oath" mentioned in the Sotheby's footnote was, in fact, the Holy Grail of printed Americana. It was nothing less than the *first document printed in America*—the first document printed in English in the Western Hemisphere. Dated 1639, it was also considered the earliest record of popular notions of freedom and democracy that would ultimately find expression 150 years later in the Declaration of Independence and Constitution. Of course, there probably were earlier printed broadsides—the form was all the rage in the early colonies—but no records of them existed. This was the only one that experts *knew*, to a certainty, had been printed. It predated by a year the famous *Bay Psalm Book*, also printed by Stephen Daye's Cambridge Press, of which only ten copies were known to exist.

Hofmann had done it again. This was, without doubt, the American antiquarian's dream. When Wade Lillywhite found out about it, he was beside himself. He had been in the Argosy Book Store not one hour before Hofmann, sifting through the same bins. "How can it be? Why him, of all people? He's made lots of terrific discoveries. Why does he have to discover it? Why not me?" It seemed all the stranger because Hofmann was a manuscript person, not a print person. "How could he look at that and know what it was?" Lillywhite wondered. "*I* wouldn't have known what it was."

(A police investigator later commented on the extraordinary coincidence: "It was as if you had never heard of the Holy Grail. Then one Sunday you go to a garage sale and you find a little silver chalice or pewter cup and you say, 'Hey, far out!' So you pick it up. You also pick up an old Sotheby's catalog. Then on the way home, you're reading through the catalog and you find a notice to the effect that the Holy Grail was lost in whatever A.D. And basically it looks precisely like the item you just picked up. You say, 'Goddam! I just bought that this morning at the garage sale!' ")

Two weeks after reporting his discovery to Schiller, Hofmann flew back to New York with the document. It should have been a triumphant return, but he could barely keep his eyes open. He had been up all the previous night, working in his basement office, and left for the airport at four that morning. Dorie knew better than to ask why, on the eve of such an important trip, he felt the need to spend all night in the room downstairs that she was never allowed to enter.

From the airport, he went directly to the Argosy Book Store and sought out the woman who had been at the cash register two weeks before. He showed her a photocopy of the "Oath of a Freeman" and the receipt.

"Oh, yes. I recognize that," she said.

Hofmann looked a little surprised. "You know this is a very valuable item. The first item ever printed in America was the 'Oath of a Freeman,' and this might be the first one."

She looked at him with friendly, vacant eyes. "That's nice. You know, other people have found some pretty valuable things here too."

At the Schiller-Wapner Galleries, the reaction was very different. They had invited Michael Zinman, a self-described "big punter" in early Americana to the meeting and to inspect the document. Zinman, the CEO of Earthworm, a manufacturer of earthmoving and construction machinery, had bought the *New England's Jonas* at the Sotheby's auction, and afterward Schiller had called him. "I have the Holy Grail," he intoned, "the 'Oath of a Freeman.' The fruit of a ten-year-long search." Zinman could hardly believe his ears. He drove to New York that very evening.

Over dinner, the group talked about just *how* valuable the discovery would be if it turned out to be genuine. Hofmann suggested maybe it was worth $20,000 to $50,000. Zinman said that was crazy. A *forgery* would be worth more than that just as a curiosity. Zinman had toyed with the idea of buying a copy of the *Bay Psalm Book* and "couldn't touch it" for $1.2 million. "That 'Oath' may only be a single page, but it's unique," he said. "It could be worth $1 million. Who knows?"

After comparing it with the copy of the *Bay Psalm Book* at the New York Public Library, Schiller sent the

"Oath" off to the most likely buyer, the Library of Congress, on April 8. The price tag: $1.5 million. Schiller explained to Hofmann that the response would take time. "They'll want to run some tests first."

38

Hofmann couldn't wait for tests. He needed money, and he needed it now. So he went back to what he knew best, Mormon documents.

Fortunately, he hadn't lost his touch.

"It's twenty times more valuable than anything purchased before," he told Al Rust, uncharacteristically breathless with excitement. "It's the most extensive and significant collection ever found."

Hofmann had good reason to be excited. He had found the fabled McLellin Collection.

The very name was enough to strike terror in the hearts of devout Mormons. William E. McLellin was an early Apostle and close associate of Joseph Smith's who left the Church in 1836 to become one of its bitterest critics. It had long been rumored that McLellin, who kept the minutes at early meetings of the Twelve, had taken with him a pirate's chest full of papers, letters, and journals, all of it incriminating, with which to destroy the Church. Over the years, tantalizing clues had turned up. But neither the Collection itself, nor any part of it, had ever surfaced. Until now.

"It includes at least fifteen or twenty letters that are very valuable and very collectible items," Hofmann continued. "There will be great demand for the material. It's much more important than the Lucy Mack Smith letter or the Joseph Smith III blessing." Rust had put up $10,000 toward each of those. But an entire collection of documents was much more valuable than a single letter from the Prophet's mother or even the Prophet himself. "To give you an idea, it's probably ten times as important as the Lucy Mack Smith letter." With numbers like that, Hofmann must have thought, who wouldn't be dazzled?

But Rust had only one question.

"Is it anti-Mormon?" He had heard of William McLellin, infamous apostate, reviler of Joseph Smith. "If it's anti, then I'm not interested."

"Oh, no," Hofmann reassured him, "not a bit. This is gonna have a lot of early writings of Joseph Smith and a lot of the early history of the Church. It's a significant collection, a big collection. There's also a facsimile from the Book of Abraham. Two or three *boxes* of material. What I want to do is bring it back to Salt Lake, then we'll sort it out, and then we can dispose of it piece by piece."

Rust had another question.

"How much money are we talking about?"

"The whole Collection should cost about $180,000."

Rust didn't believe he had heard right. The most he had ever put into one of Mark's deals was $40,000. "Boy, that is a lot of money." Then he remembered Hofmann's reputation. If he could turn little money into big money, what could he do with big money? He began to calculate how long it would take him to get a second mortgage on his house. "How do you think it would work out?"

"I believe the Collection is worth $300,000 to $500,000." The split would be fifty-fifty.

"How long would it take before we'd recover our money?" Rust was hooked.

"We can get our money out in thirty days," Hofmann said. He was all business now, like a Thoroughbred on the backstretch. "Or we can dispose of it slow and get a considerably bigger profit. A lot of people will be interested in the material." He paused for effect. "Especially people in the Church."

"Where is the Collection now?"

"In New York."

"I would want my son, Gaylen, to go with you when you pick it up." The deal was already complete. Rust was talking details now.

Hofmann looked at Gaylen Rust, a sandy-haired, round-faced, energetic young man, too extroverted for the claustrophobic profession of coin dealing—his real passion was horse racing—who had been following the discussion.

"Okay," said Hofmann.

"I want you to take a cashier's check and go together, take briefcases, and put the most valuable things in briefcases and then hand-carry them back and ship the excess back to my store. We'll inventory all of it here, and then we'll dispose of it. Instead of you just having it all to your own person."

"No problem."

For the first time in all their dealings, Rust also wanted some kind of security. It wasn't that he didn't trust Mark. It was just such a large amount of money. Besides, Hofmann already owed him $100,000 on several earlier transactions, including the Joseph Smith III blessing and the Lucy Mack Smith letter. "To go in on this big a deal, given what you owe me, I want some collateral, too, for coverage."

"No problem," said Hofmann. "I've got all kinds of collateral. I can put two or three hundred thousand in there for collateral."

"I'd feel comfortable if you'd put in a hundred and fifty anyway, since that's about what you owe me." Unlike Wilding and Bailey, Rust wouldn't demand double collateral. All he wanted was protection for the new investment.

Hofmann was a picture of cooperativeness. "Let's do it now."

Together, the two men walked across the street to Zion's First National Bank and rented a joint safe-deposit box. Later, Hofmann brought in some documents to serve as collateral. It was an impressive list: an Abraham Lincoln document, a letter signed by Daniel Boone, another one by Henry Wadsworth Longfellow.

But it didn't add up to $150,000.

Rust tried to be diplomatic. "If you want to bring in any other collateral," he said kindly, "I'd appreciate it. Because there is such a large amount outstanding, I feel a little uncomfortable."

"No problem," said Hofmann.

Soon afterward, he bounded into the coin shop with a stack of books. "Hey, let's go over now and put them in our safe-deposit box." He made it sound like fun. Rust offered to put them under both names so that if a buyer wanted one, Mark could get at it without Rust's signature. "Just let me know where it went and how much you got for it. Then bring me the money." He took Hofmann's word on the value of each item. "I wouldn't know if a book was worth a dollar or a thousand," he muttered to himself as Hofmann held up a book and said, "Twenty-five thousand." When they were done stashing the hoard, Hofmann turned to him and said with a satisfied smile, "There's about $125,000 worth of books in there." Rust accepted the number on faith. When Hofmann tried to hand him an itemized list, he waved it away. "Just leave it in the box. I can tell if you get in by the signature on the card."

"I won't be getting in there," Mark reassured him.

Hofmann came back to the shop on Wednesday, April 23. He seemed unusually agitated.

"Where's your dad?" he asked Gaylen Rust, who was manning the counter in front of the glass cases, which displayed coins from all over the world.

"It's his day off," said Gaylen. Strange, he thought. Mark knew that his father was never in the office on Wednesdays.

Hofmann was pacing a hole in the floor. "We need to go to New York immediately," he said. "We've got to get the McLellin Collection *now!*" Gaylen had heard that Hofmann would take off on a cross-country trip at a moment's notice.

"Okay."

"Have you got the check?" Hofmann asked impatiently. There was no question what he meant: the $185,000 check that Rust was putting up for the Collection. Since their last conversation, the second mortgage had come through.

"I'll have to go get it," Gaylen said, calling first the bank, which agreed to have the check ready in thirty minutes, and then his wife, who agreed to pack his bags for him.

When Gaylen returned from the bank with the check, he gave it to Hofmann while he drove home to pick up his bag. "Hang on to this," he said as he ran out the door, forgetting in his haste his father's instructions: "Keep your hands on this check until the last possible moment."

On the plane, Hofmann mentioned to Gaylen a "major document" that he was selling to the government. He wouldn't give details. He just wanted Gaylen to know that he had some other business to transact in New York. Also, Dorie would be joining them the next day.

That night, Hofmann met with Lyn Jacobs, who had come down from Boston.

The next morning, Gaylen listened as Hofmann placed a call from the hotel room they were sharing at the Sheraton Centre on Seventh Avenue. It was about their appointment to pick up the McLellin Collection. As soon as he hung up, he began rushing around the room. "I've got to go right over and meet these people. They told me they don't want anyone else with me while I finalize the details of the transaction. So just stay here and sit tight. I'll call you when we finish, and you can come meet us at the bank when they hand over the boxes."

Gaylen sat in the room all morning, nervously watching television, reading his racehorse magazines, and waiting for the phone to ring. Several times, he called the front desk. "Are you sure no one has tried to get through to me?" No one had.

Finally, Hofmann called. "The deal's been postponed till tomorrow. These people had another commitment. They had to leave before everything got settled, so we'll consummate it tomorrow morning."

That afternoon, they took care of separate business. Gaylen met with the comedian Dom DeLuise to sell him some coins he had requested.

The next morning, Gaylen, who had taken a separate room in anticipation of Dorie's arrival, went to Hofmann's room to plan the day's strategy. On the door was a note in Hofmann's scrawled handwriting: the sellers had called early. They needed to meet him right away. No time to wake Gaylen. Mark would call as soon as he could.

Gaylen spent another tense morning waiting for the phone to ring. It never did. Hours later, Hofmann knocked at the door.

"It's already done," he said.

"Everything?"

"Everything." He wanted to go to the book fair this afternoon, so he wrapped up everything at one time. "Anyway, the whole thing went very smoothly."

"Where is the Collection?" Now it was Gaylen's turn to be agitated as he pondered what his father would think of this comedy of errors.

"I went directly to the post office and sent all three

boxes by registered mail." Hofmann showed him three receipts from the post office. They were made out to Hofmann's home in Salt Lake City, not to Al Rust's coin shop.

"Why didn't you send it to Dad?" Agitation was turning to anger.

"At the time, I just felt it was better to send the stuff to myself." Gaylen didn't look convinced. "Don't worry. Each package is insured for $75,000, so we're covered. If anything happens, we'll get our money back."

Other questions raced through Gaylen's mind. How could Hofmann have made the deal, checked the materials, boxed them up, taken them to the post office, and shipped them in the six hours he had been gone? Where were the important documents they were supposed to hand-carry back? It was too late to ask, he decided. "I guess that's all right," he finally said, although he knew it wasn't.

He began to feel a little better about Hofmann later that day at the book fair. It seemed as if everybody knew him and respected him. People brought him documents and rare books to look at, not junk, of which there was an abundance, but the rare, unusual pieces. Gaylen asked him why. "There's always going to be a buyer for the important collection or the major find," Hofmann said. "It's the unimportant stuff that's hard to unload." He was in his element, Gaylen thought, sharp, impressive, on his game. He must have known what he was doing that morning.

Al Rust didn't think so. When Gaylen called him after the fair and told him the story, he could barely restrain his uncharacteristic rage. "I don't like it at all. There was no legitimate reason to vary from our accepted plan." He tried not to blame his son. He himself had had trouble handling Mark Hofmann.

When they returned to Salt Lake City the following Saturday, Hofmann told Gaylen, "I'll be into your dad's store on Monday morning with the boxes."

Monday came, but Hofmann didn't.

They managed to reach him by phone. "The boxes haven't arrived yet," he told them.

Tuesday and Wednesday came and went.

Thursday. Rust couldn't stand it any longer. When he

couldn't raise Hofmann on the phone, he drove to his house in Millcreek. Dorie spoke to him through the screen door. "Mark's not here. I don't know where he's gone." Rust couldn't help himself. He yelled at her. When she started to cry, he castigated himself and apologized.

That evening, Mark called. "I sold the McLellin Collection," he announced triumphantly.

Rust's fury disappeared. A gain of more than 50 percent in *one week!* Who bought it? he wanted to know.

Hofmann's voice dropped to a whisper. "The Church."

39 Hofmann went straight to Gordon Hinckley's office with his latest and most ambitious proposition: If the Church paid him $185,000, he would give them the McLellin Collection. In the gravest tones, he described the materials it contained—a treasure trove of early Church history, all of it, in Hofmann's tactful phrase, "impactful." Diaries, journals, Joseph Smith letters—a Pandora's box of new and unknown firsthand materials that would make the Salamander Letter sound like a Sunday-school testimonial.

Hofmann had every reason to believe Hinckley would bite. It had not been a good year for the Church's public relations wizard. The bad news started in February, when the first reports on the authenticity of the Salamander Letter began to come in. Kenneth Rendell, the Massachusetts documents dealer, wrote that the ink had passed the ultraviolet tests with flying colors, that the machine-ruled paper was the same as that being manufactured at a paper mill near Palmyra in 1835, and that the tear in the seal, the fold in the paper, and the postmark all passed muster.

Rendell was more circumspect about the handwriting, but only because there were no samples of Martin Harris's handwriting to use for comparison. The signature looked genuine. There were no signs of tracing. "It is my conclusion," wrote Rendell, "based upon all of this evidence, as well as the ink and paper tests undertaken independently of me, that there is no indication that this letter is a forgery."

Independent analysis of the ink and paper by two more experts confirmed Rendell's assessment. The ink was of the iron gallotannic type commonly used at the time. Their conclusion: "There is no evidence to suggest that the examined document was prepared at other than during the stated time period."

Steve Christensen wrote Hinckley with the "bad" news on February 26. He also gently tested to see if Hinckley would be willing to release him from the promise to give the document to the Church. The financial debacle at CFS had taken its toll on his personal finances. After his argument with Gary Sheets, he had left the company to set up his own consulting firm with his friend Randy Rigby. It would be months before any income started coming in, and even when it did, he would still owe literally millions to CFS creditors, since he was one of the officers who had personally guaranteed CFS projects. The sale of the document, Christensen wrote Hinckley, "would be most welcome in assisting me with the reduction of some extremely heavy short-term debt." But if Hinckley still wanted the document, Christensen was willing to donate it and "trust in the Lord to assist me in my financial affairs."

Hinckley still wanted it.

Three days after Christensen's plea arrived, Hinckley called and told him that, whatever his personal problems, "that letter belongs to the Church."

Christensen dutifully donated the document, and on April 18, the Church officially acknowledged the gift in a letter signed by Hinckley, Marion Romney, and the Prophet himself, Spencer Kimball. According to the letter, the document had "been placed in the archives of the First Presidency."

On April 28, more than a year after the first leaks, the Church officially released the Salamander Letter to the public. The ten-day delay was needed to word a statement as carefully (some would say deceptively) as possible:

* * *

A letter purportedly written by Martin Harris to W. W. Phelps was recently presented to the Church by Steven F. Christensen, its owner. The document is dated Palmyra, October 23, 1830, and has been the subject of much discussion and research. . . .

The original has been placed in the archives of the First Presidency as another appreciated addition to documents and artifacts dating back to the early history of the Church.

President Gordon B. Hinckley, Second Counselor in the First Presidency, who accepted the letter, stated: "No one, of course, can be certain that Martin Harris wrote the document. However, at this point we accept the judgment of the examiner that there is no indication that it is a forgery.

This does not preclude the possibility that it may have been forged at a time when the Church had many enemies. It is, however, an interesting document of the times. Actually the letter has nothing to do with the authenticity of the Church. The real test of the faith which both Martin Harris and W. W. Phelps had in Joseph Smith and his work is found in their lives, in the sacrifices they made for their membership in the Church, and in the testimonies which they bore to the end of their lives. . . ."

(Actually, Harris bore a testimony *at* the end of his life, not *to* the end of his life, having left the Church for much of his adulthood and earned Joseph Smith's condemnation as a "wicked man." But these were mere quibbles.)

If Hinckley thought that was the end of it, he was catastrophically mistaken. He had succeeded in killing the book that Christensen and his team were planning, but neither the newspapers nor liberal Mormon intellectuals would let the matter rest. Far worse was yet to come.

On April 29, Dawn Tracy, who had moved to the Salt Lake *Tribune*, reported that a "letter reportedly written by Mormon Church founder Joseph Smith describing money-digging pursuits and treasure guarded by a clever spirit seems to have disappeared from view. . . ." It was clearly a reference to the Josiah Stowell letter, written by Joseph Smith in 1825, that Mark Hofmann had sold to Hinckley back in January 1983. Hinckley couldn't have been surprised by speculation about the document's existence. A purported transcript of the letter had been circulating in the underground for at least a year. But he must have been surprised, alarmed in fact, by something else in Tracy's article: "Research historian Brent Metcalfe said he knows from 'very reliable, first-hand sources' the letter exists, and the Mormon Church has possession of it."

With its references to treasures guarded by clever spirits and hazel sticks, Joseph Smith's letter to Josiah Stowell confirmed all the worst money-digging and folk magic implications of the Martin Harris Salamander Letter—in short, everything the Church had been trying to play down. At first, Church spokesman Jerry Cahill vehemently denied the accusation: "The Church doesn't have the letter," he told Tracy. "It's not in the Church archives or the First Presidency's vault." When someone suggested that Cahill was playing semantic games—"If the exact question isn't asked, someone can wink and say the Church doesn't have it"— Cahill reiterated, "No, the Church does not have possession of the letter."

But Hinckley was trapped. With the rumors flying, photocopies circulating, and the *Los Angeles Times* set to publish an extensive article (with a copy of the letter), he had no choice but to go public. On May 9, 1985, the Church released a statement by the First Presidency: "We have acquired a letter presumably written by Joseph Smith. . . ." The next day, the *Deseret News* announced the discovery of "the earliest known surviving document written by Joseph Smith Jr. . . . The letter, believed by church leaders to be authentic, was written June 18, 1825, five years before the church was organized."

Jerry Cahill took the fall. In a letter to the editor of the *Tribune*, he acknowledged that his earlier denials had been "in error." The real hero of the story? Gordon B. Hinckley. It was Hinckley, according to Cahill's *mea culpa*, who insisted on getting the correct story before the public. "When my published statement came to his attention, President Gordon B. Hinckley of the First Presidency of the church informed me of my error." Both the Church news release and Cahill's letter carefully avoided mentioning that the Stowell document had been sitting in the First Presidency vault for two years.

Throughout the P.R. ordeal, Hinckley had to wonder

who had gotten him into this fine mess. Who was Brent Metcalfe's "very reliable, firsthand source" who had brought the hounds of the press to his door yet again? Who else knew that the Church possessed the Stowell letter besides himself, his secretary, Francis Gibbons, G. Homer Durham—and Mark Hofmann?

Coincidentally, the day the letter was announced in the papers was the day Hofmann came to see him.

Whether he was fuming over the leak or fed up with documents dealing altogether, Hinckley didn't say. He apparently wasn't about to give Hofmann the pleasure of betraying such temporal emotions. What he did say was, in effect, "go fish." He wanted nothing to do with the documents or with Mark Hofmann. Once burned . . .

Hofmann was stunned. Nothing he said about the sensitivity of the documents seemed to make any difference. It would take something more than one little embarrassment in the press to shake Hinckley's confidence in the true Church.

40 After the meeting with Hinckley, Hofmann met Brent Metcalfe for lunch at the Crown Burger near his house. Metcalfe had only recently started work as a "researcher" for Hofmann, locating descendants of prominent historical figures to see if they could provide any grist for his boss's documents mill. Both men knew it was more a favor than a real job. (Hofmann didn't seem to need any help finding documents.) After his severance pay from CFS ran out, and a six-month stint as a researcher ended, Metcalfe was badly in need of other employment. Hofmann agreed to pay him $2,000 a month and 20 percent of the profit from any documents that turned up as a result of Metcalfe's research.

While they waited for their burgers, Metcalfe wanted to know, "What's the juiciest thing you've ever seen in The Vault?" (Hofmann had often bragged to him before about seeing unknown documents there.) Metcalfe, he knew, was obsessed with the Church's secrets, and, for that matter, any tidbit of information that he could pass along to the Mormon underground.

Hofmann smiled. He seemed almost amused. Metcalfe wasn't the first person to notice that the more outrageous Mark's discoveries, the more furor they stirred up, the more amused he seemed to get. He explained it as professional detachment. He was only interested in history, and he couldn't understand why the truth should rattle so many cages.

Hofmann described a meeting with Hinckley at which he asked if there were any other accounts resembling the Salamander Letter in the Church's archives. Hinckley reportedly sent his secretary to fetch a document from the First Presidency archives and showed it to Hofmann. It was the Oliver Cowdery history.

Metcalfe nearly jumped out of his chair. He remembered the footnote in a book by Joseph Fielding Smith about an early history of the Church written by Cowdery, the Church's first historian. Smith had even indicated that the history was in the possession of the Church, but, until now, it had been just another of the many myths locked away in The Vault. A year ago, Hofmann had said he thought it existed, but now he was saying he had actually seen it.

Hofmann was into the story now, savoring the surreptitiousness of it as well as Metcalfe's breathless attention. If the Oliver Cowdery history should ever leak, he said, it would *really* shake some testimonies. According to Cowdery's account, it wasn't Joseph Smith who first discovered the gold plates, it was his *brother,* Alvin. It was only after Alvin died (from eating too many green turnips) that Joseph retrieved the plates and began translating them. In other words, *there was no First Vision!*

Metcalfe couldn't believe his ears. He himself had dug up some persuasive evidence that Alvin played a more significant role in the founding of the Church than most people thought, but this was confirmation. He couldn't have found better proof, he thought, if he had made it up himself.

Metcalfe wanted more. He always wanted more.

The Cowdery history also mentioned a salamander that appeared three times, once to Alvin, twice to Joseph, according to Hofmann, confirming the story told in the Martin Harris letter.

Hofmann later said that he swore Metcalfe to secrecy. Metcalfe remembered only that Mark had told him, "You can tell other people about this, just as long as you don't tell anyone where the information came from." Given Metcalfe's irrepressible enthusiasm for secrets, it amounted to the same thing.

As Hofmann must have foreseen, Metcalfe went straight to Dawn Tracy at the Salt Lake *Tribune*. A few days later, May 15, Gordon Hinckley had another little embarrassment to explain at the next meeting of the Twelve:

RESEARCHER SAYS LDS HISTORY
DISPUTES GOLDEN PLATES STORY

A little-known history written by an important early Mormon leader contains an account of Joseph Smith's brother Alvin finding the gold plates, rather than the Mormon prophet himself, according to a research historian. . . .

Brent Metcalfe, who worked on authenticating an earlier Mormon letter, said officials of the Church of Jesus Christ of Latter-day Saints have the history, written by Oliver Cowdery, who at one time was second in importance only to Joseph Smith. . . .

Mr. Metcalfe said his source is a private eyewitness account of the Cowdery history. The document tells of Joseph Smith's brother Alvin first finding the gold plates by means of a stone, according to Mr. Metcalfe.

Mr. Metcalfe quoted the document as saying: "A taunting Salamander appears to Alvin and prevents him and his companions from digging up the gold plates."

Early Mormon letters, recently released by LDS Church officials, link Joseph Smith to folk magic and to an "old spirit" that commanded Mr. Smith to return with his brother Alvin, who was dead at the time.

*   *   *

This time, when asked about the report, Jerry Cahill hedged his answer. "The LDS Historical Department does not have the Cowdery history," he said, *but* he refused to inquire if the document was in the "special presidency's vault." In what sounded suspiciously like a nondenial denial, he told the *Tribune,* "I have no idea if the history is there, nor do I intend to ask. I can't have my life ordered about by rumors. Where does it end?"

It certainly didn't end there.

On May 17, in an interview with KUER radio, Metcalfe repeated the stunning revelations contained in the Cowdery version, that "it was, in fact, Alvin who first discovered the gold plates and not Joseph Smith. And that at the time of the death of Alvin in November of 1823, Joseph Smith then takes over as the seer who then proceeds to try to break the enchantment to get the plates. . . ."

Have you seen this document? the interviewer asked.

"I have not, no. No, I have not seen the Cowdery history, but I did come across a source in which a person was recording his reading of the document."

"And this is a current source?"

"Yes, [a] current source."

"Would you like to name that source?"

"No . . . all I can say is that it's an extremely reliable source and I know, personally I know of no other sources that are more reliable than this one."

Just as this newest crisis was filling the local papers, the last one over the Stowell letter broke in the national media. Both the *Los Angeles Times* and *Time* magazine chastised the Church for trying to suppress its own history. Said *Time* archly: "The church offered no explanation for withholding news of the earliest extant document written by Smith." The anti-Mormons were having a field day. In the *Messenger,* the Tanners accused the Church of a "cover-up situation . . . reminiscent of the Watergate scandal." The inevitable term, "Salamandergate," made the rounds.

It was fast becoming yet another public relations debacle.

And just when Hinckley may have thought the worst was over—that there were no more bombshells out there waiting to go off—a letter, dated May 22, arrived from Steve Christensen.

In light of the recent disclosures, Christensen thought he'd better let Hinckley in on yet another skeleton in the

Church's closet: an "Articles of Agreement" dated November 1, 1825, and signed by Joseph Smith and Josiah Stowell. Confirming the Glass Looker trial record, this document virtually proved the allegation that Joseph Smith was engaged in money digging for fun and profit at the time of the discovery of the gold plates. Christensen was clear about his reason for writing. "Those enemies of the Church who would do us harm by leaning upon the crutch of magic and occultism being involved in the early beginnings of the Church do not give due credit to the way in which this activity was perceived in Joseph Smith's day."

Just in case Hinckley missed the point, Christensen added, "Please rest assured that it is not my intention to make public the existence of this legal document."

That assurance might have offered Hinckley more comfort if Christensen hadn't also mentioned who gave him a copy of the agreement in the first place: Mark Hofmann.

The next time Hofmann appeared in his office, Hinckley was ready to listen.

Hofmann painted a bleak picture. Unless he found $185,000 immediately, the McLellin Collection would fall into the hands of "the enemy." The result would be a public relations disaster of epic proportions, press so bad that the Salamander Letter would look like a release from the First Presidency, so bad that the last few months would look like the good old days. He repeated that he hadn't wanted things to happen this way, that he had planned all along for the Church to obtain the Collection.

But now the clock was ticking off precious seconds. The Collection was in the hands of a nonmember, and worse yet, an anti-Mormon. He wouldn't sell to the Church, but he would sell to Hofmann. The deal could be "wrapped up" for $195,000 (of which he had already put up a $10,000 down payment). All he needed was the balance of $185,000. He had found an investor in Salt Lake City to put up some of the money, but now that investor was getting cold feet and wanted to pull his money out. If Hofmann couldn't find the money, the deal would slip through his hands—and into those of the enemy.

They were out there too. Hofmann named them: Wesley Walters and George Smith, both "notorious anti-

Mormons," according to Hofmann. They both knew of the Collection, he warned, and were hot on its trail. If he didn't consummate the deal, one of them would.

It was the eleventh hour.

When Hinckley started to play "the game," Hofmann knew he had him hooked. They had played the game before. Hofmann wouldn't tell him any details about the contents of documents; he would wait for Hinckley to ask. That way Hinckley didn't have to know more than he wanted to know. Hofmann told friends it was a technique they had developed, without ever discussing it, for protecting Hinckley, in case he was ever questioned.

"Did you know that the McLellin Collection contained such-and-such, President Hinckley?"

"No, I did not."

"Did Hofmann discuss such-and-such with you?"

"No, he did not."

Deniability. It was a lawyerly trick, but these were lawyerly times.

Hofmann suggested that the Church come up with the money.

No, said Hinckley. It was better that the Collection not come to the Church. Too dangerous for the Church to take actual possession.

Deniability.

Now that the anti-Mormons were on to it, there was no point in trying to keep its existence a secret. The only thing to do now was to ensure that it didn't fall into the wrong hands.

According to Hofmann's account, Hinckley then suggested the Steve Christensen solution: find a wealthy devout Mormon to buy the Collection, sit on it, and then, when the commotion died down, donate it.

Christensen was out because of his financial problems, but Hofmann had another suggestion: Wilford Cardon in Arizona.

Hinckley agreed. "Go take care of your investor, and then we'll talk." If there's a problem, he added as Hofmann left, if things really get desperate and you need money, let me know.

Hofmann thanked him.

41 Meanwhile, Al Rust waited for his money. Not that he was really worried. "The Collection is in the hands of the Church," he told himself over and over, "and nothing can happen to it there."

When he pressed Hofmann for an update, it was always the same story: "Don't worry. Everything's fine." And then the inevitable warning: "Just remember, we've got to keep it quiet. The Church doesn't want this out. Only a few people in the hierarchy know, and they don't want outsiders coming in and asking to see the materials." Rust could understand that. Like everybody else, he had been following with dismay the damaging revelations in the papers. As a good Mormon, the last thing he wanted to do was cause the Church another embarrassment.

Three weeks later, Hofmann called with bad news. "We have a big problem," he began ominously. "The Church doesn't want to buy the Collection."

Rust felt the old anger returning.

"The Church doesn't want to get personally involved with this Collection. They said that if they bought the Collection, it would get out to the public and they'll have the entire public coming to them and asking to see the contents."

Could anything be done to salvage the deal?

"We've had to change plans." Rust knew who "we" referred to. He had heard Hofmann talk often about his close working relationship with Gordon Hinckley. "We've had to find a private collector to buy the Collection and donate it to the Church. That way the Church doesn't have to say it bought the Collection. They don't want to put any money out so that they won't have anybody questioning them about it. We found a private collector in Texas who is willing to buy the Collection and then donate it to the Church."

Mark ended with his usual urgent injunction: "You've got to remember that all this needs to remain confidential. Do not tell a soul. Do not call anybody. Do not do anything."

But the patience of even a patient man has its limits. Finally, Rust decided to write President Hinckley directly. There couldn't be any harm in contacting someone who already knew.

Before proceeding, however, he wanted to give Hofmann one last chance. "I need to see you in my store tomorrow," he told Mark on the phone. "We've got to settle some things."

Hofmann said he'd be there.

He wasn't.

Rust drove to Mark's house to give him another last chance. Dorie answered the door, looking unusually weary and disheveled.

"Mark's in New York," she said.

Rust was dumbstruck. "I can't believe that. We had an appointment to meet."

Dorie looked at him with her utterly vacant eyes. It was a willful stupidity, Rust concluded, too convenient to be real. "Oh, he had to go to New York."

Rust couldn't help himself. He began to yell. "If he calls, you tell him I've had it. I can't hold back any longer. I am going to the LDS Church tomorrow morning."

The next morning, he called Hinckley's office.

Mark Hofmann bragged that he could reach President Hinckley anytime. He even bragged that he could reach Hinckley immediately when he was out of the state. But could Al Rust? Even after years as a tour guide on Temple Square and a lifetime of loyalty and tithing?

Hinckley's secretary put him on hold, then, a minute later, came back on to say, "President Hinckley has indicated that you should write it all down on a piece of paper and hand-deliver it to his office."

So Al Rust wrote President Gordon B. Hinckley a letter. In it, he requested a meeting with Hinckley and Hofmann for the purpose of straightening out some questions in regard to the McLellin Collection. Nothing pushy, nothing confrontational. He came as a supplicant.

The next day he went to deliver the letter to Hinckley's office but got no farther than the security desk. Mark

Hofmann could drop in on President Hinckley anytime, without an appointment, but not Al Rust. "I have this letter for President Hinckley," he told them. Hinckley's secretary came out and took it. That was as close as Al Rust got.

Only hours after Rust returned from Temple Square, Hofmann called from New York.

"My wife says you sent a letter to the Church." He sounded very grave.

Rust was defiant. "Yes, Mark, I took it up a couple of hours ago, personally."

"Why did you do that? I told you how important it was not to do anything like that."

"You have been giving me the runaround. I told you I'm just tired of this."

"Well, you shouldn't have done that."

The next day, Hofmann cut short his New York stay and flew back to Salt Lake City. He went directly to Hinckley's office. He had come to explain the letter from Rust. "I've already taken care of that," he reportedly told Hinckley, nonchalant as ever. Rust was the Salt Lake investor whom he had told Hinckley about in their last meeting, the one who wanted his money out.

Hinckley nodded. According to Hofmann's account, he didn't ask why Rust thought the Church had the McLellin Collection when Hofmann had told Hinckley it was in a safe-deposit box. He didn't ask about money. He seemed to have only one thing on his mind.

Are you sure Rust won't make the Collection public?

"Yes, he's a good Mormon."

Are you sure he won't try to obtain the Collection?

"Yes. Wilford Cardon is going to pay off Rust's interest in the Collection."

Deniability.

Hofmann watched as Hinckley wrote a note for his file that the matter had been taken care of.

Nine frustrating days went by, and Al Rust heard nothing. Finally, he called Hinckley's office. He reached a different secretary this time. "The letter is here," she said, "but President Hinckley is gone until the ninth." Hinckley was in East Germany dedicating a new Temple. Rust considered calling or writing again to find out why there was such a delay in responding to his first letter, but decided against it. Who was he to question the Second Counselor to the President of the First Presidency or anything the Second Counselor to the President of the First Presidency chose to do, or not do? Good Mormons don't press the General Authorities. They wait to be called.

So Al Rust waited.

About a week later, Mark Hofmann called. "You probably aren't going to get an answer to your letter to President Hinckley," he said.

"Why not?"

"I've taken care of everything."

"I wonder if you really have."

In early June, Hofmann flew to Mesa, Arizona, to meet Wilford Cardon, to make his pitch. If Cardon would loan him $180,000, Hofmann said, he could buy the McLellin Collection and donate it to the Church. "It's something the Church should have," he stressed. "I'm not entirely sure what each and every item is, but what I know already is enough to indicate that the information would be devastating if it got into the wrong hands."

Hofmann said he was coming into a lot of money soon and would pay Cardon back. It was a loan, not an investment, not a gift. Hofmann wanted to give it to the Church himself. "I've got to get it and give it to President Hinckley," he said. "The Church should not buy it outright or have it loaned to them."

Cardon, a devout Mormon, found the whole proposal troubling. This didn't sound like the Church he knew and loved, all this talk of dangerous documents, clandestine purchases, and enemy hands. "Let's get Hinckley on the phone and ask him what he thinks," Cardon suggested.

"Fine," said Hofmann. "I'll place the call."

He called the First Presidency office. "President Hinckley's not there," he told Cardon. "He's in Germany."

Without Hinckley's okay, Cardon wouldn't touch the deal.

On June 14, the Library of Congress returned the "Oath of a Freeman" to the Schiller-Wapner Galleries in New York City. They were not interested in purchasing it for $1.5 million.

42

The Church needed another push.

Brent Metcalfe had been taking a lot of heat for the
Cowdery history. Interviewers were dogging him, always
with the same questions: *How* do you know? What *proof*
do you have? And all he could say was, "I have this
source, and he's very reliable." Without corroboration,
none of the national papers or magazines would pick up
the story. It would remain a local sidebar, the news
equivalent of a crank call. Certainly nothing for the Church
to worry about.

Metcalfe felt as if he'd been hung out to dry. "You put
too much responsibility on my shoulders," he told
Hofmann. "You're having me talk about these things,
without anyone to corroborate what I say. I think you
should talk directly to somebody who is known for their
integrity and for their knowledge of Mormonism, but
who is outside of Mormonism."

Hofmann had just the man in mind: John Dart of the
Los Angeles Times. Dart had written extensively on the
Church and attended several of the symposiums spon-
sored by *Sunstone* and the Mormon History Association.
His readership included some of the richest stakes in
Mormondom. As the flap over the Stowell letter made
clear, when the *Los Angeles Times* said boo, the Church
jumped.

Hofmann told Metcalfe to contact Dart and set up a
meeting.

In early June, Dart flew into Salt Lake City and rendezvoused with Hofmann at the Training Table restaurant on Highland Drive near the Cottonwood Mall. From
there, they walked to a nearby park and sat down in a
gazebo on a hill. Dart, a reserved man with an unex-

pected sense of humor, pulled out a tape recorder and Hofmann began to talk.

He described the Cowdery history as a volume bound partly in leather, with marbled cardboard covers, about eight inches wide, ten inches long and three-quarters of an inch thick, with lined pages. When asked why he agreed to be interviewed, he said he felt the Cowdery history was important corroboration for the salamander references in the Martin Harris letter, which many Mormons still considered a forgery.

What exactly did Cowdery say about the finding of the gold plates?

"I don't remember the exact wording," said Hofmann, "but the history said that Alvin located the buried gold with his seer stone. I remember clearly that it was not a private venture. Alvin had other people with him, including Joseph."

What did it say about the salamander?

The salamander appeared on three occasions, once to Alvin and twice to Joseph.

Does it sound like there was a conspiracy to keep Alvin's early role quiet?

"Conspiracy may be a bad word to use, but there must have been some sort of agreement that Joseph is the new seer now that Alvin is gone. Certainly the family and Oliver Cowdery knew. I can't imagine that any more knew, because it's an important aspect of the founding of the Church, and it hasn't come down in other histories that we know of."

Do you think this will shake some people's faith in the Mormon Church?

"There is a propensity to keep things the way they are. Dutiful Mormons would say that after Alvin died, the angel came to Joseph and told him what to do."

The interview lasted a couple of hours.

On June 13, Church leaders were awakened by telephone calls from bishops and stake presidents all over Southern California who had opened the *Times* and seen their worst nightmares on page 3 in a six-column-wide headline: MORMON ORIGINS CHALLENGED ANEW OVER PURPORTED HISTORY.

If Gordon Hinckley had sat down and made a list of everything he didn't want to see made public, it might have read like this: a complete retelling of the embarrassing details surrounding the Stowell letter, more talk of the money-digging craze at the beginning of the nineteenth century, all the most bizarre passages of the Salamander Letter, the Cowdery version of the discovery of the gold plates by Alvin instead of Joseph Smith, and references to the Church's "vague" response to questions about whether it was hiding the Cowdery history.

The article referred repeatedly to a "highly reliable source" who had seen the Cowdery book in the Church's headquarters.

> The source, who insisted on anonymity in order to preserve his standing in the church, said the Cowdery history and the role it gives Alvin Smith lend further credibility to the documents disclosed earlier, which portray Joseph Smith's involvement in occult methods to find hidden treasures without any references to religious events so familiar to present-day Mormons. . . . Throughout its history the Mormon Church has had to deal with charges that the Book of Mormon is a figment of Smith's imagination and that Smith was just a treasure seeker.

In Temple Square, the response was near panic. With Hinckley still out of the country, no one knew how to react. For weeks afterward, paranoia ran at an all-time high. The word of the day was damage control.

Hinckley was still out of the country when Mark Hofmann called Steve Christensen on Thursday, June 27. "I need to see you." His cartoon voice sounded unusually harsh and urgent. "I don't want to discuss it over the phone, but it's important." They agreed to meet the next morning at 10:30.

Christensen recorded the meeting in his journal, marking the pages "Confidential Entry":

> The meeting commenced as previously arranged and Mark wasted no time in telling the following set of circumstances. For some time he had actively pursued a collection of Mormon material in Texas which is most commonly referred to as the William McLellin Collection. At one time the Church had pursued the

collection, negotiating with the current owner's father; however they were unsuccessful in their efforts. (Mark indicated that the former owner refused to sell it at any price to the Church.)

Mark was finally successful in entering into an option to purchase with the current owner, provided that the owner neither showed nor discussed the collection with anyone other than Mark and provided that Mark could produce the necessary $195,000 needed to purchase the collection. To obtain the option Mark placed $10,000 down as earnest money deposit. The remaining funds needed therefore equalled $185,000. Mark had indicated to me that he had arranged to borrow the funds from a private party; however, in the last days remaining on the purchase option the private party withdrew his financial support.

Hofmann was desperate. The "purchase option" expired on Sunday, June 30, he said, the day after tomorrow. Was there any chance that Christensen could lend him the necessary funds? He made it clear that unless he came through before the deadline, the Collection would fall into "enemy hands."

It was too much money for Christensen, who was on the verge of declaring bankruptcy, but he wanted to help. Normally, he would have called Hinckley—he always seemed to know what to do in these delicate situations—but Hinckley was still in Germany. He suggested instead that they call another General Authority, Hugh Pinnock, a member of the Council of Seventy who happened to be a close college friend of the chairman of CFS; a man, Christensen said, who had "broad financial expertise and a wide circle of friends."

Christensen called Pinnock and quickly reviewed the situation with him. Pinnock didn't require any persuading. "I can have the funds within an hour," he said. "Bring Hofmann to my office as soon as possible."

They arrived at the Church Administration Building about 11:25. Pinnock welcomed them "most graciously," and took them into the more congenial offices of Dallin Oaks, an Apostle and Pinnock's immediate supervisor within the Church hierarchy. Hofmann repeated the dilemma, in even darker tones this time. He spelled out, "in no uncertain terms," Christensen noted in his journal, "how damaging the material could be if it fell into the wrong hands."

He told them how Wesley Walters and George Smith had somehow found out about the Collection and contacted the owner. Should Hofmann miss his funding deadline, there was no question they would rush in and scoop up the Collection. There had been some speculation in print (in the Tanners' newsletter) and considerable rumor that the Church had already purchased the Collection in an attempt to suppress it. Hofmann's message was clear: "If I buy the Collection, then you can deny that you have it." Once again, he was offering what they wanted most: deniability.

Unlike Hinckley, Pinnock and Christensen listened eagerly to Hofmann's account of what the Collection contained.

It was a chilling list. There were pieces of the Egyptian papyrus from which, according to Church doctrine, Joseph Smith translated the Book of Abraham. (The last time some of these papyri surfaced, in 1967, they had turned out to be nothing more than commonplace funerary inscriptions, throwing the divine origins of the Book of Abraham in deep doubt and causing the Church no end of embarrassment.) There were the papers and diaries of McLellin himself, all incendiary stuff. Even without seeing them, Pinnock and Christensen could imagine McLellin's chronicles of manipulation, corruption, fornication, and other assorted scandals.

And finally, most damaging, there was an affidavit from Emma Smith, the Prophet's wife, indicating that Joseph's first religious experience was the recovery of the gold plates in 1827. In other words, additional proof that there was no First Vision! The Salamander Letter and Cowdery history were right—Alvin Smith *had* been the first to hear of the gold plates. Joseph had merely stepped into his shoes—or carried on his scam, however one chose to interpret it.

There were papers connecting Sidney Rigdon, an associate of Joseph Smith's, and Solomon Spaulding, the author of a romantic novel about early Romans coming to America and establishing a civilization—a novel that predated Joseph Smith's *Book of Mormon*, about early *Hebrews* coming to America and establishing a civilization. The Church had always claimed that Smith knew nothing of Spaulding's book, despite many parallels and even common passages. Hofmann's documents would prove otherwise.

In all, there were three orange crate-size boxes filled with dynamite.

Hofmann explained that, from the very beginning, he had intended to donate the Collection to the Church. When Christensen asked him how he could afford such a sizable gift, Hofmann told him about the "Oath of a Freeman." The Library of Congress had agreed to purchase it for $1.5 million, he claimed. The contract was already signed, and the first payment was due on August 15. At that time, he could easily repay the loan.

"This way I can say that I never sold the McLellin Collection to the Church. And the Church's representatives can say they never purchased it. With any luck, no one will ever ask me if I donated the material."

Christensen commented in his journal account: "Though this form of dialogue walks the fine line of 'honest intent' behind a question, it perhaps saves the Church for the time being from having to offer an explanation on why they won't release the material and/or be under the necessity of mounting a public relations move to counter the contents of the collection."

With the fallout of the Salamander Letter, Stowell, and Cowdery fiascos still hanging in the air, it was a powerful argument.

One that Pinnock saw immediately.

Hugh Pinnock was said to have only one ambition in life, to be an Apostle. And this crisis could be his ticket. Only a few days before, he had complained to an associate, "When I was in business, I could measure my success by the amount of money I made. Now that I'm a General Authority, there is no way to measure my success."

Now he had found a way. Mark Hofmann had presented him with an opportunity to save the Church from another devastating revelation, an embarrassment far worse than anything so far. If he could successfully maneuver the Church through these tricky shoals during President Hinckley's absence, it would be an act of stewardship worthy of Hinckley himself, an act that would undoubtedly bring him to the attention of the Council of the Twelve.

He lunged at the opportunity so quickly that even Christensen was startled. He wrote in his journal: "It was remarkable to both Mark and myself that Elder Pinnock was willing to assist to his fullest extent possible with only a brief explanation. It was as though he sensed completely the potential damage this material would cause in the hands of the enemies of the Church."

The money was no problem, Pinnock boasted. He had raised funds in the past for behind-the-scenes projects that were important to the Church, always with utmost discretion. President Tanner had once asked him to find the money—"privately, quickly and quietly"—to restore the farmhouse in Fayette, New York, where on April 6, 1830, the Church was founded. Pinnock relished the story. He had called just the right nineteen men and asked for $25,000 from each. All but three had come through—no questions asked. And why not? asked Pinnock, taking off his glasses for emphasis. Their Temple covenants required them to "literally give all to the Church."

Pinnock savored the story for a few moments, like a man at the end of a rich meal, then went to the outer office to "make a few phone calls."

He returned just minutes later with a satisfied smile that said, "All done, simple as that." He said he had called Zion's Bank—the Church bank—but the chairman, vice-chairman, and president were all out of town. Undaunted, he had called Bob Ward of First Interstate Bank, on whose board, Pinnock pointed out, he served.

First Interstate would provide Hofmann with a cashier's check in the amount of $185,000. All he had to do was sign a promissory note.

Collateral?

No collateral necessary. Hofmann's word that the sale to the Library of Congress was a *fait accompli* was sufficient.

Pinnock obviously liked this—the sheer efficacy of it. Hugh Pinnock, problem solver. He was all gravity and dispatch. He handed Hofmann four phone numbers. "This way you can reach me day or night." What if the owner of the Collection tried to break the deal by arguing that a cashier's check wasn't "legal tender" on a Sunday because it couldn't be cashed? Not a problem for Hugh

Pinnock. He would have $185,000 in cash ready as a backup. Did Hofmann need use of a Church propjet for his trip to Texas to pick up the Collection? Pinnock could provide it. How about an armored car to transport the documents? Better not to take any chances. Pinnock could arrange that too.

"I think that might be overdoing it a little," Hofmann suggested, doggedly deferential. It would be enough just to send the Collection by registered mail and insure it for $195,000.

"I'll keep you updated on the negotiations this weekend," he told them. The plan was this: if all went well—and he had no reason to believe it wouldn't—he would put the Collection in several safe-deposit boxes until the check from the Library of Congress came through. Then he would pay off the loan and hand the materials over to the Church.

As the three men walked toward the door, Pinnock turned to Hofmann. "I wonder if I could talk to you sometime about retaining your services to track down two items for me."

One was the missing 116 pages of the *Book of Mormon*. Pinnock had heard of a "crazy lady" in Pennsylvania who had leads on the missing pages, as well as a hoard of materials once belonging to Sidney Rigdon.

And the second item?

"I'm not in a position to reveal the second item at this time," Pinnock said, the stiff, paternalistic tone returning. "It's too sensitive to mention."

Christensen and Hofmann went directly to the bank, where the paper work was ready. All Hofmann had to do was sign the promissory note for $185,000 at an interest rate of prime plus one, due September 3, 1985. As Pinnock had promised, no collateral was required. That didn't seem to please Harvey Tanner, the bank vice-president who had been put in charge of the transaction. An unsecured loan of this size was highly unusual. But if the Church wanted it, if his bosses wanted it, who was he to stand in the way?

Just in case, Tanner asked Hofmann to bring in a copy of his contract with the Library of Congress—at his convenience. Hofmann said he would do so gladly.

That night, Christensen wrote in his journal: "I am

convinced that Elder Pinnock's personal actions not only preserved Mark Hofmann's ability to purchase the collection, but equally important, he has saved the Church countless time and money and effort in countering what would have been an avalanche of negative publicity should the collection have fallen into the wrong hands.''

Christensen also wished Mark Hofmann well on his difficult mission to Texas, armed only with his faith and the Lord's check for $185,000.

43 Connie Smith had seen many strange things in her eighteen years of selling homes. But this pair took the prize. "How can these kids afford this house?" she asked herself, not for the first time, as they stood in the twenty-by-thirty living room of the "glorious country estate with marvelous livability and endless quality" in Cottonwood, the most exclusive neighborhood in Salt Lake City.

Partly, it was the way they were dressed. To Smith, an attractive woman in her sixties, always elegant, with good bones and twenty-four grandchildren, it was bad enough that they had worn dirty jeans and thongs to the last ten showings (thank heaven, most of the owners vacated the premises for their visits), but they had worn the *same* dirty jeans and thongs every day.

As the city's foremost broker of "quality" homes, Smith had certainly seen wealthy people wearing all kinds of crazy things, and she had learned to affect a degree of tolerance. She had learned to judge her buyers' wealth not by their dress, but by their bearing. That was the problem with these two. They not only didn't dress rich, they didn't *act* rich. They were too shy. They didn't ask enough questions. They didn't take control of the situation. He had more of an air of authority than she did, but that was damning by faint praise. They would enter a room, walk to the center, and just stand there, staring.

She expressed her concerns to the co-agent on the sale, a personal friend of the couple. "Can these people really afford this house?" she asked. "He's my childhood friend," the agent had told her. "He's *absolutely* qualified. We can trust him."

So Smith stood in the living room and ran down the house's special features one more time (this was their second visit). It may not have been a distinguished house, but it was *big:* a seven-bedroom brick rambler with big living room, big rec room, big kitchen, big tennis court, and big lawn. Smith looked at the young couple standing in the middle of the room in their dirty jeans and thongs and thought to herself, They look sort of big themselves. Sort of barrel-shaped.

Then she repeated the price, just in case they had missed it the first time: $567,000. It had first been listed at over $700,000, but the real estate market had taken a beating during the recent economic downturn. The $567,000 was "more or less firm."

The wife explained that they had been very interested in a home in Emigration Canyon. Her husband liked it because it was secluded and had an extensive security system. But she wanted a *family* house in a good neighborhood where her kids could grow up with "advantaged" children.

Smith, who worked more for pleasure than for money, took pride in her politesse, but she couldn't restrain herself any longer. She would do it diplomatically, but she had to ask.

"What exactly is your line of work, Mr. Hofmann?"

"I deal in rare documents," said the barrel-shaped man.

The co-agent on the sale was Mark Hofmann's former schoolmate, Carl Lundquist. On one of their many viewing trips, this one without Dorie, Hofmann had shared with Lundquist the security concerns that led him to prefer the fortress-like house in Emigration Canyon. "Ever since I found the Martin Harris letter," he said, "I've gotten phone calls, letters—death threats to kill me and my family."

This comment led to a philosophical debate—like the ones they used to have at Olympus High.

"Under what circumstances," Hofmann asked, "do you think you could kill a person?"

"I don't know," said Lundquist, a little startled by the question and out of practice at philosophical debates.

"Could you kill somebody for money?" Hofmann pressed. "What if you didn't even know the person, but someone offered you a lot of money to kill that person?"

Lundquist pondered the question for a minute. "If I was in a war, trying to defend my country, I could kill. If someone was breaking into my house and my family was threatened, yes, I could kill. But if I was asked to go out and kill somebody in cold blood, somebody I didn't know, and they weren't bad people, and I didn't have a reason to kill them, and I had no idea why someone wanted them dead? Could I do that? Could I take somebody else's life without justification? Without cause?"

He paused a minute, trying to give it serious consideration. "No," he finally decided. "There's just no way."

"Me neither," said Hofmann. "I don't think I could do that, either." There was a long pause. "But *if* you were going to kill somebody," he started up again, "how would you do it? Would you shoot him, blow him up, poison him, shoot him with a shotgun?" Mark had obviously done some thinking about this, Lundquist realized.

Mark thought the best way to kill someone was with a shotgun. "Shotguns are untraceable. They don't have riflings. With a rifle or a pistol you can trace the bearing marks on the bullet—unless you're using the right kind of bullet. You can use a bullet that, once it impacts, it explodes, and you can't identify that bullet." Hofmann thought about that for a moment, then added, "But you have to be at pretty close range to kill someone with a shotgun. It's something you'd have to do while you were looking at them in the face."

Then he threw out another possibility. "What about a bomb? If a bomb was well built, well thought-out, *that* would be untraceable. Your fingerprints wouldn't be on it. Nobody would know how it got there if you were careful placing it, and it would be totally impossible to trace."

"Yeah, that would be one way to do it," Lundquist agreed abstractly. "It'd make sure they were dead."

Lundquist thought how much fun it was to talk this way again—philosophically—with his old friend. "There aren't a lot of people who are this open-minded, who are willing to talk like this."

Then the conversation turned to sex: who liked what in bed and whether Hofmann, who had been to a nude "health club" on one of his trips to New York, wore gym shorts or ran around in the buff.

44

Al Rust was sick and tired of waiting for his money—$296,750 (including profits), to be precise. He had put up with unreturned phone calls, bounced checks, and bogus stories long enough. One day in August 1985, his slow burn reached the boiling point and he drove to Hofmann's house to have it out.

As usual, Mark wasn't there. When Dorie came to the door, Rust, for want of a better target, lit into her. "Mark isn't being honest with me. He's giving me a runaround again. He's never here when I want to see him. He tells me one thing one day and another thing another day. He keeps promising me all these things, and he doesn't answer my questions. I don't know what to do."

Rust had finally come to the conclusion that Hofmann was taking advantage of his devotion to the Church. It was the most despicable trick of all. "I'll tell you what I'm going to do," he told Dorie. "I am going back to the LDS Church, and if they don't do anything, I'm going to take action."

Tears came to Dorie's eyes. "I don't know exactly what Mark is doing," she said. "He's having lots of problems. I don't know what's going on."

Rust wasn't the kind of man who could watch a woman cry and not soften a little. "I'm not trying to nail him to the cross," he said. "I just need some answers. Have him contact me."

But as he drove away from the house, Rust had that metallic feeling in the pit of his stomach that told him he had been snookered again, that he was too forgiving, that Doralee was once again covering for her no-good husband. Maybe she had no choice. Maybe she was more to be pitied than censured—being married to Mark Hofmann couldn't be easy. But this time, when he stopped thinking about it, he was still angry.

That evening Hofmann called Rust from New York. "I'm taking care of everything," he said. "Everything will be fine. Just hang in there."

Rust "hung in there" until the next time Hofmann came to visit. Then he let him have it. Rust wasn't a screamer or a shouter, but he could be a stern father.

"I've heard four different stories about selling the McLellin Collection. Now you're telling me someone's going to donate the money so the Church can buy it. But *none* of it ever seems to materialize." Like a good Mormon, Rust was concerned not just about their business dealings, but about the way Mark was running his life. "It seems like you're collecting money from Peter to pay Paul. You're just trying to get money from one person to cover a debt to another person. You sell something, and instead of giving that money to pay back a person you're obligated to, you take the money and go do something else. You're running around like a chicken with your head cut off."

Hofmann sat and listened, stone still. He didn't try to defend himself. He didn't try to apologize. He just sat, not looking at Rust, not looking at anything, as vacant as a display case without the display. Al Rust was a very gentle and softhearted man—his wife was always criticizing him for it—but, at that moment, he could feel his anger rising. He felt the urge to raise his fist and smash it into that soft, blank face—just to get its attention.

When Hofmann left that night, still without a response, Rust told his wife. "I've never seen Mark like this. Nothing I said tonight got through to him. We spent two hours of wasted time." He also suspected, for the first time, that there was a side to Mark Hofmann he had never seen.

* * *

On August 12, Hofmann signed a contract to buy the big rambler in Cottonwood for $550,000, only $17,000 less than the asking price. Connie Smith wondered why Carl Lundquist had let his client pay near full price in a buyer's market where offers routinely ran $150,000 below asking price. But she didn't want to ask too many questions.

Lundquist wondered how Mark planned to pay.

"No mortgage," Hofmann insisted. "I'd prefer to pay in several installments over two or three years. I've got a bank account in Switzerland with five hundred thousand in it. I've done some deals over in Europe, some document deals, where the proceeds have gone into my Swiss account. I could pay cash for the whole thing if I wanted to. I just don't want to."

Instead, Hofmann agreed to pay $5,000 in earnest money, $195,000 at the closing, and three additional annual installments of $195,000.

The closing was set for 1:00 P.M., October 15.

45

Sometime in mid August, Hofmann brought Al Rust a check for $40,000. It bounced. A few days later, Hofmann brought a cashier's check for $125,000. He also said that if Rust redeposited the $40,000 check the next day, it would go through. To Rust's astonishment, it did. From a total of $296,750, the indebtedness had been reduced to $131,750. Mark promised to pay the balance by August 25.

Sure enough, on the 25th, Hofmann appeared in the store looking jubilant and reporting that things were going "marvelously well." He waved a check made out to Rust for $132,000.

"What's the story with the McLellin Collection?" Rust asked.

"I acquired a document that is very valuable," Hofmann

said. "It's worth over a million dollars, and it's being sold to the United States government. They are going to pay me on September 1." Just when Rust was about to ask what this had to do with the McLellin Collection, Hofmann added, "So I've donated the McLellin Collection to the LDS Church myself as tithing."

Rust was stunned. "Gosh, how can you give away a collection that you don't own? I paid the money for that collection. It's a partnership. How could you give that away when it wasn't yours?"

Hofmann tried to explain that the Church didn't want to get involved in buying it, and "this just seemed like the easy way. I was getting all this extra money and I pay tithing anyway, so I thought I would just give it to them. Don't worry. I'm going to be making so much money on this other deal."

Rust told himself that it didn't really matter where the money was coming from as long as it was coming. "Boy, that's great, Mark," he finally conceded.

"So I guess we don't need the safe-deposit box any more," Hofmann prompted.

"I guess we don't." The two men went across the street, and Hofmann retrieved his documents and books.

The next day, the $132,000 check bounced.

Steaming, Rust instructed his bank to monitor Hofmann's account daily and to put the check through for collection at the first sign of solvency.

One day toward the end of August, Jill Stone, Mark's former girlfriend, saw him at a Park West concert at the huge, circular Salt Palace on West Temple. Actually, he saw her, somehow, in a crowd of five thousand people. They hadn't spoken in almost six years. It was a brief, awkward reunion.

Two days later, he called.

She was shocked that he had been able to find her unlisted number.

"I want to see you," he said in a high, plaintive voice, like a small child.

"Aren't you married—with kids?" she reminded him curtly.

"Yes."

"Then you have no business calling me."

"But *you're* not married, are you?"

"That's none of your business. My life is my own, and it doesn't involve you in any way."

"I want to see you." An insistent edge crept into his voice. "I want to make you understand. . . ."

"I'm sorry. I needed answers six years ago—not now."

Then she hung up.

He called again the next day.

"I want to see you," he repeated, more shrill this time. "I need to see you. I need to explain things to you."

"You don't seem to understand. I don't want to talk to you any more."

It was as if a bomb had exploded on the other end of the line. Hofmann erupted into incoherent screaming— just as he had six years ago. She knew if she had been in the same room, he would have tried to hit her again. "Why can't you understand?" he railed. "Why won't you ever listen to me? Why won't anybody listen to me?" he shrieked uncontrollably, his voice filled with menace. "Why won't anybody listen to me?"

She hung up again and, terrified, called a psychologist friend. "What if he calls again? What am I going to do?"

"Whatever you do," she said, "don't make him angry. Don't make him mad."

At the First Interstate Bank, Harvey Tanner waited all day September 3 for Mark Hofmann. The $185,000 loan that Hugh Pinnock had arranged was due. Tanner's bad feeling about this whole affair had only gotten stronger, and eight hours of looking up from his desk and hoping to see Hofmann's face didn't help his fraying nerves. At the end of the day, after the bank closed its doors, he called Hugh Pinnock to give him the bad news.

Pinnock turned around and called Steve Christensen.

In his desperate search for Hofmann, Christensen called Brent Metcalfe. "I'm looking for Mark," he said, unusually frantic. "If you see him, tell him he has to call me."

"What's going on, Steve?"

"I've got to get ahold of him right away. I need to get some money from him. His $185,000 note is due. Mark has to get ahold of me quick."

A few days later, Hofmann called Pinnock and told him he was having some financial problems. Pinnock told him to call Harvey Tanner and explain. When Hofmann called, Tanner suggested that he come in and discuss the matter—and bring with him the contract to sell the "Oath of a Freeman." They set a date and time for the meeting.

Hofmann never showed up.

He did show up a few days later in Hugh Pinnock's office to offer reassurances that he was financially sound. When he left, Pinnock called Christensen. He wanted Steve to make sure the loan was repaid. Everything had to be handled discreetly, of course—Hofmann was in a sensitive position—but there could be no mistaking Pinnock's message: Get that money.

A few nights later, Metcalfe got another urgent call from Christensen. "I've got to get ahold of Mark right away."

"What happened now?"

"He's just bounced a check for $185,000. Hinckley and Pinnock are really concerned. They're thinking of pressing criminal charges."

On September 9, Hofmann visited his cousin Ken Woolley and gave him a check for $40,000 to pay off an old debt. He looked real happy, Woolley thought. "Things are going good," he said. "I am going to get the house."

46

Later the same week, Hofmann walked into Thomas Wilding's office on West Temple with spectacular news. "The Haunted Man," the Dickens manuscript, had finally sold for a *66 percent gain!* Wilding could hardly believe it. His old friend Mark really did have a Midas touch. Not that Wilding hadn't had a few doubts along the way, especially when five months went by without any word. He had even tried to see Mark's dealer, Justin Schiller, on his recent Labor Day trip to New York, but Hofmann, who was in charge of arranging the meeting, called at the last minute to say Schiller was out of town for the weekend. Now, in the midst of the celebration, he felt a little embarrassed. How could he have doubted?

"Who did you sell it to?" Wilding wanted every delicious detail.

"The Pierpont Morgan Library, in New York."

"You'll get us a sales receipt?"

"No problem."

There was one problem, however. The money, $400,000, wouldn't be paid until October 16. When Wilding asked why, Hofmann explained, "When you sell a major manuscript, there is often a delay. That's standard for the industry."

But wait, there was more good news. The Brigham Young letters that Wilding had helped him buy in August had also sold for a 42 percent gain. Almost 50 percent in one month. And that money, $34,130, was available immediately.

It was available, that is, *if* Wilding wanted to pass up an even better deal.

"You should know," Hofmann began with the twinkle in his eye that all his investors loved to see, "I now have probably the best potential investment I've *ever* had."

For Mark Hofmann, that was saying a lot.

"I can offer you a chance to get in on the biggest investment yet, an investment that is just phenomenal. I'd really like you to participate in it."

Wilding couldn't wait to hear.

It was a second copy of the "Oath of a Freeman."

"It's the first printed document in colonial America," Hofmann boasted. "I sold the first one to the Library of Congress for a million dollars. That was through Justin Schiller too. If the first one sold for a million, the second has to be worth a million and a half." He told Wilding how he had found the first one serendipitously in the Argosy Book Store. "This second one I've been offered by a documents dealer in Boston." The dealers name? Lyn Jacobs.

"I need to raise half a million dollars for it," said Hofmann, brimming with excitement. "As soon as I can get the money, I'll fly to Boston to pick it up."

Wilding didn't know beans about documents, but he did know business, and his business sense told him it couldn't help to have *two* copies of the same document on the market at the same time. "You're sure the first one has already sold?" he asked.

"Absolutely. The first one has been sold."

Wilding struggled to square up the story. He wanted to believe it was true, that the deal was really this impossibly good. "If the document's worth over a million dollars, why would Mr. Jacobs sell it to you for 500 thousand?"

"He's owned it for a year and has a gain in it sufficient enough that he's willing to let it go."

Wilding didn't need to hear any more. *All* of Mark's deals were a little screwy, but who could argue with his record? He gave the go-ahead to reinvest all the profits from the sale of the Brigham Young letters, and he arranged a meeting with some of his investors to scare up the rest of the money Hofmann needed. The deal was so good he called family first. The obvious choice was his brother-in-law, Sid Jensen. Jensen had recently come by a large sum of money in an unfortunate way: he had lost an arm in a buzz-saw accident and successfully sued the plant where the accident occurred. Now he wanted to invest his winnings. This was just the deal for him, Wilding thought: high return, no downside. Jensen came to the meeting with Hofmann accompanied by his wife, father, and mother.

After Hofmann repeated his pitch, Wilding and Jensen asked if they could call Schiller in New York to get some more information. Mark hesitated for a minute (These document dealers, Wilding thought, so secretive) but then agreed—on one condition. He didn't want Schiller to know there was a second "Oath." Wilding could ask about Schiller's opinion of the "Oath" itself, its background, rarity, value, salability, etc., but he mustn't reveal the existence of a second copy. If he did, he might "blow the deal."

Blowing the deal was the last thing Wilding wanted to do. With Hofmann listening on another phone, he treaded through the conversation very softly, very carefully—so carefully that he never bothered to confirm if the first copy of the "Oath" had, in fact, been sold. By the end of the conversation, Schiller had pushed all the right buttons—"He couldn't have done a better job if he had been selling it himself"—and Wilding was satisfied.

Jensen, too, was in.

* * *

On September 12, Harvey Tanner looked up from his desk at First Interstate Bank and finally saw the person he had been looking for: Mark Hofmann. He leaped from his chair and caught up to him at the teller's window, buying cashier's checks. "Can I speak to you privately?" he said in the most restrained voice he could muster. The two men that were with him looked startled. Hofmann looked cornered.

During their brief, tense conversation, in which Tanner demanded repayment of the $185,000 loan, Hofmann somehow failed to mention that he was carrying $173,870 in cash and cashier's checks—the money that Wilding's group was investing in the second copy of the "Oath."

Wilding and Jensen stood not far away, watching the conversation in heated pantomime. They couldn't catch any of the words, but the grim expression on Harvey Tanner's face said more than they wanted to hear. They looked at each other with identical expressions of apprehension: This man is taking $200,000 of our money. This man already *has* almost $200,000 of our money. Why does this man's banker look like he wants to have him arrested?

In the parking lot, Wilding asked, as nonchalantly as possible, "What was the problem, Mark? That man sure looked upset."

Hofmann shrugged his shoulders. "Well, I co-signed a loan, a small loan, and it's a little bit overdue. That's all. It will be taken care of." He seemed suddenly in a terrible hurry to get to the airport to catch his plane for Boston to pick up the second "Oath." No time to waste on trivial matters.

Jensen, a solid, quick-tempered man, wasn't satisfied. When they dropped Wilding back at his office, Jensen decided to stay with the money. Together, he and Hofmann drove to Hofmann's bank on 33rd South, where Jensen surrendered his check and Hofmann deposited all the checks in his account and had new cashier's checks issued.

Jensen noticed that instead of having a single check made out in the amount of the purchase price, Hofmann was having a number of checks made out in varying amounts, the biggest one only $100,000. Jensen asked what he was doing.

"I want to leave myself some room for negotiation," Hofmann explained.

"Then why don't all the checks add up to the purchase price?"

Hofmann seemed to stumble for a few seconds. "I, ah, already sent some checks to the dealer in Boston," he finally said.

That didn't sound very likely to Sid Jensen. He was liking this whole proposition—and Mark Hofmann too—less and less.

On his way to the airport, Hofmann dropped Jensen at Wilding's office. He gave him the flight information. Before Jensen had even reached the office, however, Hofmann called Wilding from his car phone. "Sid seems real nervous about something," Hofmann said. "If he wants me to buy $20,000 of his investment in the 'Oath,' I'll be glad to do it."

Wilding, who had had his own nervous flutters, was noncommittal. "I can't answer for Mr. Jensen. I'll have to talk to him."

Jensen, in fact, was way past nervous; he was mad. As soon as he returned to Wilding's office, he recruited Gary Smith, another investor in Hofmann's project, to help him investigate Hofmann's elusive financial situation. Smith immediately called Harvey Tanner at First Interstate Bank. Tanner wouldn't give specifics, but he did say that Hofmann had "a large, outstanding loan that he can't seem to pay." Hofmann had lied on at least two counts: it was a loan to him personally, and it was a loan for a significant sum. Armed with this alarming news, Jensen stalked into Wilding's office.

"Gary Smith thinks that what happened today shows up some inconsistencies in Mark's story and that we ought to get ahold of him right now and find out what the problem is." They didn't want to say it, but both men were thinking the same thing.

They tried calling Hofmann's house, but there was no answer.

They called the airport, giving the airline and flight number that Mark had given them. There was no such flight at that hour. Maybe he got the information wrong.

They jumped in Wilding's truck and headed for the airport. First, they looked for Hofmann; then they drove up and down the parking lots looking frantically for his car.

Maybe he planned to leave later that night. No, there were no more flights to Boston or New York.

They drove to his house. It was 10 o'clock. He wasn't there.

47

After a sleepless night, Wilding drove to Hofmann's house at 5:30 the next morning, Friday, the 13th of September. He had to wait an hour until Smith arrived. He wanted a witness.

Dorie answered the door. "What's going on?" she said, obviously concerned. The harassment was starting earlier and earlier in the day.

"We need to talk with your husband."

"Mark's in the shower," she said quickly, heading them off at the door to the back hall. "I'll tell him you're here."

Eventually, Hofmann came out, his hair wet and neatly combed. "What's the big deal?" he asked.

Wilding could barely control his rage. "I'll tell you what the big deal is. There are a lot of things you've been telling us that don't add up. You're *supposed* to be on a flight to Boston, but there isn't any such flight. You're *supposed* to get the money to Lyn, but you're still here. What's going on? Where's the money?"

Hofmann looked at them with a startled, slightly wounded expression. How could they distrust him so? "No problem. I still have the money, and I'm going today. I was going to go yesterday but I decided to go today, and I'm taking my son." That was a reminder: his family was in the house.

"I don't care anymore," Wilding shot back, unappeased. "The deal's off. You haven't done what you said you were going to do, and there's no way we're going through with the deal. There's no way we want to invest this money. We just want our money back. If you've still got the money, go get it."

Mark went downstairs, and came back with the back portion of a cashier's check made out to Lyn Jacobs the day before for $154,000. "I already sent the check," he said.

But he had just said he was leaving with the money later that day. More lies, Wilding thought. "Mark, I have a lot at stake here. I have investors who trust me, and I trusted you, and now there are obviously some problems."

Dorie broke in. She had heard the heated voices. She knew something was wrong. "Mark, what's going on?"

He dismissed her. "Let me handle this."

Then Mark finally began to realize what *was* going on. "You can't turn down a good deal," he said, suddenly, obviously anxious, his voice edging toward petulance. "You *can't* turn down a good deal."

"We can, and we are," said Wilding firmly. "We want our money back. And I'm going to stay with you until I get it."

Hofmann tried another expression: indifference. "Well, okay, no problem. I've got other investors who will take the investment with no problem at all. We can go to the bank and get your money. I'll meet you at the bank at 10:30."

Wilding had had enough of his tricks. "I'm not leaving here, Mark. You and I will go to the bank *together*."

They rode together in Hofmann's Toyota to the Rocky Mountain State Bank. Hofmann's account contained only $18,000—$160,000 less than they had given him the day before. He hadn't gone to Boston, he hadn't bought the "Oath," and the money was gone.

"Where's the rest of the money?" Wilding demanded, irate by now.

Hofmann avoided answering him directly. "You'll get your money back."

"Let's get it back *now*."

Hofmann said he had several business appointments that day. (But he was supposed to go to Boston today, Wilding thought.) He could call in some debts while he was out and meet Wilding back at his office with the money.

No sale. Wilding wanted to be right there with him the whole day. Who knew what other creditors, like Harvey Tanner, were waiting out there to grab anything Mark put his hands on? Wilding wanted to make sure that every dollar came to him first. "Look, Mark," he said, "I don't care who you call or what you do. Just get our money back. What you do from there is up to you."

Finally, he had evoked a reaction: Hofmann began to tremble.

The first stop was Deseret Book.

Wade Lillywhite and Curt Bench, Lillywhite's boss, had never seen Mark Hofmann so distraught. He was usually so calm, so detached, so in control. The first thing Lillywhite said, even before "Hi," was "What's wrong?"

"I'm in a little difficulty," Hofmann said, lowering his voice. "I need some money right away and wanted to talk to you about the possibility of a loan. A fairly large sum of money."

Hofmann was always pulling strange stunts, but this one puzzled even two longtime associates like Lillywhite and Bench. Just the other day, he had been in the store with a $100,000 check to cover a previous purchase. They knew the documents business had its ups and downs, but how could Hofmann have $100,000 one day and need a loan the next?

"How much do you want to borrow?"

"One hundred thousand."

Curiouser and curiouser, thought Lillywhite.

"I'll give you my collection of children's books as collateral."

Bench and Lillywhite both knew the collection well, and knew it was worth at least that much.

"I'll pay good interest." They had never heard Hofmann so eager. It sounded like more than just "a little difficulty."

There was a problem, though. Hofmann still owed them $16,000. The recent $100,000 check hadn't covered the entire debt from the previous deal.

"I've got that for you," he said quickly.

"I'll have to talk to my boss about the loan," said Bench. "Come back later this afternoon."

* * *

Hofmann got back in the car with Tom Wilding. Next stop: Al Rust.

Rust wasn't at his coin shop, he was manning a booth at the Utah Coin Show being held at the Salt Palace, a sports arena and convention center not far from Temple Square. Hofmann ran frantically from aisle to aisle until he found him. "I've got to talk to you," Hofmann called out as he approached, obviously agitated, trying to catch his breath. Rust later recalled it was the first time he had ever seen fear on Hofmann's face.

Rust noticed a man following Mark, standing a few paces back. "Let's go into the foyer," Hofmann suggested. Once they were outside, Mark threw his hands in the air in sheer exasperation. "Things are terrible. I'm losing everything," he wailed. "They're coming to get my car, my home!"

"What's the matter?"

"I borrowed $185,000 from a bank, and they're foreclosing on me today. They're on their way to lock my home up and take my car and everything. I'm going to lose my home and everything." It was unnerving to see Mark—cool, collected Mark—suddenly panic-stricken.

"Calm down," said Rust. "You're running in every direction at once. Just settle down and tell me what's going on." Then suddenly it struck him what Hofmann was saying, and what it meant to him and the money Mark owed him. The kindly, avuncular coin dealer was transformed instantly into the stern father. "You still owe me $132,000, and now you're telling me you owe a bank $185,000? What *is* going on?"

No matter how distraught, Hofmann always had an answer. "I borrowed that money to buy the 'Oath of a Freeman,'" he said. "I'm getting a million dollars for it. Also I have half ownership on a document that's in a safe-deposit box in New York."

"My goodness, Mark, how can you get in these predicaments?"

"The government promised to pay me by September 1, and then I was going to pay you. But the bank is foreclosing. They've seen my check to you, so they know I owe you $132,000, and they know I owe them $185,000, so they're locking me out." He was practically in tears.

Then he asked for a loan.

With $132,000 in uncollectable debt, a bad check sitting at his bank, and a second mortgage on his home, Rust had every right to say no—car or no car. But Al Rust took his Mormon faith very seriously, especially at times of crisis. So, reaching deep into his heart, he found one last measure of sympathy.

"I don't have any more money to help you," he said. "If I did, I would, but I just don't have it. But maybe I can help you arrange someone to loan you what you need. Let's meet in five hours to see if we can figure out somebody to help us." It was so much like Al Rust to say "us."

"Now, just calm yourself," he added as Mark left. "There's got to be a solution to all this."

The next stop on Hofmann's desperate itinerary was the Union Park Center in Midvale, south of the city, where his cousin, Ken Woolley, worked. Again, Hofmann asked for privacy. Reluctantly, Wilding agreed, remaining behind in the futuristic lobby, watching to make sure the elevator stopped at the right floor.

To Woolley, Hofmann seemed "in a panic."

"I'm in big financial trouble," he said. "I borrowed $185,000 from the bank. I was expecting to pay it back with the sale of the 'Oath of a Freeman,' but the Library of Congress didn't want to buy it. I'm desperate. I'm willing to sell it for $250,000. Do you think you might be interested?"

Woolley had had his share of problems with his cousin's crazy investment schemes. Mark still owed him $68,000 on one of them. He wasn't even slightly enticed by the offer and promptly said so.

"Well, I've got to get some money some place to pay this bank off. I wrote them a check, and it's gonna bounce."

"You *what?*" Woolley had come to the conclusion months before that Mark was a liar and a cheat, but he didn't think he was stupid too. "Why did you write them a check? You can't do that. It's illegal. It's a criminal violation. It's much better to default on a loan than to write a bad check."

But Hofmann didn't seem to be listening.

"What you've got to do, Mark, is sit down and do a financial statement of all your assets and liabilities. Then go to the bank and say, 'This is what I've got, this is how

I'm gonna work it out.' I'll be happy to go to the bank with you."

That wasn't the kind of help Hofmann was looking for. The options were running out.

They drove back to Deseret Book. Ron Millett, the president, wanted to think about the loan over the weekend. That was too late, said Hofmann. Millett agreed to see him later that afternoon.

At one point, Hofmann pulled Wade Lillywhite aside. "I can't wait till Monday," he said in an urgent whisper.

"If the deal doesn't go through and Deseret Book can't give you the money, let me know and I think I can line you up with somebody who can get you the money."

"Fine," said Hofmann. Finally, a breath of hope.

When he came out, he told Wilding, "They're contemplating investing in the document and they want to meet again at four to make the decision."

Back to the Salt Palace for a second meeting with Rust. Again, Hofmann and Rust went to the foyer to talk privately. Rust, who was rushing to get away for a fishing trip to Boulder Mountain, had only made a few phone calls—all unsuccessful. But he did have a suggestion.

"Since the Mormon Church has got the McLellin Collection, why don't you go to them and see if they will lend you some money against it until you get paid for the 'Oath' and can bail yourself out?"

Hofmann had a better idea. Ever since he gave Rust that rubber check for $132,000, Rust's bank had been monitoring Hofmann's account, waiting for funds to come in to make it good. If Rust would pull back that check, Hofmann would have a little more breathing space in which to work things out.

Rust agreed, but not without a stern warning. "Listen very carefully," he said. "I'm giving you till November 1. If you don't pay me the $132,000 by November 1, I'm taking action. Number one, I'll go back to the Mormon Church. Number two, I'll go to a lawyer. And number three, if I go to a lawyer, they're going to subpoena the Church, because the people there have a lot of answers to give."

Every time Rust mentioned the Church, he could see Mark flutter a bit. "If you give me that thirty days, there won't be a problem," Mark said earnestly.

But Rust wasn't finished. "The first mistake you make, I'm taking action—if you don't check in regularly, nearly every day. Or if you sell even one item for $5,000 and you don't turn the money over to me. I don't want you waiting until you accumulate $132,000. You go ahead and pay me the $5,000."

"Hey," said Hofmann, suddenly blithe, "no problem."

When he rejoined Wilding, Hofmann told him that Rust had come up with the name of someone he thought would put $50,000 into the deal.

Back to Deseret Book for the 4 o'clock meeting with Ron Millett. Wilding waited downstairs while Hofmann met with him for half an hour. Millett had reservations. Several times over the last few months Hofmann had "pulled a few real bad stunts," according to Millett. He wasn't sure he wanted to do business with him any longer. And then there was the $16,000 of outstanding debt. He wanted to think about it over the weekend.

But next week was too late.

Hofmann reported to Wilding: "They wanted until Monday to make a decision, and I told them, 'Look, either make a decision today or forget it.' "

"Well, as far as I am concerned," said Wilding, "any investor confronted with that kind of decision would say forget it."

About 6:30, they drove back to Wilding's office, where Sid Jensen was waiting for them. When it was clear that the day had produced nothing, Jensen began to boil.

"Where's our money?" he demanded.

"Back East," said Hofmann, suddenly, preternaturally calm. "One of my associates took the money to Boston and purchased the 'Oath.' You saw the cashier's check today—the one made out to Lyn Jacobs."

More lies. Jensen was fuming. First he said he was going to take the money back East himself yesterday, then he said he was taking it today, now he says he sent the money back East in the hands of an associate. It was all contradictions, evasions, and lies, and Sid Jensen had had enough of it.

Gary Smith had written out a list of accusations, and he fired them at Hofmann.

"Did you lie about the Brigham Young papers?"

"Yeah."

"Did you lie about having bought the 'Oath?' "

"Yeah."

"Did you lie about using the money we gave you to purchase 'The Haunted Man'?"

"Yeah."

But he insisted that the latest deal was for real. He had, in fact, used the money they gave him yesterday to purchase the "Oath" from Lyn Jacobs for approximately $420,000, and he was willing to sign a statement to that effect. But when they requested a receipt, he couldn't produce one.

"Why didn't you tell us all this earlier?" Wilding demanded.

"I didn't want to squelch the deal."

Jensen wanted to know only one thing: "How are you going to get our money back?"

Hofmann remained very cool. "I have other people who want to invest. I'll raise the money."

They didn't believe him.

"I'm telling you the truth," he insisted. "The money was sent back East to Lyn Jacobs. To be honest with you, the 'Oath of a Freeman' should have been purchased by four this afternoon."

"And how did you get the money there?"

"I sent it with one of my associates," he repeated.

"What's his name?"

"I prefer not to tell you."

That was clearly more than Sid Jensen could take. He had sat through the detached arrogance, the smug looks, the nerdy grins long enough. It wasn't just any money Hofmann was talking about, it was the money they had paid him for his arm. If anybody knew life could be unfair, he did, but to watch this arrogant little twerp *gloat* over his loss was unendurable.

"I don't think you're taking seriously what we're talking about," Jensen spat, and before anybody could stop him, raised his one arm and slugged Hofmann in the face.

There was a moment of stunned silence.

"No one's ever struck me before," Hofmann whimpered, his voice so high and soft that everyone in the room thought he sounded like a little girl.

*   *   *

After that, the meeting turned strangely businesslike, the calm after the storm. Hofmann owed Wilding's investors some $200,000, plus $100,000 promised profit. They had a lot of books and documents as collateral, but they wanted their money, as soon as possible.

They wrote up an agreement that required Hofmann to produce all the money, plus the $160,000 that had supposedly gone into "The Haunted Man," by the following Tuesday, September 17, at 3:30. Hofmann, Wilding, and Jensen all signed.

Wilding was skeptical. How could Mark raise that kind of money in that short time?

But Hofmann was confident. "Don't worry. I'll do it. I don't need any more time than that."

He had just one request. Could they keep everything confidential? After all, his business was built on reputation and without his reputation, he couldn't raise the money. And they did want their money back, didn't they? Of course, neither Wilding nor Jensen thought much of Hofmann's reputation any longer, but they saw the dilemma. If word of this scam got out, he wouldn't be able to raise enough money for a phone call. So they agreed: no inquiries, no letters, no lawyers, and, certainly, no police. At least until Tuesday.

Tom Wilding walked out of the meeting that night thinking, This is a Friday the 13th I'll never forget.

Mark Hofmann, apparently, felt differently. Early the next morning, he called Curt Bench. "Never mind about that loan," he said cheerily. "It's all been taken care of."

48

Everybody took Sunday off. Mark Hofmann went to church with his wife and children. So did Al Rust, Tom Wilding, Sid Jensen, Brent Ashworth, Steve Christensen, and, of course, Hugh Pinnock and Gordon Hinckley.

But the next day, the heat was on again.

Ron Millett of Deseret Book called to say "no go" on the loan.

By Tuesday evening, the 17th, Hofmann was back in front of Tom Wilding. It was obvious from the moment he shambled in that he didn't have the money. Wilding hadn't really expected that he would. That's why he had arranged to meet in the offices of his attorney, John Ashton.

Ashton had the papers already drawn up.

The agreement terminated the partnership and put Hofmann in a strict debtor-creditor relationship with Wilding's group. According to its terms, Hofmann not only agreed to pay back all the money invested, but also the fantastical gains that he had reported over the months. Wilding was out for blood. He was determined to make Hofmann eat his words: *100 percent gain in one month!* Indeed. Hofmann signed two promissory notes: one for $188,488, due September 17, and one for $266,667, due October 16. Total: $455,155. And just in case that wasn't enough to put the fear of God into him, there was a penalty clause: $2,000 *per day* per note.

The first penalty clause kicked in on October 15.

Wilding also wanted more collateral. He wanted the deed to Hofmann's house and the titles to his cars.

Hofmann agreed—readily, submissively.

They wanted the second "Oath of a Freeman."

Hofmann gulped. "I can't. That needs to remain confidential."

237

"I'll put it in my safe-deposit box," Wilding said. "No one has to know."

They wanted a list of all his other debts: liens on the house? None, said Hofmann. Outstanding loans? Just the one at First Interstate Bank for $185,000. Other assets? The first "Oath" was being sold to the New York Public Library for $1.5 million. Seventy-five percent of that was his.

They wanted it.

This was hardball. "*I'd* never sign this agreement," Wilding said to himself. But this was the only way, apparently, to show Mark that they were dead serious, that they weren't playing games; the only way, it seemed, to wipe that smirk off his face. "We want to get this thing taken care of," he told Hofmann with all the gravity he could muster. "You seem to have lots of financial backing somewhere. So just *do* it."

Back at Wilding's office, the ordeal continued. Gary Smith had some more questions.

"Is this a systematic scheme to defraud people out of their money?"

"No, it isn't," Hofmann said emphatically. He seemed offended at the suggestion.

"Do you intend to cheat and not pay back any of these funds?"

"I intend to pay back the money."

"Have you lied to Tom?"

Hofmann didn't answer.

The meeting was over—and still no one had threatened to call the police.

The next morning, Hofmann brought the second copy of the "Oath" to Wilding's bank. As they left, Hofmann repeated, "I don't want any of the other people involved to know you've got this."

Wilding didn't care. "As long as we get our money, that's fine."

49 In mid-September, Hofmann received a call from Kenneth Rendell, who happened to be in Topeka, Kansas, that day on business. He wanted to make sure that he had correctly understood an order that Mark had left with his secretary in Massachusetts the week before. The order was for an Egyptian *Book of the Dead* in hieratic script, the shorthand, abstracted version of the more famous, more pictorial hieroglyphic form of Egyptian writing. He had also specified that he wanted it from the first century A.D., if possible, and he wanted it on papyrus.

To Rendell, it seemed like a very strange request.

"Why do you want this?" he began. "Because, you know, if your client really knows anything about this stuff, it isn't good quality, and if they *really* know nothing about it, they're going to want hieroglyphics instead of hieratics." But Hofmann was insistent. He knew what he wanted.

On September 16, Rendell mailed him, on thirty-day consignment, two examples of hieratic script on first-century papyrus, one eight by twenty-four inches, the other, nine by three. The discounted price for both: $10,500.

It looked like the real thing to Wade Lillywhite of Deseret Book: a small fragment from an Egyptian *Book of the Dead,* written in hieratics rather than hieroglyphics, on papyrus rather than linen. Lillywhite considered himself something of an amateur Egyptologist—no expert certainly, but knowledgeable enough to know this fragment was from about the first or second century A.D. —the Roman period. It wasn't such a surprising skill for a rare-book dealer in Salt Lake City, Utah. Despite being thousands of years and half a world away from the

Nile Delta, the Mormons consider themselves "spiritually related" to the Egyptians through the religious writings that their Prophet "translated." Anything Egyptian has a certain cachet.

According to Mark Hofmann, however, this piece of papyrus had more than just cachet; it had real religious significance. He was offering to sell Lillywhite one of the *very papyri* that Joseph Smith had used in translating the Book of Abraham.

"Where did you get this, Mark?" Lillywhite thought there was a slim chance Mark might answer.

Hofmann smiled. "It's from the McLellin Collection."

A few days later, Lillywhite's boss, Curt Bench, went to the CFS offices in the old Auerbach's building to appraise Steve Christensen's book collection. Christensen knew he would have to declare bankruptcy and was selling off his most precious asset to pay debtors. While there, Lillywhite happened to mention that Hofmann was "shopping around" important papyri from the McLellin Collection.

Christensen went white.

50 By October, Hugh Pinnock and Steve Christensen were close to panic. Hofmann was a month behind on a loan that was unorthodox to begin with; he had been buying and selling documents all over town, running up unknown but probably huge new debts; there were articles in the paper daily, it seemed, about the supposedly still secret McLellin Collection, some of them saying that Mark Hofmann had sold the Collection to a third party. The Mormon underground was already salivating over the juiciest rumors and, worst of all, the Collection was still "out there," somewhere in the great Mormon-bashing unknown, ready to spring any minute onto the pages of the *Los Angeles Times*.

And to top it off, Christensen had learned that Hofmann was peddling bits and pieces of the Collection around town.

On October 2, after weeks of bounced checks, broken appointments, and unreturned phone calls, Christensen finally tracked Hofmann down and convinced him that his only hope of salvation was to face Hugh Pinnock and make a full confession. "If you want to win your way back into Church favor," Christensen admonished him, "this is the only way." Hofmann, surprisingly contrite, agreed, and the two of them drove to Hugh Pinnock's house at 10:30 that night.

"Tell Elder Pinnock your problem," Christensen prodded, drawing on his experience as a bishop.

Throughout the "confession," Hofmann's eyes remained riveted to the floor. "I'm not going to get the million and a half for the 'Oath of a Freeman,' " he told them. Why not? "Because the Library of Congress is having problems authenticating it."

"What else, Mark?" Christensen pressed.

"I won't be able to make a donation of the McLellin Collection."

What else, Mark?

"I pledged the Collection to Al Rust as security on a loan of $150,000."

And?

"And I didn't use the money to pay off the loan you arranged. I purchased other documents with it."

Anything else?

"I owe some money to a doctor."

Any other debts?

"No."

Pinnock took off his glasses in the traditional gesture of candor. He wanted to know about Mark's agreement with Al Rust. Hofmann said he was to repay $150,000 and then Rust would release the Collection. Hofmann had one key to the safe-deposit boxes where it was stashed, but two keys were required and Rust had the other one—and Rust was out of town.

Was there any money coming in?

Yes, said Mark. "The American Antiquarian Society has offered $250,000 for the 'Oath.' I'll get $150,000 from it."

Pinnock seemed to care about only two things, the

McLellin Collection and the loan. Which was not unreasonable, considering that his reputation, his standing within the First Presidency, his chances for advancement, even his position in the Celestial Kingdom were on the line. He told Hofmann to use the $150,000 from the "Oath" to pay off Rust. In the meantime, Pinnock would find someone else to buy the Collection and donate it to the Church.

By the time they were finished, Hofmann looked close to tears. "What will President Hinckley think of me?" he lamented. "I just wish I was still in a position to donate the documents to the Church." To demonstrate his contrite heart, he told them about $20,000 that he had been paid that morning. A friend had the check, but he would pick it up that very same evening and deliver it to Harvey Tanner the next morning.

Christensen volunteered to go with him.

It was midnight by the time they arrived at Shannon Flynn's house. Flynn came to the door groggy but handed Hofmann the check without complaint. Using Mark's car phone, Christensen called Pinnock. "I've got the check in my pocket."

The next evening about eight, Christensen returned to Temple Square for a meeting at the First Presidency building. On his way, he stopped at a video store in the Crossroads Mall and bought a videotape of a "Miami Vice" episode—"just to get in the mood for this event," he told a friend the next day.

The event was a meeting with Church bosses to discuss "the Hofmann problem." Clearly the Church had another crisis on its hands.

The meeting opened in Pinnock's office, then moved to the office of Dallin Oaks, Pinnock's supervisor and one of the Twelve. Then all three men walked to Gordon Hinckley's office. He, after all, was the master of damage control. Hinckley was emphatic that the Church still wanted the McLellin Collection. Finally, they asked Christensen to go back to Pinnock's office and wait while they conferred.

The jury was out only ten minutes. Pinnock came back alone.

"You know, Steve," he began in his most patronizing tone, "President Hinckley paid you a great compliment.

He said, 'We can totally trust that young man.' " Trust to do what?

The Church had a very special mission for Steve Christensen, Pinnock began. Mark Hofmann had demonstrated beyond a doubt that there were dozens, perhaps hundreds of documents still out there waiting to be discovered, many of which could harm the Church. There were now rumors that he had leads on the missing 116 pages, the seer stones, the Urim and Thummim, perhaps even the gold plates themselves. Such discoveries could hurt the Church in many ways. What if there was evidence that Smith had plagiarized Solomon Spaulding's romance in writing the *Book of Mormon?* What if Emma Smith did say, as Hofmann had indicated in his description of the McLellin Collection, that there was no First Vision? What if there was further proof of folk magic and profiteering, not just by Smith, but by his entire family?

These things were *out there,* the Brethren believed, and it was no longer acceptable just to leave them for the Mark Hofmanns of the world to dig up and sell to the highest bidder. The Church should be actively pursuing these bombshells itself—*preventive* damage control. The Brethren, especially Hinckley, believed they could no longer trust Hofmann. "We think he's too concerned with making a profit," said Pinnock. "We question his intentions. We don't think he is being totally honest with us. We are interested in finding someone who would handle these documents with the Church's concerns in mind."

Someone like Steve Christensen.

They had decided to commission Christensen to search for documents on behalf of the Church. They would extend to him a $500,000 line of credit and provide him with any services he needed. (In particular, Pinnock repeated the offer of an armored car.) This was to be a highly secret mission, said Pinnock. No one must know for obvious reasons. "You are not even to keep a private journal of your acquisition activities for the Church—that's how secret it must stay."

The next morning, October 4, the Church swung ponderously into action.

At 7:30, President Hinckley met briefly with Mark Hofmann. Christensen may have been there too. The purpose, undoubtedly, was to remind Hofmann, in the gravest terms, of his Temple covenants.

At 9:30, Pinnock met with Dallin Oaks. The purpose of the meeting: to identify a reliable "collector" to buy the McLellin Collection and donate it to the Church. Pinnock called David E. Sorensen, a wealthy Mormon businessman who had recently sold his hospital business and was therefore "very liquid." He was serving as mission president in Nova Scotia. The two men had known each other since the 1950s. Their wives had been college roommates. Just as Pinnock had expected, Sorensen agreed immediately. If Hugh Pinnock said the money was needed, then he would provide it.

Arrangements were made on the spot. Sorensen, through his attorney, David West, would purchase the Collection from Hofmann for $185,000. He would then donate the Collection to the Church, keeping it in his possession only long enough to let the brouhaha die down and, of course, maximize the tax benefits. The sale was scheduled for the next week at David West's office, and both Hofmann and Rust were to be present.

Sorensen asked only one thing: that someone be on hand to authenticate the documents. Pinnock said he had just the man.

At 11:30, Pinnock met with Steve Christensen, who agreed to authenticate the documents at the exchange. According to the plan, he would then put the Collection in a safe-deposit box under his name. (That day, he rented two boxes at the First Interstate Bank.) At the meeting, Pinnock railed against Hofmann. Oaks and Hinckley both agreed with him, he said, that Mark was "a crook" who was trying to "rip off" the Church. Christensen gingerly suggested that perhaps it wasn't dishonesty, just hard times. "Mark has hit some financial difficulties recently," said Christensen. That would account for the lies. It wasn't exemplary, but it wasn't necessarily evil.

By the end of the day, everything was ready. Now they could only wait for Al Rust to return with his key.

51

Meanwhile, frantic, Mark Hofmann scoured Salt Lake City for money. After leaving the meeting with Hinckley, he went to Glen Rowe, who had succeeded Don Schmidt as Church archivist, and sold him a Book of Common Prayer that had been signed by Martin Harris. The price: a paltry $700 in trade. The next day, the 5th, he drove to Ken Woolley's office in Midvale. Woolley had never seen his cousin so desperate. He needed to borrow $20,000.

After their last deal, Woolley had vowed never to do business with Mark again, but Hofmann was pleading with him. This wasn't a deal, it was just a loan. And he had with him a fistful of Deseret currency to put up as collateral. These were the same notes Woolley had seen in Al Rust's book on Mormon money so he knew they were valuable. And Mark promised to pay him back within a week. Woolley wrote out the check.

From Midvale, Hofmann drove back into town to the Hotel Utah, where he met with Shannon Flynn and Wilford Cardon in a room with a spectacular view of Temple Square. Cardon had chosen today of all days to fly from Arizona and "settle accounts." Hofmann calmly recounted his sale of the Jim Bridger notes: ten to Brent Ashworth, two to Charles Hamilton, and one at auction, for a total of $52,602. Cardon wanted his share of the profits immediately so Flynn wrote out a check for $19,034, knowing the check would bounce unless Hofmann made it good. (It bounced.)

Sunday was all quiet except for a phone call from Ken Rendell in Massachusetts. He called Brent Ashworth to say he was planning a trip West and would be seeing clients in Salt Lake City, including Hofmann. Ashworth relayed the good news to Mark.

* * *

At nine the next morning, in a three-way phone conversation, David West, David Sorensen, and Steve Christensen discussed ways in which the McLellin Collection could be kept secret. Christensen reported that Rust had not seen many of the papers in the Collection but may have seen some. All agreed that Rust was a potential problem. Christensen said he would question Hofmann for more details on the extent of Rust's knowledge.

Christensen wasn't the only one with questions for Hofmann. Brent Ashworth wanted to know what had happened to the money Mark owed him for two Missouri elder's licenses he had agreed to sell. Hofmann had called him that morning to say he had the money and would bring it by his office in Spanish Fork at eleven. Ashworth had delayed plans to drive to Salt Lake City to be there when Mark arrived.

At eleven, he called instead. "I'm tied up, but I'll be there at one, with the money."

Ashworth was sick of Hofmann's shenanigans and told him so. But he agreed to wait until one. Hofmann did show up at one—without the money. Ashworth couldn't believe it. He had waited around all morning for nothing. He struggled to contain his anger—"Don't blow the deal," he repeated to himself.

As always, Mark had an excuse: "I sold the document once, but that deal fell through. So I had to resell the document. That's why so much time has passed." Ashworth listened and promised himself—not for the first time—that he would never do business with Mark Hofmann again. All he wanted now was his money back.

"The guy I just sold it to will have the money by this evening," Hofmann said. "Can I bring the money down tomorrow morning at 10 o'clock?"

But the next morning, Hofmann had other fires to put out.

Just after eight, Robert Pitts was sitting at the conference table in Steve Christensen's office in the Judge Building. While Pitts and Christensen were talking, a man walked in and asked to speak to Christensen "privately." Without introducing him, Christensen took the man into the outer office. Their conversation was hushed but heated.

Suddenly, Pitts heard Christensen's voice, loud and

agitated. *"You can't hide that.!"* Then the conversation receded again into angry, unintelligible whispers. A few minutes later, Pitts saw the man leave "in a solemn mood," and Christensen came back into the office with a grave look on his face. Not a word was said about the strange encounter. Only later did Pitts learn that the visitor was Mark Hofmann.

Later the same morning, while Brent Ashworth waited impatiently in Spanish Fork, Hofmann met with Hugh Pinnock to review the Joseph Smith papyri that Hofmann said came from the McLellin Collection. As soon as Hofmann left the meeting, Pinnock picked up the phone and gave status reports to Sorensen, Oaks, Christensen, and, at 10:30, Gordon Hinckley. Then he met with Oaks and perhaps Hinckley to compare Hofmann's papyri with photographs of the other Book of Abraham papyri the Church had reluctantly acquired in 1967. There wasn't an Egyptologist among them, but they had to admit the two papyri looked troublingly similar.

The next task on the agenda was to solidify the Church's alliance with Christensen. The solution: the usual mutual back scratching. If Hinckley's itch was Hofmann, Steve's itch was money. He was in the process of declaring bankruptcy and struggling to get his new syndication company started. So Pinnock offered a partial bailout: he would find someone to buy Christensen's book collection and donate it to Westminster College. Christensen would get $100,000, the college would get the books, the buyer would get the deduction, and the Church would get some good P.R. and the insurance of Steve's gratitude. To throw an appropriately religious mantle over the day's dealings, Pinnock closed the meeting with Christensen by giving a "blessing of comfort" regarding his personal life and financial problems.

Mark Hofmann spent the same afternoon trying to appease Tom Wilding. He had good news and bad news, he told Wilding. The bad news was that the "Arizona deal" was not going to materiaize. The good news was that an even better deal was in the works with the LDS Church. A businessman named Steve Christensen was acting as the Church's agent in a "major transaction," Hofmann said, a deal that would yield $185,000. The money was already in escrow with an attorney, David West, and would be released when the deal closed the next day, October 11.

Wilding had learned enough to be skeptical. "It must be quite a significant thing if it's going to sell for $185,000."

"Well, it's a very large collection of stuff I've collected over the years. There are several boxes, so many boxes that I have to use my van to deliver them."

Sid Jensen was also at the meeting, and he wanted to know why the Church would pay $185,000 for odds and ends, the leftovers of Hofmann's collection.

Hofmann fudged. "There's just so much of it, that I was able to obtain that much. It's worth that much."

Hofmann offered to give the Wilding group $150,000 from the deal.

"No," said Jensen, "we want the entire $185,000."

Later that evening, Kenneth Rendell's secretary, Leslie Kress, received the first of several strange phone calls at her home in Cambridge, Massachusetts. A male caller wanted Rendell's home address. "Leslie, I have a gift for Mr. Rendell, and I want to send it to his home," he said in a high voice. When she asked the caller to identify himself, he said his name was "Mr. Thornton."

Kress was immediately suspicious. She didn't know a Mr. Thornton. Why did he use her first name? How did he get her unlisted phone number? Why did he refuse to give any more information? She decided not to give out the address. Rendell had just been married and was out of town on a honeymoon. Fearing that burglars might be casing his empty house, Kress phoned the police and reported the calls.

52

The first day of Steve Christensen's Columbus Day weekend, Friday, October 11, began like every other day: looking for Mark Hofmann. He called David West, Lyn Jacobs, and a dozen other names on his list. He wanted to tell him that the meeting to transfer the McLellin Collection had been reset for Tuesday, October 15.

In fact, Hofmann was in Gordon Hinckley's office—with yet another bombshell.

Joseph Smith was the butt of many jokes during his lifetime, but none more famous than the joke played on him by three men from the town of Kinderhook, Illinois. The men cut six sheets of copper into bell shapes, inscribed them with crazy letters, corroded them with acid, then buried them with some bones in an ancient Indian mound. When they were uncovered, in the presence of several Mormons, the plates were taken to Joseph Smith, who promptly "translated" a portion of them. They were a history of the man whose bones were buried with them in the mound, Smith announced, and the man was "a descendant of Ham, through the loins of Pharaoh, king of Egypt."

Smith's "translation" was lost, but one plate was later discovered in the Chicago Historical Society Museum, mistakenly labeled "one of the gold plates of the *Book of Mormon.*"

In Hinckley's office, Hofmann claimed to have found not only the missing Kinderhook plates, but, far more devastating, Joseph Smith's missing translation. It was in Orson Pratt's handwriting, said Hofmann, but it was dictated by Smith.

That afternoon, when Hofmann recounted the meeting to Lyn Jacobs, Jacobs was aghast. "What a smack in the face," he said. "Here's Joseph giving an inspired translation of these fake plates. *Doesn't* look good. The media will go mad!"

Hinckley had seen the same thing, Hofmann said. "He promised me $150,000 for it all."

"Is he going to give you cash?"

"I'll know Tuesday morning."

Later that day, Al Rust returned earlier than expected from his fishing trip to Boulder Mountain and called Steve Christensen. If at all possible, Christensen wanted to complete the McLellin transaction that day and not wait until the following Tuesday. He called Hugh Pinnock, who canceled his plans to go away for the weekend. David West was put on alert. For a few hours, it looked as if the deal might go through.

But Christensen couldn't find Mark Hofmann.

He wasn't the only one looking.

Brent Ashworth wanted his money.

"I have it," Hofmann had said again over the phone that morning.

Ashworth was blunt. "You bring it to me. I'm tired of trying to chase you down." Mark said he would be there about noon, and Ashworth told him to leave the money in the mailbox at his house if no one was home. When Ashworth returned from lunch with his family at a nearby pizza parlor, he looked in the mailbox. Nothing.

Lyn Jacobs wanted his money. He had provided the collateral for the loan from Hofmann's orthodontist client, Ralph Bailey, and felt entitled to some of the profits from the sale of the letters that Bailey had financed. In fact, he had his eye on a fabulous 1972 Jaguar that he had seen in the showroom of a local dealership. Mark said he would meet him there with $10,000 the following Monday, October 14.

Ken Woolley wanted his money. A week had passed, and Hofmann hadn't repaid the $20,000 loan and he hadn't called. Woolley phoned him to demand the money. He had learned there was no other way with Mark.

"That transaction isn't completed yet," Hofmann said. "The buyer hasn't returned to Salt Lake yet so I'm still waiting for *my* money."

Tom Wilding wanted his money. He had come into the

office early that morning for a meeting with Hofmann, but Hofmann hadn't shown up. He tried calling Mark on his car phone. No answer. Finally, about 11:30 Hofmann called. Wilding had only one question: "Do you have the money?"

"No, the transaction has been put off until Monday."

Wilding was out of patience. "I think you better come up and see me, Mark. We need to talk about this. You've been promising dollars for so long. We're sick and tired of what's going on."

Hofmann pleaded. "The transaction has just been put off until Monday. I have something I think will suffice for over the weekend."

When Hofmann got to Wilding's office, he laid a piece of paper on the desk. It was a letter on David West's letterhead, confirming that $185,000 had been placed in an escrow account. Below the statement signed by West was another statement, on a different typewriter, noting that the funds would be available on October 14. It was signed by Steven F. Christensen.

"You see," said Hofmann. "Everything is in order. The transaction is going to take place."

Wilding wanted to show the letter to his lawyer, John Ashton. He and Hofmann went together to Ashton's office.

"Well, I know Steve Christensen," said Ashton. "Why don't we just give him a call and verify this?"

Hofmann froze. "I don't think that's necessary. If you need to do it to verify the deal, let me do the talking while you listen." He said he was afraid that anything else might "cause some concerns and . . ." (he rolled out the big gun) " . . . possibly even stop the transaction from going through."

"Well, we'll give you a little bit of time," said Ashton, trying to screw the word *little* into a threat. If Hofmann didn't come through with the money, he now had a weapon to threaten him with.

"I'll have the money for you on the 14th," Hofmann vowed solemnly.

Al Rust wanted his money. On Saturday, Hofmann came into his store and announced, "We finally got the McLellin Collection settled. We've got a buyer for the Collection, but for a lot less than before. It's $185,000, and we're selling it to a man who's a mission president in Europe."

Rust had heard so many stories, he gave this latest one little credence.

But Hofmann was persistent. "Now the money will be sent immediately," he said. "It will probably be here Wednesday or Thursday. Are you going to be here Wednesday or Thursday?"

"Oh, yeah," said Rust, relaxed after the serenity of Boulder Mountain. "I'm here all week."

"I'll keep you informed. But it's definite. We will have the money."

Well, thought Rust, one way or another, it will all be settled by November 1.

Steve Christensen decided to spend the long weekend at home with his family. The months of anxiety over leaving CFS, declaring bankruptcy, and pursuing the McLellin Collection for the Church had taken a toll on his marriage. Like many wives, Terri Christensen felt that her husband didn't give her enough attention, but normally she kept her frustration out of sight. Better than anybody, she knew how Steve had suffered recently. Telling his father about the failure of CFS (and the loss of his investment) had been the hardest thing he had ever done, harder even than selling his precious book collection. At least the Church had not forced him out of his position as bishop—as he had expected they would.

But, for Terri, things were different now. She was pregnant with their fourth child, and she needed his support. She wasn't willing to look the other way when he came home and buried his head in a book.

The problems came to a head on that Friday night, October 11, when Terri demanded that they "have a talk." After a week of chasing down Mark Hofmann, talking was the last thing Christensen wanted to do. When he balked, however, Terri threatened to walk out the door. He had put her off long enough. "If you want to go off and do all those things when we need you here, okay, but you can't expect me to sit around here and wait for you," she told him flatly. When he still wouldn't listen, she made good on the threat: she walked out the door.

The gesture had stunned Steve enough that, when she

Salt Lake City. *Police dubbed it "the Beirut of the West."*

LDS Temple, Salt Lake City. *Joseph Smith believed that there were many gods, and that all good Mormons will one day be gods in their own worlds.*

LDS Visitors Center, Salt Lake City. *Someone is converted to Mormonism every two and a half minutes.*

Kathy Sheets (kneeling) with, from left to right: Joseph Robertson and Katie Sheets Robertson, Gary Sheets, Jimmy Sheets (in tree), Gretchen Sheets, Heidi Sheets Jones, and Roger Jones with son Danny. *She represented everything that was good and right about the Mormon religion.*

Gary Sheets with a portrait of Kathy Sheets. *"I did it,"* he said the day of the first bombings. *"My friend's dead and my wife's dead because of a situation I got them into."*

Steven and Terri Christensen on their wedding day, September 16, 1976. *Underneath the Boy Scout uniform, he was, by Mormon standards, a closet rebel.*

The Christensen's four sons: Joshua, Justin, Jared, and Steven. *Steven, Jr. was born on January 9, 1986—what would have been his father's thirty-second birthday.*

Cops with Hoffmann's burned-out Toyota MR2. *They feared that the water used to put out the fire had washed important evidence down the drains. So they searched the drains.*

Detectives Ken Farnsworth (left) and Jim Bell. *The police department got so crazy about leaks that the two detectives in charge of the case could only talk to each other.*

The Salamander Letter. *The letter didn't sound Mormon at all. It didn't even sound Christian. It sounded like a Grimms' fairy tale.*

Collector Brent Ashworth. *If he wanted history, he could buy another Lincoln. When it came to his religion, there had to be a "religious-spiritual payoff."*

Writers and publishers Sandra and Jerald Tanner. *They had lived in fear of this moment ever since they began their crusade of information against the Mormon Church.*

Al Rust with son Gaylen, behind the counter at Rust's Coin Shop. *Rust had only three passions in life: the LDS Church, his family, and Mormon money.*

Church leaders (left to right) Dallin Oaks, Gordon Hinckley, and Hugh Pinnock at a press conference held after the bombings. *"These guys up there weren't just people,"* said one newsman, *"they were the prophets of God, and a first-name basis with the Lord."*

THE OATH OF A FREEMAN.

I AB. being (by Gods providence) an Inhabitant, and Freeman, within the iurisdictiõ of this Common-wealth, doe freely acknowledge my selfe to bee subject to the governement thereof; and therefore doe heere sweare, by the great & dreadfull name of the Everliving-God, that I will be true & faithfull to the same, & will accordingly yield assistance & support therunto, with my person & estate, as in equity I am bound: and will also truely indeavour to maintaine and preserve all the libertyes & privilidges thereof, submitting my selfe to the wholesome lawes, & ordres made & stablished by the same; and further, that I will not plot, nor practice any evill against it, nor consent to any that shall soe do, butt will timely discover, & reveall the same to lawefull authoritee nowe here stablished, for the speedie preventing thereof. Moreover, I doe solemnly binde my selfe, in the sight of God, that when I shalbe called, to give my voyce touching any such matter of this state, (in which freemen are to deale) I will give my vote & suffrage as I shall judge in myne owne conscience may best conduce & tend to the publick weale of the body, without respect of personnes, or favour of any man. Soe help mee God in the Lord Iesus Christ.

"Oath of a Freeman." *It was nothing less than the first document printed in America.*

Hoffmann with Shannon Flynn. *They saw themselves as secret agents, jetting around the country making high-stakes deals and shooting their Uzis on weekends.*

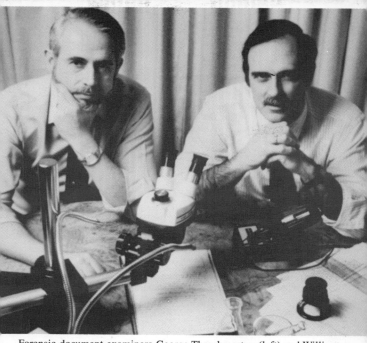

Forensic document examiners George Throckmorton (left) and William Flynn. *Their discovery of the cracked ink cracked the case.*

Hoffmann's lawyers Ronald Yengich (left) and Bradley Rich. *Yengich knew that the Hoffmann case would be fought in the court of public opinion.*

Prosecutor Gerry D'Elia (top left). *Cynical and street smart, he was a child of the sixties, always humming a Beatles or Stones tune.*

Prosecutor Robert Stott (top right). *Bob Stott had an impressive record, and no one was more impressed with it than Bob Stott.*

Prosecutors (left to right) Gerry D'Elia, Ted Cannon, Robert Stott, Bud Ellett, and David Biggs. *Before they could fight the Hoffmann case, they had to stop fighting among themselves.*

Ron Yengich gesturing in the preliminary hearing, with Brad Rich seated to his right and Gerry D'Elia looking on. *Yengich was a short, fiery man with a Yosemite Sam mustache and an unscratchable itch for confrontation.*

Mark Hoffmann approaching the courthouse on crutches with his wife, Dorie. *Mark never allowed her in his basement workroom—and she never asked why.*

Shannon Flynn (left). *He may have looked like the Pillsbury Doughboy, but underneath he was Rambo.*

Lyn Jacobs (right). *He was what people in Utah called "flamboyant."*

Mark Hoffmann with his father, William. *On pleading guilty, Hoffmann asked to be sentenced immediately. A month of prison was easier to face than a month of his father.*

Hoffmann at the entrance to Point of the Mountain prison. *He got the same sentence as an unarmed nineteen-year-old who robbed a Der Wienerschnitzel and stole a car.*

returned, he was ready to talk. "You're right and I'm wrong," he apologized. "Sure I'm worried about money. I'm worried about bankruptcy, about the business. But the only thing that's important in life is you and the kids."

To show he meant it, he went out and rented three videos, one for each night of the long weekend, and every night, after the kids went to bed, they stayed up late and watched them together. And he never even reached for a book. Terri tried to remain level-headed about it but couldn't help feeling, in her bones, that this time was different. From now on, their life together would be what she had always known it could be.

If Mark Hofmann thought the holiday weekend would bring some relief from the pressure, he was wrong.

On Saturday morning, Brent Metcalfe tried to cash a $1,000 paycheck Mark had given him. He had waited for months to be paid and finally had to beg to get it, but kept telling himself he should be grateful for the job. Then the check bounced.

That night, Metcalfe set out for Hofmann's house to demand that Mark make the check good and pay him the rest of $1,700 he was owed. But his car broke down on the freeway and he had to phone his wife, Jill, to pick him up. With their daughter, Michala, the Metcalfes finally arrived at the Hofmann house on Marie Avenue only to find that Mark wasn't there. "He's with Shannon at his lawyer's office writing his will," Dorie told them. "He'll be right back."

When Metcalfe called the lawyer's office, however, no one answered.

Instead of waiting, he and Jill drove back to his stalled Ford Escort and tried, unsuccessfully, to revive it. Then they swung back by the Hofmann house one last time to see if Mark had returned. Preoccupied by the expense of repairing the Escort, Jill Metcalfe missed the turn onto 23rd East and was forced to turn around in a church parking lot half a block farther on. The lot was empty— except for one car parked all the way to one side, near some bushes. Metcalfe recognized it immediately: Mark Hofmann's Toyota MR2. Mark was sitting in the driver's seat.

Jill muttered under her breath, "This is psychic."

She pulled up next to the MR2, and Mark looked up. There was only one word for the look on his face: anguish. His eyes seemed "filled with stress," Jill thought. His forehead was creased—so strange for the baby-faced Hofmann. He looked "scary." It was definitely the look of a man who didn't want to talk, Jill thought, but Brent got out of the car and approached him fearlessly. He opened the door on the passenger side and climbed in.

Hofmann seemed startled. He took the papers he had been poring over and hastily turned them face down on the dashboard.

"Dorie mentioned that you had been working on your will." Metcalfe pointed at the papers.

Hofmann didn't respond. It was clear even to Metcalfe that he didn't want to talk about it.

"I got a death threat," he said. "There was a call about seven this morning. This voice said, 'You're gonna die. I'm gonna kill you.' "

Metcalfe didn't think to ask how this anonymous caller had been lucky enough to get Mark on the phone. Like everybody else, Metcalfe had tried dozens of times at every hour and never succeeded. It was the subject of black humor among Hofmann's associates: Mark never picked up the phone. Except this once, apparently.

Metcalfe had only one thing on his mind: money. Specifically, the cost of repairing the Escort and the pay Hofmann owed him. "Come on, we're friends, Mark. I don't want to be begging for my salary. I'm working and deserve to be paid. I shouldn't have to ask all the time. Look, if this is too stressful for you, I can go out and find another job."

Metcalfe could believe that Hofmann was having a cash-flow problem. Dorie was always complaining about how terrible Mark was with money. "He takes checks out of the checkbook, and I don't know how much they are," she had told him, "until it comes back in the statement. One month it's feast, and the next month it's famine. I go out and buy groceries for three months so if it's famine we'll at least have food."

Perhaps this was just one of those periods of famine, Metcalfe thought. Perhaps it was his financial situation, which he always kept so close to his chest, that he was going over when they surprised him.

If Hofmann was going over his financial picture that

night in the car, it was no wonder his face showed signs of stress. In the next few days, he would be expected to repay $455,155 to Wilding's group, $171,000 to First Interstate Bank, $20,000 to Shannon Flynn, $132,000 to Al Rust, $10,000 to Lyn Jacobs, $5,500 to Brent Ashworth, $170,000 to Schiller-Wapner, $109,000 to Ralph Bailey, $185,000 as a closing payment on the "marvelously livable" house in Cottonwood, and $65,000 in other miscellaneous debts, for a total of $1,322,655, plus, if he didn't pay the Wilding group by the 16th, penalties of $4,000 per day.

"If it would be easier, you know I can always go and get another job," Metcalfe offered sympathetically.

Hofmann seemed insulted by the suggestion. "With the kind of money I make," he scoffed, "a thousand dollars every couple of weeks doesn't make the slightest difference. I'll get a check to you tomorrow."

Monday morning, October 14, Hofmann called Wade Lillywhite, who was vacationing at his parents' house in California. His voice was frantic and far away.

"I have to sell that papyrus fragment from the Book of Abraham. The one we talked about before. I need the money right away, and I have to get one hundred thousand for it."

"Is it from the McLellin Collection?"

"Yes."

"I'm surprised that you're selling off pieces of that Collection." Lillywhite had seen Steve Christensen's reaction when he told him about Mark's double-dealing.

"The Church is getting most of it," Hofmann explained, "but there are a couple of pieces that I'm going to sell off because I need to raise some cash right away." Lillywhite said he would make some phone calls, and Hofmann promised to call him back later that afternoon.

It may have been a holiday for Lillywhite, but Tom Wilding and John Ashton were in Wilding's office at two that afternoon waiting for Mark Hofmann to show up. He arrived about 2:45—a bad start to an already difficult meeting.

Things quickly went from bad to worse.

First, Hofmann didn't have the additional collateral he had promised. He also hadn't brought with him the deed to his house or the titles to his vehicles, as he had agreed to do. He didn't have the payment on the outstanding balance. He didn't have the legal description of the house that Ashton had asked for, or the releases from Dorie and his parents (whose names were on the deed).

All he had were a couple of small checks, one for $10,000 and one for $20,000. Wilding earmarked them for the smaller investors. There wasn't much else he could do, except make Hofmann promise to bring the legal description and releases by Ashton's house later that night so he could prepare the documents.

Mark cheerfully agreed.

After the meeting, he called California. Lillywhite said he had found one person who might be interested in the papyrus but he wanted to find out more about it.

"Never mind," said Hofmann, eerily calm. "I've found another buyer for it." He did, however, have a page from the original manuscript of the *Book of Mormon* that he wanted to sell for $20,000. Lillywhite told him to come by Deseret Book at three on Wednesday.

That night, Brent Metcalfe visited Hofmann to drop off John Dart's most recent article in the *L.A. Times* on the Oliver Cowdery history. Jill and Michala stayed in the car while Brent and Mark spent fifteen minutes at the kitchen table, ignoring the commotion of Dorie's trying to get the kids ready for bed.

Suddenly, Hofmann ended the discussion. "I hate to rush off like this," he said, reaching for a coat, "but I've got an appointment that I've got to go to." As they left the house, Hofmann saw Jill waiting in the car. He went over and leaned in the window. "Gosh, if I'd known you were here I would have invited you in. I'm sorry. I'm in a rush tonight. I've got to go."

Brent couldn't help wondering why Mark Hofmann, a man now in his thirties, still wore that silly, worn-out high school letter jacket.

The next morning, October 15, Steve Christensen slept late for the first time in months. He lingered in bed until quarter past seven—late for him—and, to Terri's delight, stayed for breakfast. He finally got off about 7:45 but stopped at the Country Cousins store, next to McDonald's (where his boys were always clamoring to go), and bought two six-packs of Tab and a bag of mini-doughnuts.

Terri, who was always exhorting him to diet, wouldn't like it, but she couldn't expect him to change *everything* overnight.

About the same time Christensen left his house, Mark Hofmann called Brent Metcalfe. He sounded much more relaxed than the previous evening, Jill Metcalfe thought, as she handed the phone to Brent and rushed off to work. They chatted for half an hour, mostly about the *L.A. Times* article and the Cowdery history.

At 9:30, John Ashton was shocked to hear that Mark Hofmann had arrived. The meeting wasn't until eleven. It was heartening that he would come of his own volition, even if he only had more excuses to offer. Hofmann apologized for not dropping off the necessary papers the previous evening. He hadn't been able to get a legal description of the house yet.

Ashton got right to the point. He wanted to know if Mark would have any money for the 11 o'clock meeting. Mark said he was still working on it. "We really do have to have the funds today," Ashton insisted, *"and* the legal description of the house."

Parenthetically, Ashton mentioned that he had heard a report on the radio as he was driving to work, something about a bombing at the Judge Building.

"Yeah, I heard something about that too," Hofmann said, interested. "Has the name of the victim been released?"

"I haven't heard."

When Hofmann reappeared, on time again, for the 11 o'clock meeting, he was clearly upset. "Curt Bench told me that Steve Christensen was the person killed," he told Ashton. Ten minutes later, Tom Wilding came in. He, too, was surprised to see Hofmann there. He also thought it strange that at this hour he looked as if he had just showered and shaved.

"Our problem has taken a bizarre turn," Ashton told Wilding as soon as he walked in. "Have you heard on the news that there's been a bombing?"

"Yeah, I did."

"Well, Curt Bench said the person killed was Steve Christensen."

Wilding looked over at Hofmann. He was hyperventilating.

PART THREE

Lying for
the Lord

53 Janet McDermott arrived early at the Judge Building the morning of October 15, early enough to find a parking space just a few feet from the entrance. So early, in fact, on this slow-starting Tuesday after the Columbus Day weekend, that the door was still locked and she had to punch in a combination to let herself in. So early that the big lobby chandelier hadn't been turned on yet, the store windows inside were still dark, and both elevators sat idling on the ground floor. She took one to the sixth floor.

Off the elevator, she turned right and headed down the short, ancillary hallway she shared with a new tenant in the building, Steve Christensen. As she started to unlock her door on the right side of the hall, she noticed a package, wrapped in brown paper, lying in Christensen's doorway on the left. It seemed oddly placed—not lying flat, not leaning against the door, but standing bolt upright in the doorway. She would have liked to ignore it—she had come in at this ungodly hour to get an early start on the day and this package looked like an armful. But she and Steve *had* agreed that whoever arrived at the office first in the mornings would pick up the other's mail. And a deal was a deal.

She walked over and bent down to pick it up. That's odd, she thought: no stamps, no UPS or Express Mail labels. Besides, it's too early for a professional delivery. It must have been left here late last night. But the cleaning people usually put packages in the office if they find them outside at night. The address wasn't typed, it was hand-lettered with a black Magic Marker in big block letters: STEVE CHRISTENSEN. Not "Steven Christensen" or "Mr. Steven Christensen," just STEVE CHRISTENSEN. "This looks personal," McDermott said to herself: cookies maybe, or a present. "Maybe I better leave it here." At this hour in the morning, nobody would disturb it. If Steve hadn't picked it up by the time she went out for her first appointment at about eight, she would take it into her office.

At 7:55, she ran down to put more change in the parking meter. When she came back, she had just enough time to make a few more phone calls and throw some things in her briefcase before setting off for her appointment. As she opened the door into the hall, she caught a trailing glimpse of Steve Christensen walking toward his office.

She was just about to say something when she saw the sign on her door: TURN ON YOUR ANSWERING MACHINE. She was always forgetting to do that. In mock exasperation, she put her briefcase down again and marched back to the desk. The door closed slowly on its own. She picked up the receiver and dialed 7 and 2, the code that would automatically connect her answering service. It was always a long, frustrating wait for the dial tone and the seven-digit number that would indicate the service had clicked in.

Then she heard a loud bang in the hall. It sounded like a rifleshot, only louder. The sound came from the hall but it ricocheted all around her. She thought something had happened in the room itself, but she didn't know what. She didn't see the nails that exploded through the door and lodged in her walls. She didn't see the nail that shattered the picture frame on her wall. She didn't see the nail that shot past her leg, grazing the skin and drawing blood, so quickly, so razorlike, that she didn't feel the wound until later. All she registered was the tremendous force of the explosion.

She ducked behind the desk and tried to tame her wild thoughts. Did the phone line explode? Were there men with rifles in the hall? Then she heard a sound in the hallway, a whimpering, like the crying of a child. Oh, my God, she thought, a little girl has been shot!

And the gunmen were still out there.

Then the phone began to beep loudly and she thought they would hear it. They would know she was in there and come after her!

Then she smelled sparks and fire. It was a fire! She grabbed her briefcase and coat and ran out the door.

Down the hall, toward Christensen's office, there was nothing but dust and debris. She could see his door, but it wasn't in the right place. It had been blown off its hinges. Then she saw him. All she could see was blood: his chest, his legs, nothing but blood.

She heard the crying again. It was coming from him, only now it sounded more like the moaning of a man. She moaned herself, involuntarily. The sight of him transfixed her.

At the far end of the corridor, people had begun to come out of their offices. She yelled at them, "Get an ambulance! Someone is dying!"

Christensen's partner, Randy Rigby, wasn't sure he would make it on time to their 8 o'clock meeting that morning. Like everyone else, he had been a little slow getting started after the holiday, and then he had to make a detour to his old office at CFS to pick up some things. He would have made it easily, with five minutes to spare, if he had found a legal parking space in front of the Judge Building. But he didn't, and he had too many parking violations to chance an illegal spot. So he would be a few minutes late. Steve would understand.

Rigby had spoken to him just the night before. He knew Steve was on the verge of closing a major documents deal. "How is it going?" he had asked.

"I've been going solid until just now," Steve had said, "working on the McLellin project. It looks like it's finally gonna happen Wednesday.."

And they talked about their new business venture. "Why don't we get together at eight tomorrow morning and go over things," he had suggested, "just kind of brief each other on where we're at, preparing for the future. Tomorrow looks like a pretty laid-back day."

When Rigby heard the sirens and saw the lights of the police cars, he thought it was probably a fire, but a policeman in the street told him no. Just in case, he took the stairs instead of the elevator to the sixth floor. There, amid the rubble of wall board and ceiling tile, the first thing he noticed was a can of Tab. Had the refrigerator exploded? Steve usually stopped at the convenience store in Centerville to pick up a sack of doughnuts and some pop so they could "chow down" on junk food during their morning meetings. His eating habits were atrocious. Rigby had never realized that a refrigerator could blow up.

Then he heard Janet McDermott shouting. "Steve has been hurt! Don't go down the hallway!" A policeman appeared out of nowhere and told him to move out of the way.

"I'm Steve's partner," Rigby said, suddenly feeling dizzy. "I had an 8 o'clock meeting with Steve. That's our office."

"Good God," said the cop. "What kind of business were you guys in?"

Rigby tried to get past the police to give Christensen a priesthood blessing, the Mormon last rites, but the firemen arrived and ordered everybody out of the building. They feared there might be more bombs.

In the lobby, Rigby caught up to Janet McDermott. "Is it Steve?" He had to know.

"I'm not sure."

"Is he all right?"

"I'm not sure. I heard him moan."

"How can this happen?" he said, pacing distractedly in a three-foot square. "This happens in New York, L.A., *not Salt Lake City*."

"Has his family been notified?" he asked a policeman.

"It will all be taken care of."

That wasn't good enough. He went to the nearby office of a friend and called Terri Christensen. There was no answer. Then he called Steve's father. "Mac, a bomb's gone off in our office, and I'm not sure if it's Steve—he's either critically injured or he could be dead."

Mac controlled himself. "Please let me know if you hear anything," he finally said and hung up.

Then Rigby called his wife to tell her he was all right.

Then he called Hugh Pinnock. Steve had been keeping Rigby informed about the McLellin Collection, and had even invited him to become a partner in the document searches the Church had commissioned him to undertake. "Hugh. You don't know me. I'm Randy Rigby, Steve Christensen's business partner. But a bomb has just gone off in our office, and Steve Christensen has either been critically injured or is dead."

There was a silence at the other end of the phone.

Then, in an even voice, "I appreciate knowing that. But I'm sure you have to know that this has something to do with the CFS problem."

What a strange reaction, Rigby thought.

54

As soon as he hung up the phone with Randy Rigby, Mac Christensen burst into tears. In the middle of the store that he ran like a Prussian military school, the huge man sobbed inconsolably. When he told his son Scott the news, he refused to believe it. "I want to see the body for myself," he said.

Scott went first to the police station, then to the Judge Building, but they wouldn't let him up to the sixth floor. They said they already had positive identification. He still refused to believe it until he saw the body.

Mr. Mac called a friend to take him to Terri's house.

Terri Christensen was still in the shower when the phone started ringing. In the seventh month of her pregnancy, she found everything took longer than it used to. The first call she picked up was from a friend who had heard something about a bombing in the Judge Building. One fatality. Terri brushed it off. "Steve had a meeting somewhere this morning at eight," she explained. "He wasn't in his office. There's no need to come over. It can't be him." Besides, she had to go to the dentist.

Just to put her mind at rest, though, she called Steve's office. She heard his voice, but it was only the answering machine: "Hello. You've reached the offices of Steve Christensen. . . ." That was strange, she thought, for the machine to be on this late. So she called Randy Rigby's wife—she knew Randy was Steve's 8 o'clock appointment. Sandra Rigby answered the phone but was sobbing too hard to say anything clearly. All Terri could understand was: "It's not Steve. It's not Steve."

A sense of panic began to creep over her, but she

fought it. She called Joan Christensen, Steve's mother. "I talked to Mac, and he says he's on his way home," was all she could say.

"I'm on my way there too," Terri said. "I don't want to be alone."

As she walked out the door, another friend was walking up the sidewalk, sobbing hard. She had come with a message, but was crying too hard to give it. By now, she didn't need to.

At Steve's parents' house in Bountiful, Terri sat perfectly still and quiet. She knew that if she moved or spoke a word, everything would come apart. Finally, she felt strong enough to call her parents in Montana, but they had already heard the news and were packing for the long drive to Salt Lake City. The planes were too slow for their grief.

Someone offered to get Terri's sons out of school immediately so they could be told by a family member. Someone else called her obstetrician to get some Valium for her. They were beginning to worry: she still hadn't cried. She just lay there on the couch, staring at the ceiling. "What are you feeling?" someone ventured.

"I don't want to feel," she answered. "I'm too afraid to feel." Then, to herself, "I can't have this baby alone. Why do I have to be pregnant?"

Finally, when no one expected it, she let out a terrible sound, a long, heart-stopping shriek.

Joan Christensen held out until later that evening when Don Tanner, a friend of Steve's, came to pick up his wife. He parked his car in front and walked up to the door. At that moment, Joan looked out the window and saw Tanner's dark hair and plaid shirt—the kind that Steve favored—and thought it *was* Steve, walking up to greet her. Then she realized her mistake. After hours of grim poise and brave optimism, Joan burst into tears and fell into the arms of her son Scott.

55

Tom Wilding had a different reaction to the news.

"Does this totally destroy our chances of this sale going through?" he asked.

If Hofmann thought the bombings might give him a temporary respite from his many creditors, he was badly mistaken.

Knowing that Hofmann and Christensen were friends, Wilding reminded himself to be sensitive to Mark's feelings. But as far as he was concerned, the bombing didn't change a thing. After all, he was responsible to his investors. He wanted the $185,000 that Christensen was supposed to pay Hofmann, and he wanted it now. He wasn't going to let anything, even a bombing, interfere with the transaction.

Hofmann was surprisingly cooperative. "I still think there's a good chance we can put it together. I'll just have to find a new agent to replace Steve in the deal." He said he had one in mind but didn't want to give them the name. John Ashton assumed it was Hugh Pinnock.

"Do you want to use my phone?" Wilding offered, trying not so subtly to convey a sense of undiminished urgency.

"No," said Hofmann. "I'll just use the phone in my car." He agreed to return at four, when Ashton would have ready the documents transferring Hofmann's house to HWJ, Wilding's investor group. Bombing or no bombing, they still wanted their money.

Bombing or no bombing, the Church still wanted the McLellin Collection.

But from the moment Mark Hofmann called that morning with the news of Steve Christensen's death, Hugh Pinnock knew it wasn't going to be easy. He wondered if the bombing might have been related to the Salamander

267

Letter and, by extension, the McLellin Collection, but Hofmann didn't think so. His theory was that it was CFS-related, a theory that Pinnock passed on to a puzzled Randy Rigby when he called a few minutes later. It was a remarkable piece of guesswork on Hofmann's part—the bomb at Gary Sheets's house hadn't gone off yet.

On Hofmann's heels, David Sorensen called. David West had been waiting for Hofmann to appear with the Collection at ten when he heard the news and called Sorensen in Nova Scotia. The national media hadn't yet picked up the story. "There's been an explosion, and Steve Christensen was blown up. The news people are starting to talk about the Salamander Letter. Maybe this is related to that in some way." West and Sorensen had agreed that it probably wasn't, but Sorensen wanted some reassurance from the Church. Pinnock told him that Hofmann had called and said he was still willing to go through with the deal. The meeting was reset for ten the next morning. Relieved, Sorensen called West to give him the new time and reassure him. "Hofmann will bring in all the stuff to you tomorrow."

Even though West had heard about the Sheets bombing in the interim, and accepted it as evidence that the bombings were CFS-related, he was still uneasy. "Well, Dave, I really don't know," he told Sorensen. "I'm a little bit nervous, but okay, we'll go ahead. Except that now we've got to hire somebody—we've got to get some expert in here to really look this stuff over. I don't know who to hire." Sorensen said he would check it out, but by the time he got back to Pinnock that morning, Pinnock had left the office to speak at a funeral.

While there, Pinnock learned that the second bombing victim was Kathy Sheets, whom he had known since college. Whatever the shock, the news also had to be a relief: it proved positively that the bombings weren't documents related. He went from the funeral to the home of David Burton, Gary Sheets's stake president, to console his old frat brother. Sheets, who had heard the theory that the bombings were documents related, asked him, "What do you know about Mark Hofmann?" Without flinching, Pinnock replied, "Nothing." A few minutes later, however, Jimmy Sheets overheard him on Burton's phone trying frantically to get ahold of Hofmann.

Hofmann, in fact, had gone to the First Presidency

building to find Pinnock. When Dallin Oaks found out Hofmann was in the building, he had him brought to his office. Oaks, one of the Twelve Apostles, expresident of B.Y.U., and a former justice of the Utah Supreme Court, was a shrewd lawyer and sophisticated tactician.

He began by telling Hofmann, whom he was meeting for the first time, that Pinnock had kept him informed of the McLellin Collection and of his efforts to obtain it. In other words, he could speak freely. What he *didn't* say was that he, Hinckley, and Pinnock had already concluded that Hofmann was a crook, trying in some as yet unknown way to hoodwink the Church.

Hofmann said he feared the police would question him about the Collection and he wanted to know what he should say. The message was clear. If the Church wanted him to keep quiet about the Collection, he would.

But Oaks wasn't about to be drawn into Hofmann's scheme, whatever it was. "Why would the police want to question you," he asked, if the bombings are, in fact, related to CFS? "Their business activities don't have anything to do with you, do they?"

Hofmann said they didn't.

Oaks pressed. Did Hofmann have any reason to suspect that the bombings had something to do with his documents business with Christensen?

Hofmann said no.

"Do you know anyone in your documents business who would enforce his contracts with a bomb?"

"No."

"Well, then," said Oaks triumphantly, "what do you have to worry about? The police probably won't question you, and if they do, just tell them the truth."

Oaks asked if he was planning to go ahead with the closing on the McLellin Collection the next day.

Hofmann said yes.

It was a perfect cross-examination. No open questions, no unnecessary information from the witness, no unexpected bombshells. And, on Oaks's part, complete deniability. If Hofmann had admitted wrongdoing, Oaks would have been forced either to go to the police himself or become an accomplice. This way, he was covered. He wrote up his notes of the conversation and put them away. He must have sensed that they might be needed soon, even if he didn't yet know for what.

Hofmann ran into Pinnock in the Church Office Building parking lot. He told him about the meeting with Oaks and said he was flying to New York the next day to get money to pay off the loan at First Interstate Bank. "It's fortunate that the bombings were related to Steve's business," said Pinnock. By now it had become a kind of incantation. Hofmann didn't respond. He just sat in his car and stared straight ahead.

Pinnock met immediately with Oaks, then called David Sorensen, who had phoned earlier to find out who could take Christensen's place at the meeting the next morning. Pinnock gave him a list of names but his preference was Don Schmidt, the former Church archivist who was now retired and living in Provo. Sorensen relayed the name to West, and West called Schmidt. "Can I hire you to look at some documents?—we've got some historical documents." Schmidt agreed to be there at ten the next morning.

Finally, Pinnock and Oaks met with Gordon Hinckley. By now, Pinnock was distraught. Despite his best efforts, the deal for the Collection seemed to be unraveling. Christensen was dead, Sorensen was nervous, and no one knew what Mark Hofmann was up to. No one knew if he would even show up at ten the next morning.

In the meantime, Pinnock and the others told themselves again that the bombings were related to CFS, not the documents. If that's what they had to believe to keep this deal together, if that's what they had to believe to keep the police and the press away, if that's what they had to believe to ensure that the McLellin Collection would find its way into safe hands, then that's what they would believe. They had certainly believed far more improbable explanations to reap far more intangible rewards.

An hour after leaving the First Presidency building, Hofmann returned to the office of Wilding's lawyer, John Ashton, at 79 South Main Street. Ashton presented him with the documents to be signed by his parents, whose names were on the title to the house. But Hofmann wanted to do it a different way. He wanted Ashton to prepare a deed conveying the house from his parents to Mark and Dorie, then he and Dorie would sign the trust deed over to Wilding's investor group. He was willing to come back later when the revised papers were ready.

But Ashton didn't want even one more delay. He told Mark to wait while he redrafted the documents.

During the wait, Hofmann tried several times to reach Hugh Pinnock. Each time he got a secretary: "Hello. This is Mark Hofmann, and I need to talk with Elder Pinnock. It's very important. No, I don't want to leave a message. I'll call back later."

Pinnock was with Oaks in Gordon Hinckley's office trying to figure out what to do about Mark Hofmann.

"Why are you calling Pinnock?" Ashton asked after the second or third try.

"He's a good friend of mine," said Hofmann.

When the documents were ready, Ashton told Mark to get notarized signatures from his parents and from Dorie and to bring the documents back the next morning.

"No problem," said Hofmann.

When he got back into his car, he tore the documents up and threw them on the floor.

56

October 15 also happened to be the day of the closing on the house in Cottonwood. Starting at one, Connie Smith and her clients waited at the Western States Title Co. office for the Hofmanns to arrive—and waited and waited. "I can't find Mark," Carl Lundquist said when Smith called his office.

The seller, meanwhile, was having a fit. "Connie, we've had an uneasy feeling about this all along," she huffed. "Oh, I am *not* impressed! I am not impressed with this."

Finally, Lundquist called with the explanation. "The reason that Mark isn't there is that he was supposed to have picked up $200,000 from Steve Christensen this morning. If he had been five minutes earlier, it would have worked, but Christensen was blown up and killed. Mark is somewhere in total shock, because Christensen has been killed, and because he's convinced that the bombing was meant for him."

"Now what?" Smith asked, cool as usual.

"Mark is flying to New York, where he will get fifty thousand, which he will put down in good faith to keep this contract together. He'll be back on Thursday. He wants the house and he will have the money, but there will be a delay now, because the money is going to have to come from overseas and there will be a thirteen-day delay while the check is cleared. Find out if the seller is willing to wait."

The seller said she "just wanted to forget the whole thing" but asked Smith's advice.

"We don't have another buyer," Smith told her, "so let's wait. Let's go for it."

Carl Lundquist called again. "We'll have fifty thousand, if your client will close on that."

"Fifty thousand is nothing to sneeze at," Smith told her client. "Take it. If he doesn't come through, that's good wages. If it takes you a year to reclaim the house, that's good wages for a year."

So they reset the closing for the next day, the 16th.

Smith didn't know whether to believe Hofmann's story. She was too old, she told herself, not to believe crazy things.

That evening, local television stations devoted their news programs to weather, B.Y.U. sports, and the bombings. KSL, the Church-owned CBS affiliate, gave equal time to the CFS explanation and the Salamander Letter.

Jeff Simmonds, the Utah State archivist, and his wife, Jeannie, were watching the KSL newscast in their breakfast room. When it was over, Simmonds turned off the set. "Well, by God, if it is the Salamander Letter, Mark will blow up tomorrow."

Jeannie looked at him. "If he didn't do it."

Simmonds had always known that his wife loathed Hofmann. "Ah, you're crazy," he said.

Scott Christensen still had to see his brother's body. It wasn't that he held out hope that there had been some awful mistake. He just had to see for himself. So he headed for the funeral home on Main Street in Bountiful.

He vaguely knew two of the Russon brothers who ran the mortuary. "Where's my brother Steve at?" Scott asked the one who answered the door. They led him to the room where Steve's body was laid out on a table covered by a translucent plastic sheet. There were no cosmetics. They hadn't yet covered the wounds, although they had sewn him back together. Scott took what meager solace he could in that. "At least he survived the blast in one piece," he told himself.

Gretchen Sheets, Kathy's daughter, had been in school when the policeman came to get her. "Gretchen," he said, "there's somebody waiting outside." But when they got outside, his story changed. "You need to come with me. There's been an accident at your house."

She begged him to tell her what had happened, but he wouldn't. So she got her books and drove with him to the police station. "Maybe they're bringing me in for a traffic ticket," she told herself, although she knew they weren't. She stared out the window of the police car and let the sense of shock slowly envelop her. She remembered the recurrent nightmare she used to have in high school. In it, her parents had died and a policeman came and got her out of school. When he told her the news, she screamed and pounded on the windows. She had written about the dream in her journal and talked about it with her friends, but after she started college, it went away. She figured it must have been just a high school dream.

At the police station, she saw her boyfriend's parents. She saw her sister's car and her father's car. Gary met her in the parking lot and told her the news. But she didn't scream or pound on the windows. She simply fell to the ground and wept. "I felt like someone had taken the bones from my body," she said later.

Jimmy Sheets, the quiet one, the athletic youngster with the straight-A report card, the apple of his mother's eye, was the one who screamed and pounded on the windows.

Later that evening, Kathy's friend, Cherie Bridge, walked over to the empty Sheets house to find a better photograph of Kathy. The one the police had, the one they had released to the press, showed her with glasses and wasn't very flattering. Kathy would have hated it. Cherie wanted the press to have a picture that did her justice.

Still later, Cherie's husband, Mike, a strong, solid, handsome man, father of seven, brought a pail of water and a brush over to the Sheets house. That afternoon, Gretchen had come back to pick up some things and had to walk past the place where it had happened, past the blackened wood and the patches of blood. Everyone agreed that someone needed to clean it up but no one felt strong enough. So they picked Mike. He was the strongest one. So he took his pail and brush and knelt down on the blackened catwalk and cleaned the stains of blood and sobbed the whole time.

After a day of trying, Brent Metcalfe reached Mark Hofmann that night.

"Wow," Mark said, "can you believe what's happening?"

"No. God. It's bad enough to kill Steve, somebody of his caliber," said Metcalfe, "but I can't understand how anybody could do that to his kids."

There was a long pause at the other end of the line.

"You've got to tell the police that you got this death threat," Metcalfe continued. This was the message he had been trying to get through to Mark all day. "If you don't tell the police, I will."

Hofmann seemed strangely puzzled. "Don't you feel like you can rest more comfortably tonight," he asked, "since it seems like this is all about Steve's business, Gary Sheets and the CFS thing?"

Metcalfe was taken aback. "Mark, don't you realize that Gary was the primary funder behind the research project on the Salamander Letter?"

Again, complete silence on the other end. "No, I didn't," he finally said, suddenly agitated. "Wow! I guess we can't rest easier."

57 The next morning, Wednesday, October 16, Tom Wilding waited for Mark Hofmann to call. When he didn't, Wilding called Dorie at her parents' house. She sounded distant and nervous. She didn't know where Mark was. He had driven off early that morning and, as usual, told her nothing. The best Wilding could do was leave a message for Mark to call him. For good measure, he called Bill and Lu Hofmann's house and left another message. He didn't care who knew: he wanted his money.

John Ashton, too, spent the morning waiting, waiting for Hofmann to deliver the signed papers on his house. He never did.

Hugh Pinnock couldn't find Hofmann either. When he arrived that morning, however, there was a message from Dorie. She had called at 8:15 to say that Mark "was going to see some other people" and would close the deal on the McLellin Collection at two that afternoon instead of ten that morning as originally planned. Another delay. It was a bad way to start the day.

Pinnock called David West about 9:30 to let him know that Hofmann wouldn't be there until two. That meant West would have to rearrange his afternoon appointments, even though Don Schmidt was already on his way from Provo. A thoughtful attorney, and a cautious man, West liked this deal less and less. With all the bombs going off and one of the parties already dead, he would have liked to call the whole thing off. But he called Sorensen and told him he would do whatever was necessary to get the job done. "Whatever we're gonna do," he told himself after hanging up, "let's just get it over with."

Don Schmidt arrived as promised at ten, and West asked him if he could come back at two.

"That would be okay. I'll just kind of stick around," said Schmidt, then thought to ask, "What is it that I'll be looking at?"

"Something called the McLellin Collection," said West. "Someone named Mark Hofmann has it."

Schmidt recognized that name. "Oh, yeah, I know Mark Hofmann, and I know the McLellin Collection. I'll be happy to wait around."

Schmidt returned promptly at two, and he and West adjourned to the tufted leather chairs of the conference room to wait for Hofmann to arrive with what West called "the goodies." From the picture window, they could see beyond the tall white tower of the Commercial Security Finance Building to the Temple and the Tabernacle.

And they waited. Schmidt filled the time by telling West what he knew about Hofmann. Then they waited some more. West's uneasiness returned. He wondered if perhaps there had been some mix-up on the time. After all, he hadn't spoken directly to Hofmann. He called Sorensen in Nova Scotia. "Dave, are you sure that we had an appointment at two?"

Sorensen was sure. "I thought you guys would probably have this deal all closed by now," he said.

"No. We haven't seen him. We haven't heard from anybody or gotten any calls. We're just sitting here waiting and wondering if maybe we might have gotten the wrong word or something on the appointment time."

"Well, I don't know any more about it."

But he could sure as hell find out. Like West, he had every reason to be fed up with the endless complications of a deal that had been undertaken solely as a favor for the Church. He called Hugh Pinnock, but Pinnock was out of the office, so he voiced his concerns to Dallin Oaks. Oaks turned around and called Pinnock. Just as he had the day before at Burton's house, Pinnock launched into a frantic series of phone calls in search of the elusive documents dealer. He called every number Mark had ever given him. Finally, at 2:45, he reached Dorie.

"Where is Mark?" he demanded. "Mark's supposed to be in West's office, and he isn't there. They're waiting for him impatiently." But Dorie still didn't know where he was. All she knew was that Shannon Flynn was there, at her parents' house, also looking for Mark.

Everybody, it seemed, was looking for Mark.

Within minutes of Pinnock's call, West and Schmidt heard police sirens breaking the serenity of Temple Square. West guessed immediately it was another bombing. He turned on a radio and heard a newsman saying that there had been an explosion on North Temple. Somebody had been blown up in a car.

West had a feeling he knew who it was—and that somehow the deal was off.

58 Driving back to his house in Bountiful, Brent Metcalfe remembered the strange conversation he had had with Hofmann the night before.

"Have you seen the drawing yet?" he had asked, referring to the police composite drawing of the bomber. Apparently several people had seen a man walking into the Judge Building early that morning with a package in his arms. They had given their descriptions to the police.

"Have you seen the drawing yet?"

Mark seemed very interested. "No, I haven't. Have you?"

"No. I was just wondering if it's come out yet."

"I don't think it's been released yet."

There was nothing strange about it, Metcalfe convinced himself. Mark seemed calm—too calm, in fact. Calmer than Metcalfe, certainly, who had packed his family up and taken them to his parents' house for the night.

Later that day, after stopping by Hofmann's house and finding it empty, Metcalfe called *Tribune* reporter Dawn Tracy about an AP article on the previous day's bombings that had quoted him. While they were on the phone, Tracy told him to hold: a story was coming over the wire. There had been a *third* bombing over by Deseret Gym. A car had blown up.

Metcalfe panicked.

"What kind of car was it?"

"It was a Toyota MR2."

"What color?"

Tracy left the line to check. A few seconds later: "It's blue."

"I've got to get right over there," Metcalfe cried and hung up the phone. He'd never driven faster than he did on the way to the Deseret Gym. He didn't think about where he was parking. He just stopped and jumped out.

When he saw the car, his knees turned to jelly. He began losing the feeling in his arms. It sat on the opposite side of the street from the gymnasium, near a low concrete wall that skirted the base of a tall luxury apartment complex—the Zion Summit. The road climbed steeply on that section of 200 North, just to the west of Main Street, so the scene was laid out like a tableau on a raked stage, much easier to see from a distance. The car itself was a blackened shell, the roof mangled, the insides soaking wet from a relentless dousing by an overzealous fireman. Policemen, uniformed and ununiformed, stooped beside it, hovered over it, poked inside it, and conversed in small knots. The only thing Metcalfe could recognize was the still-blue front end, strangely untouched by the blast and fire. To the left of the wreck, in the street, he could see what looked like bloodstains. If Mark was still alive, he was lucky. Metcalfe asked a policeman and was told the ambulance had just left.

He told the policeman, "I'm Brent Metcalfe. I think I know the owner of that car."

The police already knew who he was. "We need to take you into protective custody," said a detective. "Your life is in danger."

Connie Smith heard the sirens from inside her silver BMW as it sat in a parking lot at the Triad Center, a third of a mile from the Deseret Gym. A second later, a team of KSL reporters scrambled from the building and jumped into trucks, cars, and camera vans.

When her client heard that there had been an explosion near the Deseret Gym, he jumped out of the car and hitched a ride with one of the news vans, so Smith headed toward her office in Cottonwood, eager to beat the inevitable police barricades and rubbernecking traffic jams.

When she walked into the office, a chorus of voices greeted her: "No closing tomorrow."

"What?"

"Mark Hofmann was just blown up in his car. He's not dead, but we won't be having a closing."

The next day, Carl Lundquist called and said, "Mark still wants the house. Just sit tight." No matter what the police were saying, his friend Hofmann wasn't guilty of the bombings.

The seller wasn't so sure.

When Smith asked her what they should do about the earnest money, she said firmly, "If he's guilty, I am *not* going to give it back."

At about three, Jeff Simmonds was in his office when both of the Utah State archive's phones rang at once. One call was from his mother, the other from a friend, both saying that KSL had just broken into its program to announce that Mark Hofmann had been blown up in a third bombing. Stunned, his staff gathered around a radio for more news. "My God," said Simmonds. "If they're blowing people up who said something about the Salamander Letter, then I'm in trouble because I have said as much as anybody in the state."

He went into his private office and called Sandra Tanner. "Have you heard the news?"

She certainly had. "I called the police and they said that Hofmann himself was the bomber and he was in the hospital."

"Do you buy that?" Simmonds certainly didn't.

"Well," said Sandra. "Just don't pick up any brown packages."

When David West heard the news that Mark Hofmann was the victim in the third bombing, he immediately called David Sorensen. "Dave," he said, the strain of the last few days obvious in his voice. "I have absolutely no idea what's going on. I really don't. But it's time you and I get out of it, whatever it is. We don't want to have any more to do with it."

Sorensen agreed. "Absolutely."

When he went home that night, West got in his car and said to himself, "This is pretty darn scary stuff." Then he gritted his teeth and turned the key.

59

After the third bombing, everyone panicked. But no one panicked the way Hugh Pinnock panicked. No one had more to lose. In two days, his seemingly brilliant stroke to ingratiate himself with the Brethren by bringing the McLellin Collection discreetly under the Church's aegis had backfired—backfired spectacularly, backfired lethally, and, worst of all, backfired publicly. Two people were dead, one seriously injured, and the Collection was *still* out there. There had always been a danger that it would fall into enemy hands (i.e., public hands), now there was a virtual certainty. With police and press snooping around in the affairs of Christensen and Hofmann, it was only a matter of days, perhaps hours, before the details of the transaction, the Church's involvement, and Hugh Pinnock's involvement showed up on the evening news. And *that,* more than the deaths, would be the end of Hugh Pinnock in the LDS Church.

"Poor Hugh," Gary Sheets later lamented. "If it hadn't been for all this, he would have become an Apostle."

And Pinnock wasn't the only one whose position in the Celestial Kingdom was on the line. Everybody, from Hinckley on down, who had been involved with Hofmann remembered what happened to Henry D. Moyle.

Soon after Moyle was brought into the First Presidency as a counselor by David McKay in McKay's dotage, he began to think he ran the show. As McKay floated in and out of senility, and in and out of hospitals, "Money Man" Moyle took more and more of the Prophet's authority to himself. He decided, for instance, to build the giant twenty-eight-story Church Office Building. The Twelve opposed the idea, but Moyle went ahead with it anyway, and with other controversial projects as well.

Needless to say, the Twelve found such behavior unsuitable. Moyle hadn't come up through the ranks; he hadn't paid his dues in some remote, thankless outpost like the Bolivian mission. And here he was, telling the Council of the Twelve what to do. Eventually, when they couldn't take it any longer, they torpedoed him. Not publicly, of course. They didn't even announce his demotion in the *Church News*. Citing his health problems, they simply yanked McKay's authority, and with it, Moyle's. When they signed the checks, nothing else mattered. Stunned, Moyle slipped off to Florida for an "extended vacation" and obligingly died.

It was a sobering lesson, even for someone as powerful as Gordon Hinckley, who was on the Council when Moyle met his end. "You have no idea what it means to have that kind of position taken away from you," says a Church insider. "In the Mormon Church, a man's righteousness is inextricably tied to his rank in the Church. The higher up you are, the more righteous you are, the closer you are to God. If, all of a sudden, your position is taken away, it's worse than a demotion in any corporation, it's worse than a demotion in the Soviet Union—because they don't believe in God. They just have to worry about getting shot. In the Mormon Church, it means your eternal life is affected."

It must have been fear for his eternal life that prompted Pinnock to tell Gary Sheets that he knew nothing about Mark Hofmann. And it must have been the same fear that brought him to Steve Christensen's house the day after the bombings. He told Terri that he had come to "collect" Steve's confidential papers on the McLellin Collection. After all, the transaction was a "private matter," and therefore all materials relating to it should be kept under "Church control."

And it must have been his eternal life that was on his mind when Police Detective Don Bell interviewed him at 1:12 in the afternoon on October 17, the day after the bomb exploded in Hofmann's car.

"Elder Pinnock, this is the deal," Bell began, notebook in hand. "This is a homicide investigation. Do you know Mr. Hofmann?"

Pinnock paused and reflected a moment. "No, I don't believe I do."

60

Don Bell, a sixteen-year veteran of the Salt Lake City Police Department, was already in a bad mood. When it was decided that Pinnock had to be interviewed, one of the Mormon officers in the department had suggested that it be done with kid gloves. "These people are different," he said. "We have to treat them differently." Bell shot back, "This is a homicide investigation. We have people to talk to, we *talk* to them. We don't care if they're presidents of corporations, we don't care if they're ditch diggers." By itself, that exchange was enough to set him on edge. Then he called Pinnock's secretary.

"I'm sorry. Elder Pinnock's in the Temple."

"How long will he be there?"

"I don't know. Who is calling?"

"*This* is who is calling. I need to talk to him." The suggestion that Pinnock be given deferential treatment had riled him.

"Is there anything we can do for you?"

"No, there isn't. I need to talk to him."

Five minutes later, Bell's phone rang. But it wasn't Pinnock, it was Martell Bird, the head of Church Security. "Why don't you give me the message for Elder Pinnock," he suggested.

Bell was really feeling the fire now. "Because I don't *want* to give you the message. It has nothing to do with you. I want to talk to *him*. I can fit it around his schedule, if necessary. I'm sure he's busy. So am I. But I need to talk to him. If we have to do it at night, that's all right." He paused. Clearly, this guy needed a shove. "Maybe the easiest thing to do is to get an investigative subpoena and have it served."

He could hear Bird jump on the other end of the line. "Hold on! We don't need to do that."

Twenty minutes later, Pinnock called. "I have the whole afternoon free," he said in his most unctuous voice. "I can see you any time you want."

"How about right now?"

"Beautiful."

(As Bell drove over to the First Presidency building, a delegation from Church Security, headed by Martell Bird, was paying a visit to Bell's superior, Police Chief Bud Willoughby, to let him know what they thought of Detective Don Bell's manners.)

Bell already knew from an interview at the First Interstate Bank that Pinnock had arranged a loan for Mark Hofmann. Now Pinnock claimed he didn't know Hofmann. Bell choked back his astonishment and tried again. "Do you know anything about the McLellin Collection and this man who was trying to sell it?"

"Well, wait a minute," said Pinnock, apparently catching the look on Bell's face. "I think I do."

Somebody was lying, thought Bell, either the people at First Interstate Bank or Hugh Pinnock. Bell laid bets it was Pinnock. Down at the Metropolitan Hall of Justice, that bet would have been worth a lot. In sixteen years as a policeman, Bell had earned a reputation as one of the best, if not *the* best interviewer, in the department. It was Bell who had cracked Arthur Gary Bishop, extracting, within twenty-four hours, confessions to a wave of murders of young boys that had paralyzed the city. As an interviewer, he was a legend. He certainly knew when he was being fed a line.

"The McLellin Collection?" Pinnock fumbled with the pronunciation and mused another moment. "I think I remember something about that. There was a guy who came here. Now, I know nothing about him myself, but I remember that some guy came in and said something about a collection. And I remember having to get up and walk down the hall and go into Elder Oaks's office. And I asked Elder Oaks, 'Are we interested in a "McLellin Collection"' or some kind of collection?' And he said, 'No. We're not buying anything. If the guy wants to donate something, that's fine.' And I came back and told the guy, 'If you want to donate something, that's fine.' "

Bell could hardly contain himself. Lies, especially when they came in great clumps like this, could be very entertaining. "You know," he said, "we have some information that Mr. Hofmann met with President Hinckley."

Pinnock leaned back in his chair, put his feet up on the desk, and brought his hands together in prayer position. "You have to understand something," he began, summoning up all of the sanctimonious sonorities of his most patronizing tone. "People come into this building all the time. Then they leave this building, and they go and they talk to their friends. And they say, 'We've been down there visiting the First Presidency of the Church.' Or, 'We've been visiting President Hinckley.'

"This is sort of what my job is. You see, the First Presidency of the Church doesn't have the time to just listen to people who come in off the street. So they steer the people in to me and I listen to their concerns, and I'm nice to them. Then, when they leave the building, they often go say they've been meeting with President Hinckley or something. Nine times out of ten, they've just seen somebody low down on the totempole like me."

Bell had been raised a Mormon, so he knew that was true. Not just anybody could walk into the offices of the First Presidency. Perhaps Hofmann had been bragging about the visits with Hinckley. But First Interstate wasn't bragging about the $185,000 loan. Bell had held the loan application in his own hands. There was no doubt in Bell's mind: Hofmann was lying, but so was Hugh Pinnock.

"I'm afraid that's about it," Pinnock concluded. "I wish I could give you more help. But I'm sure President Hinckley has never met this man. The whole situation is very sad. Isn't it awful? In fact, I did know Steve Christensen slightly. I was friends with Gary Sheets in college, and, of course, I know Mr. Mac."

Bell pursued the subject of Steve Christensen. Pinnock said that Steve had been involved in arranging a donation of "some documents" to the Church just before his death. The donor was a private collector in Canada, and Steve was supposed to authenticate the documents.

"What kind of documents?" Bell pressed.

"Oh, some letters from Joseph Smith, something like that. Al Rust of Rust's Coin Store was somehow involved. I believe he had put up some money on some of the documents. The documents were supposed to have been donated the day Steve was killed."

Bell knew backtracking when he heard it. Pinnock had

apparently figured out that Bell was likely to uncover something about the transaction. Then he backtracked on Mark Hofmann.

"You know, that Mark Hofmann you mentioned? I think I now remember that on the 15th, his wife called my secretary and left a message saying he wanted to see me that afternoon to talk about some document collections. But we never had the appointment. There was no need to. After all, the Church wasn't interested in any collections." He was weaving an increasingly tangled web.

On his way to his car, Bell didn't doubt for a moment that he had been lied to. He only wanted to know why. Back at the department, he told a group of fellow officers about his conversation with Pinnock and other Church officials. "We've got some real problems," he said. "They're obviously stonewalling us. They're lying to us. I don't know what it is, but they're hiding something." Suddenly, one of the assistant chiefs, known to be a devout Mormon, slammed his hand down on his desk as hard as he could and leaped out of his chair. "I'm getting damned sick and tired of hearing *they*. '*They* this, *they* that.' Just who the hell is *they?*" And he continued to rant until someone took him aside and calmed him down. Everyone knew what his problem was—just as everyone knew who "they" was.

The minute Detective Bell left his office, Hugh Pinnock contacted the nearest lawyer, Dallin Oaks. It was only then that he found out Oaks had already spoken to Shannon Flynn.

61

Sometime before eleven that morning, Flynn had come looking for Hinckley. "I'm going over right now and talk to President Hinckley," he told Lyn Jacobs, who happened to be in the Church

Office Building. The police wanted to interview him and, with Hofmann in the hospital, he needed some guidance. What better place to look than Gordon Hinckley? That's what Mark would have done. "He's got to get involved in this," said Flynn. "I mean he *knows* he's involved—and, of course, I'm involved." Jacobs thought Flynn sounded more excited than worried.

About the same time, Detective Don Bell began to wonder why Flynn hadn't shown up for his 10 o'clock interview. Bell called the number Flynn had given him at his father-in-law's. Flynn wasn't there. Bell again sensed that he was being avoided. "You tell him that if I don't hear from him by noon, I'll have a warrant for him. These are *homicide* cases, you know."

Twenty minutes later the phone rang. It was Martell Bird. "I understand that you are looking for Shannon Flynn." For a moment, Bell thought the Church had tapped his phone.

"Yes, I am."

"Well, he's over here."

"He's over *where?*"

"He's over here talking to some officials of the Church."

That was curious, thought Bell—talking to Church officials before he talked to the police. "That's fine, but he had an appointment with me at ten. As I told his father-in-law, by noon I'll have a warrant for him."

"I thought you would understand."

"Understand what?"

"He's here talking to Elder Oaks."

After the events of the last few days, Shannon Flynn must have been the last person Gordon Hinckley wanted to see—next to Mark Hofmann. But it would have been too risky to turn him away. What would he tell the police? How much had Hofmann told him? The mere fact that he was showing up on Hinckley's doorstep meant he knew too much to be dismissed. For all these reasons, presumably, he was sent for cross-examination to the lawyer on staff, Dallin Oaks.

Justice Oaks was in impeccable form. He called in two men from Church Security to act as witnesses—and for protection, if necessary—and a stenographer to record every word of the conversation. Shannon Flynn, soldier of fortune, was considerably out of his depth.

"Are you a member of the Church?" Oaks began. It was a standard opening that Hinckley also used to invoke the authority of his office.

Flynn said he was, then spilled his story. He told Oaks that he and Hofmann were partners, that the police had found a check in his name endorsed over to Mark and now they were on his trail. They wanted to *interview* him, and he needed to know "what posture to take." He was particularly concerned that they might ask him about the fishy $185,000 loan from First Interstate Bank. "I know Mark's position," he said, "and I know there is no way he could get a loan for that amount."

"Do you know anything about why he got that loan?" asked Oaks. Since Oaks knew exactly why Hofmann got that loan, he must have wanted to see how much Flynn knew. Just exactly what was the Church's exposure?

"He needed those funds to get the McLellin Collection," Flynn answered. He knew that much. He had flown with Hofmann to Arizona in his unsuccessful bid to solicit funds from Wilford Cardon.

"Have you seen the McLellin Collection firsthand?" This had to be Oaks's first concern. Along with Pinnock, he had taken responsibility for bringing the Collection into the Church, and it was still out there.

Like everybody else, Flynn had seen only bits of the Collection, but he knew President Hinckley was very interested in it. Hofmann had spoken to Hinckley long distance about it recently, and twice discussed it with Francis Gibbons, Hinckley's secretary. "[Mark] told me President Hinckley had arranged the loan for him at the First Interstate Bank," Flynn added helpfully. He used Hinckley's name with stunning nonchalance. What would the police think?

Oaks broke in. "What was your relationship to him?"

Flynn explained they were "partners"—"not in business but in specifics."

"Are you partners in the McLellin Collection?" Now Oaks was revealing too much. "I am an interested bystander," he added cautiously.

"No. He came to me and told me that President Hinckley was nervous to have it." Flynn was losing what little cool he'd come in with.

"But where *was* the McLellin Collection?" Oaks demanded. It was clearly the only question on his mind.

Flynn said it was in a safe-deposit box in Texas, but Hofmann couldn't get at it until the money was paid. He had expected to be able to pay it off with the sale of another document, but at the last minute, that deal had gone sour and Mark was caught short of cash.

"The Library of Congress deal?" Oaks volunteered. For an interested bystander, he was extraordinarily well informed.

"Yes." The sale had gone through, Flynn explained, but some of the money was held up. That was why Mark had gone to see Hinckley. "President Hinckley wanted to get that Collection," he repeated. "President Hinckley arranged for a ninety-day loan from the bank." The plan was for Mark to pay for the Collection and then donate it to the Church.

How did Flynn know all this?

He had been with Hofmann when he went to Hinckley's office to ask for the loan. "I waited outside in his car. At 11:00 A.M. he went to the bank. The loan had been arranged for." In an attempt to clarify his dilemma, Flynn added, "Several banking regulations had been broken in making that loan."

Oaks jumped on that. "That is your judgment," he said quickly. This was the first mention of illegal activity. All of a sudden, Oaks's decision to have a stenographer present for this interview seemed very wise. If, horror of horrors, Flynn's allegations later proved to be true, Oaks would need to protect himself on the record from accusations of a cover-up.

Flynn only made it worse. "Obviously [the banker] was persuaded by President Hinckley."

"Did [Mark] say 'President Hinckley'?"

"Yes."

Oaks was still mulling over the last response. Undoubtedly, he had hoped that Flynn knew nothing about the loan. It was, after all, the Church's only real, *legal* vulnerability. Everything else could be explained away with the usual all-purpose denials ("the Church didn't buy the documents, etc."). Now it turned out that Flynn did know about the loan, but he knew only this cockeyed version of the story that Hofmann had fed him, a version that deeply implicated Gordon Hinckley. To correct him would be to reveal Oaks's own knowledge. He needed to find out just how cockeyed Hofmann's version was.

"Was anyone else's name mentioned in connection with obtaining this loan?"

"No."

Oaks had to be relieved. In his self-importance, Mark had failed to mention the real middleman, Hugh Pinnock. Now Oaks knew everything he needed to know. He looked at Flynn with a benign smile. "How can we be of help to you?"

"I want to find out what posture I need to take. The whole room is falling down."

Oaks was too smart to touch that question. The last thing he needed was for this overweight, overeager errand boy to go to the police and, under hard questioning, say, "Elder Oaks told me to tell you. . . ." Besides, there was nothing in his story that could hurt the Church. The allegations about Gordon Hinckley's role in the loan transaction could be easily and truthfully denied.

With the Church's deniability ensured, Oaks leaned back in his chair with a look of gravity and sincerity, and with the stenographer scribbling busily in the background, dictated a press release *through* Shannon Flynn, knowing that if Flynn didn't relay his words to the police, Oaks would.

"The Church is going to cooperate fully, and it has absolutely nothing to hide. Sometimes there are some confidential transactions but this is a murder investigation. Confidentiality is set aside. We will cooperate fully. You will not do anything favorable by assuming that you need to cover up."

There was one other point Oaks wanted to make, a point about Gordon Hinckley—although he avoided alerting Flynn to the manipulation at work by mentioning the name. He said to be careful, when talking to the police, to distinguish between "what you know and what someone told you. I would urge you not to say, 'I know this,' when all you know is what he told you. Do you understand?"

Flynn nodded.

"You are a member of the Church," Oaks continued in his best hypnotic, Sunday-school drone. "The Church has nothing to hide in this transaction. . . . We have great concern for the lives that have been lost."

Flynn nodded again. It was no longer a dialogue—if it ever was.

"I am not going to talk to the newspapers," Oaks added, suggestively. "The less said to the newspapers the better. People read the papers and get their whole ideas from the newspapers."

Finally, one last reminder, "Be sure to say what you were told," and then the meeting was over. Flynn later said it seemed like "centuries." It had been less than twenty minutes.

Soon after Flynn left Oaks's office to confront the police, Hugh Pinnock called, still shaking from his interview with Detective Bell.

62 Pinnock hadn't just lied, he had lied in easily disproved ways; he hadn't just obfuscated, he had obfuscated clumsily; he had contradicted himself and raised more questions than he answered. But worst of all, he had violated the prime directive. In his panic, he seemed more interested in protecting himself than in protecting the Church.

Not all was lost, however. The FBI agents who had interviewed Oaks the day before were coming to see Pinnock later that day. Pinnock didn't have to make the same mistakes a second time.

And he didn't. By the time the two special agents arrived, Pinnock was ready for them. Not with the whole truth, by any means, but with considerably more of it than he had given Detective Bell. He not only acknowledged knowing Hofmann, he detailed most of their dealings, including the loan from First Interstate Bank. He knew how to pronounce "McLellin." He even gave them David Sorensen's name.

But if the details were scrupulously correct, the overall picture was vastly misleading. The Church's role in the whole affair was really a minor one, Pinnock underscored. The transaction was really between Hofmann, Christensen, and Sorensen. The Church was merely (as Oaks had told the FBI in *his* interview) "an interested bystander." Christensen had kept Pinnock informed from time to time of progress on the sale, but his only substantive role in the deal had been finding Sorensen, whom he portrayed as a collector genuinely interested in the McLellin Collection who *might,* at some point in the future, donate the Collection to the Church. Which suited the Church just fine, said Pinnock, because (and he stressed this point) the Collection is "not really that significant of an item of interest for the Church."

The other thing missing from Pinnock's account—and from Oaks's account the previous day—was the name Gordon Hinckley.

This, it seems, was to be the strategy: first, the Church was merely a bystander in the deal; second, the Church didn't care about the documents; and third, Gordon Hinckley had nothing to do with it.

Someone with a sharp legal mind must have cautioned Pinnock that all of his records would be subject to subpoena, because from that time on, his journal entries took a curious turn. The conversation with Oaks itself was described not as a frantic exercise in damage control but as a friendly chat in which Pinnock expressed "concern for the safety of his wife and kids" and complained about not being able to sleep at night. The next day, he noted in his journal: "All we know is in the newspaper." And later: "Why don't we know more about what's going on?" And later: "We're saying everything we know."

The strategy worked for a day or two. Caught up in the drama of the bombings and the immediate aftermath, the papers made no mention of the Church or the McLellin Collection. Then on Thursday, the 17th, the news of Oaks's meeting with Hofmann on the day of the Christensen and Sheets bombings hit the front page of the Salt Lake *Tribune.* By the next day, the *Tribune* had wind of the Church's interest in the McLellin Collection and was speculating that it might provide the key to the motive for the bombings.

The Church did what it could to keep a lid on the speculation. Over at the Church-owned *Deseret News,* there was a determined effort to keep the public's attention off the McLellin Collection and the Church's pursuit of it. POLICE FOCUS ON EVIDENCE, NOT THEORIES, headlined the October 18 issue.

> Theories abound on killings. . . . Theories of conspiracy, elaborate forgeries and hundred-thousand dollar payoffs may make interesting reading, but police say they are more interested in solving two murders.

It didn't take the media long to put two and two together. If the Church was pursuing the McLellin Collection and Hofmann was selling it, then Oaks and Hofmann must have met to do business. According to the *Tribune:* "Hofmann was attempting to sell documents, described as the M'Lellin Papers, to various clients, including the hierarchy of the Mormon Church." Reporters were calling Church officials up and down the echelons asking about meetings with Hofmann, Flynn, and Al Rust. Some even wanted to know if it was true that Hofmann had access to President Hinckley.

On Saturday, the Church released an official statement admitting what was already common knowledge: Hofmann *had* contacted Church officials to propose that he give or sell them historical documents or artifacts, including the William McLellin Collection. But it was too little too late. After the revelations about the Salamander Letter and the backtracking on the Stowell letter, the Church had used up its credibility with the press. The story was out of control. On Sunday, on the front page of the *Tribune,* Dawn Tracy reported the unthinkable. "Complex business dealings of a document dealer accused of killing two people reach into the office of LDS Church President Gordon B. Hinckley."

Then, on Monday morning, Hugh Pinnock woke up to a nightmare.

> A member of the Church of Jesus Christ of Latter-day Saints secured a $185,000 loan for bombing suspect Mark W. Hofmann, who sources say may have used the money to purchase the missing Mormon McLellin Papers.

The article in the *Tribune* named "Elder Hugh W. Pinnock." It also repeated the accusation that Hofmann did "regular business with President Gordon B. Hinckley," and reported for the first time Hofmann's meeting with Pinnock in the Church Office Building parking lot the morning after Christensen was killed.

Pinnock had had some warning. After checking the story with several sources, *Tribune* reporter Mike Carter had called him and asked him to confirm it. Pinnock was dumbstruck. "Oh, gee, well. Yeah, gee, I don't think I can talk about that."

But Carter pressed ahead. "I am writing this story, and I'd really appreciate it if you'd clear up any misconceptions that I have." He read the first few paragraphs. When he topped, there was a moment of utter silence on the line. Finally, Pinnock said, "I can't talk to you."

The *Tribune* ran the story in the first edition.

Before the second edition went to press, Pinnock managed to formulate a new response. He called Carter back: The loan in question "was not out of the ordinary," he insisted. And the reports that the Church was planning to buy the McLellin Collection were "completely false . . . the purest of fabrication."

Later that day, Pinnock issued a terse, two-page statement to drive home the key points. It was a model of deft, legalistic, and impeccably truthful distortion. Alluding to the night on which Steve Christensen and Mark Hofmann came to his house and retrieved a $20,000 check from Shannon Flynn, which was then used to pay down the loan (the same night Christensen called Pinnock from Hofmann's car phone to assure him "the check is in my pocket"), Pinnock simply noted, "I have been informed that several weeks ago Mr. Hofmann brought the interest on the loan up to date and made a partial payment to First Interstate Bank."

In accordance with what appeared to be the Church's emerging grand strategy, Pinnock emphasized that he was not acting on behalf of the Church, that Christensen had come to him "because of the career I had had in business before being called as a General Authority," and that the Church itself had no interest in the McLellin Collection. No mention at all was made of David Sorensen or the Church's second, more recent effort to acquire the Collection.

The statement also included the bizarre observation: "I have found Mr. Christensen to be honorable and open in all dealings"—as though Steve Christensen's reputation was somehow in question. "Our thoughts and prayers have been with the families of all affected parties," he concluded, "and we pray the Lord's protecting hand will be with them."

If Pinnock thought that would satisfy the press, he was woefully mistaken. The next day, his name appeared in the *New York Times,* and the day after that, Al Rust came forward to say that Mark Hofmann had told him that the Church had bought the McLellin Collection months ago.

The Church, of course, denied it, but the Church had denied having sensitive documents before and been caught red-handed. Was this just another Josiah Stowell letter? Another damaging piece of history that the Church was trying to deep-six in The Vault? Did Steve Christensen and Mark Hofmann know that? Is that why they were blown up?

The rumors flew like shrapnel. Like it or not, the Church was now in the middle of a murder investigation —up to its clerical neck.

63

Unprecedented problems called for unprecedented solutions. On Wednesday, October 23, the Church called a press conference to "tell all" about its dealings with Mark Hofmann and Steve Christensen, and to put an end, once and forever, to the scurrilous rumors.

This wasn't just any press conference. On the elevated stage, usually occupied by some obscure spokesman from the Church Office of Communications belaboring the obvious to the oblivious, sat three senior officials of the LDS Church: Hugh Pinnock, a member of the First Quorum of the Seventy; Dallin Oaks, a member of the Council of the Twelve Apostles, and Gordon Hinckley himself, second counselor in the First Presidency and, as everyone in the room knew well, the most powerful man in the Church.

The event was impeccably stage-managed. The three officials sat behind a conference table overlooking the small, carefully chosen audience in the 350-seat auditorium in the Church Office Building. Television cameras and lights filled the back of the room. The "ground rules" were announced: like a televised presidential news conference, reporters would be allowed only one question and one follow-up. Mike Carter, who broke the loan story, remembers, "The reporters were a little nervous. The intimidation factor was definitely there. These guys up there weren't just people, they were prophets of God, and on a first-name basis with the Lord, at least."

That was the message: the Church wasn't obliged to give a press conference, it wasn't badgered into giving a press conference. This was a favor, granted to the media in the spirit of *noblesse oblige*.

To underscore that this controversy was a mere blip in the great ongoing work of the Church, it was scheduled to begin only one hour before the dedication of the Church's new Genealogy Building, an event at which the Church leaders were required to be present. One hour minus the twenty minutes needed to walk to the dedication, minus twenty minutes for opening statements, that would leave about twenty minutes—no more—for questions. Lest reporters forget, Richard P. Lindsay, Director of Public Communications for the Church, opened the press conference by reminding them: "We will try to stay carefully on schedule."

Hinckley began with expressions of sympathy to the "families and associates of those who have been victims of the bombings in our community. That such tragedies could occur here is beyond our comprehension."

Then he came out swinging.

In defense of the Church's efforts to procure documents, Hinckley said, *God told us to do it.* "The Church's interest in documents and artifacts pertaining to its history was mandated through revelation." It was an explanation worthy of Joseph Smith. As for the Church's *methods* in acquiring documents, Hinckley insisted that they had "followed the normal, accepted, and professional procedures employed by collectors generally."

As for the accusations that the Church was hiding documents, Hinckley claimed that *he personally had made the decision to make sensitive documents public*. He cited two in particular the Salamander Letter and the Josiah Stowell letter, that he had voluntarily released to the press. There was no mention of the fact that both documents were made public only after they had leaked or that one had been kept secret from the Church's own archivist for two years.

As for Steve Christensen, *Hinckley didn't really know him*. "While I had received a letter earlier indicating Mr. Christensen's desire to donate the document to the Church after research on it had been completed, I have no recollection nor any record of his ever having been in my office until the day he presented it to the Church. Nor has he been in my office since then."

As for Mark Hofmann, *Hinckley didn't really know him either*. And the meetings with Hofmann? "Many people come to see me," said Hinckley, suddenly expansive, echoing Hugh Pinnock's sermon to Detective Bell. "Many from many areas across the world, about scores of matters. I have tried to maintain a reasonable open-door policy and have met and talked with many hundreds, if not thousands." Hofmann was just one among the faceless masses.

And what about the rumors that he met with Hofmann only days before the bombing? Hinckley said that Hofmann had come to discuss "the so-called Kinderhook plates" —the bogus plates that Joseph Smith was fooled into "translating"—but Hinckley's "recollection of this episode of history was dim."

"That concludes my statement," said Hinckley, with emphasis on the word *concludes*.

Dallin Oaks was next.

"I welcome this opportunity to share what I know about what appeared to be a normal, though confidential, commercial transaction."

Oaks went immediately on the offensive. "With the benefit of hindsight, and in the feverish context of a murder investigation, and in the glare and innuendo of publicity accompanying the recent investigations, a normal though confidential proposed commercial transaction has been made to appear sinister and underhanded. My own contact with it has been seen as mysterious and questionable. I therefore welcome the opportunity to set the public record straight."

Oaks apparently wanted to convey two messages to the assembled reporters: one, the Church had done nothing improper; and two, Dallin Oaks was a very wise man indeed.

As for the McLellin Collection, Oaks insisted that he had made it clear from the beginning that the Church shouldn't be involved even indirectly in the acquisition of the McLellin Collection and had "so advised Elder Pinnock." When asked if the Church would be interested in receiving the Collection as a gift, Oaks had informed Pinnock "that the Church probably would at some future date, but in that event it had to be a genuine gift from a real donor."

Nor, according to Oaks, did the Church seek out collectors to buy the Collection, although it may have "brought the Collection's availability to their attention." In fact, by Oaks's telling, the suggestion of a donation came as a complete surprise to the Church, and his response, when asked if the Church would be *willing* to accept it, was a disinterested "I suppose so." (Missing from both Hinckley's and Oaks's accounts was the fact that Sorensen wasn't a collector at all, and never would have bought the Collection if the Church hadn't approached him.)

As for the loan arranged by Pinnock, Oaks again took pains to exculpate the Church and congratulate himself. "I said I saw no harm in that, provided it was clearly understood by all parties that the Church was not a party or a guarantor and that Hugh Pinnock was not a party or a guarantor to such a loan."

As for his meeting with Hofmann, Oaks was willing to breach the wall of confidentiality that normally protects "a conversation between a General Authority and a member of the Church," and read the unfaultable instructions he had given Hofmann in their meeting: "Hofmann came to my office and said he thought the police would question him. What should he say when they questioned him? And I said, 'You should simply tell them the truth.' "

Hugh Pinnock was next. *Except Hugh Pinnock had nothing to say.* Elder Pinnock has already issued his statement, said Richard Lindsay, and copies were available.

Hinckley and Oaks had decided, apparently, that Hugh Pinnock had already said more than enough.

Finally came the questions—barely fifteen minutes' worth.

Dawn Tracy of the *Tribune* wanted to know why Don Schmidt, the Church archivist, wasn't informed when the Church purchased the Josiah Stowell letter? And why didn't Dean Jessee, the foremost authority on Joseph Smith's handwriting, find out about the letter until after it was acquired? In other words, who exactly *did* authenticate that letter? This was a direct challenge to Hinckley's statement that the Church had followed "normal, accepted, and professional procedures" in all its document dealings. A hush fell over the room.

"I don't know why Don Schmidt wasn't advised," said Hinckley good-naturedly. "The head of the Historical Department knew about it." The head of the Historical Department, G. Homer Durham, had brought the Stowell letter directly to Hinckley. Contrary to Hinckley's implication, it was he, not Durham, who had ordered the letter kept secret.

Next question.

A young reporter mumbled his name and identified himself as KBYU News. That was all the Brethren needed to hear. This had to be a slow pitch, a B.Y.U. journalism student, all eagerness and deference, who probably knew nothing about the case. What could be safer?

"This is to President Hinckley. A few months ago the *L.A. Times* did an article on the Cowdery papers, and John Dart, who was the author, had a 'Deep Throat' source that said someone had access to the First Presidency vault. I was wondering if you could tell us who that person was and if it was Mark Hofmann."

It was a fast-inside curve ball. Oaks and Hinckley shifted in their chairs, obviously wondering who had let this rogue into the room.

On the spot, the best Hinckley could come up with was a clumsy obfuscation. "I'd like to know if someone has access to the First Presidency's vault," he said. "I don't have. Except through the one man who has the combination. I couldn't get in there if I wanted to without one individual who has the combination to go into that vault letting me go in there." What he didn't say was that the one man who had the combination was one of his subordinates, and all he had to do was instruct the individual to let him in.

This was not the way it was supposed to go. Oaks went from cocky to testy.

When Rodd Arquette of KUTV asked, "Do you believe that the McLellin papers exist at all, and if so, are you still interested in purchasing them?" Oaks commandeered the mike.

"Your question assumes that the Church is interested in purchasing them, and I stated flatly the Church is not. Would you like to rephrase your questions?"

"Do you believe they exist?"

"What I believe about the existence or nonexistence of the McLellin Collection is really quite beside the point."

Arquette picked an easier target. "Elder Pinnock, do you feel it is proper for a high-ranking official of the LDS Church to help secure a loan for any member of the Church, as has been reported that you did so for one Mark Hofmann?"

Pinnock smiled nervously. "When they came in that Friday afternoon, and when at that time I called two banks, I had not thought it improper. I was calling on what I thought was a legitimate transaction. I will say that there comes into our offices many people asking questions, but we would certainly not use our office for a favor for someone that was inappropriate." His grammar, like his poise, was falling apart.

Richard Lindsay jumped in. "One final question. Someone that's not had the opportunity." He scanned the room for someone innocuous looking. He picked another B.Y.U. student.

"Brad Mauss with KBYU News. I just have a question. Why is the Church so intent on getting the papers? Is it to secure them in the right hands so that they are not taken advantage of and make the Church look bad? And where does the money come from to purchase these letters?"

That was *enough*. Oaks grabbed the mike. "Again— why, you say, is the Church so intent on getting the papers? I thought it was clear from my statement that the Church was very intent on *not* getting the papers, so that there would be no misunderstanding about this. Could you rephrase that question?"

Oaks had successfully intimidated the young reporter

into incoherence. " . . . letters in the past, like the blessing that Joseph gave to his son and other letters," Mauss stumbled.

Hinckley stepped in to bring the conference to a close with an ink cloud of homilies and a plug for the new genealogical library. "Well, of course, I explained in my statement. I think very clearly that we are under mandate. . . . We have an obligation to keep a history of the Church, and we regard that very seriously. We are going over to dedicate the new genealogical library. It is essentially a historical library. It's cost a very handsome sum, and it's a beautiful archive. The finest in the world, and the purpose of it is historical—historical research."

The audience was ended. Lindsay thanked, not the reporters, but his bosses for discharging this burdensome duty with such grace and candor.

Reactions to the press conference varied. The Church leaders were reportedly fuming at the thorny questions posed by the B.Y.U. students. It was one thing to suffer the blasphemous skepticism of the *Tribune*, but to get blindsided by representatives from the Church's own university, a university that Oaks himself had once presided over—that was intolerable.

The next day, a letter of apology from Thomas A. Griffiths, the Director of Broadcast Services at B.Y.U., was on Oaks's desk.

> Dear Elder Oaks,
>
> Just a note to commend you on your normal preciseness and forthrightness at today's news conference regarding the historical documents issue. The information helped all of us understand what has been going on and provided valuable insight into how the Church operates.
>
> I must also apologize for one of our KBYU reporters, Brad Mauss. His final question at the news conference clearly demonstrated that he had not listened and understood what was stated earlier. Unfortunately, we are only able to discover a student reporter's weaknesses when they are actually under pressure to perform.

*   *   *

Watching the conference on television at home, Terri Christensen felt her blood rising. She remembered all the times Steve had dropped whatever he was doing because Hinckley had called and wanted to see him. She remembered the confidential files, the long, familiar letters to Hinckley—**Personal & Confidential**. Now he was telling the world that he hardly knew Steve. And she wanted to know why.

At Katie Sheets Robertson's house, Joe Robertson watched the press conference while Kathy Sheets's granddaughter Molly played nearby. He remembered the time Steve Christensen had borrowed his car. "Mine is in the shop," he said, "and I've got to go meet with President Hinckley." Mark Hofmann was standing there beside him, and Steve introduced him. When he returned the car, Steve said that he and Mark and President Hinckley were "working on some stuff that makes the Harris letter look like a priesthood manual." And now Hinckley was telling the world he didn't really know either Steve or Hofmann. And *he* wanted to know why.

In the back of the auditorium, Detective Don Bell stood against the wall and listened to the Church leaders. He felt momentarily vindicated when Hinckley admitted that he had met with Hofmann. "I knew it," he said softly to himself. Pinnock *had* lied to him. In any other investigation, he would have been on the phone that afternoon to Pinnock, saying "Listen. Don't you ever lie to me again." But as he watched the three men on the stage read their statements and deflect the softball questions, another realization crept up on him.

This *wasn't* any other investigation. That Mormon officer who ticked him off the other day had been right. These people *were* different. And they *would* have to be treated differently if he or anybody else was ever going to get at the truth.

PART FOUR

Total Faith

64

On the morning of October 17, Jim Bell returned to LDS Hospital to interview Mark Hofmann. He felt a lot smarter this time. In the eighteen hours since the last interview, he had talked to Jerry Taylor, the ATF's crack bomb man. There was no doubt about it: Hofmann wasn't a victim. He wasn't even a suspect, really. He *was* the bomber. Like any good cop, Bell hoped for a confession.

Another detective and a nurse were with him in the room. He leaned close so Hofmann could hear him.

"This is Jim Bell, Mark," he said. "I'm the guy who was here yesterday."

Mark said he recognized him.

"Can you hear me, understand me?"

When Hofmann said yes, Bell pulled out his Miranda card and read Hofmann his rights.

"Do you understand your rights?"

"Yes."

"Do you waive your rights to an attorney?"

"Yes."

"And you feel like talking to me?"

"Yes."

Now Bell was set to start again. "What happened when you got to your car?"

"I walked up to the car and opened it and a package fell off the seat onto the floorboard and exploded." It was the same answer as yesterday, only today Bell knew it was a lie.

"Were you the person who had parked your car at that location?"

"Yes."

"Where were you coming from?"

"I had just been in a meeting at the LDS Church, in the basement of the Church library. . . . After I left the

Church, I walked through the Deseret Gym, got a drink, and walked to my car. I went to my trunk first, then I opened up my car door. That's when the package fell."

"When you opened up the door, which hand did you open it with?"

"My right hand."

"Did you go anywhere else before you opened up the car door?"

"I went to the trunk."

"Who would want to kill you? Do you know anybody who would want to kill you?"

"No, I don't."

Bell decided to lower the boom. "You should know," he began slowly, "that I am confident you're the bomber."

He paused to let that sink in.

"We did a search of your vehicle and your house, and we recovered some pipe and gloves and the letter jacket. I'm interested in why you killed those people."

Hofmann said, very coolly, "I didn't, I didn't do it."

Bell pressed. "Listen, I *know* you're the guy. We've got your letter jacket, Mark, and a witness saw you wearing the letter jacket when you carried the bomb up the elevator in Steve Christenen's building."

At that, every medical alarm in the room went off: the heart monitor, the IV monitor, the respirator, the whole battery of them lit up and sang and chirped like a video arcade. The nurse asked them to leave and ushered them hurriedly out the door. Another nurse rushed in at the sound of the alarms.

On the way out, Bell turned to the other detective and said with a satisfied smile, "That's the best polygraph I've ever seen."

That afternoon, the day nurse told Hofmann's lawyer, Ron Yengich, about the interview with Bell. "When they began to talk with him, his vital signs jumped off the chart," she said. Yengich, a short, fiery man with a Yosemite Sam mustache and an unscratchable itch for confrontation, had seen this kind of thing before and it made him flaming mad. Growing up small and Catholic in the tough Mormon mining town of Bingham, Utah, where his Croatian grandparents settled, he had seen his share of bullying: by the Kennecott Copper Company, which devoured Bingham; by the company management that fought his father, a labor leader in a state where unions were considered the tools of Satan; and by local Mormons who wouldn't let their children play with non-Mormon kids like Ron Yengich.

But Yengich wasn't about to knuckle under to the system. He fought his way out of Bingham and into college on a baseball scholarship. After law school, he continued to mine the same rich vein of childhood resentments, building a profitable practice and earning a reputation as the most aggressive—possibly the best—criminal defense lawyer in Utah. He liked to say that his heroes were the Pee Wee Reeses of the world, "scrappy, little people without a lot of skills who made it big." People like Mark Hofmann.

Yengich ordered the men from the sheriff's office on duty not to interview Hofmann unless he or his assistant, G. Fred Metos, was present. Then he shot off letters to all the law enforcement authorities informing them that he was representing Hofmann and that no one was to speak with his client if he wasn't present. To prevent another incident like the one that morning, he sent a letter to the hospital instructing them that if any policeman attempted to speak to Hofmann, they were to call him, Yengich, immediately, at home if necessary. Short of standing round-the-clock vigil at the bedside, it was the best he could do.

It wasn't good enough. About 11:30 that night, the night-shift nurse, Nancy Loden, heard Hofmann's alarms go off. From her monitors, she could see that his respiratory, heart, and blood-pressure signs were rising dangerously. She rushed into his room and found a policeman and two hospital security guards around Hofmann's bed.

She had been warned about this. When she came on duty about 6:45 that evening, the day-shift nurse had told her about the interview that morning and the angry letter from Yengich. "If anyone should try and question Mark, or if Mark needs him," she was told, "notify Yengich."

Loden didn't have to hear anything more. She was already fuming over what Ken Farnsworth had said to Nurse Bowdoin the night before: "You patch him up, and we'll stand him up and execute him." That slip had quickly made the rounds of the hospital staff, and nobody was more burned up about it than Loden. As the daughter of a public defender—and a lawyer herself some day, she hoped—she knew all about oppressive police tactics. Now they were invading her territory—no one is more territorial than a night nurse—and she wasn't going to stand for it.

She walked up to Hofmann's bed, wedging herself between him and his tormentors. She asked if he needed anything. Mark said, very gravely, "I would like to make a statement, so I need a tape recorder."

Loden leaped into the breach. "Are you aware that you could have your lawyer present?"

"Yes," Hofmann answered.

"Would you like me to call your lawyer?"

"Yes."

She rushed into the anteroom, picked up the phone, and notified her nursing supervisor, Betty Townsend, to call Ron Yengich. Yengich was on his way out the door to take his girlfriend home for the night but insisted she come with him to the hospital instead. "I want an independent witness," he said, "in case the cops have him down and are bludgeoning him with their sticks." He also called Metos and told him to get to the hospital immediately.

Meanwhile, the policeman at Hofmann's bedside, Scott Hallock, rushed to the phone in the special-procedures room and called Sergeant Duffy Diamond. Hofmann had asked for a tape recorder. He wanted to make a statement. "The nurse has already called Mark's lawyer," said Hallock. "Why? I don't know. And she won't let me near his bed." Diamond called Jim Bell and told him to get to the hospital on the double. Hofmann was ready to confess.

The race was on.

Loden rushed back into Hofmann's room. His blood pressure had indeed risen, his heart rate had shot from about 100 to a whopping 180 and higher. He was shaking so badly he could hardly keep the thermometer in his mouth. When she finally got a reading, his temperature was normal, which only confirmed her suspicions that he wasn't feverish, he was just terrified. When he asked to be positioned a little differently, she cleared the men from around the bed and ordered them to back off.

After that she washed his clammy face with cool water and swabbed his mouth—and swabbed and swabbed and swabbed.

Anything, it seemed, to keep him quiet until Yengich arrived.

She talked to him, ostensibly trying to calm him down. Meanwhile, Officer Hallock grew increasingly impatient and angry. Hofmann obviously wanted to talk, and he wanted to talk *before* his lawyer arrived. Only Nurse Loden wouldn't let him.

Finally, Hallock lost his patience. "You're not a lawyer, you know, you're just a nurse."

It was absolutely the wrong thing to say.

"*Just* a nurse," she huffed.

Yengich won the race, arriving about 12:45 A.M. The first thing he did was to ask the police to step outside.

"He wants to talk to us," said Hallock, outright angry by now.

"Hey, he's *not* talking." Yengich would show him what real anger looked like. "Call your captain. Call whoever you have to. But he's *not* going to talk. And I'm staying here to make certain he doesn't talk to you. Now I want everybody out of the room so I can talk to him."

Hallock refused to leave. "He's not to be left alone."

Yengich turned to Hofmann. "Mark, are you going to follow my advice?"

Hofmann nodded. "Yeah."

"We're not talking to them. We've got to call your father. I want to call your father." Yengich had known Hofmann only since eleven that morning, when Bill Hofmann first contacted him. But he had already seen enough to know that Mark Hofmann *obeyed* his father. If the "Shut up" came from Bill Hofmann, Mark Hofmann would shut up. At the mention of his father, Hofmann's blood pressure/heart rate alarm went off.

When Jim Bell finally arrived, he told the uniformed officers to leave the room so Yengich could talk to his client. "Don't put the nurse in the position again of having to notify me," Yengich warned him as the policemen filed out. Nurse Loden remained in the room with Yengich and Hofmann.

During the conversation, Bell could hear the alarms go off several times. He had a good idea of what Hofmann was saying.

When he heard Hallock's story of Nurse Loden's actions, Jim Bell's own alarms went off. He was furious. It was one thing for her to call Yengich, but it was something else entirely for her to keep Hofmann occupied, even to *prevent* him from confessing by swabbing out his mouth endlessly and needlessly until Yengich arrived. As far as Bell was concerned, Hofmann had *wanted* to confess and she had prevented him. If it hadn't been for her, the case would be over now. They would have a confession, and the rest would be paperwork. If she had been standing there, he would have slapped handcuffs on her on the spot. Fortunately, he had time to tell himself that the case was too important to blow it with some rash mistake. Besides, she was in the room with Hofmann at that moment, listening to everything he said. Maybe he could still get that confession.

When Yengich finally emerged from Hofmann's room, Bell heard him ask Nurse Loden, "Did you hear anything?" She said yes. First thing tomorrow morning, Bell thought, he would get a warrant and find out *what* she had heard.

As soon as Yengich left, Nurse Loden sedated Hofmann. That would keep him quiet for the rest of the night.

65

The next morning, October 18, Jim Bell and Ron Yengich met at the hospital with Bud Ellett from the county attorney's office. Yengich wanted to deal. He hedged it with hypotheticals, but the message was unmistakable: "Life in exchange for a guilty plea. You give me life in prison, and I'll give you the other people who are involved."

If Jim Bell needed any more proof that Hofmann had confessed, this was it. Little Markie had spilled his guts to Yengich, and the nurse had heard everything.

As Yengich walked out with the offer still dangling, Gerry D'Elia, another prosecutor from the county attorney's office walked in on his way to see Nurse Loden.

If anybody on the public side of the case was Ron Yengich's equal it was Gerry D'Elia. Short, short-tempered, cynical, and street smart, D'Elia was, like Yengich, a child of the sixties, always humming a Beatles or a Stones tune between bursts of manic energy. Born in New Jersey and raised in an Italian Catholic family, he was also about as out-of-place as an American could get in uptight, upright Utah. What brought him here wasn't the religion, it was the skiing. The higher he could get in the mountains, the closer he got to a nosebleed, the happier he was. In the middle of winter, he was always tan, his brown hair streaked with gold highlights from hours in the brilliant white, reflected sunlight of the slopes.

On or off the slopes, he was, like Yengich, a risk taker and a poker player.

When Bell briefed him on Yengich's offer, D'Elia brushed it off. "We are not far enough into the case to even talk about a plea," but, like everybody else, he took it as a sure sign that Hofmann was guilty *and* that Nurse Loden knew he was guilty. If they could get her testimony, they wouldn't need to deal.

But it wasn't going to be that easy.

The next morning Loden arrived at the Hall of Justice with shorts on, a chip on her shoulder, and *a lawyer from the Church's law firm*. A plain, stocky woman in her thirties with brown hair, Loden radiated hostility. She made it clear that she couldn't wait to go to law school so she could save society from overreaching law enforcement officials. She and the Church's buttoned-up, establishment lawyer, Charles W. Dahlquist, made an odd pair.

He opened the meeting with a bombshell. It was the position of the hospital's counsel that the conversation overheard by Nurse Loden was subject to the attorney-client privilege.

Gerry D'Elia didn't like the sound of that one bit. This was the third time in three days he had pursued some evidence only to find the Church standing in his way. First, the person that he sent to the Church to get Hofmann's documents had come back empty-handed. "We don't trust local law enforcement," they told him. Then, they had shipped the Salamander Letter off to the FBI so the county attorneys could *never* get their hands on it.

And now, a woman who had overheard a confession by the prime suspect was being told by a Church lawyer who had nothing to do with the case not to answer questions.

Why would the Church want to protect Mark Hofmann?

"I won't have my client answer the questions you are giving me," said Dahlquist.

"Why not? Who are *you?*" D'Elia's temperature, always high, was approaching boil. "You're just here to make sure she doesn't end up in a bind, not to stop her from helping out."

"I am not letting her answer any questions against Mark Hofmann. I feel that there is an inadequate basis for you to ask the questions."

D'Elia couldn't believe what he was hearing. "What is going on here? The Church this. The Church that. Now I got the Church with the nurse." He asked himself, not for the first time, if there could be a conspiracy of some kind, headed up by the Church, and, if so, why? "Fine, then," said D'Elia. "You stay here while I go over to the court and find the first judge I can." He would get a judge to grant a motion compelling her to talk—*now*. "Then we'll sit down right now. I've already got a court reporter lined up."

It wasn't that easy. None of the judges wanted to touch it. Compel a woman to testify over the objections of Church counsel? No way. One judge suggested he go back to the judge who issued the investigative subpoena. "Get *him* to hear you," he said. "I don't want to hear it." Neither did the second, third, or fourth judge D'Elia went to.

"I have a legal issue that hasn't been assigned to anybody yet," he pleaded. "All I want you to do is to hear the legal issue."

"I don't want to hear it this morning."

"I have a criminal investigation here with a homicidal maniac out on the street planting bombs. What do you *mean* you don't want to hear it this morning?"

Finally, he got ahold of the judge who had signed the subpoena, Dean E. Conder. Conder agreed to hear the motion at two that afternoon. Meanwhile, Dahlquist called Yengich and told him to get down to the courthouse in a hurry. That only contributed to D'Elia's growing suspicion that he was up against a conspiracy.

Yengich and Metos arrived in time for the hearing.

Dahlquist represented Loden, and D'Elia represented the county attorney's office. Yengich began with a request that the proceedings be kept confidential. Judge Conder agreed.

D'Elia tore into Loden. "Mr. Hofmann began asking for the officer, or asking for a tape recorder, if I recollect, and this nurse, Nancy Loden, took it upon herself to intervene in this situation." He wanted permission, not only to depose the nurse as to the contents of the conversation she overheard, but also to look into any criminal actions that might be brought against her for obstruction of justice. "If this gentleman [Hofmann] at one time wanted to waive any right to counsel or waive any right to his silence, or whatever the case may be, we want to investigate the possibilities of this nurse being any party to the obstruction of justice."

Yengich argued that he told Nurse Loden to stay across the room but she said she couldn't leave, that it was a medical necessity for her to be there.

"I am not going to call anybody a liar," D'Elia shot back, "but regardless of what is being said, I want an opportunity to explore this myself."

Dahlquist argued that irreparable harm might be done to the hospital if Loden was compelled to testify. "I am scared we'll be held liable if it should turn out that she comes within the attorney-client privilege. We'll get sued over it."

D'Elia jumped out of his chair. "How can *you* get sued over it?" he protested. "That's totally ridiculous."

Throughout the heated session, D'Elia couldn't shake the feeling that there was a dimension to the proceedings that he was missing. "I was a non-Mormon in Mormon land," he said later—Alice through the Looking-Glass, not just pushing against the nurse or the lawyers or even Hofmann, but against a whole system.

Judge Conder decided D'Elia could depose Nurse Loden, but not on what Hofmann had said. "You can't ask her what she overheard but you can ask her about the circumstances surrounding it to see if she was really necessary," he ruled. If the deposition made it clear that the nurse's presence was *not* a matter of medical necessity, then he might reverse his decision and allow her to be questioned on the substance of the conversation overheard.

The deposition was taken at 4:15 that afternoon. Dahlquist represented Nancy Loden. Ken Farnsworth joined D'Elia. Loden lived up to her billing as surly and uncooperative. Both D'Elia and Dahlquist had to remind her to speak up for the court reporter. When she did speak up, she laced her answers with impenetrable, officious medical jargon.

Still, the facts came out.

First, Nurse Loden was not tied down to Hofmann's room. As the nurse in charge of the unit, which included twelve other rooms, she had other duties that required her to leave Hofmann's room several times. "I was in and out probably ten times," she admitted when asked to be specific, although never for "longer than five or ten minutes."

This was exactly what D'Elia had been waiting to hear. "Let's go back to the point where Mr. Yengich entered the room and he had a conversation with Mr. Hofmann. What was it that Mr. Yengich asked you, if anything, with respect to your being present in the room during his conversation with his client?"

Her face went blank. "I don't remember anything."

"Did he ever state to you that he wanted you to leave the room?"

Loden just shook her head.

Audibly, please," prodded D'Elia.

"No."

"Did he ever state to you that there was an attorney-client privilege of which you must keep secret anything that he was talking about to his client?"

"No."

"Did he ever discuss whether or not you were necessary in that room?"

"No."

"Do you remember telling Mr. Yengich or Mr. Metos that you had to specifically stay in that room with Mr. Hofmann because, if you left, you were worried about his condition?"

"I don't know if I stated it to them. I was worried about his condition at the time."

"But you don't recall whether you *stated* it or not?"

"I mentioned it. I don't know who I—you know, there were people in the room."

D'Elia asked about the links between Hofmann's room

and the computer monitors at the desk outside. "You can sit at that desk in the [intensive care] unit and *not* be in the room with Mark and *not* be within earshot of conversation and *still* monitor all the vital life signs; is that correct?"

"Yes."

The only excuse she could give for staying in the room was, "I didn't feel comfortable leaving the room at that time." In her "best nursing judgment," Hofmann could not have been monitored from outside the room.

But the hearing resolved nothing except a court date for another hearing. Even if Conder reversed his opinion (which he eventually did) and allowed Nurse Loden to be questioned, it was clear by now that Yengich could keep the police away from her for at least another month while he appealed the order, all the way up to the Utah Supreme Court if necessary.

If they wanted to nail Mark Hofmann, they would have to find another way.

66

If they couldn't get a confession from Hofmann, maybe they could get one from somebody close to him.

Somebody like Lyn Jacobs.

Even his friends wondered how much Jacobs knew. Peggy Fletcher, the editor of *Sunstone,* remembered how cool Jacobs had been at the news of the bombings—even the one that hit Hofmann. She and the rest of the *Sunstone* staff had been listening in shock, disbelief, and near panic to the first reports when Jacobs bounced in, unnaturally calm. And why, in the first few days afterward, did he play hide-and-seek with the police?

"When you heard the news, why didn't you run?" Fletcher asked. "Why didn't you run for your life?"

Jacobs told her Dorie had come back from the hospital

with good news: Mark was sure a Mormon fanatic had set the bombs.

"All the more reason to run," said Fletcher. Jacobs, after all, had discovered the infamous Salamander Letter.

"Nobody knows my face," he answered.

It wasn't an answer. Who knew Hofmann's face?

Jacobs always had some piece of inside information that proved once and for all that Mark was innocent. The day after the bombings, he came to Fletcher's office and announced, "Mark couldn't be the bomber because the bomber had a letter jacket, and Mark lost his months ago."

How did he know that?

"Dorie told me that when it happened."

Why would Dorie tell him something like that? Fletcher wondered. The next day, the letter jacket was found on the floor of Hofmann's closet.

More and more, Jacobs looked less and less like an innocent bystander. After all, if Hofmann *was* running a documents scam of some kind, Jacobs, with his command of languages and history and his Harvard credentials, could have been a very useful asset.

When the police finally sat him down in the interview room on the eighth floor of the Hall of Justice, Jacobs started chattering and wouldn't stop. "It was like putting a nickel in the slot," said Ken Farnsworth.

Jacobs began by repeating all of the old lies about how he, not Mark Hofmann, had discovered the Salamander Letter—lies that would haunt him through the early stages of the investigation. Then suddenly, in the midst of the questioning, a name popped up that no one expected to hear, at least not in this room, under these circumstances.

"Did you have an association with the man—with President Hinckley?" Detective Don Bell asked Jacobs.

"Not really."

"Does Mark?"

"Yeah. He's in constant contact with President Hinckley. They've worked together for several years. They're very dear friends as far as I can tell." Later, Jacobs told them that Hinckley "called [Mark] on his birthday and said, Happy birthday, and all that kind of stuff."

"Would it surprise you," asked Detective Bell, "if I told you that I think [Mark]'s the bomber?"

"That's what I've been hearing all day long," said

Jacobs, working his way toward indignation. "I don't buy it. I do know he's in debt. But everybody's in debt, it's just a question of how much. . . . I just don't buy it. Not in a million years. Unless he went nuts, just went cracko for some reaon. Anybody in this whole world can go cracko tomorrow. But the point is that that is not the Mark I know. I know him as one of the most level-headed, incredibly ingenious people I've ever known, as far as dealing with these documents is concerned."

Bell thought about that for a moment. "Jacobs, I think either your friend has gone crazy or you didn't know him as well as you thought you did."

Jacobs had reached indignation. "What makes you believe this?" he demanded.

"Let me put it this way." Bell spoke slowly and softly for emphasis. "There is evidence that has been obtained during the time you've been sitting in this room which a person just driving around Salt Lake City probably wouldn't have in his possession unless he was an Army ordnance-disposal person or he was a maker of bombs."

"Huh?" Jacobs looked genuinely shocked. Until now, he had never seriously contemplated the possibility that Mark might have actually committed the bombings. He hadn't let himself.

"I mean, it's not like something everybody would have with him on any given Wednesday afternoon as they're driving around town."

"So there is evidence in the car?"

"There's not only evidence there, there's evidence in a whole lot of other places." Jacobs looked so devastated that Bell felt compelled to comfort him. "For fifteen years, I have dealt with these kinds of people, some of whom have gone crazy. Okay? So I've learned that it doesn't matter what they appear like on the outside." Not to worry, he wanted to say, being fooled isn't a crime.

The next day, the 18th, Jacobs was back in the hot seat. Deputy Gaylord Dent, a sandy-haired young officer in the burglary division of the sheriff's office, had some more questions, most of them about the Church.

Jacobs said that Hofmann had told him that the reason the LDS Church was willing to trade the Joseph Smith III blessing to the RLDS Church was, one, the news had already gotten out so there was no longer any point in hiding it, and, two, the LDS Church already had in its vault a similar blessing from the Prophet to his son. Mark also said that he had turned a whole slew of sensitive materials from the same source over to the Church, on the sly.

Dent wanted to know the name of the person he gave them to.

President Gordon Hinckley. "And Hinckley said, 'This will never see the light of day,' " Jacobs told the startled Dent. "That is the first time I know of in which Mark mentioned that they had done a secret deal."

What else had Hofmann secretly sold to Hinckley?

There was Martin Harris's copy of Ethan Smith's book, *View of the Hebrews*. "It's a fascinating book," said Jacobs, giving an unprompted seminar in Church history. "The book basically provides the *Book of Mormon* story even though it was written years before the *Book of Mormon* came out. . . . Anyway, nobody's ever been able to prove that Joseph or Martin Harris or his wife or Oliver Cowdery, the four people who worked on the *Book of Mormon* manuscript, ever had a copy of that thing. And then Mark found Martin Harris's. . . . Isn't this just blowing you out of your mind?"

It was, but in ways Jacobs couldn't guess. Clearly, the Church had far more at stake in Hofmann's business than anyone else.

Jacobs continued his story: "Anyway, the point is, Mark showed it to Hinckley, and Hinckley said, 'Oh, I want it right now. It'll never see the light of day.' That was another one I understood he stashed away and paid Mark a substantial sum for it."

Like the police, Jacobs saw the potential for blackmail and had even mentioned it to Hofmann. "I said, 'Mark, all the stuff you're acquiring, all this juicy stuff you sell to Hinckley. Have you kept a copy of everything as a kind of . . .' " He reached for the word. " '. . . *insurance* for the future?' "

Dent knew what he meant.

"I said, 'You've got to. You're not that dumb.' . . . And finally, one day, he said, 'I've got some copies of what there needs to be copies of for the future.' "

So, at any point—if he needed money, for example—Hofmann could have tried to blackmail Hinckley by threatening to release what he knew: not just the documents, but the fact that the Church had bought them and stashed them away. Suddenly, the Church's strange determination to prevent Hofmann from talking to the police didn't seem so strange.

"Is [Mark] the kind of person that would consider President Hinckley, uh, two-faced?" asked Dent, trying to put it as delicately as possible. "So much so that it would finally grate on him?"

"I think he was used to it . . . because we had talked about that. As he would tell me about one of these things that Hinckley was doing, I would look at him and say, 'Well, it seems a little strange, doesn't it?'"

"Outlandish," Dent corrected.

"Well, no, I'm just saying, not necessarily from my point of view. Historically, people will justify things to say whatever they have to. I mean, they want to preserve the Church. If Hinckley wants to preserve the Church, he's going to do everything he can to protect the Church."

67

Farnsworth interviewed Shannon Flynn at 7:10 the evening of the 18th. It was almost like a joke at first. Flynn treated it like just another exciting chapter in the continuing adventure of Shannon Flynn, secret agent. He seemed eager to match wits with his interrogators.

It wasn't long before the Church came up again—something that had happened so often in the first days of interviewing that the shock had worn off, or so Farnsworth thought. He was interested that Flynn thought Hofmann was under pressure at the end, the kind of pressure that might have led to violence.

"How do you know that he's been under pressure?" Farnsworth asked. "Do you have some direct evidence?"

It was the Church, said Flynn, putting pressure on Hofmann to come up with the McLellin Collection. "Just, you know, from what he told me. He said, almost quoting, 'You cannot believe how nervous President Hinckley is about this material, and how badly he wants it here.' " There it was again: Gordon Hinckley's name. "And that's the kind of pressure [Mark] doesn't like," Flynn added. "My understanding is that President Hinckley helped arrange the loan for him at First Interstate Bank. I wasn't in the bank for that transaction, though afterwards I did see a copy of the loan agreement."

Farnsworth wanted to explore another possible motive. "Does Hofmann have any problem reputation-wise in the document community?"

"Absolutely not," said Flynn.

"So he wouldn't be suspected of forging documents, or stealing documents?"

Flynn shook his head no.

"Would stolen documents be a more likely thing if someone was dealing in the document trade than fraudulent ones?"

Flynn thought for a moment. "Ummm, I'd say it was an even split. It's difficult to steal material. It's real difficult to steal material. But it's even more difficult to forge it."

"It's a big problem either way?"

"Either way, it's a mess."

Farnsworth changed tack again. "What is your opinion of his innocence or guilt at this time, knowing what you know?"

"I believe that he is innocent."

"Any particular reason?"

"Based mainly on my association with him. I traveled a lot with him. When we went to New York, we would be twenty-four hours a day together. There were times I saw him every day of the week, practically. He's just not that kind of person."

"Okay, would he have any reason that you know of to cause harm to the Sheets family or the Christensens?"

"Absolutely none. I don't think he even knew Gary Sheets."

As usual, the discussion of motive came to a dead stop over Gary Sheets. There was still nothing to tie Hofmann to the Sheets murder. It was quickly turning into one of the imponderables of the case. Farnsworth had learned that every case had one or two.

He turned to the bombs. Did Hofmann ever show any interest in explosives? Farnsworth asked.

Flynn said no, then added, nonchalantly, "At gun shows, it's possible, you know, to pick up a fuse or this or that. In my estimation, that would have been an excellent opportunity to do it, and there was never anything like that."

Farnsworth's eyes lit up. *Gun shows?*

Flynn realized immediately that he had spilled something—a gaffe unbefitting a secret agent—and tried to backtrack. "When we would go to gun shows, he would almost never buy any guns. . . ." But he only dug himself deeper. Farnsworth was thinking: Hofmann went to *gun shows* and bought *guns?* This chubby, nebbishy documents dealer was a *gun* freak?

Then came another surprise. "I know we were both interested in things that had to do with surveillance. I know that he thought his phones were tapped."

That raised everyone's eyebrows.

"He had constant phone difficulty. They'd break, or sometimes they'd pick up a phone and they could hear somebody talking and then all of a sudden there would be a click, and things like that. So one time, when we were in New York, we went to a company that sells all kinds of defensive and offensive surveillance devices. We got the catalog."

Gun shows and surveillance devices. What next? thought Farnsworth. Flynn obviously reveled in the feeling of power these little revelations gave him. Being interrogated was fun.

But not for long. After a few questions about Hofmann and Steve Christensen, Farnsworth decided it was time to show this baby-faced James Bond that the game was deadly serious. He began by setting Flynn up. "We have already gone over the area—that neither you, nor so far as you have any knowledge, Mark, ever acquired any items that you could make a bomb with?"

"No," said Flynn.

"Have you ever bought any *directions* that would help you make a bomb?"

"Not that I recall." Flynn was beginning to catch on, but it was too late.

"Okay, I think you're a liar." The other detective

present, Mike Fierro, produced a copy of *The Anarchist's Cookbook*. "Have you ever seen this book?" he demanded.

"Uh, huh," said Flynn, his face turning red.

"When?"

"Oh, about a month ago."

"What is that book about?"

"A variety of subjects, I mean, you know. . . ."

"Does it include a large section involving how to make *bombs?*"

"Uh, huh." His face turned even redder, impossibly red.

"When I was questioning you, didn't you think of this document?"

"I didn't remember it."

"And yet this bombing incident is such a major thing in the community and you're tied very closely to a man who is accused of being a bomber?"

"Uh, huh."

"We sit here for the purposes of inquiring from you all of the knowledge that we can, and you casually forget that you in fact have bought a book in the last few weeks which described in large part how to make bombs?"

"Uh, huh."

"I find that a very convenient loss of memory. Can you explain it?"

"Well. . . ."

"You're not a dumb person, I gather?"

Flynn was distraught. "Obviously you have gone in and searched my house without my knowledge."

"How's that?"

Flynn had fallen into the trap. "Well, I haven't been to the house in two days."

"So why do you think the police have been in your house?"

"Well, I don't know how else that would come out of there." In fact, the police hadn't been to Flynn's house. All they had was a *tip* that he had bought a copy of the book. Now they had confirmation.

"This is not your book," said Farnsworth. "This is a book *like* one that you bought." He smiled broadly. "Does that make you feel better?"

"Well, not really," said Flynn, furious with himself for being tricked.

"Would you like to back up and start over a little bit?"

"Well, I don't know what to tell you."

"This is a very good time for you to get the record straight about where you fit in with this bombing business. We know Mark Hofmann is the bomber. Maybe one of several people have knowledge about this, maybe helped participate in it, maybe helped deliver bombs. The fact is, *we're going to know*. . . . And if we acquire any knowledge of your participation, we're talking death penalty for everybody who is involved in this."

If Flynn ever thought being interrogated by the police was a big adventure, another episode in the Walter Mitty life of Shannon Flynn, secret agent and ace documents sleuth, those delusions ended right there and then. Farnsworth could see it on his face. The cockiness disappeared, and the fear set in.

And everything else spilled out. He told them about buying two blasting caps for Hofmann eight months earlier. He had been on an ice-fishing trip near Richfield, Utah, and stopped at a friend's and bought the caps—farmers in the area used them all the time to blow up stumps. He tried to convince them that they were just a spur-of-the-moment gift, one pal to another, but Farnsworth didn't buy it.

Then he told them about the Uzi submachine gun in the storage shed.

The *Uzi submachine gun!* Bob Swehla, who was representing the ATF at the interrogation, couldn't believe his ears.

Farnsworth thought, first, blasting caps. Now, a submachine gun. These guys had a goddam *arsenal*.

"It belongs to Mark Hofmann," Flynn hastened to add. "The reason I'm telling you is that I'm trying to tell you anything I can possibly tell you right now before it all comes back and bites me in the ass later."

"Yes," said Swehla, still reeling, "I'll congratulate you for this particular statement. . . . Can you go into that some more?"

"Sure. I bought that for Mark. We then bought the components to convert it to an automatic."

"I take it you're fully aware that that's illegal?"

"You know, it's not the kind of information that I would normally volunteer. I'm not trying to get myself thrown in jail over some firearm violation. But, you know, I don't want to come back here tomorrow and then have you guys kicking the shit out of me, saying, 'We found this machine gun at your house.' "

"What was the purpose of having a fully automatic machine gun?"

"Just the fascination of having an automatic weapon."

"Have either of you shot it?"

"Yeah."

"How long ago?"

"Oh, probably the last time we shot it was maybe two weeks ago."

Actually, the revelation of the Uzi presented Swehla and Farnsworth with a dilemma. Flynn had just confessed to commiting a federal crime punishable by ten years in prison and a $10,000 fine. To protect that confession, Swehla would have to read Flynn his Miranda rights before going on. But reading him his rights might give him cold feet about everything else and bring the whole interview to a halt. Whatever Flynn knew about the bombings and Hofmann, whatever he *hadn't* told, might disappear forever behind the Miranda curtain.

Swehla passed a note to alert Farnsworth—"I'm at the point of Miranda"—and they left the room to talk about it. "Go as far as you can with him regarding what we're talking to him about," Swehla said. "Because once I go back in there and give him the Miranda warning, he may clam up about everything, not just about the gun."

Farnsworth decided to use the time to have one more go at Flynn, to wring him out one last time, just to make sure he wasn't holding anything back.

He began slowly, like a preacher working a guilty congregation.

"Don't you see, Shannon, that if you had come in originally and said, 'This may not be important, but it's probably very critical—I gave him some blasting caps,' that that would have established your credibility as a candid, honest person?"

"Exactly. And I should have done it. I should have done it. I shouldn't have held that back, because now, man, my dick's in the wringer, and I don't know how in the hell I'm going to get it out. You know, if I could give you more information, God, I'd tell you in a second."

"You *can't* get yourself out." Farnsworth was giving no quarter.

"Well, probably not now," said Flynn, hopelessly.

"You're so deep into this, you don't know which way to turn right now. You're sitting here. You're talking to us. We're not being mean to you, and you know we're sitting here with a ton of information and you don't know what we know, and you'd love to know what we know so that you could work around it."

"Well, can I interrupt you?"

"You *can't* interrupt me."

"Okay, I'm sorry."

"You can't interrupt me right now. That's one thing you *can't* do right now. You're sitting here thinking, my life as a paper antiquities expert, my church life, my family life, my parents, you're adding all that up and saying to yourself, 'I don't know how to respond to this thing. I can't sit here and tell these people what I know to be true, I can't sit here and tell them what I have participated in, because all of these things are on the line. . . .' "

Farnsworth stalked the room. "I'm not the kind of guy who likes to lean on the wrong person. But you have put yourself in the fix you're in with us. You lost your credibility an hour ago."

"Yeah." By now, Flynn was a beaten man.

"If anybody listened to the tape of this interview—including yourself, in a while—you'd say, 'Holy Toledo! Am I that *bad?* I mean, can't I present something better than *that* to protect myself? Did I underestimate these people and their ability to dig up information?' " Farnsworth let that sink in, then said, gravely, "I think you're in this up to your eyeballs—up to your *eyeballs*. . . ."

Another long pause. Flynn's shirt was soaking wet.

"I don't know how religious you are. I don't know how much of a believer you are. But if you are a believer, then somebody else is watching who is bigger than you are, and who already knows everything you've done, and everything you know. You may hide it from him," Farnsworth said, pointing to the other detective, "and you may hide it from me, but you ain't hiding it from some superior being." He pointed toward the ceiling in case Flynn missed the point. "So it's only a game for a while, if you choose to be honest and truthful. But later on, it's serious business." If Flynn believed in the Celestial Kingdom, his personal parcel of real estate in the world-to-come was in serious jeopardy. "Two people are dead, two very nice people as far as I can tell. I haven't heard a bad word said about either of the people that are dead."

"No," Flynn agreed meekly.

"It's a major tragedy for them. It's a major tragedy for their families. It's a tragedy for the entire community—*and you are part of this tragedy.*"

This was the moment. The moment in any interview when, if the questioner has done his job, everything is working for him: vulnerability, self-loathing, fear, all the forces that produce a confession. Not a grudging confession, not a word-by-word, question-and-answer confession, but a *willing* confession—hell, an *eager* confession, a confession that pours out like vomit from a drunk.

But Flynn just sat there, sweating and quivering and praying for it to be over. Farnsworth was sure. This well was dry.

Bob Swehla returned and read Flynn his rights.

"If you decide to answer questions now without a lawyer present, you will still have the right to stop the questioning at any time. You also have the right to stop the questioning at any time until you talk to a lawyer."

"Uh, huh."

Swehla had a few more questions about the Uzi. He wanted to know why, if it was Hofmann's, Flynn kept it at his house.

"Oh, probably the biggest reason," said Flynn, "is that Mark's wife hated it, when it was there in its semiauto form. She saw it and told him that it was really stinky and he ought to get rid of it. So he just preferred to keep it at my house."

Farnsworth asked what exactly he and Hofmann intended to use the Uzi *for.*

"We just go out and target-shoot with it."

"It's for *fun?*" Farnsworth exclaimed with an astonishment that had to have been disingenuous. He himself had spent hundreds of hours shooting pistols for fun. But a *machine gun?*

"Yeah."

"Shooting a *fully automatic weapon?*"

"Well, ya know, it's kind of like sex. You hear about it long enough, you want to do it."

Detective Fierro had one more question. He had heard that Hofmann was an atheist and wondered if Flynn knew anything about "the transition that probably took place with Mark" and resulted in his break with the Church.

Flynn seized the question gleefully, like a man coming out of a minefield and lighting on safe ground. "Oh, I don't know much about the transition. As long as I have known him, that essentially has been his philosophy. A Church authority once said the study of religious history is the quickest way to destroy religious faith. You just can't deal in this stuff very long before you start to see inaccuracies, duplicities, errors in any religion. There hasn't been one founded that hasn't been screwed up somehow."

"From what you said earlier, about talking to people in your ward, and stuff, I was getting the impression that you were active in the faith," Fierro said.

"I'm very active. I like to be active. I want to be a member of the Church. I'm not dumb, though. I know what goes on. When I talked to the General Authorities on Thursday morning, it didn't take long to get the scoop. Ya know, they weren't about to tell me anything. And what I had to tell them, they couldn't do anything about, so they just said, 'Tell the truth and do your best and see ya later.' "

"Shove it under the carpet, in others words," Farnsworth interpreted.

"Well, I realize now, man, they are doing some heavy moving over there—real heavy moving. And they weren't about to let me get in the way. I am such a small fish in the pond."

"What do you think their goal is right now?" Farnsworth asked.

"The same as it has always been—the maintenance of the Church. To have the Church continue."

It was one the next morning by the time they were finished. But Flynn had one last surprise for them. As they were booking him on the unlawful-firearms charge, they found a Philippine butterfly knife in his pocket. Secret agent, Uzi-owner, Shannon Flynn had been carrying this lethal piece of hardware throughout the interview.

Ken Farnsworth wondered, not for the first time, what

the world was coming to, when a Pillsbury Doughboy like Shannon Flynn packs a jungle knife on the streets of Salt Lake City. It was getting so you couldn't tell the bad guys from the good guys anymore.

68

A search of Flynn's house at 7:30 the next morning turned up a lot more than just an Uzi in the washbasin. Scattered among the well-thumbed copies of *Soldier of Fortune* were a .357 Magnum revolver and a Mini-14 Ruger rifle with a black nylon stock, plus reloading hardware and enough ammo to start a respectable revolution. Plus combat gear.

Next to the hardware, Flynn's copy of Charles Hamilton's *Great Forgers and Famous Fakes* looked harmless enough.

The next morning, Farnsworth and David Biggs from the county attorney's office drove to Richfield, where Flynn said he had bought the blasting caps. It was the opening day of the deer hunt, and everyone was out with rifle in hand, a sight that put Shannon Flynn's peculiarities in perspective.

The night before, thousands of men had gone out and gotten crocked. This morning, at the crack of dawn, they were out, guns in hand, shooting deer, and, if this year was like past years, at least a couple of their fellow hunters. Just the previous year, a hunter had claimed he thought he was shooting at a deer when he downed a horse and rider. So many cows, sheep and house pets were killed each season that one exasperated farmer had been reduced to painting the words COW and SHEEP in big letters on the sides of his animals to help hunters recognize them.

Despite the deadly carnival, Farnsworth and Biggs located the man who had sold Flynn the caps. He remembered the transaction, but, according to him, Flynn knew exactly why he was buying them. "I need these blasting caps for this guy I know," he remembered Flynn saying. "He likes to blow things up."

Meanwhile, Jim Bell led a phalanx of cops through Hofmann's house for the second time in two days. They came looking for the McLellin Collection. Interviews with Jacobs, Flynn, and others, as well as the contents of Hofmann's car, had made it clear that documents, in one form or another, were at the heart of the case. This time, the warrant allowed them to take "documents, papers, pictures that relate to the Martin Harris letter, McLellin letters, diaries or any other antique or ancient documents relating to Mormon history. Also any other diaries of ancient or antique nature along with any devices, tools or machines for the alteration or production of documents."

In the southeast basement bedroom, Bell found a box filled with documents on Mormon history and religion, as well as books and some information on the care and preservation of paper. Sitting on top of the box was an envelope with the name facing up. The name was Mike Hansen.

At ten that night, back at the department, while Chief Willoughby conducted yet another news conference in the next room, Jerry Taylor was drawing a picture for Jim Bell.

It was a picture of a bomb. The basic device was diabolically simple: a length of pipe nipple (a piece of pipe threaded at both ends) filled with smokeless powder, two battery packs (four C-size batteries apiece) purchased at Radio Shack, and a mercury switch. Taylor explained how the bomber had screwed metal end caps on both ends of the pipe, drilled a hole in one of the end caps, inserted a rocket igniter, then led wires from the igniter to the mercury switch and from the mercury switch to the two battery packs to create a simple circuit. When the victim tilted the bomb, the globule of mercury moved to the other end of the switch, completing the circuit and sparking the igniter, which in turn ignited the powder, and boom.

The bombs had been placed in cardboard boxes approximately six by twelve by twelve inches. (Taylor had recovered one of the pieces of cardboard from the site.)

There were some differences between the three devices. The Christensen bomb was the only one that had been packed with nails. There wasn't as much powder in the other two bombs. And the pipes used were slightly different in size. But these were distinctions without a difference, Taylor emphasized. From over sixty similar investigations, he could say without any reservations—which was the way he said everything—that the three bombs were essentially identical, meaning that they were dealing with a single bomber. Also, the person who made the bombs was the person who set them. If two different people had been involved, there would have been some safety mechanisms. There weren't.

In Taylor's judgment, Mark Hofmann manufactured and set all three bombs.

On the basis of Taylor's description, a local ATF agent, Ray Dalling, built a replica of the bomb. Then Bell borrowed a Toyota MR2 from a local Toyota dealership and drove to the exact spot on North Main where the third bomb had gone off. As Taylor had suspected, the bomb wouldn't sit on the console, the gearshift got in the way. That meant that Hofmann had to arm it while it was still in the back area, behind the seats—an awkward operation at best.

It was in bringing the bomb package forward between the seats and turning to get out of the car that he must have dropped it. That explained why his right hand, with which he must have reached for the package, had the fingertips blown off, while the left hand, which may have been reaching to open the door, was virtually unscathed. He had been holding it with his right hand when it slipped, and Bang! With a mercury switch, it took only milliseconds for ignition, according to Taylor. It had been practically instantaneous.

A few days later, around midnight, as Bell and Farnsworth slowly made their way through Hofmann's papers in the third-floor evidence room, they found a check made out to Radio Shack.

On October 19, Sergeant Sid Elliott of the sheriff's office in Cottonwood filed a report that included an interview with a young neighbor of Kathy Sheets's who had seen a suspicious van cruising the driveway in front of the Sheets house the night before the bombing. A few days later, Elliott's report arrived on Jim Bell's desk, together with a note that Mark Hofmann owned a van of similar description.

The neighbor turned out to be Aaron Teplick, a thirteen-year-old boy who lived not just near the Sheetses, but right next door, on the same tiny cul-de-sac off Naniloa Drive. Like most cops, Bell was skeptical of child witnesses—not because they weren't observant but because they were notoriously vulnerable in court. But he had Teplick brought to the Hall of Justice for an interview anyway, just in case.

It was a setting as intimidating as any courtroom. Teplick's parents didn't accompany him. The only other people in the room were five officers: Sid Elliott, the sheriff's deputy who had interviewed him first; Bob Swehla and Jerry Miller from ATF; Jim Bell; and Ken Farnsworth. But Teplick proved a trouper. In a calm, sure voice, he repeated his story that he had seen a strange van drive through the cul-de-sac the night before the bombing.

"I felt ill that night. It was really late. I woke up and was just getting up to get an aspirin and then I saw that Toyota van come down our street."

"What time was this, do you remember?"

"It was about 11:30 or twelve."

"How do you remember that?"

" 'Cause there's a clock in our kitchen and I looked." If only their *adult* witnesses were this observant, thought Bell.

"Okay, you went to the kitchen and got an aspirin and then you looked out the kitchen window?"

"It was our hall window. I just heard a car down there and just wanted to see who it was. . . . We have a little private driveway with three houses down there."

"Okay, describe what you saw, Aaron."

"Well, first I saw a light come down our driveway and then it kind of pulled in front of our house, and I looked out and it was just a gold Toyota Wonder Wagon. It was there for a couple of minutes. . . . Then it turned in the Bridges' driveway, which is the other next-door neighbors, and went back up our hill."

"You mention a Toyota. How do you know that it was a Toyota?"

"Well, that particular car is a pretty obvious car—it

was one of those new kinds of vans." And then Teplick proceeded to give the cops a complete lesson on recent changes in automotive design. The kid knew what he was talking about.

They had him draw a picture of the van as he described it. Then they showed him a series of Polaroids of various similar vans, including Hofmann's.

He pointed out what was wrong with each of the photos until he landed on Mark's. "That's it," he said—very calm, very decisive.

Farnsworth called it a "class act" (his highest accolade) and after it was over, Bell joked, "You'd think he was raised in L.A."

69

But it wasn't enough.

On Tuesday, October 29, two weeks after the bombings, the hospital announced that Mark Hofmann would be released the following Thursday. And still no charges had been filed: not for the murders, not for the bombings, not for fraud, not even for the traffic ticket the computer had spit out the moment he became a suspect.

At 2:30 that afternoon, Bell and Farnsworth and the other investigators met with the county attorney, Ted Cannon, and the U.S. attorney, Brent Ward, in a last-ditch effort to persuade them to file charges—some charges, any charges—to prevent Hofmann from walking out of the hospital a free man.

One face conspicuously missing from the meeting was Sheriff Pete Hayward's. He had already dismissed the Hofmann case, not because he believed Hofmann wasn't guilty, but because, in Sheriff Hayward's mind, the case was already wrapped up. Hayward, an amiable bulldog of a man, didn't believe in all this scientific investigation crapola. His heart (as well as his crime-solving technique) was still firmly rooted in the nineteenth century, when Utah was the Wild West and Wyatt Earp was marshal. His idea of solving a crime was jumping in his car, turning on the siren, racing to the scene, and collaring the bad guy. His idea of investigation was driving around and looking for anything suspicious. As for interviews, he could look a man in the eye and tell if he was lying.

His tactics gave bleeding-heart liberals heart failure, but the people loved him. He was the kind of cop they liked to watch on TV—no boring details, no drudgery, no paperwork, just action. In fact, they *had* watched him on TV, on the 5 o'clock news, confronting a crazed gunman in a 7-Eleven store, all alone, unarmed. The television cameras had recorded every thrilling moment as Hayward, steady as a rock, waited for his opening, and, when the man's look was averted, grabbed the shotgun from his hand. The sheer bravery of it was awesome. This was how lawmen were supposed to do their job.

And remarkably often, it worked.

Unfortunately, his department operated by the same seat-of-the-pants rules. While Jim Bell was mapping out the Christensen bomb site and collecting bits of evidence on his knees with a pair of tweezers, Sheriff Hayward's deputies were blowing through the Sheets crime scene like a twister, throwing everything they could find into a big green garbage bag. No grids, no diagrams, no tweezers, no magnifying glasses. As a result, the sheriff's men had missed several key pieces of evidence, including major bomb parts at the Sheets house. (The ATF's Jerry Taylor found them on a follow-up search days later.)

In the weeks following, interviews with important witnesses were mishandled and then, even worse, mislaid. When Bell called to get them, he was told they didn't exist. "But we have witnesses who said they were interviewed by the sheriff's department," he insisted. "They must have been talking to reporters," cracked one of the sheriff's shoot-from-the-hip deputies.

One day, weeks after the bombings, Jerry Thompson of the sheriff's office appeared on the eighth floor of the Hall of Justice and handed Bell a file. "Here is something we found pushed back behind a file cabinet," he said. "Do you want them?" They were the missing interviews, along with the evidence of Hofmann's travel schedule. Not only had the police been forced to reinterview the same witnesses—a considerable embarrassment—but the chain of custody on the travel evidence had been broken. Bell knew that a good defense attorney could "blow them out of the water" if he found out about the foul-up.

But none of that seemed to make any difference to Sheriff Pete Hayward. His business was solving crimes—let the lawyers worry about the technicalities.

Needless to say, that attitude had earned Hayward a number of enemies among the prosecutors of Salt Lake County, but none so virulent or implacable as the head prosecutor, County Attorney Ted Cannon. It was an enmity that went far beyond political differences (Hayward was a Democrat, Cannon a Republican) or working styles. The two men just plain didn't like each other. Despite having to work together on hundreds of cases a year, they weren't even on speaking terms. When absolutely necessary, they communicated through intermediaries: one man's deputy would speak to the other man's deputy.

So when Cannon said he needed more evidence from the sheriff's office to indict Hofmann on the Sheets murder, Hayward ostentatiously washed his hands of the whole matter. As far as *he* was concerned, the case was *over*. His office had done its job by fingering Hofmann. If the county attorney's office was too obstinate or obtuse to file charges, that was their problem. He wasn't about to waste any more of his men's time or the taxpayers' money just to make Ted Cannon's job a little easier. And that's exactly what he told the press.

So the meeting on the 29th went on without Sheriff Hayward.

Jim Bell began with an impassioned plea. "We've got to arrest the guy. We can't just let him go home. It was a double murder. He shouldn't be going home; he should be going to jail. He doesn't deserve any free time, even if he *is* injured."

Ted Cannon, for one, wasn't convinced. He didn't want to charge the Christensen murder without charging the Sheets murder—and he couldn't charge the Sheets murder because the sheriff's office hadn't done its job. It wasn't clear if Cannon was more interested in scoring points against his nemesis Hayward or in arresting Mark

Hofmann. As an elected official himself, Cannon also knew that if he indicted on Christensen and not on Sheets, the press would rally to the cause of Kathy Sheets. Cannon put the best face he could on an impossible situation. "If we did arrest him," he told Bell, "his lawyers would come right over and get him out."

So Hayward was out and Cannon was out.

That left Brent Ward, U.S. attorney. Would he file on the federal bomb charges? All eyes turned to the young man in the bow tie at the end of the table.

70

Bell and Farnsworth weren't hopeful. They remembered how much trouble Ward had given them when they tried to get a warrant to search Shannon Flynn's house. Right after the Flynn interview, Farnsworth had called Bruce Lubeck, Ward's assistant on the case. Because the Uzi possession was a federal violation, they needed the U.S. Attorney's Office to sign off on it.

Lubeck told them to call Brent Ward. Right then, Farnsworth knew something was wrong. Why would the top man take such a personal interest in the details of the case?

Then Ward wouldn't give them an answer. He told them to stay off Lubeck's line for at least fifteen minutes while he discussed the case with him. Fifteen minutes later, Lubeck's line was still busy. Farnsworth wondered what the hell could be taking so long. This was a simple, straightforward warrant based not on a tip but on a confession. Something was up.

When they finally talked to Lubeck again, another surprise: "I think you ought to try to arrange a consent search." That meant going back to Flynn and getting him to say, "Okay, you can search my house." This at the very same time they were arresting him and putting him in jail. Farnsworth was mystified. Why were they resisting a warrant? Surely they knew it was, in fact, *better* to get a formal warrant than to rely on a consent search that might later be challenged in court. ("My client was in the jailhouse, intimidated by police officers, placed under arrest, and under extreme duress, Your Honor. His consent wasn't voluntary!") What was Ward afraid of?

Farnsworth decided to think about it later. Right then, he wanted the warrant. "That's stupid," he told Lubeck. "Let's get the warrant. That way there will be a legal stamp on this thing, and that way we won't lose the evidence."

But Lubeck still resisted. He—and Ward, obviously—still wanted a consent search. Farnsworth finally pushed him into it, and at four in the morning, he went down to the police station and filled out the necessary paperwork. But the episode left a lot of unanswered questions in Ken Farnsworth's mind.

If Pete Hayward was the frontier sheriff, Brent Ward was the yuppie lawyer. With his red suspenders, bow tie, and horn-rimmed glasses, he could have been the rising star of some big corporate law firm on the fast track to the top. Which is exactly what he *was* before December 1981, when Orrin Hatch, Utah senator and Mormon elder, picked him, at the age of thirty-six, for the U.S. attorney's job.

They may have come from different centuries, but Sheriff Hayward and Brent Ward had one thing in common: political instincts. At the very least, Ward was in line for a federal judgeship if he chose that direction. At his age, that would put him in the running, if Senator Hatch's conservative star continued to rise, for an appeals court, or even, some day, the Supreme Court. It was no secret that one of the Church's most fervent wishes was to seat a Mormon justice on the nation's highest court.

That was the other bottom-line feature of Brent Ward: the Church. More than just a devout Mormon, Ward was an ambitious one. Of course, in Utah, political ambition and religious ambition were always closely allied. It was difficult to rise to prominent public office without the Church's backing. It was virtually impossible to do so against the Church's opposition. That was a fact of life in

Utah that any good politician understood, and Brent Ward was a very good politician.

In his four years as U.S. attorney, Ward had concentrated his activities on popular causes like pornography and child abuse—causes, not coincidentally, that the Church cared about. When the Hofmann story began to break, more than a few people wondered how the ambitious young U.S. attorney would handle himself in a case that the Church wanted to avoid at all costs.

Like Farnsworth, they soon found out.

Ward's first action was to help arrange to have a key piece of evidence shipped out of state. By the time the key investigators knew enough to ask the Church for the so-called Salamander Letter, it was already gone—off to the FBI's laboratories in Washington, D.C., for a long and very confidential analysis. When the county attorney's office requested other Hofmann documents, the Church refused to hand them over. Why would they push one sensitive document into the FBI's hands almost immediately after the bombing and fight to keep other documents out of police hands for weeks? Church spokesmen said they didn't trust local law enforcement.

But they *could* trust the heavily Mormon FBI, which worked hand-in-glove with Brent Ward.

It was Ward's FBI agents who had swooped down on all the major figures in the case in the first few days and taken statements. By the third day, however, as soon as it became clear that the Church was involved somehow, the FBI stopped sharing its information. Its agents wouldn't give local police the names of the people they had interviewed. Bell's detectives would arrive only to be told by a beleaguered witness, "What are you doing here? The FBI was here yesterday, asking the same questions. Don't you people talk to each other? Aren't you all law enforcement?" By the end of the first week, some detectives themselves were beginning to wonder.

The police asked if they could go along on FBI interviews. The FBI refused. The police asked to see the FBI interviews, a courtesy routinely extended to local law enforcement agencies on a confidential basis. The FBI refused.

At one point, Farnsworth, Bell, and others from the police department and the county attorney's office were invited to Ward's office. The purpose of the meeting, according to Ward, was to "share information." At last, thought Farnsworth, they're going to let us see what they've got. But it turned out that by "sharing information," Ward meant that the local agents should share *their* information with the federal agents, not the other way around.

The police weren't the only ones who began to wonder whom exactly Brent Ward was collecting this information for. Confidential FBI files were known to have wound up on certain desks in the Church Office Building. Was Ward running a damage-control operation for the Church, sending FBI men out ahead of local police to find out just what the Church's exposure was?

That might explain his bizarre insistence on getting a statement from Hofmann. At a meeting on the afternoon of October 24, Ward's assistant, Bruce Lubeck, demanded a "statement from Hofmann for the files." Bell and Farnsworth and Gerry D'Elia couldn't believe it. They were in the middle of a furious legal battle to compel Nurse Loden to reveal what she had heard in Hofmann's hospital room, and Ward thought that Yengich was going to let Hofmann talk to the cops directly? After the meeting, Bell turned to Farnsworth in disgust. "That's typical. If you don't go down and talk to the suspect so he can tell you to get screwed, they don't feel you've done a complete investigation." Obviously, Ward was reaching—stretching—for excuses not to act.

One thing was obvious from the moment the Church got involved in the case: Brent Ward had no intention of prosecuting *anybody* for *anything* related to the bombings. Hofmann was indicted along with Shannon Flynn for possession of the altered Uzi, but a judge quickly set aside that charge pending the outcome of the state's case. Only a few days after the bombings, ATF agents presented their evidence to Ward. They felt confident they had a federal case against Hofmann, at least for possession of a destructive device, a felony that carried a sentence of ten years in prison. They had the physical evidence, they had the letter jacket, they had the witnesses at the Judge Building. Hell, they had more than they had in most possession cases.

But Brent Ward wouldn't touch it.

And the ATF men thought they knew why. "There was too much at stake," one of them said later. "His political career was at stake. Whether he wanted to secure his political base in Utah or to further strengthen his bond with Mormon Senator Hatch—either way, it would not be helpful to put himself in a position where he had to subpoena Gordon B. Hinckley and the other Church officials, or to expose the Church's transactions with Mark Hofmann to the full light of day."

If the Church didn't want the truth out, then neither, it appeared, did Brent Ward. If the Church didn't want this case in the headlines, didn't want to get itself involved in the legal process, who was Brent Ward to put it there? As for his sworn duty to uphold the law, well, there were laws and there were laws. As one investigator on the case saw it: "Brent Ward's got motives above and beyond the law. Do you think a good Mormon in the U.S. Attorney's Office is going to hesitate for one minute deciding to do what's correct for the law or what's best for the Church? This guy was on his way to being a *god*. Next to that, U.S. attorney looks pretty insignificant."

All Ward would say, when asked about the case, was, "My gut tells me Hofmann didn't do it."

For a while, Ward even refused to convene a grand jury to *consider* if there was sufficient evidence to indict Hofmann. When finally, under pressure, he did call a grand jury, he kept it on a short leash. Police and prosecutors were excluded from its sessions. Eventually, local officials pressured him into agreeing to allow a prosecutor from the county attorney's office to sit in, but before he could attend his first session, he was informed that "a call had been placed to Washington, and Washington says, 'You can't do that.'"

In fact, he wasn't missing much. Of the more than two hundred people interviewed in connection with the case, only a dozen or so were called before the grand jury. And of those, most were questioned in what would have been considered, in any other federal grand jury room, an unusual way.

"Are you a Mormon?" Al Rust was asked during his session before the grand jury.

"Yes."

"How would you rate yourself as a Mormon between one and ten?"

"I'd like to put it at a nine or a ten, but I'm probably a five or a six."

"Have you been a Mormon bishop?"

"Yes, I have."

Even Rust wondered, "Isn't it kind of strange that religion would be a part of the questioning? What difference should it make?"

Even stranger was the determination of *which* witnesses would testify before the grand jury.

Despite their centrality to the case, no Church officials were called to testify. When people complained, Ward insisted that there was no need to subpoena them to appear. Instead, he would simply request an appointment at the Church Office Building and interview the officials himself, alone, one on one. No need for grand jury members or oaths or court reporters. And then he, Brent Ward, would decide what parts of the interview were relevant.

Terri Christensen wasn't the only one who suspected that Ward was running interference for the Church. "If you want results from the grand jury," she told him one day, "go subpoena Gordon Hinckley instead of just going along the sidelines and making a show of it. Then you might just find something."

When she stalked out of the room, Ward turned to one of the federal agents and broke into a patronizing smile. "She's a very nice-looking lady," he confided, "but she doesn't seem like a deep thinker."

At the meeting on October 29, no one was surprised when Brent Ward said he wasn't ready to charge Hofmann.

So Hayward was out, Cannon was out, and Ward was out. That meant Hofmann would remain a free man.

Two days later, at seven in the morning, Bell and Farnsworth arrived at the LDS Hospital to escort Mark Hofmann home. His attorney had requested security. After all, there was still a crazed, homicidal Mormon fanatic out there who wanted to kill him.

News of the release had been kept from the press, so Hofmann's Toyota van—the one that Aaron Teplick had picked out of a photo lineup—sat alone in front of the hospital when they arrived. Mark came out in a wheelchair, helped by Bill and Lu Hofmann and Dorie. When they arrived at the house on Marie Avenue, Bell and Farnsworth carried him into the house.

For just a split second, Ken Farnsworth fantasized that

he was carrying Hofmann into the state penitentiary at Point of the Mountain—where he belonged. But by now it was clear that if he and Bell were ever going to see that day, they would have to make it happen without help from anyone.

71

Al Rust couldn't believe Mark Hofmann would do anything so terrible. Not that he was perfect, God knows. Certainly no one had more right to complain than Al Rust. He was paying $1,500 a month interest on the $150,000 he had borrowed to invest with Hofmann. He couldn't sell off pieces from his precious Mormon collection because most of that was tied up in the investigation. Besides, the market for Mormonabilia had fallen apart since the bombings. He even had to face the possibility that he would have to sell his house to pay off his debts. Mark's debts.

But bombings? forgeries? Rust just couldn't believe it. "He's not a drunkard," he told himself. "He's not a dope addict. He's not a gambler. He's not a womanizer. None of those things." The police may have already tried and convicted him. But not Al Rust. As a good Christian and a good Mormon, he was going to give his friend the benefit of the doubt.

In fact, he was going to go to the hospital and wish him well—only, when he got there, Mark wasn't receiving visitors.

So, after they released Mark from the hospital, he decided to drop by the house. He called Dorie first.

"Well, how's he doing?" Rust asked, regretting the times he had lost his temper and exploded at Dorie.

"Pretty good," she said.

"Will he have visitors?"

"Yeah. I think he'd like to see you." Rust was pleased

that she didn't seem to hold a grudge. Boy, this must be a hard time for her, he thought.

"Why don't you ask him?" he suggested gently.

While she was away from the phone, Rust thought again how wrong they were to suspect Mark of committing those bombings. A moment later she returned. "Yeah, he said he'd like to see you."

So Rust went home and carefully chose a book from his library, one that he felt sure Mark hadn't read, and took it to him.

As soon as he got there, he looked Mark straight in the eyes, and asked him point-blank: "Mark, did you commit these murders?"

"No. I didn't."

Even though he had never believed it, Rust felt a great weight lifted from his shoulders. "Do you know who did?"

"No."

Rust believed that too, but he was still mindful of Mark's shortcomings. "And what about all these lies on the McLellin papers?" he asked.

"Well, right now, I'm confused on the McLellin papers," said Hofmann. "I don't know just how to handle this. But right now I can't talk about the McLellin papers. My lawyer won't let me."

Rust didn't want to let it drop. He wanted to clear the air between them. "Word is that you and I were to deliver them there that day, and you know I haven't seen them, and I don't have them in my safe-deposit box, which is where you told them the papers are."

"I can't talk about that."

"Mark. You know my financial position. Shoot, I had to borrow that hundred and fifty thousand, and we kind of made an agreement that I would get it back within thirty days. It's six months now, and I'm paying fifteen hundred a month interest. I need to recover it."

"No problem," said Hofmann, fidgeting in his wheelchair. "I'm working with my attorney to go back to New York and sell some things."

Rust thought that sounded suspiciously like another Hofmann story. After all this, were they just back to square one? He refused to believe that the pain and suffering Mark had been through hadn't taught him something. Besides, given the condition he was in now, it was wrong to press him on it.

But he did see Mark's civil attorney, Robert Schumacher.

Schumacher told him that there was no plan to go to New York, no plan to sell anything. Mark had lied to him again. "Something's sure wrong here," Rust concluded. "I just keep getting stories." So he filed a lawsuit, a process that produced nothing except the distressing news that Hofmann didn't have a nickel to his name.

Rust visited Hofmann twice more at home, once by himself and once with Mark's attorney. Both times, Mark sat impassively in his La-Z-Boy recliner and listened. Except every once in a while, when Rust caught Mark off guard out of the corner of his eye, he had the most offensive smirk on his face.

But he still didn't believe that Mark was capable of murder.

72

The day after the third bombing, The Word came down from the offices of the First Presidency.

It was quick, but not quite quick enough. The day *of* the Hofmann bombing—before the edict filtered down through the Church hierarchy—Detective John Foster, a soft-spoken, self-effacing man with a dry sense of humor, visited Martell Bird in the Church Office Building. He was following up on Hofmann's statement, given almost as soon as he regained consciousness, that he was being tailed by Church Security in a tan pickup truck. Foster told Bird, "Some allegations have been made that Mark had been followed by Church Security."

Bird denied the story adamantly. And he was willing to cooperate with the police in any way necessary to clear himself and his colleagues.

When Foster brought him a list of all the owners of

trucks resembling Hofmann's description, Bird pulled out the Church employee records and cross-checked them with Foster's list. They found one "kid," who worked for Church Security, with the same last name as one of the owners on the list. The lead turned out to be a dry hole, but Foster was impressed with Bird's cooperativeness.

Like the way he offered the information about President Hinckley's meeting with Mark Hofmann, a meeting that took place at the unlikely hour of 7:00 A.M. on October 4, less than two weeks before the bombings. Foster didn't have to ask about it. Bird just volunteered it, strangely enough, while emphasizing how little involvement there was between Hofmann and the Church. He considered the meeting "insignificant."

Foster didn't. Despite his laconic humor and easygoing manner, Foster was a good cop, and, like all good cops, suspicious. He found it strange that a man who supposedly had no real involvement with the Church would be visiting its President at seven in the morning—and even stranger that Martell Bird would "blow it off" as insignificant.

"I was curious about it myself," Bird admitted when Foster pressed him. "So I went and asked President Hinckley about it. President Hinckley told me it was a guy named Mark Hofmann. 'He came to tell me about some people who had transcripts of the conference agenda,' he said." The semiannual Church conference was scheduled for the second week in October. Before each conference, transcripts of the talks to be given by Church officials are prepared and translated into various languages so they will be available at the time of the conference. But they are supposed to remain secret until officially released.

Bird continued: "Hofmann was here to tell President Hinckley that somebody had copies of the transcripts and was about to let them out." Bird said he had checked the Church Administration Building log and that Mark Hofmann had indeed paid a visit to President Hinckley at the unusually early hour of seven.

When Foster told him about it, Ken Farnsworth was astonished that nobody had bothered to inform the police about the meeting—a meeting that might be crucial to understanding the pressures on Hofmann prior to the bombings. But at the same time, he was encouraged that Martell Bird, apparently, *wanted* to cooperate. Given the way everybody else was balking, he certainly welcomed the openness.

The next day, The Word came down.

Foster found that out when he officially requested copies of the Church Administration Building log—the log from the First Presidency guard station, not Hinckley's personal log book. "I'd like to get a copy of that sign-in sheet," he said, "to show that Mark was there on that day."

Martell Bird called back a few minutes later. "It wasn't that day. I was mistaken about the day." He said it was the latter part of September. He offered to provide a photocopy of the sign-in sheet for the *right* day.

But when Foster went to pick up the photocopy, every entry except the one relating to Hofmann had been whited out. The day-timer had been copied, then expurgated, then copied again, giving the police no way to determine if relevant entries had been whited out along with irrelevant ones.

When he asked for a photocopy of the sheet for October 4, the date originally mentioned, Bird refused. His attitude had completely changed. Instead of eager and cooperative, he had become cool, suspicious, and recalcitrant. Foster recognized the signs. "Somebody's told him to shut up, or told him that he shouldn't have ever said anything about it in the first place."

On the same day, Nurse Nancy Loden walked into the county attorney's office with a Church lawyer. The Word, apparently, had also been passed from the boardroom on Temple Square to the boardroom of LDS Hospital. Jim Bell heard from friends on the nursing staff that the higher-ups had been very explicit: "Don't talk to the cops, no matter what happens."

Just how much things had changed didn't hit them until they went to the hospital to serve an investigative subpoena on Hofmann to obtain new fingerprints and photos of his injuries. At the security desk, they were told they would have to explain their business both to the security team and to the hospital administration. Both groups would need to see the paperwork and hear what they needed.

"Is it okay if I call the defense attorneys?" asked the hospital director.

"Okay," said Bell. "You can give them a call, but we're here, and we'd like to do it and get it done and get on with our own work. We've got things to do." Hell, they weren't going to ask him any questions, they just wanted his fingerprints.

But it was another fifteen minutes before the security officer found the time to take them to the area where Hofmann was being kept. And when they arrived, a staff member rushed in front of them with a portable X-ray machine. "Oh, looks like they've got to do some X rays first before we can go in there," said the security guard, like a bit player in a high school drama. "We'll have to wait." They waited, coincidentally, until Yengich's associate, Brad Rich, arrived.

By the time Bell and Farnsworth talked to Hugh Pinnock on December 2, the relationship between the Church and the police had turned from chilly to ice cold. Pinnock seemed to understand that: he shook throughout the meeting. In his fourteen years of police work, Farnsworth had never seen anybody more nervous. In a relatively short fifteen-minute exchange—the primary purpose of which was only to reassure him that they were not "out to get him"—Pinnock drank what seemed like an entire pitcher of water. Bell wondered how he would handle the real interview the following Friday.

In fact, he was a basket case. With Dallin Oaks and the Church lawyer, Oscar McConkie, looking on in dismay, Pinnock led Farnsworth and questioner from the county attorney's office and the FBI on a wild three-hour ride through the last five months of his life.

His chronology was a mess: July, October, August, July, September, August, October. Farnsworth, who had prepared carefully, hardly had a chance to ask a question. He rarely knew what Pinnock was saying. It wasn't until afterward, when he deciphered his notes, that he began to see the gaping holes and inconsistencies.

It wasn't that Pinnock hadn't kept a record. In fact, he had kept a meticulous record, a journal of every phone call, every meeting, with the names of everyone in attendance. He used a personal shorthand, with initials for names, to keep the entries brief, but they were complete—"down to the last sneeze" according to Farnsworth.

So why was the presentation so incoherent?

Because Pinnock didn't have the journal with him.

Farnsworth couldn't believe it. Instead of reading from his journal, Pinnock had copied onto separate sheets of paper all the "relevant" entries. He even positioned them on the paper so they corresponded to the entries in the journal. The result was an incoherent patchwork of secondhand notes. Whenever somebody expressed confusion, Pinnock would simply say, "This is how it's written in my journal, but I don't have the journal here."

Why *didn't* he have his journal?

"I don't want to show you all those personal things having to do with the Church," he said, shaking just as he had at their last meeting. "I could read from that if I wanted to," he added defensively. "I could do that."

But he never did. He just returned to the cryptic entries and read verbatim, without expression. And if anyone asked him to elaborate, he simply said, "I can't remember."

Not surprisingly, the interview produced few surprises.

In retelling the events immediately following the bombings, Pinnock did seem genuinely touched. Farnsworth noted, "When he's talking with us, he's crying. He was just devastated by this. He wasn't concerned for his own personal safety—he was worried about his wife and kids. You can see him reliving his whole emotions. Talk about confusion, everybody was dying all around him. He didn't know what was going on. It was a hard time for him."

On October 25, Pinnock said, he had paid off Hofmann's loan from First Interstate Bank—$ 171,243.76. Doing so had wiped out his liquidity. But, he said, "If I hadn't made the referral, the loan wouldn't have been made. It's mine and mine alone."

The Word had finally gotten through to Pinnock: protect the Church.

Farnsworth came out of the interview believing Pinnock's pain was genuine, but little else. "Just not telling all," he wrote in his notes.

The next day, December 7, was Mark Hofmann's thirty-first birthday. Farnsworth, who felt an obligation to keep the victims' families informed, reported the conversation with Pinnock to Terri Christensen, now eight months pregnant. He wasn't surprised by her reaction.

"I am going to go to that man and talk to him myself,"

she fumed. "I'm tired of all this . . ."—Farnsworth supplied the word *crap* " . . . that I'm hearing."

But he talked her out of it. Confronting Pinnock now couldn't do any good, he argued. Even worse, it might put other Church leaders on their guard.

73

On December 9, Farnsworth interviewed Gordon B. Hinckley.

It had been almost two months since the bombings, two months since Hinckley's name first surfaced in connection with Mark Hofmann's, two months since he became a key figure in a major police investigation. If he had been anybody else, the police would have paid him a visit long ago, before his memory faded, before he had a chance to revise his story to fit with the other stories appearing every day in the newspapers. But Hinckley wasn't just anybody else.

Even without the police badgering him, it hadn't been an easy two months for Gordon Hinckley. Right-wingers in the Council of the Seventy were already meeting and talking in low, frustrated voices about how President Hinckley had mishandled the case. Mark Hofmann had fooled him. Where was his *inspiration?* Some were already calling him a "fallen leader." Hinckley fired back by circulating a statement within the General Authorities casting himself as a warrior fighting a stupendous, mortal battle against all the forces of Satan (a.k.a. Mark Hofmann) arrayed against him. How lucky the Church was to have escaped with only a little allegation of fraud.

But the militants weren't fooled. They had already begun a whispering campaign: "Hinckley isn't inspired. The Church needs a spiritual cleansing. He should step down."

The last thing he needed now was a police interrogation.

* * *

Duffy Diamond, the sergeant of Homicide, wasn't about to send just any detective to do the job. Although not a Mormon, Diamond had enough Irish savvy to know when to take his hat off. He knew the first question out of Hinckley's mouth would be, "Are you a member of the Church?" quickly followed by, "In good standing?" The third question would be, "Where did you do your mission?" It was their standard way of asserting their claim—a claim that transcended anything so temporal as a job.

That's why Diamond picked Ken Farnsworth for the job. He was, to all appearances, a good Mormon, even if he wasn't married. The county attorney's office sent Mike George, one of its investigators, to join him, and an FBI man tagged along. As a Catholic, George didn't think the pomp and circumstance would cow him, but he was wrong. Passing the big Corinthian columns and being led through the hushed, paneled halls, he felt as if he was having an audience with the Pope.

This Pope wasn't above playing power games. Hinckley let them cool their heels in his outer office for half an hour before instructing his secretary to usher them into his presence.

Even Popes, however, need legal counsel. So Hinckley had invited the Church's lawyer, Wilford Kirton, to join them.

The lighting was so subdued, thought Mike George, it could have been a funeral parlor.

Curiously, Hinckley singled out Mike George, the Catholic, for his standard opener: "Are you a member of the Church?" George had to wonder if the Church didn't already have a readout on the religious affiliations of all the key investigators in the Hofmann case.

From the first question, Hinckley never relinquished control of the meeting. Normally, George would have seized the offensive by stalking the room, leaning over the witness's desk, or even sitting on it. But somehow he didn't feel right just getting up and sitting on the desk of the man who ran the Mormon Church—even if it was almost bare.

Not surprisingly, the interview produced no revelations. Hinckley's memory had not improved one jot since the press conference in October. If anything, the controversy had driven details right out of his head. So many truly *important* things to worry about. He did have one addition to make to the record. "If you read the transcript of the press conference," he said, "you will see that I said I dealt with two documents with Mark Hofmann, and I couldn't remember the second one. The first was the Josiah Stowell letter. The second one was he David Whitmer letter." (That was a brief document that confirmed the testimony of a witness to the *Book of Mormon.*) Then he added the real point. "Actually, the Church bought them, and I simply handled the transactions."

Hinckley went on to review his contacts with Hofmann, from the Anthon Transcript to the Kinderhook plates. And, oh, yes, there was something called the McLellin Collection, but he had told Hofmann to take care of Al Rust before he would talk about it. That was the last he could remember hearing about it.

And what about Steve Christensen?

After the press conference at which Hinckley had said he hardly knew Christensen, the police and prosecutors had been flooded with calls from Steve's friends—good, upstanding members of the Church, even a bishop—who said that wasn't true. They were confused and angry. Someone like Hofmann might have exaggerated his relationship with Hinckley, but not Christensen.

Hinckley sighed, clearly signaling his exasperation with answering the same questions again and again. He had met with Steve Christensen one time only, on April 12, 1985, when Mr. Christensen donated the Martin Harris letter to the Church. In other words, for the third time, "I don't know him."

Farnsworth asked if there had been any special blessing conferred on Christensen or if the Church had made any special business agreement with him. Both his wife and his business partner had told Farnsworth about such an agreement. Kirton broke in. "A lot of people have egos and feed off of that stuff. They like to feel that they're very important people."

Farnsworth wanted to say, "Who the hell do you think you are lecturing me, with my job, about human nature?" but said instead, as politely as possible, "Steve was different. Steve wasn't that way. That wasn't his nature, from what I know." He decided to hang them with their own rope. "And he was a bishop. I grew up in the Mormon Church. All of my bishops were honorable people. I had the highest respect for all of them, each and every one. A carpenter, a lawyer, you name it, they were the tops, in my opinion. They always conducted themselves properly, they were always sagacious people."

Kirton sighed. "Ah. We have ten thousand bishops, and they have problems just like everybody else."

Farnsworth said to himself, "I get the picture you're trying to paint here. Steve was just another person. This didn't all happen, and there's no way we're gonna tell you anything about it even if it did."

President Hinckley said he had no further information relevant to the investigation.

When they came out of the building, one of the investigators said under his breath, "Why, that lying son of a bitch." Without blinking, Farnsworth and the FBI man nodded their heads in agreement. George was startled. *He* was the non-Mormon.

Down at the department, Farnsworth recapped the interview and repeated their assessment of Hinckley. Duffy Diamond agreed. "Those guys think they're dealing with a bunch of dumbbells," he fulminated. "A bunch of dopes. Well, I've got news for them. We ain't no dummies over here."

74 Everyone agreed that it was a good thing Fred Harmon wasn't there to hear Farnsworth's account.

Harmon, a solid family man from Sacramento, California, joined the Hofmann case soon after the bombings. He was the ATF's operations officer, the man who kept track of all the information and gave out assignments. Like Jim Bell, he saw everything.

He arrived a devout Mormon.

Fifteen years before, Harmon had turned to the LDS Church after the crib death of his eight-month-old daughter. With their firm belief in the afterlife and in the reunion of families in the Celestial Kingdom, the Mormons offered Harmon hope and he grasped at it. "If it looks bad," they explained to him in his grief, "it's because you're not seeing the whole picture. If you just have *total faith*, everything will eventually be made clear."

That lesson had gotten him through his personal tragedy, and in gratitude Harmon had surrendered himself to the Church: studying the gospels—including those of Joseph Smith—raising his children in a devout Mormon household, and living a rigorously Mormon life-style—not an easy thing for an adult convert outside Utah.

Then he began to read the reports.

It was the interviews with Church officials that first made him wonder. What were they covering up? If they were really the victims of a fraud and not the perpetrators, why were they afraid of the truth? But he told himself there had to be an answer. He just couldn't see the whole picture. He just needed to have *total faith*, and eventually everything would be made clear.

Then he listened to the press conference. He listened closely, hoping he might finally hear from the leaders of his Church the explanations that would make everything right again. Instead, he heard "lie after lie." Dallin Oaks he pegged for an unwitting accomplice. The others had lied to him, Harmon figured. Pinnock was just ambitious. Like a functionary in any organization, he realized that pleasing Hinckley, handling his unpleasant little jobs, was the key to advancement. Pinnock, at least, looked chastened at the press conference. To Harmon, he acted like a man who knew he had erred. He had the grace to look chagrined.

To Fred Harmon, devout Mormon, the real villain was President Gordon B. Hinckley. He saw no chagrin on Hinckley's broad, implacable face. No repentance. No apologies. No admission of wrongdoing. Just arrogance—plain, unbridled arrogance. As far as he was concerned, Hinckley had fallen for Mark Hofmann's blackmail, bought up damaging documents and hidden them away in his private vault, and in so doing, indirectly contributed to the deaths of two innocent people.

And then lied about it. As Harmon saw it, Hinckley had lied outright by saying he had met with Mark Hofmann only casually and with Steve Christensen only once; he had lied indirectly by allowing Church spokesmen to deny that the Church owned documents he had bought. And where did the money come from? If it was the Church's money, what kind of accounting procedures were involved? To whom did Hinckley account, if anybody? Or did Hinckley consider himself answerable only to God?

Fred Harmon, gentle man, loving father, faithful husband, devout Mormon, couldn't contain his anger.

He knew his religion well. Facing temptations and overcoming them were the essence of a religious life. Who was Gordon Hinckley to decide what the members of the Church could or could not know about the Church's history? Who was he to decide what temptations were too tempting?

Hinckley, he concluded, was no different from any other powerful man.

If absolute power corrupts absolutely, surely spiritual power corrupts spiritually.

And what did it say about the Church? If the Church was run by men who told lies, was the Church itself a lie? Harmon refused to believe it. "If it looks bad," he repeated to himself over and over, "it's because I'm not seeing the whole picture. If I just have *total faith*, everything will eventually be made clear."

But it wasn't. In fact, the more deeply he became immersed in the case, the more interviews he did, the worse the whole picture looked. He could feel his faith slipping away. He began to hate Gordon Hinckley, not just for the arrogance, not just for the lying, but for coming between him and his religion.

Harmon heard that Terri Christensen shared his anger at the leaders of the Church and wanted to talk to her. "My wife is not the type to bite her tongue or keep her silence," Harmon told Ken Farnsworth, "but if I had been in Steve Christensen's place, she would be standing on top of the state capitol building with a megaphone screaming to the world what had been done to me and yelling about the lies that were being told and *demanding* justice."

But the meeting never took place. Around Thanksgiving, a fellow officer saw Fred Harmon sitting in his car outside the Hall of Justice, alone, sobbing. Soon afterward, he went home.

Back in Sacramento, he met with his stake president and related his ordeal in detail. He didn't have to describe the agony he had been through; it was written all over his face. The stake president listened sympathetically, then said, "There must be something missing. There has to be an explanation. There probably are a lot of things wrong with the administration of the Church, but still there *must* be an ultimate answer somewhere. You must have more faith."

Poor Fred still lacked *total faith*.

75

The Word came down to KSL-TV.

In the lobby of the station's plush new offices on the first floor of the Triad Center, opposite the huge Palladian window, under the massive, brass-studded barrel vault, hung a picture of the chairman of the board of the Bonneville International Corp., the parent company of KSL. It was a picture of Gordon B. Hinckley.

This wasn't the first time The Word had come down to the station. In the 1970s, it had been rocked by a series of scandals over Church intervention in news decisions. Programs considered by Church leaders to be "not in the interests of the faith," programs like "Mormon Women and Depression," had been summarily canceled. Other news stories were axed or modified either directly as a result of pressures from Church officials or because KSL management feared offending them. Scathing memos shot back and forth, journalists accusing the station of "handling stories sensitive to the Church in an arbitrary manner," and devout Mormons on the staff accusing the journalists of Mormon bashing.

Spence Kinard, KSL's news director, remembered it well. Although a devout Mormon himself and an occasional spokesman for the Church, he had resigned over the flap. He even went public with his grievance, telling an AP reporter that he had been under "longtime constant pressure in the news director post" from both the Church and from the station, "concerned about the impact of news stories on its business and ideological concerns."

Since that brouhaha and fearing FCC intervention, the station had tried hard to re-establish its credibility as an independent news source, even luring back Spence Kinard as news director. Reluctantly, the Church accepted the fact that if KSL was going to compete successfully with the two non-Church stations in Salt Lake City, and not run into FCC problems, it would have to be able to report on the state's paramount institution with at least the appearance of objectivity.

But the reality remained largely unchanged. Whenever a reporter forgot to call a Church leader by his title, referring to "Gordon B. Hinckley" rather than *"President Gordon B. Hinckley,"* angry memos would blanket the station like snowflakes on the nearby ski slopes. When KSL reported that a young man who had hijacked a plane out of Salt Lake and demanded a $500,000 ransom was "a former B.Y.U. student," the Church raised a hue and cry. They didn't want to have the name of the Church's university associated with a common criminal.

If such flare-ups were rare, it wasn't because independent journalism had finally triumphed. If Church officials weren't jerking KSL's leash very often, it was because KSL, like every other television station and newspaper in Utah, mindful of its Mormon audience, rarely tested the limits. Stories that cast a negative light on the Church were routinely downplayed.

If anything, the *appearance* of undue influence at KSL was greater than it had been in the seventies. Gordon Hinckley wasn't the only key figure with one foot in the KSL newsroom and the other in the Church Office Building. Bruce Lindsay, KSL's anchorman, although an ardent advocate of journalistic independence, was also the son of Richard Lindsay, chief Church spokesman; and one of the station's investigative reporters, Lynn Packer, was a nephew to Apostle Boyd Packer. But no one was more intimately tied to the Church than Kinard himself, who delivered "The Spoken Word" for the Church, often introduced the Tabernacle Choir, and sometimes traveled with Church leaders and acted as their spokesman. In addition, everyone suspected that there were two or three "moles" on the news staff who alerted Church officials to anything in the works that might conceivably meet their disapproval.

And nothing met their disapproval like the Hofmann story. After years of a virtual blackout on negative reporting about the Church, it represented what one reporter called "open season on the Mormon Church." Suddenly, reporters were doing dozens of stories on Church-related issues, *sensitive* Church-related issues.

And the Church wanted it stopped.

As much as Gordon Hinckley hated the story, Lynn Packer loved it. Tall and dark, with the chiseled good looks of a TV newscaster, Packer, a part-time KSL reporter, rushed into the Hofmann story with full-time abandon. If ever there was a story to investigate, this was it. That he was a Mormon, that his uncle was an Apostle—an ultraconservative one to boot—that he would be, in essence, investigating his own company, all those things only made the story more irresistible. By Utah standards, it was a shocking attitude, but hardly surprising for a reporter who had come of age in the journalistic hothouse of Vietnam as a cub reporter for the military's internal news operation.

Like any eager reporter, Packer occasionally went beyond the bounds. One Saturday, he called the newsroom from inside the county attorney's office, a place that had been officially declared off limits after reporters were discovered sifting through the office garbage in search of leads.

Eventually, Packer's aggressive reporting helped put KSL in the uncomfortable position of providing some of the most extensive, most in-depth coverage of the Hofmann case. Not because the Church allowed it, not because Spence Kinard approved of it, but simply because *KSL couldn't stay away from it.* From the standpoint of local TV news, the story had everything: murder, mystery, big money, local characters—everything but sex. It was a certainty that the other two stations in town, both aggressive competitors for market share, would go after the story with everything they had. With November sweeps looming, KSL couldn't *afford* to concede the story of the decade to the competition just because it made the Church uneasy. Subordinating journalistic ethics to the needs of the Church was one thing; sacrificing market share and advertising revenues was something else entirely.

But there were still limits.

In November, Packer prepared a story that went way beyond those limits. On the basis of extracts from Steve Christensen's letters and journals that had been leaking piecemeal to the press, as well as other sources, Packer put together a report on the relationship between Christensen and Hinckley. Although carefully worded, the story clearly contradicted the version of events that Hinckley had presented at the press conference, particularly the fiction, carefully nurtured by the Church, that Hinckley and Christensen had met only once and remained virtual strangers.

On a morning in November, Packer met with his allies in the newsroom and circulated a draft of the Hinckley piece. It included part of an interview in which Shannon Flynn said he had sat in Hofmann's Toyota MR2 a couple of times when Hofmann was meeting with Hinckley and that, another time, Hofmann carried on a cozy conversation with Hinckley on his car phone while Flynn listened. Everyone agreed it was an important story, but no one was optimistic about its seeing the light of day. "There's no use trying to get it on the air," said Ernie Ford, the assistant news director and managing editor. The problem, everyone agreed, was Kinard, whose approval was needed.

Someone suggested that if they could put their hands on Christensen's journals and letters—the hard evidence— then the station couldn't sit on the story. Embarrassment or not, they would have to air it.

Packer knew that if he tried to push it through now, he would have to reveal his source for Christensen's papers, and within fifteen minutes that information would be on Gordon Hinckley's desk. Hinckley would make a few phone calls, the heat would come down on the source, and they would *never* see copies of the actual letters and journals.

It had happened before. The day before the Church's

press conference, they had prepared a story about a cop who claimed that the Church wasn't cooperating in the investigation and the police were considering subpoenaing documents from the Church. Someone had leaked that to Church officials, who had turned around and put pressure on the station's senior management to kill the story.

They agreed that, for now, the best course was to run only the part of the story relating to Christensen's departure from CFS and to leave the bombshell about Hinckley until more information came out. When word of the story leaked within the newsroom, Packer was approached by another reporter, known to be in regular contact with Church officials.

"Doing such stories would be unwise," he cautioned gravely. "And we shouldn't do them."

"That's why I'm checking it out further," Packer said.

The voice lowered to an ominous whisper. "Care should be taken in making such inquiries."

To Packer, it all sounded familiar.

He had been working for AFVN, the television network for American forces in Vietnam, on the night in 1970 when the military police surrounded a TV station in Saigon and arrested a newscaster. His crime: he had announced, on the air, "All the news you're getting here about the war is censored."

The military didn't *officially* permit censorship. But the men in charge had other ways of spreading The Word that certain stories were better left unreported. Packer, like the newscaster in Saigon, was among a small group of journalists who weren't playing by the informal rules. For example, the rules said you didn't report incidents of unprovoked hostility against local civilians. It didn't make the American Army look good. So the story of the My Lai massacre broke in the United States two or three days before it broke in Vietnam.

And Lynn Packer was the reporter who broke it.

The army threatened to court-martial him, but after a series of congressional hearings on military censorship, he became part of a compromise deal. The military kicked him and four other men off the network, but they didn't prosecute them for disobeying orders.

So Packer knew how big institutions worked in little

ways, mostly painless, invisible ways, to cover their big crimes.

The Hinckley story never ran.

Packer also did a story about Hugh Pinnock and the loan at First Interstate. Kinard viewed the tape and said it didn't add up to much. And he didn't trust Packer's source.

Packer argued that the same journalistic suspicion should be directed at the General Authorities. "That's the role of a journalist—to treat information skeptically and check it out no matter who said it, whether it's Hinckley or Hofmann."

The argument was lost on Kinard. As far as he was concerned, it was only further proof of what he had suspected all along, that Packer was out to get the Church.

Ernie Ford called Packer in to let him know what kind of havoc his stories were causing. "You're getting us all in trouble." Surely he remembered Kinard's tantrum when another reporter, Con Psarras, did one Hofmann story too many. "Goddam it, you guys are trying to cost me my job," he yelled in the middle of the newsroom. "You are out to attack the Church!"

Packer suddenly realized that the heat on the station management from the Church was far worse than he had imagined.

Don Gale, the vice president for news of Bonneville International Corp., took the opportunity to express his view that Pinnock had acted alone in helping to arrange the First Interstate loan, perhaps even against the feelings of the more senior General Authorities on how the matter should be handled.

The Pinnock story never ran.

Finally, Kinard and the station's senior management tried a more general deterrent. They decided that the station had been running too many Hofmann stories. One day, Kinard looked at the calendar of proposed Hofmann stories and said, "That's ridiculous!" Soon afterward, the station officially limited the number of stories it would do. "The public doesn't understand the difference between the documents story and the murder story," said Don Gale in an effort to explain the move. From now on, Kinard would personally review all stories relating to the Hofmann case.

Eventually, word leaked out to other news organizations that the reporters at KSL were complaining that their stories weren't getting on the air.

One reporter called a KSL staffer and offered to act as an intermediary. "I hear KSL has a hell of a lot of information they won't let you use," he said. "Our station could take the information and put it on the air without saying where it came from."

"I'm unhappy," the reporter admitted, "but we still hope the story will get on the air."

At the first inconspicuous opportunity, Lynn Packer was fired.

76

When November came and went and still no charges were filed—against Hofmann or anybody else—Bell and Farnsworth could feel the public turn against them.

The press was having a field day. Bored with the Hofmann angle, they had made it into a story of police incompetence, of bewildered and desperate investigators grabbing at straws, manufacturing evidence, and hounding innocent citizens. An article in the January *Utah Holiday* recounted, inaccurately, Farnsworth's encounter with the nurse at Hofmann's bedside that first night. It quoted an unnamed policeman as telling Mark directly, "You son of a bitch. This is what you deserve, and we're looking forward to getting you out of here so you can be executed."

Another issue of the same magazine accused the police of not running a "thorough investigation." It also reminded them that vast numbers in the community doubted whether Hofmann was guilty at all. "As *Utah Holiday* went to press in December with the article," it pointed out, "Mark Hofmann had not been charged with murder, and police sources said that investigators are still scrambling for enough solid evidence to make charges stick. Friends and associates of Hofmann claim it is ludicrous to believe that a man of Hofmann's impeccable credentials—religious and professional—could bomb his former associates. Some people close to Hofmann believe he was 'set up' as a suspect."

Picking holes in the police case had become a kind of local pastime. The eyewitness had said the suspect was wearing a jacket with *brown* sleeves, and Hofmann's jacket had *gray* sleeves. The witness said he had a mustache, but Mark was clean-shaven. One witness said he wasn't wearing glasses, but Mark always wore glasses, and on and on.

Over at the *Tribune*, Mike Carter, a friend of Ron Yengich's, had a field day with the biggest hole of all: motivation. "Sources close to the investigation say detectives have not yet come up with a scenario that would explain the second bomb that claimed the life of Mrs. Sheets," Carter wrote on October 26, "or a third device that exploded and critically injured Mr. Hofmann a day after the killings."

Carter didn't think much of the police explanation that Christensen was killed because he had uncovered evidence of Hofmann's double-dealing or of the McLellin Collection scam (by now, it was generally accepted that the Collection never existed), or the even more incredible theory that the Sheets bomb was intended merely as a diversion, to make the killings look CFS-related. "If that is the case," wrote Carter, "they are left with no viable explanation as to the target of the third bomb that exploded in Mr. Hofmann's car."

When the police composite leaked to the press, there were howls of derision. No one thought it looked like Hofmann. Bell and Farnsworth knew the problem: the public watched too much television. They were used to the portrait composites they had seen on police dramas. By *real* police standards, John Johnson's composite was pretty damn good, they thought. It had Hofmann's chin. Besides, the purpose of a composite wasn't to make a positive I.D., it was to exclude false suspects. But that distinction was lost on a press and public raised on "Dragnet" and "The Rockford Files."

* * *

Meanwhile, Mark's neighbors eagerly fanned the flames of public outrage over police incompetence. One told a sheriff's deputy that Mark was at home at the time of the bombing. "It doesn't matter if he was there or not," she went on to say, "because you've got the wrong guy. You're crucifying him. I'll go into court and lie for him if I have to."

Even some cops were beginning to have their doubts. It was a well-known maxim in the department that if you didn't nail a suspect in the first month of an investigation, you weren't going to nail him. And they had passed that deadline weeks ago. Hundreds of detectives had spent thousands of hours and hundreds of thousands of dollars, and they didn't have a whole lot more on him than they did only three days into the case.

The police knew the case was in trouble when they saw their hard-nosed chief, Bud Willoughby, walking through the office with a piece of string wound around his finger, holding it up in different directions trying to pick up "vibrations." Apparently, Gwen Wilcox, a psychic Willoughby consulted occasionally, had told him that this procedure might turn up some missing clues in the Hofmann case.

If anybody still doubted that the police were hounding an innocent man, Hofmann's attorney, Ron Yengich, was always there to drive the point home.

Every time Bell and Farnsworth went to search the Hofmann house, Yengich and the press showed up soon thereafter. At a search on Sunday, November 3, the police offered to stay in their cars until Dorie could arrange for someone to take care of the children. When Yengich arrived, Farnsworth gave him a receipt for the search warrant.

"What's up, Ken?" Yengich asked informally.

"We found some more information in the laboratory, and we need to do another search. Here's your warrant." It listed the specific items they were looking for. "This is what it's all about. Any questions?" Yengich said no.

Later, while the police were still searching, a reporter asked Farnsworth for an interview.

"We don't have anything to say," Farnsworth said firmly.

But Yengich did. That night, Farnsworth saw him with

the same reporter on the evening news. He was complaining that the police have been here twice before and they're here again. They can't get it right. They just keep coming back. I don't know *what* they're after this time. Beats me.

Farnsworth hit the ceiling. He had shown Yengich the warrant. Yengich knew *exactly* what they were after. It was all simply a play for sympathy, an attempt to make people believe that the police were pestering the Hofmanns, that they didn't have a case so they were digging for something that wasn't there.

And, worst of all, it worked.

A few days later, Bell and Farnsworth saw Bill Hofmann on TV telling reporters that the police were fabricating evidence to make the case against his son: that no matter how hard they searched, they couldn't find the evidence, because it didn't exist, so they were making it up.

And if that wasn't enough, Bill Hofmann then had a *revelation from God* that his son was innocent.

Soon afterward, Dorie Hofmann called Brent Ashworth's wife, Charlene, and told her Mark had been on a mission to locate Mormon documents and that *the Devil* was bringing him down. She swore that Mark had been with her the entire night before the first bombings and couldn't *possibly* have been the bomber. He was on a mission, and the forces of evil were combining against him.

When he heard the story, Farnsworth decided that, by the forces of evil, Dorie must have meant him and Jim Bell.

In mid-November, Yengich called David Raskin at the University of Utah. Raskin was the dean of American polygraphers, or, as he preferred to call them, "human psychophysiologists." He had done the polygraphs for Patty Hearst and John De Lorean, as well as a host of defendants whose results on the test had *not* been revealed to the public.

Yengich wanted him to perform a test on Mark Hofmann.

Raskin, a full-bearded, academic looking man, may have wondered if it was appropriate for Yengich to be doing business with him at that moment, because Yengich was also representing him in a civil suit. But that would have meant questioning one of the most prominent defense attorneys in town, and the bulk of his business came from defense attorneys.

They agreed that the test would be performed in Yengich's office by Raskin's associate, Charles Honts. Everything was done with the utmost confidentiality, of course. Everyone knew the drill. If the defendant passed the test, the defense attorney would call a press conference, shout the results, and heap praise on the test and the examiner. If the defendant failed, the test would never see the light of day. For obvious reasons, even the fact that he had taken a test would be kept secret. That was what happened when he tested Ted Bundy—and dozens of other defendants. One of the reasons for the polygraph's bad rap, Raskin often said, was that the public only heard about it when a defendant passed the test. Yet in the vast majority of cases, he didn't.

On November 13, Honts showed up at Yengich's office. He was a huge man, six feet, four inches tall, well past two hundred pounds, huge face, huge belly, and a corona of sandy-colored hair and beard, looking like a cross between a mountain man and an absent-minded professor. Hofmann was already there. Honts began with the usual pretest interview in which he asked about the events surrounding the three bombings a month before. Hofmann denied any direct involvement in the bombings except for being a victim of one of the blasts.

Then Honts hooked Mark up to a four-channel Lafayette Polygraph machine, Model 76163, which recorded on a single strip chart Mark's finger-pulse amplitude (flow of blood through the fingers), relative blood pressure, thoracic respiration (breath rate), and skin resistance (sweating on his hands—usually the most telling indicator).

The test itself was divided into three groups of questions: control questions, filler questions, and relevant questions. The control questions were designed to elicit a "violent" response even from innocent subjects, questions like "Have you ever broken the law?" or "Have you cheated on your income taxes?" These questions, supposedly, established a standard for "guilty" responses. The filler questions were innocuous inquiries designed to elicit a passive response, even from guilty subjects. They established the standard for "innocent" responses.

The relevant questions were the real test. Honts had already gone over them with Hofmann during the pretest interview, but there was still palpable tension in the room when he began to ask them with the machine humming and scratching.

"Before it exploded, did you know there was a bomb in your car?"

"No."

"Did you plant either of the bombs that exploded on October 15?"

"No."

"Did you, yourself, cause any of the bombings of October 15 and 16?"

"No."

Through it all, Hofmann remained completely calm.

In accordance with Utah state law, Honts went through the three sets of questions—control, filler, and relevant—three times.

After the third round, Honts stroked his wild beard. Hofmann's results were inconclusive. Something about the scores bothered Honts. There were too many inconsistencies. He wanted to go through the questions a *fourth* time. From the psychological profile, he knew Hofmann was clever. And he was holding his legs together in a strange, awkward way. Could he have read David Lykken's book, *A Tremor in the Blood,* that explains how to fool a polygraph? Or was Honts just imagining things?

Could Hofmann be a pathological liar? There was evidence that psychopaths and sociopaths could beat the test, but Honts dismissed it. He felt that psychopaths take so much pride in their lying and get so much pleasure from it, that their physiological *pleasure* responses are almost identical to the "healthy" defendant's guilty responses. He and Raskin had done some studies on the accuracy of polygraphs on psychopathic subjects and determined, not surprisingly, that they were in fact quite accurate. After all, Ted Bundy had failed the test.

But the fourth time around, all Honts's doubts were cleared up.

Hofmann was telling the truth.

When Honts announced the good news, Yengich couldn't wait to share it with the world.

At 5:15 the same day, John Harrington, a reporter for KTVX, Channel 4, received a call from Yengich's associate, Brad Rich. "I'm gonna tell you something, but it's embargoed until after six," he said, "because we promised it to Channel 2 first. We want them to have it first, because we promised, but you should be aware that Mark took a lie detector test and passed it with flying colors."

"Why are you telling me this at 5:15?" asked Harrington.

"Well, I just thought you needed to know."

Harrington hung up. He was steaming mad. What kind of reporter did Yengich and Rich think he was? Did they really think they could call up with a story fifteen minutes before the early evening news went on the air and he would *not* run it? Did they think Harrington would sit on it until after six?

Harrington immediately typed up a story to the effect that the defense had secretly announced that Mark Hofmann had passed a lie-detector examination and had leaked it to another news station on an exclusive basis. In the report, he quoted Rich saying that the story was confidential and off the record. "This is just something you need to know," he quoted Rich. "But we're embargoing it."

And they ran it on the next news program as a hot flash.

The next day Rich pretended to be piqued, but Harrington already knew he had been tricked. If Yengich and Rich hadn't intended for him to use the story, Rich wouldn't have given him the story. By making it the subject of a rivalry between the stations, he had turned it into big news.

And it *was* big news. Honts went on television and said it right out: Mark passed his polygraph. He was telling the truth when he denied knowing a bomb was in his car and denied planting the bombs that exploded on October 15. Then Rich went on. Hofmann is innocent, he said. Go look for somebody else. Then Bill Hofmann went on. My son didn't do it, he insisted again, more plausibly this time. I asked him, and he said he didn't. And look, he passed the polygraph. So he isn't lying.

At the police department, the switchboard lit up. Every police witness, and every member of the victims' families, every reporter called demanding an explanation: If Mark was guilty, how had he passed the test?

Jim Bell, who had taken a polygraph test as part of his

police training and failed repeatedly, explained that there were ways to fool a polygraph, like putting something between your toes and pressing on it. Or simply focusing your mind on some irrelevant thought. Ken Farnsworth explained to Terri Christensen that Hofmann's medical condition could have interfered with the test. "With major damage to his leg, he might be on medication that could alter the results. Besides which, from the best we can tell, Mark is a sociopathic liar. He could probably walk right through a test because he has no fear of it. And if there's no fear, there's no test." Terri was easier to reassure than the others. She *knew* Mark Hofmann was guilty. Her only question was how a guilty man could pass the test.

At the county attorney's office, Gerry D'Elia railed against polygraphers. "They're so full of shit it comes out of their ears." "Give us the charts," he yelled at Rich. "Let *us* read them. You've administered the test. We don't care what the test shows, just let us interpret it. Let's see what the control questions are." But Yengich never released them.

The next day, D'Elia said to Brad Rich, "I bet the results surprised *you* a lot more than they surprised me."

The next week, Dorie Hofmann took the test in the conference room of Yengich's offices. Unlike her husband, she was terrified. Honts asked her if Mark had been with her the entire night before the bombings. She said yes.

She, too, passed the test.

When Carl Lundquist heard the news about his old friend Mark Hofmann, he remembered a conversation they had had one night many years ago after stopping at the Safeway to buy some doughnuts and a Coke. It was another of their stimulating, free-ranging talks about everything from religion to nuclear war.

"Do you think you could trick a lie-detector test?" Mark asked.

"I don't know," said Lundquist.

"Well, I think I could. I know how they work, and to trick one, all you'd have to do is train your brain and your thinking to do what you want it to. If you're ultimately in control of yourself, you could tell the lie detector anything, and it would register as a truth."

77

Duck-hunting season came and went, and Jim Bell missed it.

He couldn't even find time for jogging. Instead, he hibernated in the Hofmann "war room," developed a passion for Crackerjack, and put on weight. So did Ken Farnsworth, who hadn't been out to the department shooting range since the day of the bombings. The paranoia and night sweats returned, for the first time since his undercover days. He started leaving his gun on the nightstand next to his bed again, a habit that had taken him six months to break after the sting operation. It wasn't the physical danger, it was the anxiety.

He didn't get to play much basketball either. The one time he did, it was a pickup game, one-on-one with Ron Yengich in the department basketball court next to the evidence rooms.

They couldn't get away from the case.

But they couldn't talk about it either. There had been so many leaks from the department, from the sheriff's office, from the county attorney's office, from the defense counsel, that Bell and Farnsworth barely spoke to each other anymore.

Hell, they couldn't even talk to Chief Willoughby about it. In the first weeks of the investigation, Bell had briefed Willoughby almost every day, sometimes two or three times a day. "You don't talk to your lieutenant, you don't talk to your captain," the chief had told him. "You just come and talk to me." The discussions had been outrageously frank, Willoughby not being the kind of man to stand on rank.

But one day Willoughby called him in to say he didn't want to know what was going on anymore. He didn't want anyone to be able to accuse him of leaking information to the press. "I don't want you and Ken to be neutered by the people across the street," Willoughby said, referring to the county attorney's office. "I don't want them to say, 'We can't share information with you because you've got to tell the chief, and we think he's telling everybody.' " Their daily meetings stopped. That's how paranoid everybody was.

Bell couldn't even go home and talk to his wife, Patti. Even if he could, his thoughts were so deep into the minutiae of the case, she wouldn't begin to understand. It got to the point where he broke into a sweat if he thought she was going to ask him a question about it. He knew he would either say nothing or go on for five hours. Either disappear or explode. He would come home, always late, and just stare at the wall. He would go to bed and not sleep.

The *entire* case was in his head. In the beginning, they tried a computer program to organize all the information, all the leads and rumors and possibilities, but it proved woefully inadequate to the task. So Bell's head remained the computer. At times, he was afraid that if he broke his concentration even for a minute, the whole case would disintegrate. No wonder he couldn't sleep.

Or he would wake up in the middle of the night with a thought that he *had* to write down, one more memorandum to assign, one more question for one more cop to ask one more witness. And when he couldn't get back to sleep, he would dress and drive down to the Hall of Justice to join the graveyard shift of rookies, sifting through the mountains of evidence.

When Farnsworth stole a day to attend a family get-together, he couldn't sit down to dinner without his mother or his sister or his brother or his niece or *someone* asking him something he couldn't tell them about the Hofmann case. Or, even worse, volunteering advice: "You've got the wrong guy. I watch TV, and your case against Hofmann doesn't look good."

Around the eighth floor war room, the humor only came in black. Kyle Jones brought in some fortune cookies in the shape of white salamanders, each one labeled with the name of one of the cops working the case. Inside were fortunes from FU-LING-YU: "Office space available in Judge Building, real cheap."

It was a sign of the times that the only diverting moments were provided by another murder case, the first to come their way since the night of October 15. In the middle of a jealous spat, a twenty-nine-year-old Mexican woman accidentally killed her sixty-two-year-old lover by beating him to death with a pair of Sears binoculars.

But the next day, it was back to overtime in the war room, back to what Bell had dubbed "the royal pain in the butt": Mark Hofmann.

It didn't take a close friend to notice that the case was taking its toll on Jim Bell. Old "Stretch" just wasn't the congenial guy he used to be. He yelled at friends, snapped at subordinates, ate nothing but junk food, and looked like hell.

They could only imagine what was happening at home.

In fact, it was worse than they imagined. Patti tried to maintain her own grueling schedule as an emergency-room nurse while assuming full responsibility for keeping the family and the household going. Even under the best of circumstances, it would have been trying. But the Bells had recently sold a video rental shop, and there was still a drawerful of paperwork to be taken care of. And there was Steven, their second child. The doctors suspected that he had cystic fibrosis. More than once, he became so short of breath that Patti had to rush him to the hospital in the middle of the night. Where was Jim at these moments of crisis? Where he always was, down at the Hall of Justice, working late on the Hofmann case.

Patti was a strong, self-reliant woman, but there was a point beyond which even she couldn't bend. One day she called Ken Farnsworth, desperate and sobbing. "When is this going to be over?" she cried. "I can't take it anymore. I never see him. He doesn't know his kids. When is this going to be *over?*"

78 But they kept working. The city stopped paying overtime, ATF cut its contingent by half, the sheriff's office wouldn't show up for meetings, the U.S. attorney wouldn't share information with them, the press ridiculed them, Ron Yengich reviled them, and Bill Hofmann seemed to be accusing them of conspiring with the Devil, but they kept working, clinging to the hope that maybe the next search, the next interview, the next lead, would convince *somebody* to charge Hofmann with *something*.

Ever since Jerry Taylor told them that the bomb had been made with C-cell-battery packs from Radio Shack, they had been trying to track down the clerk who sold them to Hofmann. There were nineteen Radio Shack stores in Salt Lake City alone, and each of those had thousands of receipts for September and October. And maybe Hofmann used an alias, so they had to try for every possible variation on Mark Hofmann, including any name with the initials M. H. And maybe someone else, an accomplice, bought the stuff for him, so they had to check for Brent Metcalfe, Shannon Flynn, and Lyn Jacobs, and possible variations on those names.

At first, they hoped they might find a shortcut through the huge sea of paperwork. Bell called the parent company in Dallas, Texas, and discovered that all the receipts were computerized. Theoretically, anyone who bought anything at Radio Shack had his or her name added to a computer mailing list. In reality, however, it wasn't that easy. When they ran the names Bell gave them through the computer, they came up empty. Sometimes, a name doesn't make it onto the list, they explained. A clerk forgets to write it in.

So they went back to the stores.

At the very first one they visited, the Cottonwood Mall

branch, an ATF officer found a receipt for a battery pack and a mercury switch. The name on the receipt: Mike Hansen—the same name Bell had found in Hofmann's papers. The customer had given a false Salt Lake City address—a vacant lot. The lot was about a mile and a half from Hofmann's home. The next day, at the same store, they found a second receipt, also made out to Mike Hansen, with a different address, also false.

For a few days, the results looked encouraging.

Then they found a clerk who routinely made up names to avoid his boss's wrath when he forgot to enter the customer's real name on the receipt. One of the names he used most often: Mike Hansen.

They tried the search in reverse, pulling out all the receipts for mercury switches and tracking down *all* the buyers. From September 1 to October 15, thirty-seven mercury switches had been sold between the Idaho border and Spanish Fork, Utah, between Nevada and Wyoming. They tracked down and cleared as many as they could, thirty-two. Of the remaining five, three were eliminated for other reasons, one was sold with a D-cell-battery pack to an M. Hansen, and one with two C-cell-battery packs to their old friend, Mike Hansen.

But how could they prove Mike Hansen was really Mark Hofmann?

The first step was to prove that he wasn't anybody else. To do that, they had to contact every Mike Hansen in the state of Utah to see, first, if one of them had made the Radio Shack purchases, and second, if he matched the description of the man seen carrying the bomb into the Judge Building the morning of Steve Christensen's killing. Using the telephone book, drivers' license directories, and Polk consumer directories, they had made a list of fifty people in the Salt Lake City area alone. It was a long, slow process—they always seemed to be about three addresses behind—and it had only just begun.

While still in the hospital, Hofmann had said that he left his car door locked the day he returned to find the bomb on the seat. So if Hofmann was telling the truth, the bomber must have broken in.

But what if that particular car was jimmy-proof? It wouldn't prove Hofmann was the bomber but it would shoot another hole in his story.

The Wagstaff Toyota dealership could not have been more helpful. The manager gave them the pick of his cars, and they put their best lock man on the job—a man who popped cars every day of the week with slim-jims. With a video camera rolling, he went to work, scratching and banging at the lock until the car was a mess. But the door wouldn't open. He finally had to take the entire door panel off and study the lock mechanism before he could get into the vehicle.

They offered to pay the Toyota man for the damage but he said not to worry, he would take care of it.

When they got back to the department, they discovered that Hofmann's MR2 was a 1984 model. They had been working on a 1985. So they went back to the Toyota man for another car. But the result was the same: one more frustrated locksmith, one more torn-up car, and one more Hofmann lie.

Toyota also provided a list of six hundred people in Utah who owned vans like Hofmann's. Bell was determined to interview all six hundred, but that would take all winter.

Hofmann had also said that he was driving around in Emigration Canyon on the morning of October 16, before the third bombing. Then Shannon Flynn confessed that he and Hofmann had shot their Uzi up in Emigration Canyon. Then they discovered that Mark had been looking at a house in Pinecrest Canyon, an offshoot of Emigration Canyon. Maybe he had done other things up there. Like build bombs.

On November 23, Farnsworth and a team of detectives canvassed Pinecrest Canyon, which was dotted with rustic cabins and isolated estates. There was only one way to do it: knock on every door up and down the two-mile canyon.

They found a sixteen-year-old girl who had been riding home on a school bus when she saw a car just like Hofmann's MR2 parked in front of a shed near a Swiss chalet-style house—the house Hofmann had considered buying. Later, at the Hall of Justice, she repeated the story to the police. Both she and her mother knew of the Hofmann investigation and were terrified at being dragged into it, but felt duty-bound to help however they could. Farnsworth found that a refreshing attitude.

The girl also led them to another student, a ninth-grade boy, who had been sitting on the right side of the bus and saw the open shed. When they talked to him, he said he noticed it because every other day when the bus drove past, the shed had been closed. He, too, was nervous about being a part of the Hofmann investigation.

Like the girl, he told them they should talk to the bus driver.

The bus driver had actually *seen* Mark Hofmann—or somebody who fit Hofmann's description. "He actually walked right in front of the bus, as if he wasn't paying attention to what he was doing," said the driver, a sharp, dark-haired man from Kamas. "He was so deep in concentration. I almost hit him." Then he gave them the precise time of the incident.

How did he remember the precise time?

He drove the same route every day, and he knew what time it was by where he was on the route.

There was only one problem. He said it happened on Tuesday, the day of the first bombings, not Wednesday, when Hofmann said he was there.

On December 4, they did the drains. Because they hadn't found the mercury switch or wires used in the bomb that destroyed Hofmann's car, they decided to dredge the gutters near where the car had been parked. They started at nine in the morning. It was filthy, cold, back-breaking work. And it turned up nothing.

For Bell and Farnsworth, the investigation had hit rock bottom.

79

One more time, Jim Bell made his pitch. "There might not be enough evidence to take the Hofmann case to court yet. But at least we should get the ball rolling. Let's arrest Mark. Let's get the warrants. Let's get it started. If we arrest him, it will generate confidence in the case. It will bring witnesses out of the woodwork. And at least it will get the community off our backs. If we don't file soon, we'll never be able to convince anybody that there's a case."

But Bell was wasting his breath. The man on the other side of the table wasn't even listening.

Bob Stott, the deputy county attorney, rarely listened. It was his way of controlling a conversation. No matter how short or simple the explanation, Bob Stott always had to hear it one more time. After an hour-long explanation of a complex case, he was always the one who asked a question that took the discussion back to square one. "You have to pull him through a case by the nose," says a colleague.

Bell and Farnsworth had hoped, prayed, in fact, that the day would never come when they would have to lead Bob Stott by the nose through *this* case. At first, it looked as if Gerry D'Elia, the street-savvy prosecutor from back East, would take the case into court. He had arrived at the bombing scenes soon after the police and had stuck with the case ever since, assisting the searches and fighting the legal battle with Nurse Loden. Unlike so many people, he had done everything he could to make the investigation easier, not harder. They liked him. He was a cop's lawyer, quick-thinking, kick-ass, combative.

Or if not D'Elia, then David Biggs, a dapper young prosecutor who had joined the county attorney's office only five months earlier. Like D'Elia, he had worked with the cops from the beginning. They hadn't always seen eye to eye. Biggs, in particular, didn't think they had enough on the Sheets murder for an arrest, and he wasn't shy about telling them so, but at least he pulled in the same direction.

Not Bob Stott. He just looked at them with his startling cerulean-blue eyes and tilted his big round head to one side in what could have been either a nervous tic or a sign of total incomprehension.

Stott told people that as a youngster growing up in a devout Mormon family in Geneva, Utah, he had developed his verbal skills as a way of besting his belligerent brother. "I could never win the physical battles, so I had to try to win the other ones." But it took only five minutes of listening to him in the courtroom to know that his verbal skills had never won any battles. He mispronounced words, rambled incoherently, dangled participles, mangled syntax, and, despite mighty efforts, often failed to get subject and verb to agree. With all that, the fact that he often forgot names—not just personal names but simple nouns too—went almost unnoticed. Although no one in the office would forget the day when, in the middle of a trial, he forgot the defendant's name.

No, Bob Stott became a lawyer because lawyers were in control. Or at least that was the impression he got from watching Perry Mason. In nine years at the Salt Lake County Attorney's Office, he had worked his way into a supervisory position where he had control both over cases and over other lawyers. In court, he was a plodder. Determined to maintain control, he spent hundreds of hours preparing for every possible contingency, writing out every question and every conceivable answer beforehand on yellow legal pads.

If the case was simple and everything went according to plan, he looked good. Juries sometimes took to his low-key manner and workmanlike approach. Sometimes, they just felt sorry for him. "If you put the proper makeup on him, and do his hairstyle for him, and walk him into the courtroom, and tell him everything he has to say, then he can do a good job," says a colleague. "But set him on his own, and he can't organize a ham sandwich."

Of course, as a supervisor, Stott made sure to pick and choose his cases and control his work load in such a way that he always looked good.

Still, Stott *had* helped prosecute a variety of famous defendants during his nine years at the county attorney's office, including Ted Bundy, the serial murderer; Ervil LeBaron, the fanatic polygamist; Joseph Paul Franklin, the white racist; and, most recently, Ronnie Lee Gardner. Gardner was already on trial for murder when, using a gun slipped to him in the courtroom by an accomplice, he tried to shoot his way out, killing one man and wounding several others in the process.

It was an impressive record, and no one was more impressed with it than Bob Stott. Others may have considered him slow-witted and dull, but Bob Stott considered himself a very successful advocate—he was the best lawyer on the county payroll and he wasn't shy about saying so. In his eagerness to demonstrate his superiority, in fact, he had more than once appropriated credit for brilliant ideas that originated elsewhere on his staff—a practice that won him no friends among his colleagues.

In fact, it was Bob Stott's vanity that had gotten him into the Hofmann case in the first place.

At first, he didn't want it. As a devout Mormon—a very devout Mormon—the last thing he could have wanted was a case that involved the Mormon Church. From the second day, anyone could see that this case was filled with trapdoors. As lead prosecutor, he would have to interview leaders of the Church who most definitely did not want to be interviewed. God forbid, he might even have to subpoena Church records and, even worse, call Church leaders to testify in court. The thought of putting President Gordon B. Hinckley on the witness stand in a murder trial was enough to give Bob Stott chills.

On the other hand, it *was* the case of the century, the highest-profile case ever to come along, and if Bob Stott didn't take it, somebody else would. And it would be *his* feather, not Stott's. Inevitably, he would lose some status— and that, too, was enough to give Bob Stott chills.

For the first month of the investigation, he tried not to commit himself, tried to stand back and see where the case was going, letting D'Elia and Biggs work with the police and take the heat. If it turned out the Church wasn't that deeply involved after all, he could always jump in and grab the case without taking the risks.

Eventually, vanity won out over caution.

By mid-November, County Attorney Ted Cannon had to have an answer. The case was getting complicated, both legally and politically, and D'Elia and Biggs were getting too far out in front. Soon, it would be impossible to turn the case over to Stott, even if he wanted it. "Today is it," Cannon told Stott on November 18. "You've got to stop kidding around. Either you want to be the case manager as far as the county attorney's office is concerned, or it's going to be Gerry D'Elia. But whichever way, I'm going to have the decision by 4 o'clock."

Stott chose to interpret Cannon's ultimatum as a plea. He needed his "best man" on the Hofmann case, and there was no doubt in Bob Stott's mind who the best man was.

*　　*　　*

"Please, Bob, tell us *exactly* what you want in order to file a complaint on Hofmann." Jim Bell tried not to sound as if he was begging, but it was hard not to betray his frustration.

Stott couldn't give them an answer—or wouldn't.

So he and Farnsworth went back to the war room and sat around in stunned silence. What could they do, that they hadn't done already, to get the county attorney's office off its butt to file a case? Someone suggested that perhaps the problem was partly theirs. Perhaps they had made the case too complicated. Perhaps Stott didn't really understand it. Perhaps they hadn't done enough to make it understandable. Maybe it was all just a failure to communicate.

If the prosecutors wouldn't put together the case against Hofmann, then the police would do it for them. They would show them in the clearest possible terms exactly what they had to work with.

So that's what they did. A group of ten or twelve officers directly involved in the investigation—about half police, half ATF agents—sat down in front of the chalkboard and listed the evidence against Hofmann item by item:

1) Two eyewitnesses who saw him carrying the bomb.

2) The letter jacket found in his home corresponding to the eyewitnesses' description.

3) Robert Pitts's statement that Hofmann was in Christensen's office one week prior to the bombing and they were arguing.

4) A witness who saw Hofmann wearing his letter jacket the day of the bombing.

5) Jerry Taylor's rock-solid conclusion that the three bombs were distinctive and consistent.

6) Hofmann clearly holding the bomb in his car.

7) Crease on his pants showing that his position in the car was not what he said it was at the time of the third bombing.

8) Brad Carter's statement that Hofmann was inside the car at the time of the bombing—also inconsistent with Hofmann's statement.

9) Aaron Teplick's identification of Hofmann's

van in front of the Sheets house the morning of the bombings.
10) The Radio Shack receipt for a mercury switch purchased by an M. Hansen, and the Mike Hansen envelope in Hofmann's office.
11) Shannon Flynn's testimony that Hofmann was knowledgeable in the use of explosives.
12) A Radio Shack catalog found in Hofmann's house in which someone had circled the type of C-cell-battery pack used in the bombs.

Next they made a second list outlining the case *for* Hofmann, Yengich's case, all the holes and hurdles prosecutors would face if they indicted Hofmann immediately. They typed up both lists and made copies for everybody. Then Bell called the county attorney's office and asked for a rehearing, with the whole staff: Cannon, Stott, D'Elia, the works. It was do-or-die time.

A few days later, Bell and Farnsworth led a contingent back across the street to the county attorney's office and made their pitch again. Unlike Stott, Cannon, a genial, white-haired man with an off-center sense of humor, welcomed them. He inquired about the status of the effort to compel Nurse Loden to testify (the Utah Supreme Court was scheduled to hear the appeal) and seemed to share their determination to bring the case to trial soon. For the first time since the case began, Farnsworth felt as if the police department and the county attorney's office were working on the same team.

"By golly," said Cannon, "we still have to work on the Sheets case, but I think we can get a conviction on the Christensen case." To the cops' ears, it was music. Finally, someone agreed that they had a prosecutable case. Farnsworth wrote in his notes of the meeting: "It worked out really well. . . . They were being so difficult a couple of days before because Bob Stott was running the case."

Optimism was still running high the following Monday when Cannon called Chief Willoughby to say, "We can convict Hofmann on the Christensen case." Even the Utah Supreme Court's decision on December 5 refusing to compel Nurse Loden to divulge what she heard in the hospital couldn't dampen Jim Bell's spirits.

Any day now, they could arrest Mark Hofmann.

80

Three weeks later, Hofmann was still a free man.

And everybody knew why: Bob Stott wasn't ready yet.

Again Bell requested a meeting with the county attorney's office to "review" the case; that is, to light a fire under Stott. This time, he pulled in his biggest gun: Jerry Taylor. He was embarrassed to do it. Taylor had already flown into town four times for this investigation and, as far as he was concerned, his work was long since finished.

"Jerry, can you come back?" Bell asked sheepishly when he called Taylor in San Francisco. "We have one county attorney we want you to talk to, because he doesn't buy what's going on."

"Jim. There's more goddam evidence in this bombing case than in 99 percent of my cases. That son of a bitch should have been tried and found guilty by now." Taylor had a way of getting right to the point.

He wasn't happy about it, but as a favor to Jim, he agreed.

On December 11, Bell and Farnsworth met with contingents from the county attorney's office, ATF, the state crime lab, and the U.S. Attorney's Office. It was a huge meeting but there was no mistake who the guests of honor were: Jerry Taylor and Bob Stott.

As he always did, Taylor took control of the meeting, laying out the case in the simplest possible terms. One, all three bombs were planted by the same person. Two, that person had to be Mark Hofmann. It was exactly the presentation he would give in court, and it was a virtuoso turn, from beginning to end.

When he finished, Gerry D'Elia stood up to cross-examine him. D'Elia was a bomb expert, too, and he went after Taylor with a barrage of questions that had even the old pro on his toes. If Taylor could weather this assault, he could handle anything Ron Yengich threw at him in court. Compared with Gerry D'Elia, Yengich knew nothing about bombs. It was a duel of wits that had everyone in the room riveted.

Everyone, that is, except Bob Stott.

Out of the corner of his eye, Farnsworth noticed Stott squirming in his chair and looking at his watch. A few minutes later, in the heat of an exchange, he got up and started putting on his coat. The room fell silent with astonishment. Stott actually intended to get up and *leave* the meeting, a meeting that had been called especially for him, a meeting for which Jerry Taylor had flown into town. Then Farnsworth remembered. Every day at noon, Stott played racquetball.

As Stott started to leave, Farnsworth cut him off. "Where are you going?" His tone wasn't friendly.

"I have an appointment for lunch," said Stott.

Farnsworth moved in close. "You ain't going anywhere. We flew this guy in for *you*. Everybody else here already knows the case. You are the only one who doesn't understand what the fuck's going on. You're staying *here*."

Stott looked at Farnsworth, then looked at his watch. Then he looked at his watch again. Finally, he took his coat off. "Excuse me," he said in a huff. "I've got to make a phone call." A few minutes later, he came back and sat down again quietly.

When the cross-examination was finished, both Taylor and D'Elia were invigorated. "I want that young kid cross-examining me on this case," Taylor told Jim Bell. "That's as effective a cross-examination as I have ever had in a courtroom on a bombing case. No better than that." From Jerry Taylor, it was a hell of a compliment. But it didn't make Bob Stott very happy.

Speaking to the whole group, Taylor continued. "Now I'm going to tell you what I can't tell you in court—my own personal opinions of Mark Hofmann."

The room was absolutely quiet.

Taylor addressed himself to those who speculated that Hofmann's actions were those of a basically good man in desperate straits, a man who may have intended to commit suicide with the third bomb, out of guilt and remorse. "The idea that Mark intended the third bomb for himself," said Taylor, "is a bald-faced lie. If he intended suicide, if he entered the car with the purpose of connecting two wires and blowing himself to hell and gone, then he wouldn't have knelt with one knee on the seat, he would have gotten all the way into the car. He wouldn't have reached for the box with one hand; he would have reached with two hands and not just one but both would have been hit by the full blast of the explosion. In fact, his whole body would have been destroyed.

"Mark Hofmann is not just a sweet kid in over his head, blowing himself up out of remorse. He is your basic all-American serial bomber. He *likes* setting bombs. He gets off on it. I've dealt with hundreds of people just like him. I know the type."

He closed on a chilling note. "In fact, that third bomb won't be his last. He will continue setting bombs until you catch him or until he blows himself up."

To a group of men who had lived and breathed Mark Hofmann for two months, it was a breathtaking display. "Now," he said, fixing the sole of his shoe, which had come loose during his presentation, "if you've got any questions, just shoot."

Bob Stott cleared his throat portentously. As the lead prosecutor, it was, of course, his place to speak first.

"Now, tell me, Jerry," he began blankly, "do you really think the guy did it? What do you *really* think?"

81

George Throckmorton had been following the Hofmann case with growing indignation. He had read all the newspaper articles and watched all the TV reports and couldn't get one thought out of his head. "I know there's something wrong with the way the documents have been checked," he told his wife, for the umpteenth time, after watching the umpteenth Hofmann story on the evening news, "but I can't get anyone to listen to me."

For Throckmorton, a conscientious Mormon, that wasn't just armchair speculation. Unlike most of the people commenting on TV, he happened to know something about documents. He was, in fact, the *only* practicing forensic document examiner in the state of Utah, the only person for miles around who was trained to study documents and testify about them in court.

But had anybody bothered to ask *him* about Mark Hofmann's documents?

Of course, most of his experience involved everyday documents, not historical ones. Once he had cracked a serial rape-and-murder case by matching the handwriting of a note the rapist left at the scene to the suspect's handwriting. But that was unusual. Most of his time at the state crime laboratory was spent checking medical records to see if a doctor had made changes to protect himself in a malpractice suit or looking for forged signatures on bad checks or credit-card slips. He certainly didn't have much experience with historical documents.

But he didn't need much to know something was wrong with Hofmann's story. Simple common sense told him that one man couldn't have turned up so many key documents over such a short period of time. Others, including Jim Bell, had harbored the same suspicions at first, only to be told that all the experts back East had authenticated Hofmann's documents and attested to his reputation.

George Throckmorton had heard the same thing. Only he knew better.

He knew, for example, that those "East Coast experts" may have been experts in something but they weren't experts in authenticating documents. Most had no training or experience in forensics. In his opinion, some of them weren't even *equipped* to authenticate a document.

Throckmorton had tried to call attention to this travesty. Despite an order from his boss, the state attorney general, not to talk about the Hofmann case, he had hinted broadly to reporters that *someone* needed to get a qualified examiner to look at the documents in the case. As far as he could tell, they had never been "authenticated" in the true sense of the word.

When that didn't get any attention, he went to the sheriff's office. "You should be aware that these documents have never been really authenticated," he explained, "in spite of what everyone's saying. Because I'm not sure if anyone has authenticated them who knows what he's doing." Like so many other things, his warning disappeared into the black hole of the sheriff's office.

So Throckmorton turned to the press. He called both the *Tribune* and the *Deseret News*, which were in a journalistic dogfight over the bombing story, mounting massive investigations over every crumb of gossip that could be conned from officialdom. But neither paper was interested in Throckmorton's abstruse quibbles with the East Coast experts.

The three top local television stations, KSL-TV, KTVX, and KUTV, also turned him down. In the end, only one person, Paul Larsen of *Utah Holiday*, Salt Lake City's glossy monthly magazine, showed any interest, and by now, Throckmorton was too dispirited to think much would come of that.

But he didn't give up the fight. If no one else would authenticate the documents—*really* authenticate them— then George Throckmorton would.

He called Dean Jessee, whom he had met the year before at a seminar for the Southwest Association of Forensic Documents Examiners. At that time, Throckmorton discovered that Jessee, who routinely "authenticated" documents for the Church, had been educating himself to the task out of a single book. If that wasn't discouraging enough, Jessee was now in the midst of preparing a magazine article for *BYU Studies* on "why the Salamander Letter is authentic."

Nevertheless, Jessee met with him at the Church library and showed him a copy of the Salamander Letter along with the reports that had been written to authenticate it. As Throckmorton suspected, the ink report from Albert Lyter at Federal Forensic Associates in Raleigh, North Carolina, said only that the ink was iron gallotannic and consistent with those in use at the time. Bill Crueger's report on the paper said essentially the same thing: the paper was 100 percent rag, consistent with paper in use at the time. But, as Throckmorton explained to Jessee, iron gallotannic ink had been around since the seventh century and cotton rag paper had been available since about A.D. 1100, when it was introduced to Europe from the Orient. The paper and the ink could have been produced anytime within that period. They were, essentially, undatable.

The report of Kenneth Rendell, the East Coast documents dealer, was even worse. "The letter was examined under ultraviolet light," he wrote of his examination of the Salamander Letter, "and the ink fluoresced in accordance with other inks of this period." As Throckmorton, and any forensic documents examiner worth his salt, knew, ink never fluoresces, it luminesces, and it does so under infrared light, not ultraviolet. And besides, gallotannic ink should *neither* fluoresce *nor* luminesce.

Then Throckmorton researched Rendell's involvement with the famous, forged "Hitler diaries." Despite what many people seemed to think, Rendell had waffled for a long time on their authenticity and attacked those, like Charles Hamilton, who questioned them. Eventually, he agreed they were bogus—but only after the consensus of experts had shifted against them.

And this was the expert who authenticated Hofmann's documents?

A week later, Throckmorton was on the phone with Mike George of the county attorney's office.

"I'm not saying these documents are forged, all I'm saying is that they need a serious looking into."

Like everybody else, George thought it sounded like quibbling. "Jeez," he said, like everybody else. "You've got authentic paper, authentic ink."

Throckmorton tried to be patient. "Listen," he said. "I could go out and find 'consistent' paper right now, and I could make 'consistent' ink in the bathroom. And all you have to do to make ink look old is to bake it in an oven."

That got George's attention. Maybe this was worth looking into. He asked Throckmorton to come down and give his pitch to the prosecution team.

When he arrived in the war room on the third floor of the county attorney's office, everyone was sitting around the big conference table reading copies of *Utah Holiday*. Paul Larsen's article had just come out.

After talking to Throckmorton, Larsen had contacted Dean Jessee, who stood by his earlier assessment that the Salamander Letter was authentic, but added, "I'm not an expert. I'm not a forensic document examiner. I'm not qualified to testify in court. It's my personal opinion. That's all." When Larsen pressed him on *why* he thought the document was authentic, he fudged, claiming that he wanted to save his reasons for the paper he was writing.

Then Larsen called Rendell in Massachusetts to get a fuller explanation of his "authentication" of the letter. Rendell was instantly defensive. "I don't think forgery is a possibility," he said peremptorily. "Mark Hofmann, for example, is too sophisticated to try that."

Rendell added that, as far as he knew, the police had long since given up looking into the Salamander Letter as a motive for the bombings. "The deal was completed on it over a year ago. Everybody seemed happy with it."

But not Larsen. "How *do* you authenticate a document?" he pressed.

"We look at the paper it's written on, the ink used to write it, and the handwriting," Rendell explained. "The paper and ink are tested to see if they are of a type that was actually in use at the time the document was supposed to have been created." From what Throckmorton had told him, Larsen knew how much that was worth.

And what about the handwriting? "I did not authenticate that the document came from Martin Harris's hand," said Rendell. "That would have been impossible with what little I had." Dean Jessee had told Larsen that Harris left behind precious little of his handwriting for comparison purposes, just a few signatures and one short note, maybe fifteen or twenty words long. And where was that note? In a Book of Common Prayer that had been sold to the LDS Church by Mark Hofmann.

Rendell concluded: "All my report said was that the handwriting was consistent with the handwriting of the time and that there were no signs of forgery." It was hardly the ringing authentication that the press had made it out to be.

When Larsen asked Jeff Simmonds, Hofmann's old mentor at Utah State, what he thought of the Salamander Letter, he didn't mince words. "I think it's a forgery," he offered enthusiastically. "It's too pat." But he didn't think Mark had forged it. He guessed it was a nineteenth-century forgery by anti-Mormons trying to discredit the Church.

Larsen wasn't so sure. His article didn't directly accuse Hofmann of forgery, but it did raise some scratchy questions, speculating that the Salamander Letter and other Hofmann documents might have been part of a larger scheme to defraud the Church with even more spectacular, more controversial forgeries.

> It should be asked whether these pieces might be a prelude to some other great discovery—the 116 pages of the *Book of Mormon,* which Martin Harris lost while he was a scribe for Joseph Smith and which appear in his own handwriting. Hofmann has indicated to several people that he had an interest in finding this lost manuscript. If forgeries exist, were they ends in themselves or were they meant to be used as the samples against which other more valuable documents might be compared? Did the limitations on authentication of the salamander letter create an opportunity for forgery? Was the inexperience of Mormon scholars with that process of authentication a temptation to test it? These are speculative questions, but they are the sort which must be posed in a thorough investigation.

After reading that, the men sitting around the table in the county attorney's office greeted the arrival of the tall, thin, academic-looking Throckmorton like the Second Coming. They took one look at his reassuringly grizzled, graying beard and hired him on the spot.

Throckmorton said he needed two things. First, the original documents. He couldn't work from photocopies. Second, he needed a partner—a *non-Mormon* partner. "If I can prove these documents are forgeries, there will be a lot of people who say I am just protecting my Church by tarnishing documents that are against the faith."

Not that he doubted his own objectivity even for a second. He couldn't have cared less what was *in* the documents. He hadn't read them and didn't plan to. When he looked at a document, it was one letter at a time. It was the appearance of objectivity he was concerned about.

The man he chose was William J. Flynn, the chief questioned-documents examiner for the state of Arizona and one of the most highly regarded forensic specialists west of the Mississippi. It didn't hurt that he was also president of the Southwestern Association of Forensic Documents Examiners, and the director of a private forensic laboratory. Of the 233 documents examiners in the United States, Flynn, who had handled a staggering fifteen thousand cases over the years, was the cream of the cream. Thockmorton was taking on the big boys back East, and he knew he needed all the help he could get.

"I have just one question," he told Flynn when they talked on the phone. "What religion are you?"

Flynn, who knew almost nothing about the case, thought it was an odd question. "I'm not practicing," he replied, "but I'm a Catholic."

"That's perfect," said Throckmorton.

82

Flynn understood the question a lot better when he arrived in Salt Lake City for a brief visit on December 17. Throckmorton met him at the Holiday Inn off I-15, the one with the indoor pool that Flynn would never get to use, and drove him directly to a meeting on Temple Square. The Church wanted to look him over.

Dallin Oaks was there, along with other top brass, the new Church archivist, Glen Rowe, and the by-now unavoidable lawyers. At first Flynn thought the purpose of the meeting was to turn over the documents, but there were no documents in sight.

The real purpose of the meeting was quickly made clear. The Church wanted to know what Throckmorton and Flynn intended to do to their prized possessions. As they pointed out repeatedly, this was an unprecedented situation. They were being asked to open the Church vault to *outsiders,* to people beyond their bureaucratic control, to a non-Mormon, no less. Not that they trusted Throckmorton any better. His attacks on Mark Hofmann and his documents were, by now, well known, and they didn't please the Church. Someone accused Throckmorton of "picking on" Hofmann.

The mood was not friendly.

How did they plan to test the documents? Would the tests damage the documents in any way? Would they be handled with appropriate care by a Gentile? From their skeptical faces, Flynn got the feeling "they thought I was going to dump these things in grape juice.

The Church's dilemma was clear. As later described by a Mormon in the county attorney's office, "It was damaging enough to think that the documents were genuine and that the first leader of the Church might have been nothing more than a con man who duped the faithful. But it would be even *more* damaging if the documents turned out to be forgeries, and the *current* leaders of the Church had been duped by a con man."

Caught between a rock and a hard place, the Church reached for its favorite defense: secrecy. They agreed to let Throckmorton and Flynn look at the documents, but they were determined that absolutely no one else should see them.

That meant that under no circumstances could the two examiners make photocopies, or copy down the contents of the documents.

It meant the documents could not leave the Church premises. Throckmorton and Flynn would be given a conference room in the historical library. The locks would be changed, and they would be given the only two keys.

It meant that they would have to enter and leave the room together. Neither one would be allowed to stay in the room alone.

It meant that the documents would be brought to them every morning in a locked briefcase and returned every night to The Vault, where the briefcase would be handcuffed to a pipe so that it could not be opened again until the next day.

The Church lawyer who was doing most of the talking repeated again and again: "We don't want these divulged. We don't want the writing disseminated."

Throckmorton couldn't understand the paranoia. All of the documents they intended to review had already been published in Dean Jessee's book, *The Letters of Joseph Smith*. But when he repeated that, three times, the lawyer didn't seem to hear him. "I have to protect Hinckley," he kept saying. "I have to protect the Church."

*   *   *

They began work the next morning at eight, laying out their equipment on a huge wooden table in an ample conference room on the third floor of the Church Office Building. Flynn had brought his portable infrared equipment as well as some test plates. Throckmorton brought the microscopes, the ultraviolet equipment, measuring devices, and miscellany. They arranged everything around the table in stations until the place looked, according to Flynn, "like a mad scientist's laboratory." The plan was to move the documents from one station, one machine, to the next. Documents examiners were nothing if not methodical.

The Church provided them with five documents, including the Anthon Transcript, the Josiah Stowell letter, and a letter from Joseph Smith to the Lawrence sisters. The RLDS Church sent the Joseph Smith III blessing, and Brent Ashworth contributed the Lucy Mack Smith letter, the Martin Harris letter, and another letter written by Joseph Smith from the Carthage Jail. In addition, the Church provided a number of documents by the same authors that had not come through Hofmann's hands, for purposes of comparison: in all, eighty-one documents. Despite repeated requests, however, the FBI refused to surrender the Salamander Letter.

They worked for four days straight, from eight in the morning until eight at night, leaving only occasionally for Flynn to get a cup of coffee—he was shocked to discover that none was sold in the building. Despite a bank of windows in the conference room, they never saw the sun; it rained the whole time.

They put every document through what they called the "round robin," starting with the infrared machine, which was equipped with a camera that took pictures directly through the infrared apparatus. Because infrared radiation reacts differently to different chemical compositions in different inks, it was easy to spot any later additions to genuine documents.

At the microscope station, they checked for signs of alteration, obliteration, abrasive or chemical erasure, and any anomalies that would betray the date or region of manufacture. They looked to see how the paper had been cut. They could tell the difference between a cut made with a razor blade, with scissors, or with a papercutting machine. They could tell how the paper had been manufactured, how the ink had spread into the paper over time, and whether there were any fox marks (oxidation spots).

Then they compared the handwriting with other examples from the same writer that had not come through Mark Hofmann's hands. Using a rigorous set of seventeen tests, they looked for such things as lift points, pressure points, embellishments, and the relationship to the base line. The handwriting in a single document took as many as three hours to analyze thoroughly.

Almost from the start, little things bothered them. Under the microscope they noticed that on some of the documents, the ink had cracked into tiny scales—they called it "alligator skin"—invisible to the naked eye. Since neither man had worked with old documents before, they assumed it had something to do with aging but couldn't imagine why it would affect some documents and not others.

The handwriting in the Josiah Stowell letter looked too elegant for a messy writer like Joseph Smith. "If all you can play on the piano is 'Chopsticks,' " Flynn told Throckmorton, "you can pound on the keys with your fists but you can't play Mozart. If you only have a certain degree of skill, you can always write worse, but can never write better."

The letter that Smith had supposedly written from the Carthage Jail wasn't on the same kind of paper as two other letters Smith wrote the same day, letters that had been lent by the RLDS Church. What were the chances that a man in jail would have access to two different paper stocks on the same day?

And something was wrong with the Anthon Transcript. If the ink used to make the characters was so acidic that it burned through the paper and left reverse images on the other side, why didn't it leave similar ghost images on the pages of the Bible where it had lain, supposedly, for more than a hundred years? And why was the inscription in that Bible written in one ink, and the signature—which proved it belonged to the Smith family—in another? Why were several different inks used in one document, and why had the date on another been changed from 1722 to 1822?

But all this only suggested that a few of the documents might be forged, in whole or in part. Even if true, it didn't tell them *when* they were forged or *who* forged them. They would have to wait and pursue that when Flynn returned in January.

On the day Flynn left for Arizona, a Church delegation led by Gordon Hinckley visited the conference room. They looked suspiciously at all the equipment while Throckmorton and Flynn explained the process. They asked some questions but, to Flynn's astonishment, never asked the most obvious question of all: Are the documents genuine?

Not that he could have answered. Their tests to date had shown no sign of systematic forgery by Hofmann or anybody else. Sure there was a signature added here, a line removed there, but in any group of eighty-one historical documents, you were likely to find some anomalies. Most of the documents looked surprisingly "right." The paper, even on the doctored documents, looked genuine. The ink looked genuine. The writing instruments looked genuine. The handwriting looked genuine. They all seemed to have aged the appropriate length of time. The only unanswered question was the nagging one about cracked ink.

Maybe the East Coast experts had been right all along, Flynn thought.

But there was another explanation, admittedly a bizarre one, and he tried it out on Throckmorton as they drove to the airport on December 20. Was it possible that someone had gathered the old paper, the old ink, the old writing instruments and then artificially aged all the documents?

Nah, he concluded, jumping out of the car. Impossible.

83

On Christmas Eve, the gang met again in the county attorney's office: Ted Cannon, Bob Stott, Jim Bell, Ken Farnsworth, both national and local ATF men, representatives from the FBI, even Brent

Ward, the U.S. attorney, and Pete Hayward, the county sheriff. At least twenty men in all, few of them friends. Hayward still wasn't speaking to Cannon; Brent Ward wasn't speaking to Bob Stott, at least about this case. The police were furious with Hayward for copping out of the Sheets investigation; the ATF men were furious with Ward for copping out on the explosives charge. The county attorney's office was angry at Ward for locking them out of the grand jury proceedings, and Stott was angry at everybody for trying to push him into filing charges before he was good and ready. In short, the meeting was noticeably lacking in holiday cheer.

One more time, the investigators summarized the evidence. Then they repeated their plea: Won't somebody please file charges against Mark Hofmann?

No one had to ask Sheriff Hayward where he stood. For months, he had been telling everyone, especially the press, what he thought of Ted Cannon's office. "Those guys aren't *prosecutors*. They aren't prosecuting the case."

Not too long before, D'Elia had visited Hayward's office only to be greeted by a hail of verbal abuse. "How stupid can you guys be? When the hell are you going to file? What's it going to take? You can't imagine the public pressure that's on us to have this case filed. The county attorney's office doesn't know what the fuck is going on. You *gotta* file this case."

D'Elia took his coat off and dropped it, a gesture with a clear message: "If you want a fight, I'll give you a fight." He wasn't the kind to "take shit" from anybody, even Hayward.

"Listen," he yelled back. "Two weeks after the bombing, you and your men had already pulled out. I can't even get your men to do anything. They're not even in there with the investigation. It's total uncooperation. You're sitting here, doing nothing, and you're telling me to file. You go out there and get the damn facts and maybe I'll file it. You don't have a case yet, you don't have a motive yet." It was a full-scale screaming match by now.

Hayward ended on a threat. "I'm sending my detective over with the papers tomorrow, and I'm gonna have him screen this case in front of you. And then I'm gonna call the press and tell them."

D'Elia wasn't an easy man to intimidate. "Fine," he

said, stalking out of the room, "but you tell your man to bring a kick-out letter with him tomorrow morning." Hayward got the message: a kick-out letter was the form a prosecutor signed when he officially refused to file a case.

All eyes turned to Brent Ward. He looked completely uninterested in the proceedings. Someone asked if he would file separately on the bomb charge.

Not a chance. At first, his argument was technical. "We would have to get an exception to file simultaneously on the bomb charge," he explained. "Your filing would oust us from jurisdiction." Not everyone understood the details, but they understood the bottom line.

"Besides," Ward added nonchalantly, "nobody has convinced me that we have the right person. How do we even know we don't have the wrong guy?"

There was a long stunned silence.

Duffy Diamond broke it. "Whose fucking side are you on, anyway? Who are you working for here, for Christ's sake, the fucking defense counsel?"

"I'm the devil's advocate," Ward offered lamely. The time for devil's advocacy was long, long past.

When no one jumped to support him, Ward scurried to explain. "We need to find where the bombs were made. We need to go down other avenues, talk to other witnesses." Bell and Farnsworth looked at each other in astonishment, thinking of the hundreds of witnesses they had already spoken to. But Ward went on. "We need things that you don't have any prospect of getting. Mostly physical evidence." Like the *fake mustache,* for instance. "The man in the elevator was wearing a mustache. Where is the fake mustache?" Unless the police could get a lot more information than he had seen, Ward would not file, and if the county attorney's office did, they would be "walking into an absolute disaster." A disaster that, if it failed, would reflect badly on all of them.

In other words, it wasn't really a question of guilt or innocence, or even of good law enforcement or bad. In the final analysis, it was a question of P.R.

Then and there, it was clear to everyone that Brent Ward was signing off on the case. For a man with political ambitions, it was just too hot to handle. (Colleagues who saw Ward after Christmas said he looked "as if four hundred pounds had been taken off his shoulders.")

That left only the county attorney, Ted Cannon.

This time, to everyone's astonishment, he gave the go-ahead. First thing after Christmas, he said, his office would file charges.

Then Bob Stott spoke up. He didn't think it was the right time. "We can't do that," he said. "How's it gonna look? Here it's been two or three months, and then, all of a sudden, between Christmas and New Year's, we go ahead and do it. That'll look stupid." Or, even worse, vindictive—an attempt to destroy the Hofmann family's holidays.

So the filing was put off until January sometime, and everyone, including Mark Hofmann, spent Christmas at home.

84

Flynn wasn't scheduled to return to Utah until January 7, but he couldn't wait that long to return to work. While the rest of Phoenix sweated through last-minute shopping and hung Christmas lights on the cacti, Flynn buried himself in the literature on antique ink. For some reason, he couldn't get one question out of his head. Why the cracking?

He canvassed the libraries and called every forensic expert he knew hoping to find someone else who had experience with cracked ink. He examined the stampless covers that the county attorney's office had supplied him with. No cracking. He called a friend at the FBI labs in Washington and asked for all the information he had on iron gallotannic inks. No reference to cracking.

There was only one thing left to do: make his own ink and see if he could get it to crack.

Making it was easy. Anybody could do it in the kitchen

sink. The formula was available in several places, including Charles Hamilton's book *Great Forgers and Famous Fakes*. Teaching himself how to cut quill pens from turkey feathers was harder. (Although not as hard as locating turkey feathers in Phoenix. He finally found them in an Indian supply store for $1.50 apiece.)

Once he had made up a fake document, he had to age it. Iron gallotannic ink, like iron, rusts with age. The trick to aging ink was to speed up this oxidation process. One way to do that was to apply heat—simply to bake the document. Flynn tried it, and succeeded in aging the ink from black to a rust-brown color, but in the process, aged the paper dramatically. Instead of remaining supple like Hofmann's documents, it turned dry and brittle. In aging the ink a hundred years, he had aged the paper a thousand. And still no cracking.

So he tried speeding up the oxidation process chemically, using oxidizing agents like oxalic acid, which he had seen mentioned in the literature. That aged the ink all right, but it also took it off the paper. Sodium hypochlorite, nitric acid, sulfuric acid, hydrochloric acid, and hydrogen peroxide were equally unsuccessful. When he tried ammonium hydroxide (common household ammonia) and sodium hydroxide, the ink turned a lovely shade of rust-red, but there was still no cracking.

He decided to stick with the ammonia and change the ink, mixing up several batches using different additives common in the nineteenth century. One of those additives was gum arabic, a form of complex sugar used to preserve and improve the viscosity of ink. When he exposed the gum arabic solution to the sodium hydroxide, the ink once again turned the requisite reddish-brown color. Then he put the sample under the microscope and saw what he'd been waiting for. The ink had cracked.

When Flynn and Throckmorton reunited in Salt Lake City on January 7, they had only one thing on their minds. They wanted another look at the documents. Even with all the work that had been done, there were still important unanswered questions: Which documents showed the cracking? What other circumstances—besides gum arabic and artificial aging—might explain the cracking? For example, the Church routinely deacidified documents that came into its archives. Or was there something about the way they were stored?

It wasn't long before they started getting answers.

First, they realized that they had seen the cracking only on Hofmann's documents. It had to be more than a coincidence.

Throckmorton tested the theory. "Hand me a document and don't tell me where it came from," he told Flynn. After looking at it under various instruments, he announced, "This one came from Mark."

"Right."

He examined a second document. "This one didn't come from Mark."

"Right again."

Then a third document.

"Hofmann?"

"Right again."

They started putting the documents into two stacks, one stack for the documents that showed the cracking, Hofmann's stack; and one for documents that showed no cracking. Before long, they were both feeling cocky.

Flynn handed him another document, and Throckmorton pronounced it "Mark's."

Only this time it wasn't.

Suddenly their theory didn't look so good. They could have understood it if a document from Hofmann had *not* shown the cracking and had been genuine. It only made sense that *some* of Hofmann's documents were real. But to find a document that did show cracking but didn't come from Mark blew a gaping hole right through the middle of their theory.

Then it happened again. Another document that didn't come through Hofmann showed the cracking.

They tried to pass it off as a minor glitch. Throckmorton started a third pile with the two documents, but said to himself, "This theory doesn't hold water."

That night he took the two documents to Glen Rowe, the Church archivist, and asked him to check again on where they came from. Who donated them to the Church, and where did the donors get them?

The next day Rowe came by to say that both documents had been donated to the Church by the same man. And he had gotten them both from Mark Hofmann.

* * *

A day later, they found the clincher. It looked harmless enough, a simple promissory note made out to one Isaac Galland and signed on the back by Joseph Smith. Only when Throckmorton and Flynn looked at it under the microscope, they discovered a curious thing. The ink on the front was not cracked. The ink on the back was. The same piece of paper, stored under the same conditions, deacidified in the same way, and yet one side was cracked and the other wasn't. Clearly, the signature had been added and, like all the other documents with cracking, artificially aged.

And it came from Mark Hofmann.

85 Ken Farnsworth was visiting friends in Los Angeles when Jim Bell phoned from Salt Lake City on February 3. The county attorney's office had called Bell and told him to be at their offices at seven the next morning. No explanation, just be there.

No explanation was needed. Bell knew why they wanted him there, which was why he was calling his partner. "They won't tell me what they're doing," said Bell. "So you and I both *know* what they're doing."

It was that son of a bitch Stott. "Hell, if you can't trust the guy who's a detective on the case," Farnsworth sputtered, "who do you trust? What's the point?"

He flew back that night at ten.

The next morning at seven Farnsworth showed up at the county attorney's office. Bob Stott was more than a little surprised.

"I don't appreciate being left out of the arrest," Farnsworth snarled at Stott. Then he found out that they had also left his name off the information. He demanded to know why.

"Well, we were just gonna let Jim sign it because we

didn't know you were gonna be here," said Stott, squirming.

It was all Farnsworth could do to keep from slugging him. "That's bullshit. This case is assigned to me. The Christensen murder is specifically assigned to me, and it's my responsibility to sign a complaint. I'm gonna put my name on it. You got a problem with that?"

Stott fumbled for a few seconds then finally came out with it. "Well, you know that Mark and his family and Ron think that you haven't looked at anything else. All you've looked at is Mark. And they think that it's real, that you're real prejudiced."

Prejudiced! Farnsworth was livid. Who the hell was running this case, the law enforcement agencies or Mark and his family? He shot Stott a black look. "Hey, pal, I'm not going away on this case. I'm part of it. No choice, I'm here. You got me whether you like it or not. I don't care." He pointed at the information. "So you change that puppy right around, right now. I'm not going back to my department and say, 'Hey, they took my name off my own case because they don't want me on it.'"

Stott's mouth twitched. It was a standoff. Finally, he looked away.

"Okay, for you, we'll put your name on it." So they added Farnsworth's name to one of the informations, the one that listed the two counts of murder. Two of Stott's investigators, Dick Forbes and Mike George, signed the other three.

That defused the situation, but it didn't leave Farnsworth feeling any better about it. Stott had kicked him in the teeth, and it still smarted. "Mark doesn't like you," he repeated to himself. "Bullshit." It wasn't Hofmann. It was Stott.

Bell, Farnsworth, Forbes, George, and D'Elia took the paperwork to the chambers of Judge Paul Grant in the county court building for signing. When they were finished, Bell said, "Let's go to jail." Hofmann had denied them the pleasure of hauling him in. He had agreed to come to the jail on his own. The five of them would go wait for him there.

On the way across the plaza to the Hall of Justice, the two investigators stopped. "Look," said Mike George to Bell and Farnsworth, "this is you guys' case. All we've been doing is helping. It's your deal. You guys go and book it." If anybody deserved to be in on the arrest, it was George and Forbes, thought Farnsworth, so he persuaded them to come along. But it was a class gesture.

Bell and Farnsworth walked through the main floor of the Hall of Justice and out the other side. Because of construction in the building, they would have to take one last detour. Standing on the other side of the parking lot at the entrance to the booking room, they could see Channel 2 reporter Rick Schenkman and his cameraman. They looked around. That was it for press. And Schenkman didn't even notice them. Just as they were entering the tunnel that led to the booking room, they heard him call out to his cameraman, "Hurry, get the picture of that guy over there!" He was pointing at Gerry D'Elia. So they walked on, uninterrupted, with the arrest warrant in their hands.

At the end of the tunnel, the garage door opened in front of them. They passed through the electrically controlled security gate and into the long, concrete booking room lined with the iron bars of holding cells. At the far end of the room, on a bench next to the booking window, sat Mark Hofmann.

Sheriff Hayward and Lieutenant Ben Forbes were also there, but it was Bell and Farnsworth who approached Hofmann and said, "You're under arrest."

Filling out the booking sheet took only fifteen minutes. But it was still a high. Farnsworth heaved a sigh of relief. "Finally, we got the little prick in jail."

Later that day, they drove to Centerville to explain the arrest and probable-cause statements to Terri Christensen. For the first time, they saw her new baby, now almost one month old. Knowing he would be a caesarean, Terri had chosen to have him delivered on January 9—on what would have been Steve's thirty-second birthday. She named him Steven.

PART FIVE

Contending with Lucifer

86

Now it was the prosecutors' turn to approach Gordon Hinckley.

Bob Stott must have prayed this day would never come, but by late March, he could no longer avoid it. Church functionaries like Don Schmidt could testify at the preliminary hearing about most of the documents Hofmann had sold the Church, and Hugh Pinnock could take the heat for Dallin Oaks on the McLellin Collection, but only two people knew about the Josiah Stowell letter, Mark Hofmann and Gordon Hinckley.

Ironically, Stott had assigned himself the documents side of the Hofmann case, allowing him to control—some said contain—the Church's involvement. Now, as the prosecutor in charge of the documents scam, he was leading his team into the sanctum sanctorum of Church power, Hinckley's paneled offices.

Before they even sat down, Hinckley asked the first and most important question: "Are you members of the Church?"

David Biggs answered, "Yes. But I'm not a particularly good one." He wasn't sure if Hinckley heard him, he seemed so preoccupied with picking up "vibrations." He was, after all, first and foremost a spiritual man with the Lord's business on his mind—and a lawyer, Wilford Kirton, at his side.

Stott explained that they needed to know more about Hinckley's meetings with Mark Hofmann. In particular, they needed to know what kind of pressure Hofmann might have been under to produce the McLellin Collection. Was it the kind of pressure that might lead to murder?

Hinckley looked at them with a *Mona Lisa* smile. Far from putting pressure on Hofmann, he said, he only vaguely *remembered* Mark Hofmann.

Stott and Biggs shifted uneasily in their chairs. With all the time in between to recollect those meetings, he *still* couldn't remember a thing.

"Was he ever in your office?" Stott asked.

"Probably," said Hinckley.

Probably! thought Biggs. Now he was even forgetting what he had admitted in the press conference.

"Have you ever bought anything from him yourself?"

"Not directly. A couple of documents may have come through me, but only as a vehicle by which the Church made the purchases."

They tried, ever so gently, to refresh his recollection. Surely he remembered the morning, only days before the bombings, when Hofmann came to tell him the Kinderhook plates "might be available for the right price"? He did remember the Kinderhook plates?

"I don't know a whole lot about them," Hinckley said dryly.

Biggs thought, This is *Hinckley*. He's telling us he doesn't know a whole lot about the Kinderhook plates. My God, even I have learned a little about them in this investigation. He *has* to know what they're about. They're a big thing in Mormon history.

In a show of cooperativeness, Hinckley walked to his bookshelf, pulled out a book and began to read a passage about the Kinderhook plates as if it were all news to him, like a person who has just heard an interesting word for the first time and wants to look it up—just out of curiosity.

Stott and Biggs pressed. Surely he knew that Steve Christensen had been called by Church officials at all hours of the night to go out and find Hofmann and get him to repay the First Interstate loan?

Hinckley shrugged his shoulders.

Surely, he knew that phone calls had flown back and forth from the Church Office Building and that Christensen was pounding on doors all over Salt Lake City? Surely this indicated that the Church was bringing pressure to bear?

Hinckley could recall nothing.

No matter how evocatively they painted the picture of those last desperate days, Hinckley could recall nothing.

Biggs decided it was time to push a little harder. One

thing that had always amazed him, he began innocently, was why no one had investigated the documents the Church bought from Hofmann, not *really* investigated them, not checked their provenances, for example. True, Hofmann, like many documents dealers, kept his sources confidential, but the Church had never even *tried* to verify its purchases. And yet it was spending tens of thousands of dollars on these documents.

Biggs wanted to ask: Were these the actions of parties who barely knew each other? Is it credible that you would put that much trust in someone whom you knew only "vaguely"? But he decided instead to ask only half the question, "How is it that you felt comfortable relying on Mr. Hofmann as a sole basis for purchasing these documents?"

Hinckley looked him in the eye. "We relied on Mark Hofmann's integrity," he said gravely. "If we were deceived, then it's to *his* eternal detriment."

Wow, thought Biggs. Heavy stuff. But hardly responsive.

They tried another approach. As per Joseph Smith's instructions, every good Mormon is supposed to keep a detailed daily diary of his or her activities. Over the years, the Church's leaders had been extraordinarily conscientious in obeying that injunction. So they asked to see Hinckley's diary entries for his meetings with Mark Hofmann. "I don't keep a diary," Hinckley responded quickly, as if he were prepared for the question.

After another hour of evasions, memory lapses, and sermonettes, Biggs lost his patience. "President Hinckley. This has been in the news—people have *died*—isn't there any way we can get some information about your meetings with Hofmann?"

Hinckley couldn't contain his indignation. "This is the *least* of my concerns," he huffed. "I am an extremely busy man. I have worldwide concerns. Mr. Hofmann is a postscript . . ." he reached for the rest of the phrase, ". . . in the walk of life."

You wish, thought David Biggs.

When Bob Stott finally worked up the courage to talk about Hinckley's testimony at the upcoming preliminary hearing, Wilford Kirton jumped in.

"President Hinckley doesn't wish to testify at the hearing. We think it would be in everyone's best interests to not have him testify."

Someone suggested that he would have to testify at trial.

You don't understand, said Kirton imperiously. President Hinckley does not wish to testify at the hearing, at the trial, at anything.

Even Stott had to be outraged. This was putting him, as a devout member of the Church, under wholly unacceptable pressure.

Hinckley had obviously wanted to stay out of this discussion, but it was clear from the prosecutors' reaction that nothing less than his personal intervention would calm the furor that Kirton's comments had unleashed. So he decided to give another sermonette, this one on the subject of "priorities." He sat down with Stott as a father would sit down with a wayward son.

"This isn't that significant, as it relates to Church matters," he said softly. "It's the Church that matters. You have to consider the Church first. I don't wish to testify."

This time Stott said nothing.

But that wasn't all Hinckley wanted. "I think it would be in the best interests of the Church," he added in the same mellow voice, "if you simply dismissed the charge."

Dismiss the charge? Biggs was aghast. It took them a moment to realize that he meant only that Stott should dismiss the charge on the Stowell letter, which would let Hinckley off the hook as far as testifying at the preliminary hearing.

Despite the months of investigation, Stott and Biggs had only the vaguest idea of how much Hinckley had to lose if Mark Hofmann told all in open court, or even if the complete details of his relationship with Hinckley came into the open. They knew nothing of the forces at work within the ranks of the General Authorities to oust Hinckley from power for his failure of vision, his failure to see the trap that Hofmann had laid for him. If Church conservatives were to read the full details of his misadventures in newspaper accounts of a trial, the consequences for *him*—apart from the consequences for the Church—could be catastrophic. He could disappear from the upper reaches of power or, even worse, of the Celestial Kingdom.

More fervently than the prosecutors could have imagined, Gordon Hinckley must have wanted to say "dismiss the charges" on *all* of Hofmann's crimes. Close the public record, lock him away or buy his silence, put the matter to rest. Make him, as quickly as possible, "just a postscript in the walk of life."

But Bob Stott wasn't ready to do that. "We are not going to drop the charge," he said after he regained his composure. But he did have a compromise suggestion. "If we can get the defense to stipulate as to your testimony, we won't have to call you. But if they won't stipulate, and if we think it's important for you to testify, you will have to testify."

As they left the room, Biggs slapped Stott on the back. He knew that couldn't have been easy.

87 The preliminary hearing began on April 14, 1986, in the midst of an early-spring heat wave. It would have led the news stories in both local papers if Ronald Reagan hadn't ordered an air raid on Libya the night before. And some people were surprised that even *that* knocked the biggest local story out of the lead spot.

Ron Yengich and the Hofmann family had been shouting Mark's innocence from the media rooftops for three months, and most of the press and public believed them. It had taken so long for *anyone* to file charges that when they finally did, many people figured the police were just trying to cover their backside: pinning the crimes on Hofmann because they had to pin them on *somebody*.

It was only a preliminary hearing—a proceeding before a judge to determine if the evidence warranted a trial—but there was nothing preliminary about the media hoopla or the police security precautions. The circuit court building swarmed with uniforms. There were guards in every corner of the courtroom, guards at the doors, guards in the halls, guards downstairs, guards upstairs, guards in the bathrooms. Spectators passed through a metal detector both on entering *and* on leaving the courtroom. Briefcases, purses, camera bags, rolled-up newspapers, everything was checked. Those who wanted to avoid the search had to listen to the proceedings on loudspeakers set up in an anteroom. Ron Yengich argued that because Hofmann was innocent, the *real* killer was still out there and Mark was still a target. Police said they feared an attack by some crazed Mormon, mad at Hofmann for hoodwinking Church leaders. Most people thought Yengich's explanation sounded more likely.

Paranoia, like spring, was in the air. After technicians from KSL finished installing the wiring system in the courtroom, several detectives on duty wondered, seriously, if the men from the Church-owned station might have secretly arranged to transmit the proceedings directly to Church headquarters.

The day before the hearing, Jim Bell had left a message with Yengich's secretary. "Tell him that if Mark wants a bulletproof vest, the police department will provide one free of charge. We'll be happy to bring it over to him, and he can keep it through the entire proceeding."

It was an especially strange offer given that Hofmann, free on bail, had been seen in local restaurants dressed in nothing more protective than a T-shirt emblazoned with a white salamander.

Circuit Judge Paul G. Grant entered the courtroom and strode to his place in the corner behind an altar-like dais of blond oak. He was a huge man, with cowboy boots showing beneath his tent-size black robe. The fifty or so spectators, half of them press, who filled the padded pews of the stark, concrete courtroom, quickly settled down. Grant stepped up on the dais and slumped his vast frame into a big leathery chair. Everything about him seemed huge: hands, feet, head, eyes, even his glasses.

At six-feet seven, Grant was used to being the center of attention. He had presided over the preliminary hearings in the Ted Bundy, Ervil LeBaron, and Frances Schreuder cases. After the last, he had lost his taste for high-profile cases and generally let the younger judges take them now. If he wanted attention, he would say, all he had to do was show up at church with his twelve children, most of whom were also more than six feet tall.

A devout Mormon and former bishop, Grant brushed off questions about his ability to sit in judgment on a case that involved the Church so deeply. Every judge brings some baggage to the bench, he would say; at least he was honest about it. Just in case, though, he had sounded out Ron Yengich on the issue. Yengich assured him that he felt Hofmann could get a fair hearing in Grant's courtroom.

In fact, the only thing that really bothered Grant about the trial was that it threatened to interfere with the basketball season.

"I have perceived that it's going to get warm in this courtroom," Grant announced in his comforting, avuncular voice. "So I will invite everyone to take off their coat and not suffer through this."

Bruce Passey, the co-owner of a jewelry manufacturing firm on the third floor of the Judge Building, took the witness stand first. He looked like a man who spent most of his time indoors doing close work: pale, balding, slightly overweight, bespectacled. Early on the morning of October 15, he had stood in the foyer and ridden up in the elevator with a man wearing a green letter jacket and carrying a brown package addressed to Steve Christensen.

Gerry D'Elia questioned him. "Did you notice anything with respect to any kind of glasses on this individual, hearing aid, anything of that sort, that you would recognize?"

"No eyeglasses."

"How about facial hair? Did you notice anything about facial hair?"

"He was not clean-shaven."

"Would that be a beard?"

"Well, more of a five-o'clock shadow, as if he hadn't shaved for the morning."

"I am going to show you, Mr. Passey, what's been marked Proposed Exhibit No. 2. I'm holding it up, for the record, and showing you the front of it, and then showing you the back of it, and then putting it up right in front of you. Are you able to recognize that jacket, Mr. Passey?"

"Yes."

"From where?"

"That was the color of the jacket that was on the fellow that was in the foyer."

"How about the remainder of the jacket? The sleeves are gray on that, are they not?"

"Yes."

"You originally described the sleeves as being a light tan color. Is that correct?"

"Yes."

"Why the difference between your original description of tan sleeves and the gray sleeves right now?"

"Because the light in the foyer; they use a little bit dimmer light."

"Now, with respect to the person that you saw in the elevator and in the foyer of the Judge Building in the lobby on October 15, 1985, are you able to recognize that person again?"

"Yes."

"Do you see that person in the courtroom today?"

"Yes."

"For the record, would you indicate where that person is seated and point out the person and tell us what the person is dressed in?"

Passey pointed to Hofmann. "He is sitting next to Mr. Yengich wearing glasses and a blue suit."

On cross-examination, Yengich tried everything to impeach Passey's identification. "Did you say whether or not he was wearing glasses?"

"He was not wearing glasses."

Yengich smiled. "I note that you wear eyeglasses."

"Yes."

"Were you wearing them on that morning?"

"Yes."

"I'm nearsighted," Yengich confessed congenially. "What's yours?"

"I'm nearsighted also."

"When is the last time you had your eyes checked, sir?"

"About a year and a half ago."

And what about the mustache, Yengich wanted to know.

"I said I was not 100 percent sure on the mustache."

"The composite does have a mustache on it?" The composite had been based partly on Passey's original description to the police.

"Yes."

"It's easily identified as a mustache? You would agree with me on that, wouldn't you?"

"Yes."

On the letter jacket, Yengich circled warily. Reading from the notes that Detective Johnson had taken at the time of Passey's original description of the letter jacket, Yengich said, "It goes on to say, 'with dark brown leather sleeves.' " Not just brown, but *dark* brown. It was easy to mistake light gray for light tan, but light gray for *dark* brown? "Is that correct?"

"No, I did not tell him dark brown."

"Is that what it says on State's Exhibit 4?"

"It does say it, yes."

"But your testimony today is that you did not tell the detective that?"

"No, sir."

"The detective must have been in error when he put dark brown leather sleeves. Is that correct?"

"Correct."

As for the identification of Hofmann, Yengich wanted to suggest that it was based not on Passey's own recollection of the encounter in the elevator but from what he had seen in the media.

"Do you take either newspaper, either daily, in Salt Lake?"

"Yes, sir."

"Have you seen any photographs of him in those papers?"

"No, sir."

Yengich hadn't expected that answer. "You have not? Why is that, sir?"

"Because ever since the bombing, I saw him the first time they put him on television, and then, after that, I just quit watching. I don't read the paper anymore."

If there was anything Yengich hated, it was a witness who knew how to protect his testimony. "You don't read the paper at all anymore?"

"No, sir. If I do, it's more the sports page or the Wall Street section."

"You don't watch any of the TV news?"

"If anything comes on about it, I just turn the opposite way or think of something else. I do not watch it."

Later that day, D'Elia called to the stand Margene Robbins, a receptionist in Tom Wilding's office. Hofmann had visited the office on the morning of the bombings.

What time did he come in? D'Elia asked.

"Well, it was probably about 9:15 or something."

"How was Mr. Hofmann dressed?"

"He was wearing a green fabric, a green fabric jacket that had gray leather sleeves and a striped knit collar." She recognized it because her son had a letter jacket very much like it. "Except," she added, her son "didn't wear it after he was out of high school."

"Have you seen any other men over thirty wearing an Olympus High School jacket without a letter on it, to your recollection?"

"No."

Janet McDermott, a businesswoman in her mid-thirties with the large eyes and high cheekbones of a fashion model, took the stand next. She had been across the hall when the bomb exploded in Steve Christensen's hands. In the audience, Terri Christensen told herself she was prepared to listen. Two days before, Ken Farnsworth had visited her at home to warn her about McDermott's testimony. "She will be saying that she thought Steve was alive when she came out into the hall," he had said, "that she heard Steve crying." Farnsworth wanted to reassure her that the testimony was both ugly and inaccurate. He swallowed hard and explained that what McDermott thought was crying was probably just air being released from the lungs. The medical examiner would testify that Steve had died instantly. Farnsworth wrote in his notes that Terri handled the explanation "pretty well."

McDermott testified she heard an explosion and crouched down behind her desk.

"What did you think when you heard that?" asked Gerry D'Elia.

"I was very scared. I thought that if there was somebody out in the hallway, that they would know for sure I was there."

"Did you hear anything at that time while you were over at the desk?"

"Yes, I did."

"What did you hear?"

"A very high-pitched crying." McDermott began to cry.

In the audience, Terri Christensen braced herself.

"When you opened your door of 610 Judge Building, what did you see?"

"Steve Christensen was laying on the floor."

"Where was he?"

"He was partway in his office, partway out in the hallway."

"Did you see any wounds on Steve Christensen?"

"Yes."

"What were the most extensive wounds that you saw that caught your attention?"

"His entire chest was bloody."

"How about the noises that you had heard from inside your office? Did you ever hear them again once you got to your door and looked at Mr. Christensen?"

"They were coming from Mr. Christensen. They were much deeper by now."

Terri Christensen put her head down and began to cry as softly as she could. She had thought she could handle it. "I want to know everything," she had said two days before. "I want to be there." But she didn't really. She believed what Farnsworth had told her about Steve dying instantly, and she was prepared for McDermott's story—intellectually at least. But the image, true or false, caught her unawares, and the tears just came of their own accord.

Only a few feet away, close enough to hear her crying, Bill and Dorie Hofmann sat stone still.

Throughout the testimony, Steve Christensen's younger brother, Scott, sat in the courtroom staring at Mark Hofmann. Only occasionally did his eyes stray briefly to the witness or to a piece of evidence being admitted. No one would have guessed that the handsome, sandy-haired, burly young man with vengeance in his eyes was, in another world, a sweet-tempered, easygoing family man. But then, no one could have guessed how much his brother had meant to him.

At the end of the day's session, one of the officers

assigned to watch the courtroom approached Ken Farnsworth with a worried look. "Watch the big guy," he said ominously, pointing at Scott Christensen. "He's going to kill Mark. He's going to get up and go over and beat the fuck out of him."

88

Gerry D'Elia circled the next witness for a long time before asking his first question. He wanted the judge, the media, and the audience to look long and hard at a man whose life had been shattered by Mark Hofmann.

"You were married to Kathleen Sheets?"

"Yes." Gary Sheets shifted in the witness chair looking uncharacteristically nervous.

"For how long?"

"Twenty-seven years and a few months."

"How many children did you have in total?"

"Four."

"And the names, besides, I think, Gretchen, and Jimmy, that I can recollect?"

"Kathryn Robertson and Heidi Jones."

"How old is Gretchen?"

"She's twenty."

"How old is Jimmy?"

"Jimmy is fifteen."

"How would you describe Kathy's relationship with the family?"

"She was her grown daughters' best friend. Two or three times a week, I would come home at night, and Kathy would come up and say, smiling at me, we have got all three grandchildren tonight, which meant tending them. Her children and her grandchildren were her life and her love, and me. We had a very close family."

In the audience, Jimmy, Gretchen, Katie, and Heidi, along with their Aunt Joan, listened to their father's testimony and relived the pain with him. Like everything in their lives for the last six months, it was an ordeal, but this one they welcomed.

For months after the bombing, Gretchen couldn't walk down stairs without thinking something terrible would happen. Every time she opened the dryer, she closed her eyes and waited for the explosion. She wouldn't go near the mailbox. One day, she opened the front door and saw a big cardboard box from AT&T. She just looked at it in terror and shut the door again. Eventually, she worked up the courage to kick it a few times, then Jimmy poked it with a long pole. It turned out to be telephones.

When Gretchen went to give blood, the nurse recognized her name. "Oh, you're not related to that *Gary* Sheets are you?"

"Yeah, that's my dad."

"Well, I don't think that Mark Hofmann is guilty."

Then one day Katie took Danny, her nephew, to a hamburger place. They were about to sit down when she saw Mark and Dorie in the next booth. Her mother was dead, and her murderer was sitting there eating a hamburger and fries. She took Danny's hand and left. But that did little to ease the anger and she brooded for days.

Now, finally, it was Hofmann's turn to suffer. This was *his* ordeal. And they wouldn't have missed it for the world. They had spent so many months hating him and hating the thought that they were suffering and he wasn't, that Kathy was gone and he was free.

The next morning, Ron Yengich cross-examined Gary Sheets.

Since the bombings, Sheets had been at the center of a storm of rumors accusing him of everything from adultery to homosexuality. One of the more fantastical versions involved a sordid love triangle between Sheets, Steve, and Terri Christensen. Another story making the rounds as the hearings began was that Gary and Kathy had been involved in an ugly divorce at the time of the bombings and that Gary had since remarried. The point of the stories was always the same: Sheets himself had killed his wife—and maybe Christensen—either in a jealous rage or in order to make room for some other liaison.

They were outrageous lies, but Yengich had to use what was available. He had heard the rumors—some suspected the defense team had generated its share of them—and he knew they could support at least one red herring. In a case heavy on circumstantial evidence and weak on motive, it took only one red herring to hang a jury.

"You considered Steve to be a very bright young man?" Yengich asked.

"Extremely so. The brightest in the company."

"And he voiced to you his concerns about directions that CFS was taking. Is that a fair statement?"

"Yes."

"But they never boiled over into any arguments or anything such as that between you?"

"No."

"Not even the type of argument that a father and son might have—is that correct?"

"No."

"And so any dispute between you and Steve at that point would have been, again, coupled with the genuine affection that you held for him—is that correct?"

"I think so. But I don't think we really had disputes."

Sheets was making it easy for him. As Yengich knew, Christensen had had many serious disputes with his boss, in front of witnesses, as the CFS ship sank. But all that would come out at trial. It was enough just to suggest it here.

Yengich floated another red herring.

"Having been in the insurance industry for a period of time—and you did consider Steve Christensen to be an important part of J. Gary Sheets & Associates—correct?"

Sheets: "And CFS."

"And CFS—is that correct?"

"Yes."

"Was Mr. Christensen insured by either of those companies?"

"Just by CFS."

"And was that insurance policy still extant at the time of his death?"

"Was it still what?"

"Did it still exist at the time of his death?"

"Yes. We bought some buy-sell insurance on all of us in the early part of '85."

"Who was the beneficiary of that?"

"CFS."

"Has that been paid?"

"That has been paid."

"What was the amount of that insurance?"

"Five hundred thousand."

On redirect, D'Elia made bouillabaisse of Yengich's red herring.

"Now, with respect to the insurance on Mr. Christensen, that is known as a key-man policy, isn't it?"

"That's right."

"And is that customary for CFS, and other corporations that you have ever been a part of, to have this on key men within the group?"

"Yes. We were far too long in coming to do that. We felt, for a few years before, we needed to have key-man insurance. Just slow getting around to it."

D'Elia asked if CFS was "the sole beneficiary of that key-man insurance policy."

Sheets: "That's right."

"And has that all gone to the bankruptcy?"

"Yes."

"Have you received any part of that insurance policy?"

"Personally?"

"Yes."

"No."

"I don't have anything further. Thank you."

When Aaron Teplick, a curly-haired thirteen-year-old with a serene, Buddha-like face, took the stand, his head barely showed over the witness box. The microphone was set as low as it would go and it still pointed at his forehead.

But nothing fazed Aaron.

Before the hearing, D'Elia and Ken Farnsworth had prepared him for this moment.

"Do you know how important you are to this case?" Farnsworth asked.

"Oh, I don't know," said Aaron offhandedly, as if he had been asked what he wanted for lunch.

"Do you know *why* this is so important?"

"Does Mark Hofmann have a van like that?" No doubt about it, Aaron was a smart kid.

Teplick Senior was more of a problem. D'Elia and Farnsworth spent more time reassuring Aaron's father, Dr. Stanley Teplick, than Aaron. Would testifying against

Hofmann expose his son to any danger, he wanted to know?

"The crisis is over," D'Elia assured him. "Mark isn't going to go out and blow up everybody who testifies. There are just too many of them. Besides, he can't even walk."

From deep inside the witness box, Aaron repeated, in the same calm, assured voice, his account of the night of October 14 when he saw a van pull up in front of the Sheets house off Naniloa Drive.

"I looked through the Levolor blinds and saw some lights coming down the drive. It was going quite slow. . . . It was a gold-colored Toyota van, a Wonder Wagon. . . ."

When he was finished, Farnsworth, who was sitting in the courtroom, wanted to stand up and applaud.

Like D'Elia, Yengich knew how unreliable child witnesses could be, how easily discredited. And if ever a witness needed to be discredited, Aaron Teplick was it.

"Aaron, have we ever met before?" Yengich adopted a pleasant, avuncular tone that he used often if never entirely convincingly.

"No."

"Okay. Just shook hands out in the hallway—is that correct?"

"Yes."

"Introduced myself to you—right? You don't have any problem answering my questions, do you?"

"No."

"Have you ever been down to a Toyota dealership and looked at the books that they have about these vans?" Yengich wanted to get Aaron to admit that the police had manipulated him into identifying the van as a Toyota. After all, doesn't one van look more or less like any other to a thirteen-year-old? Especially in the dark.

"Not the books," Teplick answered. "I've seen them in magazines."

"In magazines." Teplick was certain it was a Toyota because he *knew* the differences between various vans. At that moment it became clear to everyone in the courtroom, especially Yengich, that Hofmann had had the misfortune to drive by a young car buff that night.

"Did the police officers, at any time, actually take you and show you a van, an actual van?"

"Yes."

"When was that, son?"

"It was *after* I drew the diagram and the picture and everything." Thirteen-year-old Aaron Teplick knew exactly what Ron Yenich was driving at.

Yengich quickly changed course. "And you described it [to the police] as a gold van, right?" Yengich had discovered that Toyota listed Hofmann's van as "copper."

"Yes."

"That was the phrase you used—is that correct?"

" 'A gold Toyota Wonder Wagon' was the phrase I used." Aaron was a match for Yengich.

"A gold Toyota Wonder Wagon. And you meant, by gold, you meant gold in color—right?"

"Right."

"Now, you know the difference between the color gold and the color copper, don't you?"

"Yes."

"What color is a penny?"

"Copper."

"Is that copper color to you?" Yengich asked, holding up a penny.

"Yes."

"What color is this?" He held up a gold wristwatch.

"Gold."

"For the record, I have a 1983-D penny and my law partner's watch." Yengich sat down with a satisfied look on his face.

But in the back of the courtroom, Ken Farnsworth was also smiling. He knew what Yengich didn't, that a representative of Toyota had already submitted a statement that the Wonder Wagon didn't even come in gold. It came *only* in copper—whatever you called it. D'Elia knew it too. Holy shit, he thought to himself as Yengich sat down, are you in for a big surprise when we go to trial.

After Aaron Teplick's testimony, Jim Bell noticed a change in the press. In the lobby outside the courtroom later that day, he was approached by a TV reporter who had proclaimed Hofmann's innocence loudly and often during the long months of investigation. "Well, do you think he'll plead guilty now?" the reporter asked eagerly. "There's no question what the kid saw."

89 The last person to testify that day was an attractive woman in her early twenties. She gave her name as Kelly Maria Elliott.

"Kelly, directing your attention to the month of October of 1985," D'Elia began, "where did you work?"

"Radio Shack."

"And where is the location of that Radio Shack?"

"Cottonwood Mall, Highland Drive."

D'Elia sensed some movement at the defense table. He had already noticed that Yengich didn't have the case under control, that he hadn't begun to read all the thousands of pages of materials the county attorney's office had dumped on him in the last two months. Could it be, D'Elia wondered, that the defense hadn't read the report on this witness yet? That they didn't know what she was going to say? That only Hofmann knew what she *might* say?

"And now, directing your attention, Kelly, to the 7th of October, 1985," he continued, "were you working on that day?"

"Yes."

"Do you remember what day of the week that happened to be?"

"Monday."

D'Elia approached her with a copy of a Radio Shack receipt. "And do you recognize that receipt?"

"Yes."

"What is it a receipt for?"

"Battery holder, a small switch, and lamp."

"Now, the battery holders, what size battery holders are they? To fit what size battery?"

"A C-cell."

"And now, on this date, do you remember making this sale to any individual?"

"Vaguely."

"Do you remember anything about the individual . . ." Again, he heard shuffling at the defense table, Mark scribbling something on his pad, perhaps, ". . . the name that they gave to you?"

"Mike Hansen," said Elliott. She spelled it.

"What do you remember, if anything, about the actual transaction that day, Kelly? First of all, do you remember what time of day it was?"

"Probably in the afternoon."

"Why do you say that?"

"Mornings are usually very slow."

"And do you recollect anything else about that actual transaction?"

"Just the merchandise that was purchased."

"Why do you recognize that merchandise?"

"Because it is not a common switch, and it is not common to buy the switch and battery holders at the same time."

"Now, you have worked at Radio Shack for a year and a half. How many mercury switches like that have you sold to any individuals at any time?"

"Maybe a dozen."

"And how many C-size battery holders had you ever sold two of to any individual in either Decatur, Illinois, or here in Salt Lake City?"

"Including this situation, maybe twice."

"And how many times have you ever sold a mercury switch like this along with two C-size battery cell packs at Radio Shack during your entire year and a half experience?"

"This is the only one I can recollect."

D'Elia moved in closer to the witness stand. "Now, do you remember anything about the individual who purchased these items?" Out of the corner of his eye, he could see the defense table "tighten." It was a physical movement, unconscious, of course, everybody pulling closer together, wincing collectively. Clearly, they feared that this woman could identify the man who bought the C-cell battery packs and mercury switch from her on October 7, that she was going to wheel around on the witness stand and point her finger at Mark Hofmann. Of course, if Yengich had done his homework, he would have known, as D'Elia did, that Elliott couldn't make a positive identification. This will teach him to read the summaries we send him, thought D'Elia.

Through all the testimony so far, Hofmann had played the great stone face, his expression never changing from the fleshy ennui of a bored choirboy. Now D'Elia saw a chance to make him sweat.

He stepped back to include both Hofmann and the witness in his line of vision. "Would you ever be able to make an identification of that individual again?" he said slowly, separating his words with pauses and waving his arm to encompass the entire courtroom.

"Possibly," said Elliott. Great response, D'Elia thought.

"Possibly?" he repeated. "How about looking around the courtroom right now. . . ."

At that moment, Hofmann looked away. He squirmed around in his chair and *actually looked away* as D'Elia watched in astonishment. His face turned pink, and he tugged at the collar of his shirt. For the first time, he looked scared.

D'Elia finished his question as slowly as he could, "Would you take a look around the courtroom and see if you can recognize anybody that is either similar or not."

Elliott dutifully scanned the courtroom from left to right, saving the defense table for last. Fortunately for Hofmann, Yengich had positioned him so that he was partly hidden from the witness stand by a lectern that the lawyers used. If he hunkered down in his chair, Kelly Elliott might hardly see him at all.

And with D'Elia staring right at him, that's exactly what he did. Trying not to be noticed, he began to slink lower beneath the defense table. While Elliott looked from face to face, still on the other side of the room, taking her time, Hofmann began to disappear from view.

The courtroom was absolutely quiet.

Oh, God, thought D'Elia, he thinks he's going to be identified this time, and he's going down. The next sound D'Elia expected to hear was that of "everything dropping into his pants."

Finally, Elliott looked back at D'Elia. "I don't see anyone."

And Hofmann sighed. For the world to hear, he actually *sighed.*

90 Judge Grant was looking at Kelly Elliott at that moment and missed the drama at the defense table. He had already come to the conclusion that Hofmann was a tough nut, an emotional cipher. Normally, he could tell from a defendant's posture when a witness said something that was true but was disputed by the defense. He could see what he called "aspects of denial" either in the body language or, if the defendant was a particularly hard case, in the eyes. But not with Mark Hofmann. As far as Grant could see, Hofmann had given away nothing. The only other person he had ever had in court who was that way was Ted Bundy. "If Hofmann is guilty," he said to himself, "then he must have no value system in any way, shape, or form."

Ken Farnsworth was one of the multitude of people watching Mark Hofmann closely. Because Jim Bell was scheduled to testify as a witness and therefore couldn't attend the hearings prior to his appearance, Farnsworth sat through the early sessions, watching Hofmann's reactions and thinking about his interview with Eric Nielsen, the police psychologist.

In March, Farnsworth had asked to see him. He wanted to know as much about Hofmann's mind as possible. Like any good cop, Farnsworth had a sharp instinct for people and their motivations, but if Ron Yengich ever let him interview Mark, he wanted to be sure to "ring all the right bells."

The meeting took place at Farnsworth's dilapidated bachelor pad in a peeling turn-of-the-century house northeast of downtown, furnished sparingly with a weightlifting machine, an antique Chinese carpet, a small dining table, and the piquant odor of cat litter. A huge safe stood in the bedroom. It held all of Farnsworth's guns and shooting medals.

Nielsen, who had lost an eye (and a fast-track career as a professional soldier) in the Vietnam War, listened as Farnsworth reviewed the facts of the case. Then he offered his opinion. "Mark sounds basically like the classic sociopath, although he doesn't show the vicious aggressiveness that most sociopaths show."

It was the pressures on Hofmann at the end—from Wilding, from the Church, even from his wife in regard to the new house—that had transformed him into "a sociopath out of control."

"My general sense is that we are dealing with a paranoid personality disorder," Nielsen explained. "His fondness for his children would not suggest psychopathology. Also, he's methodical. He is capable of very long-term planning, which is atypical of psychopaths. Psychopaths tend not to think about the consequences of their actions.

"Often, when people think of a paranoid personality disorder, they think of the suspiciousness. With Mark, suspiciousness isn't the salient feature in his personality. Grandiosity is the salient feature. He really thinks he is a superior person. And he obviously is bright, bright enough to pull off a number of things."

For Nielsen, that explained why Hofmann wore the letter jacket when he delivered the first bomb to Steve Christensen's office, an action that seemed uncharacteristically stupid. "He had come to believe that he could get himself out of anything," said Nielsen. "This is just speculation. But he was a solitary kind of kid, who probably retreated a lot into fantasy. Since he never belonged to a group of kids, he probably retreated more and more into his grandiose fantasies."

And what about his bizarre relationship with the Mormon Church? Why the elaborate scam and the forgeries discrediting the Church, an effort that, in the end, didn't net him very much money?

"Among his grandiose fantasies were some that involved his parents," said Nielsen. "I think he's real ambivalent about his dad. I think that, if anything, his effort was probably to destroy something in the long run that was of tremendous value to his dad, to discredit the Church, that is, and thereby to shake his dogmatic beliefs. And also to assume the dominant position in their relationship.

"In a way, the Church hierarchy became a symbol for his father, so in harming the Church officials, he was also harming his father."

That's why Nielsen thought the third bomb was intended for Hugh Pinnock. "Pinnock was intimately involved in bringing all the pressure to bear on him. Obviously, Mark was trying to take out people whom he saw as sources of stress. It sounds as if it was related to the fact that he was being replaced by Steve Christensen. He was no longer going to be the Church's finder of rare and controversial documents, Christensen was."

Suddenly, it was all obvious, Farnsworth thought—as if Nielsen had opened up a window on the impenetrable darkness of Hofmann's motivations and let in a shaft of sunlight. The third bomb had to be for Pinnock. What better way to shut down the McLellin deal and get the creditors off his back? If a bomb had exploded in the First Presidency building, no one would have ventured out for a month. The media would have gone mad. It *had* to have been for Pinnock. Nobody else could have given Hofmann that much "bang for the buck."

Nielsen didn't think that ten to twenty years in prison would do anything to improve Hofmann's personality. "That personality type doesn't get any better. If anything, a prison environment will just solidify that paranoia."

Why did Mark keep up the facade of being a good Mormon, going on a mission and attending church? "I suspect he went on a mission, not because he wanted to, but because the failure to go would have put him in direct conflict with his father, which he preferred not to do. So he did that under a fair amount of resentment."

Nielsen speculated that the legal proceedings could only exacerbate tensions within the family. "I think that's likely in *any* family, but I think that members of the LDS Church are more likely to get goodness and family wrapped up together. Family is part of the route to heaven, if you will. If somebody in the family does something bad, it reflects on the whole family. It erodes the eternal family. So a wayward child tends to pull the family down together."

As for Hofmann's anger at his father: "It's hard to

know. He may have been compliant but pissed off all the time. He may have expressed it all internally. Or he may have acted it out in a fantasy life. It got acted out symbolically in the end."

Farnsworth asked about an incident that had been bothering him ever since it came up on a routine police check following the third bombing. On January 8, 1981, after the discovery of the Anthon Transcript, after he was established in the documents business, Hofmann had been arrested for stealing a 76¢ bag of sliced almonds from Smith's Food King on East Sixth Avenue. Why would he risk exposure and ridicule for a 76¢ bag of nuts?

"Sociopaths get a kick out of doing illicit things," said Nielsen. "They do them just for the thrill of it. Like a lot of things he did, Mark may have done it for the kick of getting away with it.

"In the end, I think his grandiosity got the best of him. He lost his ability to harness it and to restrain it. He started to do things that were just too risky, thinking things like, 'I could wear my letterman's jacket, plant a bomb, and walk out and nobody's going to remember me.'

"But," Nielsen added cautiously, "one thing is absolutely clear, and that is, Mark is never going to tell you what was going on inside Mark. He will tell you about the brilliance of his actions, but nothing about his motivations. He will tell you what he *did*, but he will never tell you what he *thinks*."

The next day, Jim Bell took the stand.

Gerry D'Elia led him methodically through the mountain of evidence that had been accumulated in six months of investigation. Bell described arriving at the Judge Building on the morning of October 15, described the bomb scene, the position of the victim's body, the condition of the doorway. He identified photographs of the body and the scene that were taken at the time.

"Is this an accurate representation of the wounds you saw when you first entered the Judge Building on the morning of the 15th?" D'Elia asked.

"Yes, it is."

Then began the laborious process of identifying the evidence, beginning with the diagram Bell had drawn at the scene on which the location of each piece of evidence was carefully marked.

"Were you in charge of the scene as far as collecting the evidence at the Judge Building, Detective Bell?"

"Yes, I was."

D'Elia showed him the first batch of plastic bags, each with its own number—C-1, C-10, C-20, C-34, etc.—corresponding to its location on Bell's diagram. Together, they were State's Proposed Exhibit No. 41.

"What these are, are items of all types of batteries that were removed from the Steve Christensen bombing scene at the Judge Building. They're battery tops and batteries."

"What size batteries are they?"

"C-cell."

Next came State's Exhibit No. 43, pieces of the cardboard box that contained the bomb. Then No. 46, including bits of wire, an Estes rocket igniter, and a mercury switch. Then No. 45, which contained item C-33A, a three-inch glass vial.

"What is in the vial within that package, Detective Bell?"

"This is a carpentry nail. Those were the type of nails that were in the bomb in the Judge Building and were scattered throughout the whole building."

"About how many nails did you happen to find scattered throughout the building as a result of the explosion?"

"I didn't totally count them. It got so ridiculous, I just quit picking them up after a while. I would guess somewhere about a hundred or so, a hundred and fifty."

"Where did that specific nail come from?"

Bell looked at the package. "This specific nail came out of Mr. Christensen's body at the autopsy."

"What part of his body?"

"His head, his brain."

Bell looked directly at Hofmann. He had determined in advance that he was going to look at Hofmann as much as he could while on the stand, especially when he described the gruesome evidence at the site of Steve Christensen's death. Like everybody else, he wanted to elicit *some* reaction from that fleshy mask.

"Now," said D'Elia. "Would you open up the packet and take out C-179." Bell pulled from the packet a mangled, nine-inch piece of twisted steel. When he first saw it, he had called it "the ugliest-looking weapon I ever saw as a policeman." He held it up in front of him to make sure the entire courtroom got a good look—especially Mark Hofmann.

"What is that, Detective Bell?"

"This right here is a piece of pipe that was removed from Mr. Christensen's chest."

A faint gasp, more like a change in air pressure, swept the room. Joan Gorton and Kathy Sheets's children covered their eyes in a reflex of anguish. Terri Christensen gathered her things, clinging to her composure, and walked quickly from the room.

Bell looked at Hofmann. His eyes had glazed over, his chest was heaving, his body had gone rigid, his neck had tensed till the tendons stood out, his knuckles went white, his mouth slacked open. Suddenly Bell realized what was happening—and others in the courtroom later confirmed it. "Did you see Mark?" Jerry Taylor asked him at the next adjournment. "When they showed that piece of pipe, he had a goddam orgasm!"

91

Later in Jim Bell's testimony, D'Elia returned to the elusive Mike Hansen.

Bell recounted how, on the morning of October 18, he had sent agents to canvass the local Radio Shack stores in search of receipts for the components used to make the first two bombs.

"Did you receive a report from any of them at any time?" asked D'Elia.

"Yes. Agent—Sergeant—Larry Stott of the Salt Lake Police Department and Agent Jim Thompson from the ATF in Sacramento, who had been here in Salt Lake, had called in to the police department and informed us that they had located a receipt where a person had purchased a mercury switch and a battery pack and the address was bad and the name on that receipt was M. Hansen."

The same day, Bell had obtained a search warrant for Mark Hofmann's house.

"Who was in charge of the execution of the warrant?"

"I was."

D'Elia approached the witness stand with State's Proposed Exhibit No. 63. "I'm going to ask you just to take that from the packet and tell us whether you can identify what's in there or not."

"Yes, this is the MIKE HANSEN envelope that was located in Mr. Hofmann's house."

"Where in the box in the southeast basement bedroom was it that you saw that?"

"It was laying right on top. . . ."

"What else was in that box?"

"There were documents on Mormon history, Mormon religion."

"Now, when you specifically seized this envelope, No. 63, why did you seize it?"

"Because prior to going in there, we'd heard of M. Hansen, who had purchased the mercury switch and the battery pack, and that's Mike Hansen and that's why it was taken."

"Now, this Radio Shack receipt that you originally referred to, Detective Bell, that the Mike Hansen was on, did you ever have a subsequent opportunity to see that Radio Shack receipt?"

"Yes, I did."

"And there was an address on it?"

"Yes, there was."

"Did you ever go to the address . . . ?"

"Yes."

"And what did you find?"

"I found a vacant field and a parking lot."

After lunch, David Biggs resumed the questioning. He handed Bell the envelope with MIKE HANSEN written on it. "Is there something else on that envelope, some other writing that was there, previous to it being seized?"

"In the center here, it says it was mailed to Utah Engraving at 231 Emerson Lane, Salt Lake City."

"Did there come a time when you visited Utah Engraving?"

"Yes, on March 3rd of 1986."

*　　　*　　　*

On that day, Ken Farnsworth and David Biggs had gone together to the small shop on Emerson Lane, a tiny back alley between First and Second East, and talked with the owner, Julius Andersen, a seventy-year-old Dane. Andersen served as honorary consul to Utah from both Denmark and Sweden and proudly displayed a huge Royal Danish seal on his office wall. Given half a chance, he would lapse into stories about trips to his native land and hobnobbing with its royalty.

Farnsworth showed him the envelope that they had found in Hofmann's basement with the name MIKE HANSEN written on it. Andersen looked at it and said immediately, "Jorgen wrote that."

He introduced them to Jorgen Olsen, a short, blunt man, who darted around the shop like a mechanical figure in an eccentric old clock. Andersen had imported him from Denmark some time ago but had taught him pitifully little English in the years since.

As soon as Olsen saw the envelope, he pointed to it and said something in Danish. "Oh, yeah, I wrote that," Andersen translated. To prove it, Olsen wrote out MIKE HANSEN several times in the same capital letters. It meant that Olsen had, at some point, made a plate for this man named Mike Hansen.

Farnsworth and Biggs searched through boxes and boxes of Andersen's receipts, which were stored in no particular order, but came up empty. "Maybe we can find the negatives," Andersen suggested helpfully. "When do you think these plates were done?"

Farnsworth and Biggs had no idea.

The negatives were stored in huge photographic boxes, each containing thousands of negatives, six months' worth to a box, again in no particular order. They asked for everything from October 1984 through April 1985 and settled down for another interminable search.

Farnsworth lifted the lid from the first red-and-yellow box and looked glumly at the massive pile of black films. He picked up four or five, looked at each on a light table, then tossed them aside and reached for another batch. After the second one, he let out a whoop. "Bingo!"

It was a negative for a promissory note, one of the notes that had been "signed" with Jim Bridger's *X*.

* * *

On the third day of the hearing, April 17, Jack Smith, a photoengraver at Debouzek Engraving Co. in Salt Lake City, took the stand. A forty-year veteran of the printing and engraving business, Smith had a gentle manner and leathery smile.

Biggs showed him an invoice from Debouzek Engraving, marked State's Exhibit No. 69.

"Do you recognize specifically that particular invoice marked State's No. 69?"

"Yes, I do."

"How do you recognize it?"

"Because I made it out."

"Is it in your handwriting?"

"It's in my handwriting."

"Let's go through it briefly. Tell the court, what it is that was ordered on that particular receipt?"

"It was a Jack London signature." He explained that the customer had ordered an etched plate made from a sample signature provided by the customer. The plate was then mounted on wood "so the customer can use it for letterpress work or to print."

"Can you tell how State's 69 was paid for by the individual?"

"It was paid in cash."

"What was the name of the individual that ordered that particular plate?"

"A Mike Hansen."

Ken Farnsworth had accompanied Biggs to Debouzek Engraving about a month after the arrest, led there by a $2 check found among Hofmann's papers, made out to Debouzek on March 8, 1986.

Sitting in his little office surrounded by samples of artwork the firm had done at the turn of the century— "Wasatch Brand Butter," "Popularity Chocolates," "Vernal Honey"—Mr. Debouzek, the son of the founder, seemed baffled by their questions. "Gee," he said, "I'm the owner, but I don't really do all this stuff." He sent them to Jack Smith, who sat at a long, low counter against the back wall next to a tall filing cabinet filled, undoubtedly, with pink invoices in no particular order, Farnsworth feared.

Smith said he had seen Hofmann on television and in the newspapers but didn't remember having done work for him. Farnsworth explained what they were looking for and began showing Smith copies of Hofmann's most important documents.

When he got to the "Oath of a Freeman," Smith took one look at it and said, "I made that."

Farnsworth was afraid to look at Biggs. "Come again?" he ventured.

"Yeah," said Smith nonchalantly. "I remember making that one."

Farnsworth struggled to maintain his professional composure. "Do you think maybe you could find it for us?"

"Yeah, sure." He loped into the back room and a few minutes later returned with the negative for Mark Hofmann's "Oath of a Freeman." He pointed at Farnsworth's copy. "That was printed from this negative."

Farnsworth couldn't hold back any longer. "Don't you realize," he shouted, "this is a one and a half million dollar fraud!"

Smith looked at Debouzek, who was standing next to him, and the two men said, almost in unison, "We didn't know." They were obviously afraid the police might consider them part of the scam—accessories after the fact, or something. "The plate has a disclaimer at the bottom," they pointed out.

A few more minutes and Smith produced the receipt. It was dated March 26 and made out to "M. Hansen." Smith also produced a second receipt for another version of the "Oath of a Freeman." The customer's name on that order was "Mark Harris," but the telephone number he gave was Mark Hofmann's and the receipt was dated March 8—the same day Hofmann, apparently short of cash, wrote a $2 check to Debouzek Engraving.

After the fourth day, Scott Christensen stopped coming to the hearings. Farnsworth asked Mac Christensen why.

"You convinced him Mark's the guy. He doesn't need to hear any more. All he wanted to know was whether Mark was the guy who did it. He's absolutely convinced."

So was Mac Christensen. So convinced that he wondered why they bothered to go on with the hearings. "Do we have to do any more?" he asked Farnsworth. "Is there any more point in going farther? Does anybody have any doubt in their mind that this guy did it?"

Farnsworth couldn't help gloating. "It gets better than this," he beamed. "We are saving better things for later. The best evidence we're saving for the trial."

92

There was one more twist to the Mike Hansen story. David Biggs called Sonda Gary to the stand.

"Where do you work?" asked Biggs.

"At Salt Lake Stamp."

Biggs showed her State's Exhibit No. 68, a copy of a receipt from Salt Lake Stamp. "Can you identify that particular receipt?"

"Yes, I can."

"How?"

"I am the one that wrote it out."

"To whom was this particular receipt made out for?"

"It was made out for Mike Hansen."

"The address?"

"He didn't give me an address. It was P.O. Box 9421, Salt Lake City, Utah, 84109."

"Can you tell me what it is that was requested to be produced by Salt Lake Stamp by Mr. Hansen?"

"A stamp."

"Did Mr. Hansen bring in something to show you to give you what it is he wanted you to produce?"

"Yes, he did. He brought me in a copy of the stamp that he wanted made." Biggs pointed to some writing at the bottom of the receipt. "It says, in parentheses, 'Needs to be exactly' and, underlined three or four times, 'like above' exclamation point. Who wrote that?"

"I did."

"Can you tell me why you would have written that?"

"I asked him if he just wanted a rubber stamp to say

that and he said, 'No. It has to be exactly like the one I brought in,' and so I wrote that down underneath so our typesetter would know he would need to make a photocopy of that."

"What is it that he wanted reproduced?"

"It's just a rubber stamp."

"What does it say?"

"It says Austin Lewis, and it looks like—it's an address, 301 Harper, Berkeley, California." It was the name and address of the friend to whom Jack London had, supposedly, given a first edition of *Call of the Wild* complete with a "dream inscription."

Biggs himself had found the receipt in the attic of the Salt Lake Stamp Co., a big outfit that made rubber stamps for almost every business in town. He was, as usual, going through boxes and boxes of papers surrounded by dim light and dusty rafters, thinking that this was, without doubt, the most ridiculous search of all. What was a suave, ambitious young lawyer like David Biggs doing searching through crates full of old receipts anyway?

They had chosen Salt Lake Stamp for no reason other than it was the biggest stamp-making company around and therefore the most likely one for Hofmann to use. They had already been through all the receipts in the attic (and the basement) once. They had gone all the way back to 1978 and come up empty. Now they were starting the search all over again.

Then Biggs hit paydirt. "Look," he called out, "a Mike Hansen!" The receipt was stapled to two other pieces of paper: one the original artwork submitted by "Hansen," the other a proof of the finished stamp. (Later, they found in the same crates an order for stamps used to print notes for the "Spanish Fork Cooperative Institution." That one was made out to Mark Hofmann.)

Biggs was proud of his discovery, so when Jim Bell brought it over to the county attorney's office two weeks later, he took a special interest in it. As he watched his colleagues pass it around, he had a crazy idea. "Jim, has this thing been dusted for prints?"

"No," said Bell, thinking, Give me a break. Fingerprints dry up and fade away, in months sometimes, and these had been around since 1982.

But Biggs didn't care about what *usually* happened. He

just had a feeling. He put the stapled papers back in the envelope. "I want these analyzed for prints. And I want it done today."

"Okay," said Bell, shaking his head, "but it's not going to show anything."

They sent it off to Scott Pratt, the latent-prints examiner at the state crime lab, a former FBI man and a real Da Vinci of his craft. If anybody could find a print on that document, Pratt could.

Biggs called Jim Bell back to the stand after Sonda Gary stepped down.

"I would like to show you what's been marked State's Exhibit No. 75 and ask if you have seen that before."

"Yes. This is fingerprints that were taken off Mark Hofmann up at the LDS Hospital."

"What hand?"

"Left hand."

"Were you present when Mark Hofmann's left fingerprints were taken?"

"Yes. They were done at my request, and I was present in the room when it was done."

Then Biggs called Scott Pratt to the witness stand. He was an unlikely hero, soft-spoken and nondescript in his regulation police-force mustache.

"Who do you work for?"

"The State of Utah crime laboratory."

"What position do you hold at the state crime lab?"

"I am the latent-prints examiner."

Biggs showed Pratt State's Exhibit No. 75. "I ask you if you can identify that?"

"This is a fingerprint card that was shown to me by Detective Bell representing Mark Hofmann."

Biggs then showed him State's Exhibit No. 68A, containing the three pieces of paper that Biggs had recovered from Salt Lake Stamp.

"What were you requested to do, if anything, with 68A?"

"My request was to process these documents, three documents, for the possibility of finding any latent fingerprints contained upon the documents."

"Did you do that?"

"Yes, I did."

"What, if anything, did you find?"

"On the document which I marked as No. B which has

a 'l' and a stamp of 'Austin Lewis' and down at the bottom says 'Needs to be exactly like above'—I found some identifiable prints on that document.''

"Were you able to identify the latent print on 68A with any known prints that you were shown?''

"Yes. On the document that's State Exhibit 68A, up in the upper left-hand side of the document I found a latent fingerprint which was found to be the same as the left ring finger on the fingerprint card bearing the name Mark Hofmann.''

After the Mike Hansen testimony, the mood of the press and the public changed overnight. When Ken Farnsworth came to the courtroom that day, he could feel the audience "rolling over" from the defense to the prosecution. Jim Bell, who had been going over to the courthouse during breaks to see if the prosecution needed anything from the evidence room, sensed a complete transformation. Mark Hofmann was no longer the innocent victim of a bungling police department, he was the calculating, cold-blooded killer of two innocent people. The police were no longer closed-minded clods, they were intrepid investigators, guardians of the peace.

One female television reporter approached Bell after the Hansen testimony and put her arm around him. "We would *really* like to interview you and Ken,'' she said, nuzzling him. (They had never been introduced. He recognized her from TV.) Bell was too polite, too chivalrous, too diffident to say what he was thinking: You bitch. After all this crap you've thrown our way, in one day you want us to be friends and tell all.

The only apology came from Mike Carter, the court reporter for the *Tribune* who had roused the cops at every turn in the investigation and earned a nearly permanent place on the police shit list. In just three days, Carter's courtroom dispatches had gone from championing Ron Yengich (DEFENSE ATTACKS KEY WITNESS IN HOFMANN CASE) to congratulating the prosecution (FINGERPRINT ON RECEIPT MATCHES HOFMANN'S.) "I thought I knew everything there was to know in this case,'' he told Bell and Farnsworth's boss, Captain Oran Peck. "I thought

I had all the sources. And I didn't know shit. You guys kept things secret from us that I had no idea about."

When Peck relayed the apology, Farnsworth thought it was about time. "No shit, shinola," he said. "What does he think we've been *doing* over here?"

93 On the fifth day of hearings, Bob Stott began presenting evidence on charges related to the documents, and the courtroom fell, almost instantly, into a profound slumber. Stott led a parade of witnesses through minute descriptions, often confusingly detailed, of dozens of documents and the circumstances under which each one was acquired from Mark Hofmann. On cross-examination, Brad Rich, Yengich's second, compounded the ennui by taking each witness back over the same flat ground a second time, sometimes a third time. By the sixth day, reporters felt free to put down their pencils whenever Rich rose to speak, and members of the audience were openly expressing their disdain for his endless quibbling.

About the only exciting moments were provided by a crazy lady in scarf and glasses who sat in the back of the courtroom and every now and then yelled out in a strident voice, *"The Church is railroading Mark Hofmann! He's taking the fall for people in the Church!"*

In the witness room, Ralph Bailey, Wilford Cardon, Al Rust, and other Hofmann victims occupied themselves talking still more deals. A collector from Arizona tried to buy a "packet of gold," an extremely rare, early form of Mormon currency, from Rust. When Rust steadfastly refused to sell, Ralph Bailey turned to him sympathetically. "Al, do I know where that packet came from?"

Rust rolled his eyes and nodded sheepishly. "Yeah."

Amid all the talk of irresistible deals and rates of

return and double collateral, Brent Ashworth's appearance was a jolting shot of humanity. Two weeks after the bombings, while Ashworth was out of town, his seven-year-old son, Sam, had been hit by a car driven by drunken teenagers. For three months, he had languished in a coma. Then, for three more months, he seemed to get better. Charlene Ashworth stood by his bed all day and Brent all night. Then, on the Friday before Ashworth was scheduled to testify, Sam died.

He blamed Mark Hofmann. He was not there when the accident happened partly because he feared for his life, because Hofmann had sent a message from the hospital that he should get out of town, that he might be the next victim.

David Biggs, Ashworth's cousin and law school classmate, offered to put off his testimony, but Ashworth said, "I'd like to get it over with before the funeral so I can go to the funeral without having this thing hanging over me." Earlier on the day he was scheduled to testify, Ron Yengich—another of Ashworth's law school classmates—had approached him. "I'm sorry to hear about your son," he said. "Would it be agreeable to you if we came down and talked to you privately in a few days? And we'll waive our cross-examination?"

Ashworth considered it a gracious gesture.

Later that day in court, when Yengich stood up and announced he wasn't going to cross-examine Ashworth, Hofmann shot him a startled look that said, You're *not?*

There was one element of suspense still hanging over the hearings: Would Gordon Hinckley testify? As late as April 19, the defense had been telling reporters that they expected to see Hinckley on the stand the following week. Bob Stott's brave determination to subpoena Hinckley seemed to have dissolved in the three weeks since the meeting in Hinckley's office, although no one knew exactly why. After that meeting, David Biggs and everybody else in the county attorney's office had been cut off from any further contact with Church officials. Stott insisted that he, and he alone, would deal with the Church.

Farnsworth, for one, was not reassured. He had seen the way Stott dealt with other, lesser Church officials. Like Hugh Pinnock. In briefing Stott in preparation for Pinnock's testimony at the hearings, Farnsworth had told him about Pinnock's statement to the effect that he considered the piece of papyrus that Hofmann showed him to be genuine—that is, one of the papyri from which Joseph Smith translated the Book of Abraham. Stott refused to believe it. "I won't ask Pinnock that on the stand," he snapped, "because I think he's lying."

"But Bob, this is an important piece of evidence," Farnsworth insisted. "You've got to ask the questions." Stott refused to do it. He refused to be a party to exposing a General Authority to ridicule: either for lying, or for being unable to distinguish between commonplace hieroglyphics and a genuine Joseph Smith papyrus. At the preliminary hearing, Stott stuck to his pledge and skipped over the subject entirely.

If Stott was that deferential to Pinnock, his colleagues wondered, how could he stand up to Hinckley? The fact that he was known to have had several one-on-one meetings with Hinckley in the interim only fueled speculation that a deal, explicit or implicit, had already been cut.

But Hinckley still had a problem. If he wanted to be certain to avoid the witness chair, somebody else needed to sign off on any deal: Ron Yengich. And with the day approaching when Stott was scheduled to put the Stowell letter into evidence, Yengich was still making noises about calling Hincley to the stand.

That's when Bob Stott paid an unusual visit to the counsel for the defense. For the record, he took David Biggs with him to Yengich's office on 4th South.

"President Hinckley doesn't want to testify," Stott told Yengich. "And we don't want to call him any more than we want to call any other recalcitrant witness. How would it be if we set up an appointment for you to talk to him? And then you come to us, after you talk to him, and see if you can enter into a stipulation as to what his testimony will be." Stott made it sound like his idea, but everyone assumed he could never have offered a meeting if Hinckley hadn't cleared it first.

Yengich accepted the offer.

It was a brief, tense, businesslike meeting. Different as they were, both men had something the other wanted. Hinckley wanted a stipulation that only Yengich could give him. But what did Yengich want? What he *got* was an agreement by Hinckley that Church officials would argue against the death penalty at Hofmann's sentencing.

Hinckley undoubtedly wanted more (a guarantee that Yengich wouldn't call him to testify at trial, for instance), and so did Yengich (an agreement that the Church would push for a plea bargain, perhaps), but those deals would have to wait.

For now, it was a sure sign of how Yengich thought the hearings were going that he was already hedging his bets against the death penalty.

94 Mark Hofmann had his own way of responding to the deteriorating situation in the courtroom. On April 23, after seven days of hearings, he reinjured his knee. As Ron Yengich told it, he had tried to take a step without crutches, fell, and fractured his kneecap. Between the surgery and the sedatives, Yengich argued, Mark would not be able to exercise his constitutional right to assist in his own defense. The hearings came to a sudden halt. Judge Grant was not pleased. It was a shame, he said, to interrupt a preliminary hearing already so complicated. But better that than to go through with it, only to have some higher court order him to repeat the whole thing. With great reluctance, he granted a continuance until May 5.

Local media scrambled to fill the news vacuum.

At KSL, a reporter, Jack Ford, suggested keeping the story alive by doing an extensive recap of the hearings to date.

It was a suggestion that almost cost him his job.

It wasn't the recap itself that got him in trouble. In fact, the station, like all the local stations, had long since learned that Hofmann was a ratings winner and the idea won instant approval. The problem was what he *said* in the recap. In reviewing the testimony that Hugh Pinnock had arranged a loan for Hofmann from the First Interstate Bank, he said the *Church* had helped to arrange a loan for Hofmann to buy the McLellin Collection. He also mentioned that the Church had arranged for the mission president in Nova Scotia to buy the McLellin Collection from Hofmann.

The moment the story aired, the roof caved in. The Church spokesman, Richard Lindsay, father of KSL anchorman Bruce Lindsay, called the news department raving mad. Spence Kinard buckled instantly and ran a retraction even before calling Ford at home to brief him on the situation. When Ford saw the retraction, *he* went through the ceiling. He set fire to the newsroom phone lines but Kinard was unapologetic. "You hung me out to dry," he said.

"Spence, it's not *you* who got hung out to dry," Ford shot back. "The Church is upset because we said they helped arrange a loan. Well they *did!* They say it was an individual, not the Church, but that's baloney. It may have been an individual who placed the call, but he was a Church official, sitting in his Church office, on Church time, using a Church phone, and he did it for the benefit of the Church. Nobody else wanted that McLellin Collection except the Church. And the Nova Scotia mission president doesn't *collect* documents. He was just a big-bucks guy who said, 'If you need help, I'll help you out.' If the Church says they weren't helping arrange any buyers for anything, how do you explain the fact that the Church volunteered to get an armored car to go down to Texas and pick the Collection up?"

The arguments were lost on Kinard. The only arguments he cared about were the ones that came from up the line, from senior management and higher.

The next day, Ford spent eight hours on the carpet, explaining his actions four times at four different levels of bureaucracy, right up to and including a meeting with the vice-president of Bonneville International, Don Gale.

And then it happened again.

In another report, Ford repeated a direct quotation from the testimony of Curt Bench, head of the rare-book department at Deseret Book. Bench had said that a high Church official—police later determined it was Hugh Pinnock or Gordon Hinckley—called Steve Christensen to say that Hofmann hadn't paid back the loan yet and to ask him to tell Hofmann that if he didn't get his act together, they were going to excommunicate him.

This time, *Hinckley* went through the roof.

The Word came down through the bureaucracy like a thunderbolt from Mount Olympus. Several General Authorities called the KSL station manager, Jack Adamson, who called Kinard, who called Ford, and threatened to fire him on the spot. The report was in error, they argued, because Christensen did not have the *authority* to excommunicate anybody, and if he conveyed that message to anybody, he was doing so entirely on his own initiative.

But there was no mistaking what had really brought down the whirlwind: *Ford had spoken Gordon Hinckley's name in connection with the Hofmann case.* For months, everyone in the media had been tiptoeing around Hinckley's involvement, and now Ford had dared to jump on it with both feet. It was only a passing mention, but someone still wanted his head.

Once again, Ford tried to defend himself: "Christensen was relaying information from the Church Presidency," he explained. "All he was saying was that if Mark didn't straighten up, it might prompt the Church to bring excommunication proceedings. Christensen wasn't saying that *he* would excommunicate Mark, only that the *Church* might do it." Somebody upstairs was quibbling over legalistic turns of phrase, and Ford guessed who it was.

Then came the final warning. If he stepped out of line one more time, he would be fired. It was a clear, unequivocal message, and it came, unlike Christensen's warning, on the highest authority.

Ford had had enough. He told Kinard, "Okay. From now on, I'll just give you the information, and you write the stories. Whatever you want, you do it. You can write the story, then have three different people go in and change it around so that it doesn't make the Church look bad."

That seemed to satisfy them.

95 When the hearings resumed on May 5, the prosecution woke the courtroom up with its last two witnesses, William Flynn and George Throckmorton. Flynn spent nine hours on the stand explaining, for the first time in public, the key to Mark Hofmann's forgeries: the cracked ink.

Bob Stott began the direct examination with the most important question of all. "Are you a member of either the LDS Church or the Reorganized Church?"

"No, I'm not," said Flynn.

Stott got quickly to the point.

"Did you find any unusual or unnatural, abnormal characteristics on any of these documents?"

"Yes. On many of the documents, there appeared a microscopic cracking on the surface of the ink. These appeared on the questioned documents that we were examining."

"Besides the cracking, were there any other characteristics?"

"Yes. Under ultraviolet examination on several of the questioned documents, there was a one-directional running of the inks, or a constituent part of the inks, as if they had been wet."

"Were you able to determine if there had been any additions on the documents, any additional applications of ink?"

"Yes. On several of the documents, there were inks that were not consistent with the body of the document. That is to say, that data had been added to the document with a different ink."

"Now, besides these characteristics, was there anything common about the documents that you found these characteristics on?"

"Yes."

"What was that?"

"These anomalies that I spoke of all occurred on documents that had been dealt by the defendant in this case, Mark Hofmann."

By now, the courtroom was wide awake. Even Judge Grant had some questions.

After Flynn described the techniques by which a document could be artificially aged, he produced a sample "antique" document that he had created himself just the previous month using those techniques.

"Let me clarify," Grant jumped in. "The paper is modern paper aged by heating?"

"Correct, Your Honor. Everything about these documents is modern. It's modern paper that's been artificially aged, modern ink of an old formula that has also been artificially aged."

The following Monday, May 12, George Throckmorton picked up the story. In the course of the investigation, he had examined 688 documents written in iron gallotannic ink. Of that total, "I observed twenty-one that had this characteristic cracking effect."

"Out of the twenty-one or so that you have exhibited with the cracking effect, where, to your knowledge, did those documents come from?"

"All of them were purported to me as coming through Mark Hofmann."

Throckmorton also explained the printed forgeries, like the Deseret currency and the Jim Bridger notes. He and Flynn had found "trash marks" on the documents corresponding to microscopic flaws in the photographic negatives the police had found. These indicated that the documents had been printed from the negatives and not vice versa. If the documents had been photographed, Throckmorton explained, the microscopic flaws would not have been picked up by the camera and therefore would not have shown up on the negative.

Gerry D'Elia asked about the Spanish Fork Cooperative notes, the early Mormon money that Hofmann had sold to a number of collectors.

"Now, did you have any opportunity to make an ink comparison from the colored red, green, yellow, and blue inks on those Spanish Fork notes with any known inks that you received?"

"Yes, sir."

"What kind of ink was it that you had in your possession that you made the comparison with in those?"

"The red inks I examined on the Spanish Fork notes, on all four sets that I examined, I found to be indistinguishable from the Carter's brand red ink that is used to put new ink in rubber stamp pads."

The same was true of the green, yellow, and blue inks. All were the Carter's brand inks available in any stationery store. In addition, the paper contained optical brighteners that were not introduced into paper manufacturing until the 1940s.

D'Elia held up three sheets of rub-off letters that had been found in Hofmann's house.

"And now, when you had occasion to review the Spanish Fork Co-op notes that were printed, along with the transfer rub-off sheets, were you able to form any relationship or comparison through your analysis?"

"The Spanish Fork Co-op notes contained three different styles and sizes of printed letters, hand-printed letters. And I observed that the rub-off letters on these sheets were of the same size and style as found on the three different sizes and styles on the Spanish Fork notes."

"Were there any styles and sizes on the Spanish Fork Co-op notes that you did not have on the rub-off sheets so that you were able to conclude there was a relationship?"

"All of the sizes and styles I was able to find on these three rub-off sheets."

"And what was your conclusion with respect to the quantity?"

"The quantity of the letters that were removed from the rub-off sheets were consistent with what was found on the Spanish Fork notes."

Throckmorton had an additional observation on the Anthon Transcript, the only one of Hofmann's documents that did not show the characteristic cracking. (He had used an ink that didn't contain gum arabic and had aged the paper with heat rather than with chemicals.) The brown marks on the Transcript, said Throckmorton, could be easily explained. "Those characteristics are very similar to the characteristics I have observed when a document has been wet and subsequently dried and heated.

In fact, it almost looks like an iron, a regular iron that you would use to iron your clothes, has gone over it."

On cross-examination, Brad Rich went straight for Throckmorton's weak spot: the possibility that his findings had been influenced by his faith.

"Are you familiar with a document known as the *Book of Mormon?*"

"Yes, sir."

"Do you have a particular belief about from whence that volume came?"

"I do."

"Can you tell us what that is?"

"I believe my beliefs would be what would be considered the conservative point of view for a member of the Mormon faith, and that is that the *Book of Mormon* was translated from the plates that were given to Joseph Smith."

"And who gave those plates to Joseph Smith?"

"That would have been Moroni, the Angel Moroni, as he is called."

"An angel. Do you believe that either a salamander or toad was involved in any way in that process?"

"I don't believe so."

In their summations, both Stott and Yengich focused on the issue that had stumped everybody from the beginning: motive.

Stott added up the hundreds of thousands of dollars that Hofmann owed at the time of the bombings. He recounted the pressure Hofmann was under to pay back that money, and the possible consequences if his forgery scheme was exposed. "He had to get rid of Steve Christensen," Stott told Judge Grant. "He was the center of the pressure. Maybe it wouldn't solve all the problems, but at best it would buy him some time. And we all know the only thing a con artist needs is time . . . maybe just one more day." Kathy Sheets had been killed to divert attention away from the Salamander Letter and toward CFS.

Because the third bombing wasn't being charged, Stott didn't have to speculate on the intended target of the third bomb.

* * *

The next day, Yengich tore into Stott's neat scenario. The prosecution hadn't satisfactorily explained the motive for the Christensen murder, Yengich charged, and had glossed over the Sheets murder entirely. "What is the motive for Hofmann to perform all these vile acts?

"Steve Christensen was helping Mark. They were friends. Hofmann didn't owe money to Christensen. He—Christensen—was offering his hand in friendship, not offering a threat that all of the others had. The death of Steve Christensen does Mark Hofmann no good at all."

Yengich scoffed at the suggestion that Christensen had been killed to buy time. And if the killing was designed to avoid an investigation of his document dealings, well, the result had been just the opposite. In relaying warnings from the Church, Yengich said, Christensen had been acting as a friend. If Hofmann had reason to kill anyone, if he would have benefited from murder, then the targets would have been either Hugh Pinnock or Gordon B. Hinckley, not Steve Christensen.

As for the Sheets murder: "There is no evidence that the death of Sheets advanced the scheme to defraud." It was, he concluded, a case based on maybes. "And a case based on maybes is no case at all."

For Judge Grant, the cracked-ink testimony cracked the case. From the outset, he had been worried that some might question his impartiality in assessing documents antagonistic to his faith. How could a Mormon judge rule on this case? Flynn's and Throckmorton's objectivity had saved him from the whispers. And he was the first to admit it. They were a "godsend," he would tell people later. "With their cracked-ink finding, they delivered a totally objective forensic test as to the validity of the documents. That meant we never had to deal with what they said or what they meant."

During the hearings, Grant also began to develop a theory about Mark Hofmann's *real* motivations. When people asked, "How could all this evil come from a clean-cut young Mormon kid, a kid like our kids?" Grant had the answer. Sitting on the bench, watching Mark, he had seen into his dark heart.

He would begin his explanation by telling a story. "This case makes me think of a story I heard from a man I respect a great deal, a very bright person with a law degree from Columbia. Just one of the top people I've known in my life in terms of brightness and congeniality. A people person, an idea person, and a things person.

"And he told me this story about the time when he was a missionary in London many years ago. He would go to Hyde Park, where the missionaries would preach, and he got to the point where he could contend with the hecklers and the ministers from other faiths. Then one day, while he was in the midst of it, he met a man, rather large of stature, with swarthy skin and eyes like fire.

"And he got into a contention with this man that nearly destroyed him. All the proven arguments just didn't hold water. This big man with the swarthy skin and eyes like fire was just so bright that he simply destroyed my friend.

"Accepting defeat, he returned to the mission home, and the mission president asked him what was the matter. The mission president happened to be an Apostle. My friend reviewed what had just happened, and the mission president said, 'I hope you learned a valuable lesson. The individual you were contending with was Lucifer himself. There is not a living soul on the earth who can match wits and contend with Lucifer. Just cannot be done. If you take him on individually, he will defeat you every time.'

"That story introduced me to the possibility that there was in fact a satanic involvement in this case." That was how Hofmann was able to trick the top members of the Church hierarchy. They were dealing with no mere mortal.

Judge Paul Grant, father of twelve, had decided that Mark Hofmann was, in fact, Lucifer.

What else could he do but bind Lucifer over for trial.

PART SIX

Follow the Brethren

96 David Biggs wasn't the only one who looked forward to a real courtroom cockfight beginning on March 2, 1987, when the first of Hofmann's five trials was scheduled to begin. Ron Yengich had been scratching the dust in anticipation ever since the preliminary hearing. So had Gerry D'Elia.

D'Elia especially seemed eager to mix it up. During the hearings, he and Yengich had already had one altercation over a media motion to release the probable-cause statements (which included the names of witnesses who could be cornered for interviews). In a small corridor outside Judge Grant's chambers, D'Elia tried to explain the prosecution's objections to the media attorney.

"Don't interrupt!" Yengich snapped.

D'Elia wasn't one to let a challenge go unanswered. "Why don't you stop talking, then, so someone else can say something."

From there, the exchange quickly degenerated into a name-calling shouting match.

"Asshole."

"Son of a bitch."

Oh, yeah?

Oh, yeah.

Someone said, "Okay. Let's have it out right here," and suddenly both men began to square off, ready, aching to put the matter to the ultimate test of manhood. No need to go outside, just decide it right there in the hall outside the judge's chambers.

At first, Biggs, Stott, and Brad Rich were too startled to stop them. Biggs, proud of his cool, couldn't believe the lapse of professionalism. Having been to school with Yengich, he knew his confrontational style. It was his job to hate prosecutors. But if he could work up this much venom over a motion to release probable-cause statements, what would he be like at a murder trial?

Bob Stott stepped back and looked at the two men, who were literally inches apart, in total bewilderment.

Finally, somebody said, "Okay, it's time to cool it," and the two roosters backed down.

Then Judge Grant, who had been towering over the skirmish from what seemed like a great distance, issued a stern warning. "Look. This is a high-profile case. I am sorry, but in any other case, if you fought in my courtroom, that would be okay with me—at least until it got to the point where I felt I had to cut it off. But in this one, it just won't fly. If you two don't behave, I am personally going to get into it with you. You won't just have to fight each other, you are going to have to fight me personally."

Coming from the huge-handed, six-foot-seven Grant, that was enough to keep both Yengich and D'Elia in line for the rest of the hearings. But Grant wouldn't always be there, and the stakes at trial would be far higher. All the signs pointed to a real street fight.

Then, in November, strange things began to happen.

The first began with the arrival of David Yocom. In the November 4 general election, Ted Cannon lost his bid for another term as county attorney to Yocom, a criminal lawyer—and friend of Ron Yengich's—who had worked in the county attorney's office from 1970 to 1979 and prosecuted such high-profile criminals as Ted Bundy. Normally, Cannon wouldn't have turned over his office until January, but other problems forced him to leave prematurely. When Cannon's interim replacement, Bill Hyde, proved insufficiently malleable, Yocom arranged to be sworn in as acting county attorney on November 19, two months before his term officially began.

Almost the minute he got his hands on the reins of power, Yocom pulled Gerry D'Elia off the Hofmann case. Yocom accused him of insubordination, but people who knew the history of their relationship suspected otherwise—that Yocom had long carried a grudge against D'Elia for refusing to deal on a case involving some of Yocom's pals. At the time, Yocom, acting as their defense attorney, had called D'Elia a liar, an asshole, and, worst of all, "a lousy prosecutor."

"Screw you, Yocom!" D'Elia shouted back. "Let's go to trial."

"If we go to trial," Yocom boasted, "I'll clean your clock."

But in court, it was D'Elia who cleaned Yocom's clock.

After the election, to no one's surprise, Yocom came gunning for D'Elia. One of his first official acts was to drop D'Elia from an arson case that he had been working on for six years and instruct the other prosecutors to arrange a plea bargain that was "satisfactory to everybody." Yocom knew the defense attorney and knew he wanted to settle. The case was weak and, even after a trip to the Supreme Court, dead in the water, Yocom insisted.

When D'Elia showed up in the courtroom to hear the sentencing of the case, Yocom hit the ceiling. He called D'Elia into his office and ranted. "You can't beat me, D'Elia. No one can beat me. The people voted for me." Later that week, drunk and belligerent, Yocom approached D'Elia in a bar. "Why don't you get a haircut?" he muttered under his breath—breath that, according to D'Elia, "you wouldn't want to light a match near." Jabbing his finger in D'Elia's chest, Yocom ranted about the case three years earlier, when D'Elia had "fucked him over."

The following Monday, D'Elia got a call from Bud Ellett, the chief criminal deputy. "That's it," he said. "Tomorrow Yocom is shifting you to the satellite office. You're being relieved of all of your duties on the Hofmann case."

D'Elia reacted with, for him, surprising cool. "He's dumber than dog shit. I always knew it."

The next day, he left for Carson City to be married and then to Lake Tahoe for a honeymoon. When he came back, he took a few weeks of sick leave and then quit. A television reporter asked him on camera, "Mr. Yocom says you're absolutely not necessary to the Hofmann case. How do you respond to that?"

"Well, either he's incredibly stupid or he's a liar. Take your pick."

The victims' families picked stupid. With D'Elia gone, the prosecution lost its killer instinct. Putting Bob Stott alone in a courtroom with Ron Yengich would be like putting a tuna alone in a pool with a barracuda. When

Jim Bell and Ken Farnsworth heard the news, they suspected immediately that Stott had no intention of getting wet.

Just about the same time Yocom pulled D'Elia off the Hofmann case, Bob Stott started disappearing frequently from the county attorney's office. No one knew for sure where he went or whom he saw, but Biggs, for one, was sure something was up and that the something had to do with the Hofmann case. It crossed his mind that Stott might be meeting with officials from the Church, probably Church lawyers, possibly even Hinckley himself, briefing them—unofficially, of course—on trial preparations. But by the end of November, a year after the bombings and three months before the trials were scheduled to begin, the secret meetings, whatever they were, whomever they were with, were obviously heating up.

Soon, work on the Hofmann case ground to a halt. Stott diverted Biggs from trial preparations into a morass of paperwork on motions: a thankless, eight-to-eight job. As soon as he climbed out of that hole, Stott put him to work on a pointless synopsis, condensing thousands of pages of evidence into readable form. Biggs spun his wheels for weeks, producing a twenty-two-page document that Stott pronounced "too long. It sounds like a book," he said. "You've got to cut it down." So he spent more time cutting the twenty-two pages to seven.

Biggs knew it was all busy work, designed only to keep him occupied while Stott, the demon for control, continued to conduct his secret business.

97

To drivers who glanced into the windows of the stylish black Chevy Blazer as they passed, the two men inside must have looked like an odd couple. Behind the wheel, Ron Yengich, with his long hair and medicine-bow mustache, looked like one of those redneck ranch hands who descended on Salt Lake City from Price and other distant towns every weekend to terrorize the townsfolk. He was dressed better, of course, but he sat too low in the seat for passersby to see the cut of his suit.

In the passenger seat, Bob Stott squirmed uncomfortably. Next to the lean, hungry Yengich, Stott looked unusually well fed and burgher-like. He couldn't have been entirely at ease, perched on the white sheet that Yengich had thrown over the seat to protect Stott's suit from the sheddings of the seat's usual occupant, Yengich's big dog, Little.

In fact, both men had good reason to be nervous. Two months before the opening of what promised to be the most publicized trial in Utah history, after more than a year of investigative work by hundreds of state, federal, and local officials, after hours spent preparing, not just for one trial but five, they were meeting in the secrecy of Yengich's black Blazer to cut a deal that would bring the whole huge enterprise to a quick, quiet end.

After the preliminary hearing, Yengich knew that he was in deep trouble. For the first time, he had seen the prosecution's case in its totality, and it was a frightening sight. They had the eyewitnesses, they had the letter jacket, they had the Radio Shack receipts, the Mike Hansen alias, the bogus printing plates, the cracked ink. They hadn't cracked Nurse Loden, but Hofmann's clumsy lies in the hospital were almost as damaging.

The case was short on motive but that was a two-edged sword. If a jury was positively convinced that Hofmann did it, the lack of a strong motive would only make the act look more wanton and senseless. It's a lot harder to show mercy to a man who kills people for flimsy reasons —as a diversion, for example—than for a man who kills in the heat of passion, or even out of revenge. Yengich had often said that it was easier to understand killing a friend than killing a total stranger. And what if the prosecution convinced the jury that the third bomb was intended for someone else? Then Hofmann would look like a mad serial bomber with total disregard for human life. It was a formula for a death sentence.

In fact, the only weakness in the prosecution's overwhelming case was that it was *too* overwhelming. In his compulsiveness, Bob Stott had loaded so much information into a single case, much of it arcane and confusing, that a jury could easily get lost in it—especially with a little help from defense counsel. "I'll have a chance to try a myriad of other people other than my client," Yengich boasted.

It was one of his favorite tactics: working up sympathy for the criminal by working up contempt for the victim—or for the prosecution, or for the judge, or for the system. In this case, it was easy. The victims of Hofmann's frauds, men like Thomas Wilding, were, in his opinion, just greedy fat cats out for a fast buck. It was almost comic the way they climbed all over one another to get at Hofmann's documents, to make the big, easy score. Why the hell didn't one of them blow the whistle on his client before things deteriorated to murder? If Wilding had just called the police when he uncovered Mark's shenanigans, Kathy Sheets and Steve Christensen would still be alive. But no. He wanted his money first, justice second.

They were all the same way. They didn't call because they were all getting rich. They were either going to go to another kingdom of heaven, like Brent Ashworth, or they were going to get rich in this kingdom.

In Yengich's mind, however, no one was more culpable than the Mormon Church. "Documents are coming up every six months," he explained to a reporter, "located by the same guy. And what does this guy do? This guy is a student. He's planning to go to medical school. And all of a sudden, he's turning up major document finds every time we turn around. Well, doesn't somebody sit back and say, 'Okay, we want to compare this document and that document?' But they don't ever do it. You know why?

"Greed. Incredible greed on the part of a number of members of the hierarchy of the Church who wanted to get these documents and salt them away somewhere where the Brethren's faith wouldn't be shaken by them." If it hadn't been for that greed, Yengich believed, Mark's whole scheme would have come to a quick end, and Kathy Sheets and Steve Christensen would still be alive.

Between the avarice of Mark's clients, the CFS scandal, the Church's complicity, the confusing documents, and the huge cast of very public characters, including everybody from well-known TV pitchman Mac Christensen to Church bigwigs like Hinckley and Oaks, Yengich knew he could develop enough red herrings to confuse the already muddy waters and hope that the jury, unable to see its way clearly, might mistake its confusion for "reasonable doubt."

If *he* were the prosecutor, he would have handled it all very differently, he told himself. He would have focused on "the woman who's dead and the man who's dead, and eliminate all the rest of the garbage." But he was certain Bob Stott wasn't clever enough or brave enough for a bold stroke like that. In fact, Stott was so deeply involved in the Mormon side of the case that he was more likely to give up the homicides than the documents.

Except even Bob Stott wasn't myopic enough to do that.

Yengich also had troubles in his own camp. If Stott's case was too overwhelming for its own good, Yengich's client was too smart for his own good. In public, Yengich later praised Hofmann's savvy and clucked about how helpful it was to work with a client who understood the legal ramifications of his actions. But privately, Yengich had torn his hair more than once over Mark's stupidity—or arrogance (he was never sure which it was).

Early in the case, against Yengich's specific instructions, Hofmann had met with several reporters in the office of Jimmy Barber, Shannon Flynn's attorney.

The next morning, Yengich called Mike Carter, one of the reporters at the meeting. "Come over to my office," he barked.

When Carter arrived, he could hear Yengich yelling at Hofmann through the walls, calling him a "dumb shit." When Carter joined them, Yengich instructed Mark, "You've never met this guy, have you?"

Hofmann cowered in his wheelchair. "No," he said in a tiny voice.

"I want to introduce you to Mike Carter. Shake hands." After they shook hands, Yengich wheeled Hofmann out of the room as if looking for the nearest cliff.

He returned a few minutes later still in a tizzy of rage, swearing and knocking things off his desk. At first he tried to threaten Carter—"You know you might be in trouble"—then he promised him "great things to come" if he kept the previous day's visit with Mark "under his hat." Carter agreed, and Yengich kept his end of the bargain by giving him first look at the polygraph test results.

That wasn't the only time Yengich had been surprised by his client. Mark had an annoying habit of withholding important details, especially details that made him look stupid as well as evil. So Yengich had to wait for each new packet of discovery materials from the prosecution to find out what bombshells Hofmann had conveniently forgotten to share with him.

Like when he used the Mike Hansen alias at the same time he wrote a check in his own name. That one drove Yengich crazy. It was bad enough that he had been so stupid, or so brazen, as to try to pass himself off as Mike Hansen while writing checks on a Mark Hofmann account. It was bad enough that he tried it not once but *twice.* But then not to tell his lawyer about such a disastrous miscalculation, to let him learn about it from the *police!* That was just too much.

Hofmann tried to win his way back into Yengich's favor by telling him, "I've confided more in you than in anybody else in the world." But Yengich couldn't help wondering what other surprises were waiting out there, and how could he trust a man who had beaten a lie detector?

The case was also costing too damn much money. So far, by some accounts, the Hofmanns had been able to produce only about $25,000 even after Bill Hofmann mortgaged his house. Yengich could have billed twice that much just for the preliminary hearing. Who was going to pay for six months of trial preparation and two months of trial, taking up two-thirds of his staff? As long as a stunning upset was a possibility, the case was worth the red ink. Dramatic, highly publicized acquittals are the criminal lawyer's loss leaders. But with conviction almost a certainty, the dollars and cents no longer made sense. Was it worth his time just to save Hofmann from the death penalty—assuming he could do even that?

A plea bargain was the only way out. If Mark could plead to a second-degree murder and a manslaughter charge and the sentences ran concurrently, he could get out of prison eventually. At thirty-two, he could serve ten or fifteen years and still have twenty or thirty years as a free man. It wasn't great, but it was a lot better than a capital murder conviction. In Utah, very few capital murderers *ever* walked out of prison.

There was only one problem. Why on earth would the prosecution want to bargain this one? With an unmuffable case, mountains of evidence, hundreds of man-years of investigation, and with the eyes of the media and the world watching, what possible reason could Bob Stott have for trading it all away?

As the black Blazer sped through the early morning dusk in the suburbs of Salt Lake, Yengich made his pitch, outlining for Stott the "advantages" of a plea. He started off by reflecting on how often law enforcement officials had said to him, "Boy, I'd sure like Mark Hofmann to explain this to me." Once a week, as regular as clockwork, Ken Farnsworth had called his office and requested an interview with Mark. Stott himself had asked on numerous occasions, "When can we talk with Mark? Are we going to be able to talk to Mark?"

It was more than just personal curiosity—although there was plenty of that too. There were all sorts of "pressures" —Yengich let the word sink in—to find out what Hofmann knew. Pressures from the public, pressures from the press (who weren't about to let the police off the hook until their questions had been answered), and, of course, pressures from the Church.

No one wanted to know what Hofmann knew more than the Church. Were the documents authentic? *Which* documents were authentic? Hofmann had sold or given or traded hundreds of documents to the Church. Only a handful were covered in the indictment. A trial would determine the authenticity only of those entered into evidence at the trial. The rest would be cast into permanent shadow—*unless,* of course, Hofmann were to talk and tell everything he knew.

The same was true of all the nasty rumors connecting Hofmann to the Church. A trial would resolve only a few of them, leaving the most destructive ones—like the rumor that the Church was railroading Hofmann to cover up its complicity—intact. How much better it would be for the Church if Hofmann told everything he knew. "If we go to trial, and he's convicted," Yengich later said, "the vast majority of the public out there may believe he's guilty, but there's going to be a lot of people who still say he's *not* guilty. They're going to have this conspiracy theory. It may only exist in the minds of a few people, but if it exists at all, it's really going to make life difficult for the people at 47 East South Temple."

The public wanted answers, the press wanted answers, the cops wanted answers, Stott wanted answers, and, more than anybody, the Church wanted answers. And the only person who had the answers was Mark Hofmann.

Stott made an offer. "He can plead to one first-degree murder charge or two second degrees."

"I want to go lower on the murder charges," Yengich countered.

"That's impossible," said Stott.

"How would you like to interview him on the charges?" Stott looked as if he could barely contain his excitement.

Yengich dangled it some more. "You can interview him and get a complete confession as to the cases charged." Stott's eyes widened.

"But for that, I want to have a manslaughter."

That's what Yengich had to bargain with: answers. And he made it clear: no plea, no answers. "If we go to trial, pal," he said, "you're never going to know. Because I can assure you—look me in the eye—that my client's *never* going to tell you."

It was a persuasive argument that played to Stott's obsession with the documents as well as his courtroom insecurity. But just in case it wasn't enough, Yengich decided to show his trump card.

At the preliminary hearing, he had agreed not to call Gordon Hinckley to the stand but instead stipulated to certain statements about how Hinckley had acquired the Josiah Stowell letter.

Now, Yengich made clear, all previous bets were off. If this case went to trial, not only could he call Hinckley and Pinnock and Oaks to the stand, he could use his subpoena power to "rummage to his heart's content" through the deepest, darkest recesses of The Vault.

The very suggestion was almost enough to give the jittery Stott a nervous breakdown. He and D'Elia had already argued about the chances of impaneling an impartial jury in a case that involved high officials of the Mormon Church. Stott thought it wouldn't be that difficult. D'Elia thought he was either crazy or willfully blind. Every potential juror would be asked, "Are you a Mormon?" and then, "Would you believe President Hinckley more than the other witnesses in this case simply because he is who he is?" And if the juror was wearing his garments, and he said no, then he was a liar, and D'Elia didn't want him on *his* jury.

On the other hand, non-Mormon jurors with axes to grind against the Church might convict Hofmann only if the prosecution managed to serve up a piece of the Church as well. The resentment out there ran deep. On a recent skiing weekend in Alta, D'Elia had sat on the deck downing beers with some friends who wanted to talk about the Hofmann case. They particularly wanted to know all about President Hinckley's complicity, which they took for granted. The more they drank, the rowdier they became and the more they demanded Hinckley's head. Banging their tankards on the table, they chanted in unison, "Hinckley did it. Hinckley did it. Hinckley's a fucking jerk. Hinckley did it. Hinckley did it."

And they *believed* it.

Now Yengich was threatening to put Hinckley and other Church leaders on the stand and grill them like unindicted co-conspirators. The Mormon bashers would have a field day. The foundation for their testimony alone would be devastating to the Church.

"What is your name?"

"Gordon C. Hinckley."

"What do you do for a living?"

"I run the LDS Church."

"How often did you see Mark Hofmann?"

"Why did you meet him so often?"

"Did you ever personally give him any money?"

"Under what circumstances?"

"Isn't it true that most people have to make an appointment to see you?"

"Isn't it true that most members of your Church never see you at all? Or if they do, they have to first see their bishop, then their stake president?"

"Did Mark Hofmann always call for an appointment?"

"Isn't it true that he just walked right into your office?"

"Doesn't that indicate that you attached a great deal of importance to what Mark Hofmann was doing for you?"

"Doesn't that indicate that your public statements to the effect that you barely knew Mark Hofmann were in fact misleading?"

"If you were lying when you said that, why should this jury believe you now?"

And the farmer in Genola, Utah, who pitched hay all week and went to his ward house every Sunday would read about it in his paper or see it on the evening news and say, "Golly. When I got into trouble with my farm down here and I needed to talk to somebody from the Church who has some authority, I couldn't even get past my bishop." And a lot of basic, decent people who were members of the Church would start asking themselves the same questions.

And nobody wanted that.

98

On Sunday, December 28, Judge Kenneth Rigtrup lingered late at church. He had a lot on his mind. A genial, portly man who managed to maintain his Santa Claus disposition despite being confined to a wheelchair and suffering through endless bouts of ill health, Rigtrup thought again that maybe he just wasn't cut out to be a judge. Maybe that was why, during his four years on the bench, he had never gotten a capital case. All cases, of course, were supposed to be assigned randomly, but it was an open secret that lawyers could "jiggle the system" by slipping a little money to someone in the clerk's office to get the *right* judge for a case. And in four years, no one, apparently, had considered Rigtrup the right judge for a capital murder case. Perhaps the defense attorneys were fooled by his stern courtroom manner, and prosecutors who knew him saw the buoyant humanity beneath the somber black robes.

But all that changed when, after a lot of bad press, the clerk's office instituted a new calendar system by which docket numbers were randomly assigned to cases, and the numbers were then blindly divided among the judges.

Only then did Judge Kenneth Rigtrup get a capital murder case: *The State of Utah* v. *Mark Hofmann.*

Like almost everyone else, Rigtrup had been personally touched by the crimes, if only lightly. He always bought clothes at Mr. Mac's, and his next-door neighbor's son had lived in Hofmann's ward and knew him.

Since the case was assigned to him, Rigtrup had seen Hofmann only once, at the arraignment the previous February. Ron Yengich had ambushed Rigtrup in the courthouse on the Friday before the Monday when the arraignment was scheduled to take place. He said something about having to be in Wyoming for a case on Monday, but Rigtrup suspected it was all just a ploy to dodge the press. "It's set for Monday, and we ought to do it Monday," he said. But when Yengich pressed, he relented and, against his better judgment, arraigned Hofmann not just on the murder charges but on everything. Hofmann stood in the empty courtroom with only his father at his side and said "Not guilty" in his high, disembodied voice as Rigtrup read each of the charges. By the time the press arrived—on his way into the courtroom, Rigtrup had told the clerk to alert them—the show was over.

The next time Rigtrup was scheduled to see Hofmann was Monday, December 29, the first of three days he had scheduled for hearings on motions.

When Rigtrup returned from church about 12:30 that frigid December Sunday, his wife told him that Jack Ford of KSL-TV had been calling every fifteen minutes trying desperately to get ahold of him. Minutes later, he called again.

"Are you going forward with motions tomorrow?" Ford asked.

"Yes."

"Well, hasn't there been a change?"

"Not that I'm aware." Rigtrup knew what he was driving at.

It wasn't the first time Ford had suggested that a plea bargain was in the works, but Rigtrup wasn't about to explore the subject with him. Utah state statutes forbade judges from participating in plea discussions prior to an agreement being reached between prosecutors and defense counsel. So he would just as soon not know what was going on.

In fact, Rigtrup had suspected that something was in the works for a long time. For the past month, neither Yengich nor Stott had been approaching this case as if he really intended to go to trial. Yengich had waited until ridiculously late to file his motions, and then seemed totally unconcerned about the hearing dates. Stott wasn't beating down his door either. Rigtrup had been forced to call Stott's office to tell him to tell Yengich to come to his office so he could set the date for the motions. It was not the behavior of attorneys who planned to go to court.

Jack Ford's phone call only confirmed the obvious.

"No one has conferred with me," Rigtrup told him officially. "We have the matter set for hearing in the morning. So, as far as I know, we have a motion set for hearing."

The next morning, before the hearing began, Yengich and Stott came into Rigtrup's chambers together. "We want to talk to you before you take the bench," one of them said as the other closed the door. Just by the tone of voice, Rigtrup knew what it was about.

"If I change the plea," Yengich began, "would you let Mark out on bail between the plea and sentencing?"

Rigtrup didn't like the idea, but he didn't want to commit one way or the other without hearing more.

Yengich said he would enter a guilty plea on the Sheets case, but he wanted it to be sentenced one degree lower than the charge. So a guilty plea to second-degree murder would be sentenced as if it were manslaughter.

Rigtrup liked that even less.

Stott had agreed, Yengich insisted, subtly reminding Rigtrup that a judge's only duty was to ensure that a plea bargain was "carried out in good faith and that there was some rational basis for it, not to substitute his own views." Yengich just wanted to make sure that Rigtrup would honor the agreement he and Stott had reached on sentencing.

But that wasn't all.

Yengich also wanted a commitment that the sentences would be concurrent rather than consecutive.

Rigtrup liked that least of all. In fact, he was offended. Yengich was sandbagging him. He couldn't imagine how Stott had agreed to these outrageous terms.

"I don't really care for this kind of negotiation," he finally said, restraining his indignation.

But Yengich was undaunted. Unless Rigtrup agreed to both terms, he said, the deal was off. Hofmann wouldn't plead.

At that point, to Rigtrup's utter astonishment, Bob Stott jumped in and argued fervently *for the deal*. He had talked to the victims' families, and they were foursquare in favor of a plea. Besides, a jury would never hand down a death sentence in this case, so the plea bargain gave them as much as they could get in a trial—almost— with considerably less time and expense.

But under this agreement wouldn't Hofmann get only five to life, making him eligible for parole in about ten years, rather than a near certain life sentence?

Yes, Stott admitted, but the Board of Pardons probably wouldn't let him out anyway, so the results would be the same. Besides—and on this point he grew especially impassioned—this way we are going to find out all of the information we need to know. And that, he said again and again, was absolutely crucial.

Rigtrup detested the deal, but as long as Stott agreed to it, his hands were tied.

99

Contrary to what Judge Rigtrup thought, Bob Stott did have reservations about the plea bargain, but they had little to do with whether or not it was fair or whether or not Ron Yengich was, as one cop put it, "getting away with everything but Bob Stott's wallet."

Stott's concern was to make sure Mark Hofmann told *everything* he knew—or at least everything that Bob Stott wanted to know. "How do we know Mark is going to be open with us?" he demanded of Yengich. "We can make this agreement, then Mark could clam up. We go ahead and he pleads, and then he says, 'Ha, ha, fooled you. I got my plea, and I'm not going to talk to you.' "

Yengich's solution was to offer a "sampler." He would let Stott talk to Hofmann, off the record, before officially submitting the plea agreement. That way Stott could test the merchandise, so to speak, and see just how forthcoming Hofmann would be.

And what was to prevent Hofmann from pretending to be an open book in the brief interview before the plea and then clamming up afterward? Nothing. But Bob Stott didn't seem to care. He was so eager to get a plea, so eager to talk to Hofmann that nothing else seemed to matter.

The interview, which took place at Yengich's house, turned out to be not just off the record, but top secret. Stott didn't tell Jim Bell or Ken Farnsworth, or his own investigators, Mike George and Dick Forbes, the four people who knew the most about the Hofmann case— and were best able to detect if Hofmann's answers were evasive or contrary to the evidence. This was Bob Stott's show, and he wasn't going to share the spotlight with anybody. At the last minute, he relented and brought along David Biggs, who, unlike Stott, knew *something* about the homicides.

On January 7, Hofmann and Yengich were waiting for them in the living room of Yengich's small, red brick, white-trimmed Victorian house in a suburb of Salt Lake City. The four men took seats surrounded by books on famous defense lawyers and baseball players, companion volumes to PBS series, and general bachelor clutter. They knew this was serious business when Yengich locked Little out of the room, although his odor lingered.

They began by asking Hofmann about his experience with bombs. He described the wood-alcohol concoction that had left the scar on his neck.

And there was another one. "My friend Brian and I made a black powder incendiary device, which we put in a Sterno can. We put a fuse of black powder in the can, and Brian took it to explode at the schoolyard, which was near his house on Connor Street. Brian took the cap off to ignite it but it didn't explode."

How did you know how to make an incendiary device?

"I knew quite early how to make black gunpowder. I

started making it in elementary school. I got the formula and the percentage makeup of black gunpowder out of the *World Book Encyclopedia*. Another friend, Mike, and I made black powder out of sulfur, saltpeter, and charcoal."

And there was another incident with another friend. "We made some black powder and went over to a park and detonated it." And another one. "I made a sort of cannon out of a pipe along with a kind of extension-cord ignition system. I shot rocks out of the pipe and knocked leaves off the trees. I also blew up a bottle with dry ice. I liked firecrackers ad cherry bombs. I thought they were fun."

What about the bombs that you made in October 1985? How did you put those together? Where did you get the supplies?

"The idea for the nails packed around the Christensen bomb came out of a book I bought at a gun show that Shannon and I went to. The purpose was to make the bomb more lethal—to make sure it resulted in death."

Why did you kill Christensen? Why Sheets? These were the questions everybody was asking. Perhaps for that very reason, Hofmann backed away from answering.

"I knew I was going to make two bombs to kill two people. At first, I just didn't know for sure who the victims were going to be. I thought of several scenarios for the bombings. First, I thought that one of the bombs would kill either Tom Wilding or Brent Ashworth, and the second bomb would kill me."

It was an absurd idea. Why would he kill anybody else if he was planning to kill himself? But Hofmann went right on, undaunted.

"Then I thought maybe the bombs should be for Christensen and Wilding, and finally I thought about killing Wilding and Ashworth with the two bombs. It wasn't until the morning of the 15th of October, when I made the bombs, that I settled on the actual targets."

Could that be true? Could Hofmann have been playing that kind of game with people's lives? Or was *this* a game, throwing out several scenarios and watching in secret delight as Stott struggled to believe first one, then the next, then still another?

He *admitted* that the Mike Hansen alias was a game. "It was my way to play detective. I used it as early as

1978. I used it in 1979 at the University of Utah special-collections library. I also used it at the LDS Church archives, the Utah State University archives special collections, and the New York Public Library. I once bought a tire from David Early Tire using the name Mike Hansen."

Why would you use an alias for something like that?

"Oh, I don't know. I must have felt like being secretive that day."

Hofmann recounted the events that led up to the October 15 bombings.

He bought the equipment for the bombs on October 5, taking care to cover his tracks. "I bought the end-pipe caps, the nails, and the gunpowder all at the Allied store at 6200 South State. I knew I shouldn't buy them all at the same time, so I first bought two cans of Hercules Bull's-eye gunpowder. I carried them to my MR2, then went back to the store and bought the end pipes and the nails. I used different cashiers at Allied's—one for the gunpowder and another for the end pipes and cement nails.

"When I had the bomb components, I went home and put them on a blanket in my downstairs den. That's the same room I did my forgery work in. But one night, just before I made the bombs, Shannon came back to inspect the house because he wanted to buy it when we bought our new house in the Cottonwoods. I threw the blanket over the parts and Shannon walked into the room, walked around it, and walked out without noticing a thing."

Hofmann thought that was very funny.

Did he test the bomb components?

"I went to an area off of I-80 near Grantsville. I connected the wire of the rocket igniter to a fifty-foot extension cord, walked back to a small gully, and connected the extension cord to a battery pack. The bomb went off, so I knew if I made a bomb twice that size I could kill someone with it. When I was testing the bomb in the desert, I felt it was still going to be for Tom Wilding. I wanted to kill him."

So he did have victims in mind.

They asked him to describe how he set the bombs.

"The evening of October 14, I went with Shannon to [a friend's] house to talk about polygamy. Afterwards, I dropped Shannon off at his house at Quailbrook Condominiums. When I got home, Dorie was still up. It was about 11:30. We talked for a little while, and then she went to bed. I went downstairs and made the bombs. I drilled the holes into the pipes in the garage and made sure I picked up all of the filings. It didn't take long, probably two hours or less, to construct the two bombs. I mean, they were very simple devices . . . not nearly as complicated as the ones in the *Anarchist's Cookbook*."

They asked him why the bombs weren't equipped with safeties. This had puzzled investigators all along. To carry a bomb without a safety was such a daredevil thing to do, and bombers, as a rule, were not the daredevil kind.

For the first time, Hofmann couldn't suppress a smile. The bombs *did* have safeties. "I wouldn't have carried the bombs without it," he said, confirming that he indeed wasn't a daredevil. He made small holes in the box with an ice pick, then threaded the wires from the bomb through the holes and taped them separately to the outside of the box. "When I delivered the bombs, I took the tape off the wires and connected them. At the preliminary hearing, I looked at some of the remnants of the boxes that were introduced into evidence and I found one of the small holes."

His disdain was palpable. If he could find the holes, why couldn't the police?

"I finished putting the bomb packages together by writing the names Steve Christensen and Gary Sheets on them. I didn't know Sheets's address so I looked it up in the phone directory. In fact, I underlined Sheets's address in the directory with the same Magic Marker that I used to write the names on the boxes. That directory was still there when you did the search."

More disdain. For all the searches of Hofmann's house, for all the grief Yengich and the press had given them for taking everything that wasn't tied down, including Dorie's recipe box, they had missed the telephone book.

"When I was released from jail on bail, I destroyed the directory."

"The bombs were finished by 2:00 A.M. the morning of the 15th. I constructed the bombs at night because that's when I did my best work, my forgeries."

The choice of victims came up again, and Hofmann grew evasive again. "It was while I was making the bombs that I finally decided who they would be for. I wasn't rational at the time." Biggs for one sensed that Hofmann was already laying the groundwork for his appeal to the Board of Pardons: "I didn't know what I was doing. I wsn't rational. I was just lashing out." The idea was to transform a calculated, cold-blooded killing into something approaching temporary insanity. Obviously, Yengich and Hofmann had decided that the only way to pull off that sleight of hand was to argue that *building* the bombs may have been calculated and cold-blooded, but *using* them was an irrational, last-minute, impulsive act.

"I decided that Steve Christensen would have to be killed to stop the McLellin transaction. Steve was an honorable man, but closemouthed. From some cryptic things he said, I knew that CFS and Gary Sheets were in trouble. CFS was going under, and Sheets might be liable for some legal troubles."

Why did he resort to bombs, with their inherent risk of harming innocent bystanders—like Kathy Sheets?

"The thing that attracted me to bombs as a means of killing was that I wouldn't have to be there at the time of the killings. I don't think I could pull the trigger on someone if I faced them, but I could do it if I didn't have to be around. I only filled the Sheets pipe bomb half full of powder, and I didn't think the rocket igniter would work because it was three-fourths chipped away." Earlier, he had said that he knew he was going to make two bombs to *kill* two people. The story shifted a little every time he told it.

"It didn't matter to me if the Sheets bomb went off or not because the purpose was to establish a diversion, so that everyone would believe that the bombings were the result of the CFS business problem."

On that count, at least, the police had been right all along.

"For that purpose, the death of someone was unnecessary. Of course, I knew a bomb left at a residence could kill or severely injure someone, but it really didn't matter to me."

Everyone knew he meant to say that it didn't matter to him if the second bomb killed somebody or not, but the words, said in that tinny, deadpan voice, still sent a chill through the room: "It really didn't matter to me."

"When I finished making the bombs and the packages,

I cleared up the area and put everything that might incriminate me into two bags—a full can of Bull's-eye powder, battery packs, the old blanket I used as my work area, the Marks-a-Lot pen I used to address the packages, the drill bits I used to make the holes in the pipe, my soldering iron, solder, the rags I used to wipe off the grease from the threaded ends of the pipes, tape, and unused rocket igniters."

Biggs asked himself: Are these the actions of a man who intends to kill himself?

"Later that morning, I dropped the two bags into Dumpsters. One was put in a Dumpster at an apartment complex near 2100 East and 3300 South. The other, I dumped into a Dumpster at the apartments where Shannon lived, the Quailbrook apartments." Mark Hofmann, true friend.

"Sometime after 2:45 A.M., I put the two bombs and two bags into my van and left for the Sheets residence."

"Aaron Teplick was a good witness at the preliminary hearing." Finally, an acknowledgment of competence elsewhere in the world. "But he was wrong about the time I drove by the Sheets home. It was more like 3 A.M. than midnight. After driving by the Sheets home, I went back up, parked, walked to the garage, and placed the bomb package upright in front of the garage door closest to the front door. Then I connected the two wires, which were taped to the box. The bomb was ready to go off if the package was tipped. I had tested the mercury switch with the light tester and knew that if the box was tipped at a ninety-degree angle or knocked over, it would explode. I placed the bomb about five feet from the garage door, thinking that a car leaving the area would hit it. I can't understand why a car didn't hit the package and detonate it before Kathy Sheets found it."

In other words, it was all a terrible mistake.

"I got back home about 3:30 in the morning. While I was downstairs, my daughter woke up. Dorie, who was upstairs, asked me to take care of our little girl, which I did until she went back to sleep a while later.

"Sometime between 6:00 and 6:30 that morning, I went to the Judge Building to deliver the second bomb. I parked my van in front of the building on the south side of Third South. I first went into the building and up to the sixth floor without the bomb package to see the lay of the land. Then I went back to the van and sat in it for a moment, then went back to the building with the bomb. I got into the elevator with [Bruce] Passey and [his] father.

"I pressed the sixth-floor button and left the elevator on that floor. I walked directly to Steve Christensen's office and placed the bomb package inside the doorjamb. I fastened the wires together and returned to the street level using the elevator.

"To eliminate fingerprints, I wore gloves while I was delivering both bombs. In front of the Judge Building, I took off the gloves and threw them into a trash can. I did it to test fate."

The disdain again.

What were you wearing when you delivered the bombs?

"I wore tan pants, a striped shirt, black shoes, my green high school jacket with tan sleeves, glasses and gloves."

What about the mustache?

"I hadn't shaved, but I didn't have a mustache. I wore my jacket and used the name Mike Hansen to leave little clues."

More disdain. A smile quivered at the corners of his mouth. "I was kind of hoping to get caught . . . and I thought if you could catch me, you should."

But that was just the prelude to Hofmann's tale of regret and remorse. At 8:30 that morning, only an hour and a half after returning home from the Judge Building, Hofmann said he called the Sheets home, but no one answered. "If someone answered, I would have disguised my voice and told them there was a bomb in their driveway and not to touch it."

This, too, Biggs thought, was fodder for the parole hearing.

"I was already regretting the Christensen bomb and was considering calling Christensen. I called his office. The answering machine picked up so I hung up without leaving a message."

Biggs thought, Right. And just how did you think Christensen was going to answer the phone without picking up the package that was sitting in front of his office door? If he felt so damn contrite, why didn't he call the *police*?

Later, they asked him how he had passed the polygraph test.

"I'm very good at masking my emotions," he said, without a hint of irony.

And how did Dorie pass the test when she said he was home all that night?

"I guess because both times she woke, at three and seven, I *was* home. Also, my youngest son told Dorie that 'Dad was downstairs all the time.' She had no idea that I had left the house that night."

Finally, they asked the other question that had been on everybody's mind for more than a year: Who was the third bomb for?

Hofmann drew his lips taut and looked straight ahead. "That was a suicide attempt. I was distraught over the killings the day before. I thought I deserved death, and it would be the best thing for my family. I also placed a number of inconsequential papers in the car so that people would think that the McLellin Collection, which didn't exist, was blown up in the explosion and fire."

Earlier he had said that he planned suicide from the beginning. Now it was out of guilt for the two bombings.

Hofmann told them how he bought the bomb parts in Logan and assembled them in Logan Canyon. "I wanted a quick and clean death, so I made the pipe sixteen inches long. It was substantially larger than the ones that killed Kathryn Sheets"—he couldn't even remember her name—"and Steve Christensen. Then I drove down to Salt Lake, parked in my normal spot across from the Deseret Gym, and walked in to get a drink of water to bolster my courage. I went back to the car. The bomb was in a paper sack on the passenger seat. I put it on the driver's seat, touched the two wires together, and the bomb exploded."

If he wanted to spare his family the stigma of his crimes, why did he leave pipe parts and surgical gloves in the trunk that would identify him as the bomber?

If he only wanted to blow himself up, why did he bother to cover his tracks by driving to Logan to buy the bomb parts?

And given his level of expertise, why did he place the bomb in the car rather than in the trunk with the papers, or the papers in the car with the bomb? Certainly he knew that from that distance, the blast wouldn't destroy the papers.

And why would he arrange to have the bomb blow up on a city street where no bomber could plausibly find him?

And if he twisted the wires together to set the bomb off, why was only one hand mangled? You can't twist wires together with one hand.

And why was he leaning into the car with one foot still outside the door when the bomb went off? People don't duck into their cars to commit suicide. What would Jerry Taylor say?

And what about the childhood of cherry bombs and black powder? Only serial bombers think first about making bombs and then about who the targets will be.

The explanations raised more questions than they answered, but Bob Stott didn't ask them. At the final session on January 22, he moved on to the only subject that really seemed to interest him, the documents.

Hofmann admitted the Salamander Letter was a forgery. He spoke proudly of it. "To write it, I researched the matter thoroughly. . . . I had also read books on magic at the University of Utah library and had discussions about it with Brent Metcalfe.

"I composed the letter in about two hours when I was visiting the Church historical library. I called Lyn Jacobs in Boston and read the draft to him."

He had stolen the authentic 1830s paper from a book at the University of Utah special-collections library. "The handwriting style of the letter was copied basically from the available Martin Harris signatures, the samples of letters and styles from that era, and the common style and standards that were employed at that time. I attempted to keep the handwriting of the letter consistent with the handwriting of the known Martin Harris signature. I researched the mail schedules from and to Palmyra and the surrounding areas and knew what post office date and mark to affix. I knew that, prior to 1829, the Palmyra postmark was black and afterwards it was red. The beginning of the letter, 'I received your letter today and hasten to respond,' was from words I had seen in actual letters from that era and place. So I was sure the time sequence was proper.

"Basically, I created what I believed the actual history to be. I believed Joseph Smith was involved in magic. The early writings of Joseph Smith didn't characterize his experience as a First Vision but as a dream. I was aware that salamanders and toads are commonly associated with magic literature. My Salamander Letter was a magic forgery."

Hofmann went on to brag about his other creations. "The postmark on the Lucy Mack Smith letter was from a plate I created myself from a photograph of an original postmark. I did most of the printing myself from plates I made. I did my own photography, chemical work, etching, and printing. People would be surprised at how much I did to ensure that the 'Oath of a Freeman' would pass the forensic tests, but I got lazy and had the 'Oath' plate made professionally. Obviously, I should have made the 'Oath' plate myself."

He was the only one in the room who laughed.

"At one time, I told Dorie that the Anthon Transcript was a fake, but because it so greatly affected her, I later told her that I was only joking and that it was genuine. Although she probably felt or suspected that many of my items were forgeries, she still thought the 'Oath of a Freeman' and the Salamander Letter were authentic."

Through the harangues of creditors, the endless police searches, and the public shame, Dorie had stuck with him, and no doubts about her innocence had ever been raised. Now he was implicating her in a scheme of criminal fraud with breathtaking nonchalance.

They never asked about the bombings again. And despite the evasions and outright lies, Stott maintained that Hofmann had been cooperative and agreed to proceed with the plea.

It was clear to everyone by now that Bob Stott was determined to avoid a trial no matter what. Said one policeman when news of the bargain began to spread through the department like the smell of a gas leak, "Even if we'd had a *confession,* Stott would have given Yengich anything he wanted."

Later, when a *Los Angeles Times* reporter flew to Salt Lake City to cover the breaking plea-bargain story, he told Dawn Tracy that the most surprising aspect of the entire case was the attitude of the prosecution. "The typical prosecutor," the reporter said, "goes out and gets bad guys. He goes out and stirs things up. Here, they're so nice and cooperative. What a *nice* plea bargain. In any other state, you'd see this thing go on trial, because that's how prosecutors' reputations are made. Going to trial and getting bad guys, big splashes, lot of exposure. Here you have a nice plea bargain."

"Hey," said Tracy, "you don't rise in this state embarrassing the Mormon Church or making them look bad."

100

There was one last obstacle to the deal, an obstacle that even Bob Stott's inexplicable enthusiasm couldn't overcome.

That obstacle was Bill Hofmann.

At the hospital, only a day after the third bomb exploded and the police announced that Mark was their primary suspect, Bill Hofmann had gone to his son's bedside and said, very gravely, "If you did it, you should turn yourself in and ask for the death penalty, because that's the only way your soul can be saved." Bill Hofmann believed in Blood Atonement.

But Mark had assured him: "I didn't do it."

Since then, Bill Hofmann had gone on television to proclaim his son's innocence. He had mortgaged his house to pay for his defense. And finally, he had announced that God Himself had reassured him that his son was blameless. No one who knew Bill Hofmann was surprised. When he was right, he was a rock.

Lu Hofmann, on the other hand, apparently had doubts, even in the beginning. After Ron Yengich's first long interview with Mark, she had asked him in her tiny, knowing voice, "Do you still feel good about the case?" Only days after the bombings, she called a relative and shared her dilemma. Her husband was absolutely convinced of Mark's innocence, she said, but she didn't know if her son was innocent or guilty, and the uncertainty was tearing her apart. She had been so proud of his accomplishments.

For Lu Hofmann, the uncertainty must have ended at the preliminary hearing. After that, according to friends, she barricaded herself in her house, quit her job on Temple Square, stopped going to church, and hid when the phone rang. Already small as a child, she began to lose weight at a dangerous rate. Relatives described her as "a fraction away from a nervous breakdown."

But Bill Hofmann continued to believe. Like Dorie, he protected his certainty by refusing to read newspaper accounts of the case or watch reports on television.

A year after the bombings, Mac Christensen came to see Bill Hofmann. He had been carrying around the anger and bitterness too long, Christensen decided. His children and grandchildren would grow up with hate unless he put a stop to it. So he made up his mind to forgive Mark Hofmann for killing his son. It wasn't just the religious thing to do, it was the healthy thing to do.

But Bill Hofmann didn't want to hear anything about forgiveness. "Before you say anything," he told Christensen, "I want you to know my son didn't kill your son. And I know that because I gave him a father's blessing. And I had a spiritual manifestation."

That left Mac Christensen with nothing to say, except, "Bill, if you ever change your mind, I would like you to come talk to me." Then he walked away.

Another time, Joan Gorton, Kathy Sheets's sister, found herself face to face with Bill Hofmann on an elevator. She wanted to say, "If you're a good Latter-day Saint, tell your son to confess, tell your son to admit his guilt. Then maybe he can be forgiven. Until he admits it, no one can forgive him. We can't begin to forgive him as long as he says 'I'm not guilty.' " But her tongue got caught in her throat, and all she could manage was, "I'm Kathy Sheets's sister, and I want you and your wife to know that we sympathize with you."

Bill Hofmann looked at her and said blankly, "We have sympathy for you too."

Brent Metcalfe was visiting Mark one day when Hofmann Senior walked into the living room and found several books on evolution that Mark had bought for his kids. He looked at them and said in a grave voice,

"These kinds of books should not be lying around the house. This isn't the view presented at the Temple." Mark Hofmann was thirty-two years old, and he still hadn't found the courage to tell his father about his views on evolution.

How could he ever tell him he was guilty of murder?

By January 1987, Ron Yengich was desperate. The deal was set, Bob Stott had agreed to everything, Judge Rigtrup had given the agreement his reluctant approval, but *Mark Hofmann refused to sign it.* He had submitted to Stott's questioning and confessed almost everything—including the most outrageous crimes, the two bombings—but he still refused to sign the deal or to confront his father with the truth face to face.

The first time someone mentioned the possibility of a guilty plea in Bill Hofmann's presence, his response was immediate and unequivocal: In that case, Mark should ask for the death penalty. Only by submitting to a death sentence could he atone for his sins and assure himself of even the possibility of entering the Celestial Kingdom.

Ever helpful, Bob Stott volunteered to convince Hofmann Senior that Blood Atonement was no longer official Church policy. He even brought along a copy of an article on the subject by Bruce R. McConkie.

But Bill Hofmann was a rock.

Ken Woolley, Mark's cousin, was the next to try to solve the impasse. He went to Bill Hofmann's home and pleaded with him to consider the possibility that Mark might be guilty, and not to spend all of his savings supporting Mark's defense effort. If he went into bankruptcy over this, it was all going to be a loss.

To prove his point, Woolley brought along some of the evidence of Mark's forgery and double dealing (provided by Ken Farnsworth). He also mentioned, gingerly, that a plea bargain was in the works. Bill Hofmann shoved the evidence aside. "Ken, they are lying to you. There is absolutely no plea bargaining. Believe me, he's innocent. I don't care what you say." He pointed at the evidence. "I don't understand these things. I'll have to talk to Mark, and you'll have to talk to Ron Yengich. You ought to talk to Ron Yengich, because I'm sure there is an explanation for this."

Woolley later said, "Bill Hofmann is a salesman, and

salesmen want to believe everything." Bill Hofmann wanted mightily to believe his son was innocent. Yengich told Mark repeatedly: You *have* to tell your family. You can't keep leading them on this way. But no matter how Yengich pleaded, Mark still couldn't face them with the truth.

Finally, disgusted and desperate, Yengich decided to force Hofmann's hand. He invited Bob Stott and Mark to his house in an effort to re-create the confessional atmosphere of the interviews. Then in the middle of the meeting, by prearrangement, Bill Hofmann arrived at the door. As Yengich got up to greet him, Mark went white. "Get that guy out of here!" he said to Stott in a frantic, choked voice. "I don't want to talk to that guy. Get that guy away."

A few minutes later, Lu Hofmann arrived with her daughter and Dorie. Yengich had also arranged for them to be present at Mark's confession—but the confession never came. Mark sat glumly, saying nothing.

With the date for entering the plea only a few days away, Yengich was out of tricks.

In fact, it wasn't until the evening of the last day before the plea was scheduled to come down that Bill Hofmann finally heard that his son was planning to plead guilty. But the news didn't come from Mark. It came from John Harrington on the Channel 4 news at 5:30. Mark Hofmann, he announced, was going to change his plea from innocent to guilty.

Ron Yengich went through the usual show of fist pounding and finger pointing. He called up Biggs and Stott in a rage. Did they realize what anguish this was causing the Hofmann family? Bill Hofmann was terribly, terribly hurt. What a terrible, terrible way to hear the awful news. The very idea that his son had *really* been guilty of the murders and forgeries was a blow from which this man might never recover.

He even threatened to scuttle the deal. "We're just flat not going to do it," he said. "When you guys learn to shut up and tell your people that whoever told the media has to shut up, then we'll go through with it."

"But we've already signed the document," Stott protested. The renewed threat of a trial sent him into a meltdown panic.

"Bullshit," snapped Yengich. "We're not going to do this. Because it's not fair. I don't think it's fair to the victims' families. I don't think it's fair to my client's family. We come to an agreement. We agree it won't be released to the press. And then you guys shoot your mouths off. I don't think anybody can comprehend how difficult it is for Mark to deal with his family on this. And you're making it more and more difficult."

It was vintage Yengich, full of sound and fury, but some suspected that it signified nothing. No one gained more from the leak than Yengich himself. The press had done what Mark—and Yengich, for that matter—had failed to do: break the bad news to Bill Hofmann. A few even suspected that Yengich himself or someone in his office had planted the story in an eleventh-hour ploy to force Mark's hand and save the deal. And even if he didn't do it, he had to be pleased it was done.

That night, the Hofmanns had a family meeting. Yengich, who attended, described it as a gut-wrenching experience. By the end of the meeting, he said, every single person there, including him, was in tears. David Biggs wasn't the only one who found it hard to work up a genuine sympathy. "Mark could have told his father a long time ago and saved everyone a lot of pain."

Early the next morning, Yengich called Judge Rigtrup at home. "Mark's not gonna come in," he said. The reports in the media had come at the worst possible time. "Mark was in the process of trying to spend his last quiet evening at home with his family when they saw the plea announced for the first time on television. Let me tell you, we're shocked, and incensed, and infuriated."

They weren't the only ones.

When Heidi Jones heard the press reports that Hofmann would be charged only with manslaughter for killing her mother, Kathy Sheets, she seethed with indignation. Contrary to what Stott had told Judge Rigtrup, the families of the victims had only generally endorsed the *concept* of a plea bargain. They didn't know the details of the deal until they appeared, sometimes in mangled form, in the press. In fact, the deal called for Hofmann to plead guilty to a second-degree murder charge for the Sheets killing but to be *sentenced* on a manslaughter charge. It was a subtle distinction, but one that made all the difference to the relatives of Kathy Sheets.

Heidi called her aunt, Joan Gorton, and Gorton, equally irate, called the county attorney, David Yocom. "This is Joan Gorton. I am Kathy Sheets's sister. Is it true that Hofmann is only pleading to a manslaughter on Kathy's murder? Kathy's daughter and I are very upset."

Yocom's naturally short fuse was made even shorter by the growing public criticism of his handling of the Hofmann case. "Listen," he snapped, "I don't have the time to hold the hand of every sister or daughter or cousin of a victim."

If Heidi and Gorton were irate before, now they were beside themselves. Gorton called Gary Sheets that night and related the conversation with Yocom. Sheets tried to calm her down. "If they don't have an explanation," he said, "then we simply won't agree to the plea." Sheets called Stott at home and told him that Yocom had all but caused a collapse in the plea bargain. Stott knew that if the families of the victims came out against the deal in the press, the public would spit it up like a hairball. They were already choking.

"Why don't you come in to my office tomorrow morning," Stott suggested, "and I'll explain the whole situation to you."

In the meantime, Sheets did the best he could to explain the situation to his children. "People are saying Hofmann will be out in ten years. Stott says if we waited and went to trial, because of all the publicity in the state, he doesn't think a judge would give Hofmann a long sentence.

"Stott says he thinks we have a strong case, but we take a chance. He says he thinks we can get as much time served out of him here in this plea bargaining as we would going to trial. And we don't have the risk of going to trial and having some nutty juror giving in to Hofmann's personality. He's a con man. The kid's persuasive. You get the kid on the stand, and who knows what'll happen in a trial. And here, Stott says, we're sure he's going to jail for a good long time."

Besides, said Sheets with a deep sigh that he hoped would end the conversation, "in the eternal scope of things, I'm going to be with Kathy."

The next morning, Sheets went to see Stott and agreed to support the deal.

101

Ken Farnsworth sat in the small circular courtroom and thought about his partner, Jim Bell. "He should be here," Farnsworth muttered to himself as people, mostly reporters, crowded into the seats around him. A few weeks ago, before he left to give some talks to a nursing convention in South Dakota, Bell had said, "I can tell you exactly what day Mark Hofmann is going to plead guilty. It will be the day I'm in South Dakota."

And he was right.

In just a few minutes, the room was full, and the bailiffs directed members of the Sheets and Christensen families to seats in the jury box, and then to chairs set up in front of the jury box. From there, they would be close enough to Mark Hofmann to feel his breath when he said the word they had waited more than a year to hear: "Guilty."

Jim Bell should have been there.

But perhaps it was all for the best, thought Farnsworth ruefully. The press had made so much of their "vendetta" against Hofmann. The last thing he wanted now was to give them an eight-by-ten of Ken and Jim leading a handcuffed Mark Hofmann to the state prison at Point of the Mountain—as sweet as that moment would have been.

At the last possible minute, Hofmann walked into the courtroom wearing a dark-blue pinstripe suit like the one he always wore to his meetings with Hinckley and other Church officials. Only Mark was twenty pounds heavier now, and the coat barely buttoned. He was flanked by his father and Ron Yengich. Mark looked at neither of them, keeping his eyes straight ahead of him, fixed in the middle distance. A moment later, Judge Rigtrup wheeled himself into the courtroom and took his place at the dais.

482

Looking very stern, Rigtrup reviewed the terms of the deal. Hofmann agreed to plead guilty to two counts of second-degree murder and two counts of felony theft by deception. In exchange, the prosecutors would drop twenty-six other felony charges against Hofmann. In addition, the U.S. Attorney's Office would drop federal charges of unlawful possession of a machine gun, and New York authorities would agree not to prosecute Hofmann for any alleged criminal conduct surrounding the "Oath of a Freeman."

Finally, Hofmann agreed that within thirty days, he would "meet with the prosecuting attorneys and answer, truthfully and completely, all questions said attorneys may have on any or all of the charged offenses . . . and the surrounding circumstances of those offenses and any other related activities." Distaste clung to every syllable as Rigtrup read the four-page agreement.

When he was done, he turned to Hofmann, who stood but refused to look him in the eye.

"Did you intentionally and knowingly cause the death of Steve Christensen?" Rigtrup asked.

"Yes," said Hofmann in a faint, tightwire voice. It was the first time the victims' families had heard him speak. Throughout the preliminary hearing, he had never said a word. Now, the sound of his high, squeaky voice, came as a shock. "He's a fag! He's a fag!" Jimmy Sheets whispered to his sisters.

"Did you intentionally and knowingly cause the death of Kathleen Sheets?"

"Yes."

Kathy Sheets's daughter, Katie, put her head down and breathed a bottomless sigh. Now, finally, she could start putting her life back together.

"Do you desire to enter these guilty pleas because you are in fact guilty?"

"Yes."

Under normal circumstances, the proceedings would have ended there. Judge Rigtrup would have set a date in three or four weeks for sentencing and ordered a presentence report. But these were not normal circumstances. There would be no delay, no presentence report. Rigtrup would sentence Mark immediately after the plea was entered and he would be led directly from the courtroom to prison.

Mark Hofmann wanted it that way.

At first, he had wanted a month's delay in both the pleading *and* the sentencing. Rigtrup insisted that the plea go on as scheduled but offered to delay the sentencing a month, giving Mark another month of freedom. If that was the only alternative, Mark responded, he preferred to plead and be sentenced the same day. Yengich tried to explain his client's decision by saying Mark knew he was going to prison eventually anyway so why wait around for a presentence report.

The truth was he didn't want to spend an entire month explaining to his family why he had lied to them for so long. He didn't even want to spend a day. Prison was easier to face than his father.

So Rigtrup pronounced sentence.

He had read through more than a thousand pages of evidence, including transcripts of the preliminary hearing, and was struck most by the "indiscriminate nature" of the bombings. "The deaths were inflicted consciously and knowingly," he concluded, "after considerable planning and scheming." The devices Hofmann employed were sensitive, and he had virtually no control over who would be killed by them. A neighborhood child could have been killed by the Sheets bomb. An innocent woman from across the hall had almost been killed by the Christensen bomb.

Finally, Rigtrup announced the sentences dictated by law: an indeterminate term of five years to life for the murder of Steve Christensen and indeterminate terms of one to fifteen years on each of the counts of theft by deception. In accordance with the deal, however, the sentence for the murder of Kathy Sheets was reduced from five-to-life to one-to-fifteen.

One-to-fifteen. Joan Gorton sat in the courtroom and shook her head. Even Kathy Sheets, who could find humor in almost anything, wouldn't find any humor in that.

Rigtrup turned to Hofmann again. "I feel very personally involved in this particular case," he said, with all the gravity he could summon. "I do not have any authority with the Board of Pardons, but I can express my opinion and I will. Mr. Hofmann, it is my personal opinion that you should spend the rest of your natural life at the Utah state prison."

In the back of the courtroom, Ken Farnsworth wanted to stand up and applaud.

Rigtrup said to Mark, "Do you want to spend a moment with your family?"

With his father sitting directly behind him, Mark kept his eyes fixed straight ahead. "No."

But he was ushered into the judge's chambers anyway, where his father embraced him before the bailiff led him off to jail.

102

The first session at which Mark Hofmann was supposed to "tell all" began at 2:25 on the afternoon of February 11, 1987. As at the test debriefing, only Bob Stott, David Biggs, Mark Hofmann, and Ron Yengich were present.

As before, Bob Stott controlled the questioning, going over documents damaging to the Church in excruciating detail while virtually ignoring non-Mormon forgeries like the "Oath of a Freeman." Most astonishing of all, despite public reassurances at the time of the plea, Stott never returned to the subject of the bombings.

Only once did the remarkably genial questioning stray near the murders. Hofmann began to talk about his rationalization for the bombings. "It was half a joke," he began. "Well, joke is not a good word, but it was more, thinking that I have the parts, I have a way out, than actually saying to myself when I purchased the parts, this is what I'm going to use them for—these are the people I'm going to take out. None of that was in my mind at that time. As far as the idea of Mrs. Sheets . . ."

"Let's back off that a minute," Stott interrupted, "and get back to the documents."

Later, when Biggs protested, Stott insisted that the murders had already been thoroughly covered in the test debriefing, and, in any case, they would get to them eventually. But the test debriefing had been off the record, and they never did get around to the murders again.

Ron Yengich later expressed his own theories as to Stott's curiously selective questioning.

"You've got a very devout Mormon who is in charge. He's a good guy, but, on the other hand, he had more than one interest. Bob's interest goes beyond solving the crime. I don't know if he's talking to Church leaders or not. I find it hard to believe that he wouldn't be. I think Bob has dual motivations. And one of the motivations is to explain some of these things to the Brethren. I think that's going to become clear when the transcript of the Hofmann meetings is available. Bob asks and reasks and reasks the same questions when it comes to anything that affects the Church."

Hofmann admitted that the Anthon Transcript was "a clumsy job," but described its manufacture in proud detail.

For the ink, he picked a recipe containing tannic acid, ferric acid, gum arabic, and logwood, and went to the chemistry stand in a local hobby store in Logan for the ingredients. "Perfect Chemicals is the brand name," he enlightened them.

After the ink had dried, he soaked the document in hydrogen peroxide—William Flynn had been right—dabbing it on with a piece of tissue. That oxidized the black ink to an "appropriate brown color." To make it look as if the Anthon Transcript had been in the Bible for many years, he wadded sheets of aluminum foil the size of the folded Transcript, heated them with an iron, and placed them in the Bible where he intended to put the Transcript itself—"to make it look like the acid from the paper had browned the leaves of the Bible."

The paper came from an end page of a book in the Institute Library at Utah State.

"Did you rip it out? Cut it out?"

"Yes. Probably at this time I would have used a razor blade to remove it, being careful to only remove the one blank page and not cut into the rest of the book. So I doubt you will find other traces besides the cut end page. You won't find other traces of razor blade." He also trimmed all four edges of the sheet with the razor blade.

being careful to remove any oil stains where the paper had come in contact with the leather binding.

Then he dipped the paper in a hot gelatin solution to give it a new sizing—since sizing tends to wear off as paper ages. Without the sizing, the ink would have "feathered," or spread out too much, when it came in contact with the old, absorbent paper. After writing the text, he applied heat with an iron—he *ironed* the document—then poured hydrogen peroxide on it to age the ink and to remove the sizing where it wasn't protected by the ink.

"Why did you do both the hydrogen peroxide and the heat?" Stott asked.

"Well, I was trying to make it look old. The hydrogen peroxide made the ink look old. The heat made the paper look old."

"But the paper was already old."

"Yes, but it made it look like it had seen some use. It was ragged, it was well aged. It is true that it was genuine paper from that period but I thought it would be more convincing rather than being pure white to show that it had the high acid content. Also, I wanted it to have high acid content so it would stain the page in the Bible."

Finally, he sprayed the document (Mark had taken to calling it "the Hofmann Transcript") with a solution of gelatin and milk in order to create "foxing," or rust spots.

Stott wanted to know how long this elaborate process had taken.

"It was completed in a day. When I say completed, I mean the Transcript was written in a day. Obviously it took longer than that to research it. In one day, the Transcript was written, aged, the Bible was aged, and the Transcript was inserted in the book. All of the forgery work would have been done in a day."

For some time, the Tanners and others had been demanding that Hofmann provide a sample of his forged handwriting. There was no other way, they claimed, to be absolutely sure that he operated alone, without an accomplice. So Stott asked Hofmann to write the signature of Samuel Smith, the supposed relative of Joseph Smith's whose name had been appended to the genuine insert in the Anthon Bible. Hofmann signed the name effortlessly, proudly, then signed his own name underneath it.

At the next session, on February 17, instead of plowing ahead, Stott returned to the Anthon Transcript.

"Let me ask you about some of the spelling—words like *characters*. Do you remember why you misspelled it? Where you came up with that idea?" The interview was becoming a game of Mormon trivia.

Later Stott asked about Joseph Smith's "characteristic formation of certain letters and words." What does that mean, he asked?

"In other words, the shape of the letters are the same as Joseph Smith's shaping. The words also," Hofmann added, his exasperation showing for the first time. "I mean, it's *supposed* to be a forgery of Joseph Smith. That's what it's intended to be. So I don't think it's surprising that it looks like his handwriting."

Stott went on and on about Joseph Smith's handwriting until finally *Hofmann* changed the subject. "You will probably want to know what the glue was," he offered helpfully, referring to the black glue with which the Transcript had been pasted in the Bible.

"I'm sure they shall," said Ron Yengich, whose short attention span had long since expired. "Why don't you tell them."

"It was some charcoal ground up with a wheat paste which I found was not terribly sticky, and so, believe it or not, I added a couple drops of Elmer's Glue to it."

"What kind of Elmer's Glue?" Stott asked with a straight face.

"Not the carpenters' but the school stuff."

"The white stuff?"

"Yes, the white glue. Just a regular bottle with the orange top."

"Where did you get the idea for this charcoal and wheat paste?" Stott wanted to know.

"I thought to myself, I need to glue this in here. What looks like old glue? I had the idea of getting an old book and soaking the end page of the spine where it's glued down and retrieving some glue that way, which I figured was too much work. I was in a hurry. I wanted to get this thing done that day."

"Why?" Biggs asked.

"I don't know. I'm always rather impatient. That's probably part of my personality. I wanted to get it done before Dorie came home from work. My wife. So anyway, just sticking Elmer's Glue on there, or rubber cement, didn't seem to quite do it. They usually didn't use white glue back then."

Hofmann had folded the document into quarters, glued it along the edges into the Bible, and closed it up. Then he cleaned everything up, pouring the leftover ink down the sink and throwing away the extra glue and paper, and waited for Dorie to come home and bear witness to his first great "discovery."

"Was your intention to sell it at that time? Was the money a factor?"

"Yes, but not so much. Originally, initially, it was more [a matter] of the fame involved—although I thought all along that it would be sold, and the more publicity I got the better."

At the session on February 27, Brad Rich substituted for Ron Yengich. Taking advantage of Yengich's absence, Stott tried to broach a sensitive subject. "I think this is a good time as any to ask, what were your feelings at this time, generally, to start out, say, with your faith?"

"Well, previous to this, I had lost faith in the Mormon Church."

"Do you want to tell us when—or was it a gradual thing?"

"Right around the age of fourteen."

Suddenly, Hofmann broke off. "This is something that I guess Ron wants to be here [for] when I start talking about [it]. Well, I will finish what I was saying."

He looked to Rich for guidance. "We are very close to an area that I know Ron wants to be here [for]," said Rich, "but I think you can finish this."

"I wasn't fearful of the Church inspiration detecting the forgery," Hofmann continued, referring to the Church leaders' alleged ability to read minds and see into men's souls. "That's all I was going to say."

"What was your feeling about Mormon history and, specifically, early Mormon history with Joseph Smith at this time?"

"I won't go so far as to say I wanted to change Mormon history. Let me take that back. Maybe I did. I believed that the documents that I created could have been a part of Mormon history. I'm speaking specifically, for example, of the magic-related items. The 1825 Stowell letter, the so-called Salamander Letter. In effect, I guess, the questions I asked myself in deciding on a forgery—one of the questions—was what *could* have been. I had a concept of Church history, and I followed that concept."

The questions finally moved on to the Joseph Smith III blessing, which Hofmann considered "a better forgery than the Anthon Transcript."

Where did he get the idea for the blessing?

"It's pretty common knowledge in the Church, RLDS Church, that there's been a debate going on as far as whether or not such a blessing was ever given. Because of that controversy, I figured such a blessing would be worth a lot of money to certain people. So again, as far as motivation, it is true that partially it had to do with my rewriting of Mormon history."

But mostly it was money, he admitted. "As I remember, my first son was born around the time of this."

Stott wanted to know where he had gotten the words for the blessing, but Hofmann couldn't remember the source. "I'm wondering where I got this," he said, " 'And he'll be wafted as on eagles' wings.' I must have taken that from someplace."

"Sounds like it's taken from someplace all right."

"Sounds real lyrical," Biggs added caustically.

"I must have read that someplace and thought that it was something that Joseph Smith might say. I can't say. Hopefully it is not from Shakespeare or someplace."

"Do you recall where the inspiration for the second paragraph came from?"

"As I remember, the first paragraph said basically everything that I needed to say. But it seemed to take up such a little amount of paper, and Joseph Smith had a tendency on occasion to say more than what was needed, perhaps."

Reading a line, "His days shall be lengthened upon the earth and he will be received in an instant unto myself," Stott asked: "That's kind of quaint—you know, a stylized way of putting things. Where did you come up with it?"

"Just seemed like words Joseph Smith would use."

* * *

Stott wanted to know if Hofmann intended to harm the LDS Church when he forged the blessing.

"That was not my original intent, because, like I say, I didn't think it would see the light of day."

"Did it become an intent later on?"

"It cast me in a rather bad light with some people in the Church, I believe, yes."

"But that wasn't part of your motivation?"

"That's right."

The techniques for forging the blessing were similar to those he had used for the Anthon Transcript, except he invented a more sophisticated method for applying the hydrogen peroxide. He laid the document against a metal screen—"such as you would find on storm doors"—sprayed the document with hydrogen peroxide, then sucked the fluid through the document and the screen using the hose on an old vacuum cleaner. This saturated the fluid through the document, instead of just letting it rest on the surface. "The purpose of the sucking is to bring the characteristic aging or brown of the ink through to the back side," he explained.

Was Mark ever concerned that he might have been forging "a document the Church already had but never made public to anyone?" Stott asked.

"No. That didn't concern me. For one thing, I thought if they had such a document, it wouldn't still be in existence. Not to say that the Church nowadays would go around burning documents or anything. And if another blessing *was* given presumably if the Church had a copy, it would not have matched my words since I made mine up and I don't feel like I was inspired at the time."

When the fourth session was held on March 12, Bob Stott was vacationing in the Bahamas, Ron Yengich in Arizona. David Biggs took advantage of Stott's absence to ask questions about some of the documents in which the Church had no interest, like Al Rust's Mormon money.

Hofmann chided the police for missing the plates for the Deseret currency notes during their numerous searches of his house. "The plates were on the top shelf in the closet of my downstairs office until I destroyed them after returning home from the hospital after the bombings."

"How did you destroy them?"

"They were burned in my fireplace. The metal burns a bright white, incidentally, but I knew that it was flammable, the wood backing and also the metal, and that was their fate."

"Did anybody in your family know you did that?"

"They knew I had a fire but not that I was burning plates in that fire."

"Where was the fire in your home?"

"In my fireplace in the front room. People were there when the fire was going. My children, my wife, was there, but they did not participate in helping me in constructing the fire and they thought it was a lot of fun to have. My son was there when I was doing it, when I was building the fire, and since he is young, just turned six, I wasn't afraid of him seeing anything or understanding anything."

"Was this when you were still in your wheelchair?"

"Yes and no. I was able to jump around somewhat on one leg before I really went on crutches. But it was in that time period where I would have been out of my wheelchair, when I went downstairs. I obtained them the first time I went downstairs, which would have been a few weeks after I returned home, I imagine. I wouldn't have gone. downstairs in the wheelchair. I would have slid down the stairs on my behind. I went in the room, in my office, and whatever incriminating evidence that wasn't already taken, I put in a bag and probably that same night is when I built a fire."

Stott's absence also allowed Biggs to ask about the "Oath of a Freeman."

Hofmann described the extraordinary lengths to which he had gone to formulate the ink. "I knew that this document would be scrutinized so I took pains to ensure that the ink would not differ from the seventeenth-century printing ink. . . . I obtained some paper from the same time period, approximately, from Brigham Young University library. The paper did not have printing on it, which I guess they'll be happy to hear. That paper I burned in an apparatus to make carbon black. The reason I went through this trouble is because I thought that there was a possibility that a carbon 14 test would be performed on the ink."

"Do you know what book this paper came out of that you used to produce the carbon black?"

"If you want to take me in shackles to the library I could point it out to you, but I don't know that I can describe the exact location."

He then took the carbon and mixed it with linseed oil. "It was just chemically pure linseed oil, which I treated to some extent."

"How did you treat the linseed oil?" Biggs asked.

"Well, I'm going into all of this. You are just *dying* to hear this, aren't you?"

Biggs was.

"The linseed oil was heavily boiled, which thickens it, and then it was burned." To that, he added a solution of tannic acid that he created by taking a piece of leather binding from a book of that period and boiling it in distilled water "until it turned a nice brown color." With a final touch of beeswax—"just ordinary beeswax, nothing special to it"—the ink was ready.

The paper was a piece of seventeenth-century paper that approximated as closely as possible the paper used for the *Bay Psalm Book*, the other product of Stephen Daye's press. He actually found a piece that was within five years of the alleged date of the "Oath," and almost precisely duplicated the spacing of the laid lines of the paper used for the *Bay Psalm Book*.

Before printing the "Oath," he aged the plate by grinding down some of the letters, chosen at random, with a small drill fitted with a fine grinding-tip stone. A final rubdown with steel wool rounded off the corners of the lettering.

The printing was done in his basement workroom. He rolled ink onto the plate, placed the paper on the plate, covered it with a layer of felt and a second thick copper plate, then pressed everything together with a C-clamp.

"Did you have only one piece of paper at that time to print on?"

"Yes, I did."

"Were you a little concerned that maybe you wouldn't get it right the first time?"

"I don't think so. For one thing, this was the first attempt by the Daye print shop to make an impression, and if it was crude or didn't look quite right, I didn't think it would be too great of a concern."

"Did you test out your final product on a piece of modern paper to see how it looked on the paper?" Rich asked.

"Yes, I'm sure I did."

"He's a lot bolder than I am," Rich confessed admiringly. "A lot of things, he just did it, knew it worked, and went ahead and printed it. I would take a ream of paper and go through it to be sure it worked."

Hofmann wasn't one to shy away from a compliment. "By the time I forged the 'Oath,' I considered myself a pretty good forger. I thought I had a pretty good knowledge of different techniques that would be used in analyzing it."

In fact, Hofmann himself had noticed the cracked-ink phenomenon before Throckmorton and Flynn pointed it out.

"Oh, really?" said Biggs, genuinely surprised. "You had seen that cracking before yourself?"

"Yes, although I didn't know the cause of it until the preliminary hearing—as far as the gum arabic. Undoubtedly, when somebody reads this transcript, they'll keep gum arabic out of the formula."

"We are doing an invaluable service here, I guess."

For the "Oath," he had aged the ink not with hydrogen peroxide, but with ammonia.

"Did it concern you that it might be tested by the cyclotron method?"

"No."

"Why not?"

"Because I felt that the document would pass. I'm sure if it wasn't for the other suspicion, i.e., the bombings, etc., I believe it would have passed very well."

As long as Hofmann had brought it up, Biggs couldn't resist pursuing it. "Hypothetically," he said, "if the American Antiquarian Society had been able to, and did vote to purchase your 'Oath' on October 15, 1985, for about a million dollars, what would that have done to the financial hole that you dug yourself into by that time?"

"It would have relieved me from it. Hence, I guess you want me to say the bombings would not have taken place."

"I don't want you to say that unless it is true."

"I'll say it, since it's true."

* * *

By the session on April 7, Stott and Yengich had returned and the questions concentrated on Hofmann's desperate financial situation in the months leading up to the bombings.

"Weren't you in a pretty frenzied state at this time?" asked Biggs.

"Yes."

"Weren't you desperate for money?"

"Yes."

Biggs recited the list of victims. "[So] you just defrauded people out of hundreds of thousands of dollars. Wilding, Pinnock, First Interstate Bank, Rust. We could go on forever."

"Now just a second," Hofmann interrupted. "I want to clarify all of this, how all of this fraud and stuff took place, if I can. My view was, when I forged a document and sold it, I was not cheating that person that I was selling it to because the document would never be detected as being a fraud. Obviously, if I would have known they would someday be detected, I wouldn't have done it."

It was a rationalization he had used since childhood. He told them the story of how he had electroplated a mint mark on a coin to make it valuable and when he sent it in, the Treasury Department pronounced it genuine. "And my feeling was that if the Treasury Department pronounces it genuine, that it is genuine, by definition."

"Is that the same kind of rationalization you used on these documents?" Stott asked.

"Yes. I never would have done them, obviously, if I thought they could be detected. I thought I was clever enough to avoid that, which obviously I wasn't."

"If the experts say they're real documents, then the people who buy them really aren't hurt?"

"Yes, that's right." Reality and appearance were one and the same thing, as long as nobody knew otherwise.

"Was there any concern on your hand," Stott pressed, mangling his phraseology as usual, that "these people who perhaps had given you money were now investing sentiment and emotion and belief in these documents— but it was based on a false premise? Did that enter your mind?" It had obviously entered Bob Stott's mind. "Did that cause you any concern?" It had obviously caused Bob Stott concern.

"No, that didn't cause concern in my mind. My feeling is, it's not so much what is genuine and what isn't, as what people *believe* is genuine. My example would be the Mormon Church, which may be a bad example, since I'm sure you're both believers in it. I don't believe in the religion as far as that Joseph Smith had the First Vision or received the plates from the Angel Moroni or whatever. It doesn't detract from the social good that the Mormon Church can do. To me it is unimportant if Joseph Smith had that vision or not as long as people believe it. The important thing is that people believe it."

It was an attitude worthy of Joseph Smith. Hofmann may have rejected the Church's doctrines but he had taken to his bosom its attitude toward truth: faith before facts.

"The Oliver Cowdery [history] was made up by you?" Stott asked, eager to put the damaging rumors to rest.

"Right."

"Never saw it in the First Presidency's vault—or anywhere?"

"Right."

"Why did you make the story up?"

"For a couple of reasons. First of all, I remember distinctly, when I did make it up, we were eating at Wendy's. Indigestion, perhaps. . . . The other reason, obviously, would have been that part of the Oliver Cowdery history was about a white salamander and Alvin's involvement [in the First Vision], and that would have validated the history presented in the forged Salamander Letter."

"Again made up by you?"

"Again made up by me. One forged idea to validate another forged idea."

On the last day of questioning, May 15, Stott asked what Hofmann would have done if someone had loaned him the money to pay off Al Rust and he had been forced to produce the McLellin Collection.

"What was in my mind is, President Hinckley would be happy if eventually I could tell him that I had seen to it that the documents would not fall into the wrong hands. . . .

He wasn't so concerned, especially when he found out other people knew about this material, to actually *obtain* it, as to just see that the right people got it."

In other words, Hofmann could claim that he had sold it to a devout Mormon who would never breathe a word about the McLellin Collection, and Hinckley would never breathe a word either.

It would have been the *ultimate forgery,* a collection of documents that existed only in Mark Hofmann's imagination and Gordon Hinckley's fears.

103

Mark Hofmann entered the Utah state prison at Point of the Mountain on January 24, 1987. Soon afterward, he wrote a letter to the family of Kathy Sheets:

> Of course it is difficult to explain my actions of October 1985. I cannot justify what occured [sic]. My actions have caused irreperable [sic] harm to your families and to my own.
>
> Saying I'm sorry sounds so hollow as to seem meaningless, but with all my heart I want you to know that although my actions were inexcusable, I am sorry.
>
> I have tried in small measure to rectify my crimes by fully exposing them to the authorities, and putting to a halt the further trama [sic] of the trial process.

In Utah, the plea bargain arranged by Ron Yengich and Bob Stott was not greeted warmly. Informal polls conducted by local papers showed that a majority of people in the Salt Lake area felt Hofmann should have been tried and, if found guilty, sentenced to death.

In the criminal-defense community, Ron Yengich was hailed as a hero. The consensus was that he had "raped the prosecution" on the deal. "We were envious as a group," says one fellow attorney. "Envious of his ability to have gotten such a good plea bargain. And a lot of that had to be attributed to Ron, because the prosecution's case wasn't that weak. In fact, it was so good, we all hoped it would give us leverage in pleading some of *our* cases."

John Harrington, a reporter for KTVX, ruefully recalled the case of a nineteen-year-old kid who stole a car and robbed a Der Wienerschnitzel, a fast-food chain. He was caught before any money was turned over. He didn't have a weapon, but they *thought* he did, so he went to prison on armed robbery and car-theft charges. He got five-to-life for the "armed" robbery and one-to-fifteen for the car theft—exactly the sentences imposed on Hofmann for murdering Steve Christensen and Kathy Sheets.

At the county attorney's office, George Throckmorton, the documents examiner who broke Hofmann's forgeries, lost his job. David Yocom claimed he was just making good on campaign promises to cut costs by cutting personnel, and Throckmorton was expendable. "We'll never have another case like this again," said an official. "We don't need an expert like that." Soon afterward, Throckmorton left Salt Lake City.

He was followed by David Biggs, who quit when the Byzantine politics of the county attorney's office got to be too much even for his considerable political savvy.

Of all the original Hofmann prosecutors, that left only Bob Stott, the architect of the plea.

A few months after the plea, Al Rust called Bill Hofmann. He wanted to express his sympathy for the pain that the Hofmann family had suffered. "I also want you to know that I don't hate Mark," said Rust. "I probably have analyzed him in my mind as much as anybody. I probably know, right now, nothing more than before this happened. I can't understand it. I don't think there's a qualified psychologist who could talk to Mark and come up with the answers. But I forgive him for what he's done to me, I probably will never visit him, and I know what a heartache it must be to you. I'm going ahead with my life. I hope all of us can."

For the first time, Bill Hofmann didn't reject the offer of sympathy or challenge the suggestion of his son's guilt.

As soon as Mark entered prison, the members of his ward rushed to Dorie Hofmann's aid with money, food, and clothes. She and her four children were, they reasoned, as much victims as anyone else. Once a week, she would bundle the kids into the car and drive them to Point of the Mountain to visit their father.

Several months later, Shannon Flynn and his wife, Robin, called. They wanted to make sure Dorie was all right. "Some members of my family have tried to talk to me about divorcing Mark," she admitted, "but I think I should stand behind him. I go see him every Friday with the children." Had she come to terms with Mark's guilt? All she would say was, "I realize Mark has made a few mistakes."

When Flynn related the remark to Brent Metcalfe, he was, like everybody else who heard it, stunned. "A few *mistakes?*" Metcalfe gasped. "Don't you get the feeling that that doesn't quite capture the magnitude of what's happening here?"

Eventually, both Terri Christensen and Gary Sheets remarried.

On Temple Square, the Mormon Church had its own unique way of responding to the events of the previous year.

Hugh Pinnock was promoted. On October 4, 1986, almost exactly one year after the bombings, he was "called" to the presidency of the First Quorum of the Seventy, a position just below his ultimate ambition, Apostle.

Francis Gibbons, Gordon Hinckley's secretary who had sometimes dealt with Mark Hofmann in matters of the greatest sensitivity, was promoted to General Authority.

Gordon Hinckley was promoted. Eighty-nine-year-old Marion G. Romney was "released" as First Counselor on November 5, 1985, making room for Gordon B. Hinckley to rise from Second Counselor to First Counselor in the First Presidency. He remained third in line to become Prophet, Seer, and Revelator.

Under the ironic headline, HISTORICAL RECORDS NOW MORE ACCESSIBLE, the Church announced a new policy that would virtually shut the doors to its archives. "Great numbers of the Historical Department's current records will be catalogued and microfilmed over the next several years," said Elder John K. Carmack, G. Homer Durham's successor. "Although confidentiality, respect for the sacred, and laws of privacy necessitate that some records will be closed, we expect that most records will eventually be open to the public."

"The public," however, would be required "to register with the archives, state their research purpose, and sign a research agreement." This agreement, not described in the article, required that anyone using the archives would henceforth have to agree to Church censorship, not just on books or articles being researched at the time, but on any books or articles published at any time in the future.

In a speech to the faithful, Hinckley attacked those scholars of the "new history" who ran around trying "to ferret out every element of folk magic and the occult" surrounding Joseph Smith. Yes, folk magic and superstition existed in Joseph Smith's day, but there "is no evidence whatever that the Church came of such superstition."

Finally, the Brethren called upon all those who had questioned the leadership of the Church during this time of trial, who had wondered how the representatives of God on earth could have been so easily and repeatedly bamboozled by Mark Hofmann, to *have more faith.*

"Safety lies in loving the Brethren," the faithful were told at the October 1987 General Conference. "To follow them is to build one's house on a rock. . . . Read the scriptures, especially the *Book of Mormon.* . . . Do as the prophets request. . . . Pray for the prophets."

The benefits to be derived from loving and following the Brethren would be many, they were told. Wives would be more obedient to their husbands; children would be more obedient to their parents. "Declare in quiet tones that you love the Brethren and you are going to follow them. Add exclamation marks to your words as you quietly and faithfully follow the Brethren."

EPILOGUE

On January 29, 1988, a little more than a year after Mark Hofmann entered Point of the Mountain prison, the Utah Board of Pardons met to consider his eligibility for parole. In a letter to the board, Hofmann wrote how he had rationalized the murders of Steve Christensen and Kathy Sheets. As always, he found himself easily convinced of things he wanted to believe: "I told myself that my survival and that of my family was the most important thing. That my victims might die that day in a car accident or from a heart attack anyway."

To the surprise of all and the gratification of many, the Board of Pardons ruled that Mark Hofmann should be denied all possibility of parole.

Index

About the Authors

STEVEN NAIFEH and GREGORY WHITE SMITH are both graduates of the Harvard Law School. They co-edit the biennial directory *The Best Lawyers in America*, and have contributed articles on legal subjects to various journals, including *The New York Times*. In eight years of working together, they have written more than ten books, including two bestsellers— most recently *The Human Animal*, which they wrote with Phil Donahue. Mr. Naifeh is a native of Tulsa, Oklahoma; Mr. Smith, of Columbus, Ohio. Currently, they both live and work in New York City.